Integrating and Streamlining Event–Driven IoT Services

Yang Zhang
Beijing University of Posts and Telecommunications, China

Yanmeng Guo
Chinese Academy of Sciences, China

A volume in the Advances in Web
Technologies and Engineering
(AWTE) Book Series

Published in the United States of America by
  IGI Global
  Engineering Science Reference (an imprint of IGI Global)
  701 E. Chocolate Avenue
  Hershey PA, USA 17033
  Tel: 717-533-8845
  Fax: 717-533-8661
  E-mail: cust@igi-global.com
  Web site: http://www.igi-global.com

Library of Congress Cataloging-in-Publication Data

Names: Zhang, Yang, 1970 September 6- author. | Guo, Yanmeng, 1976- author.
Title: Integrating and streamlining event-driven IoT services / by Yang Zhang
   and Yanmeng Guo.
Description: Hershey, PA : Engineering Science Reference, [2019] | Includes
   bibliographical references.
Identifiers: LCCN 2018031665| ISBN 9781522576228 (h/c) | ISBN 9781522576235
   (eISBN)
Subjects: LCSH: Internet of things.
Classification: LCC TK5105.8857 .Z43 2019 | DDC 004.67/8--dc23 LC record available at https://
lccn.loc.gov/2018031665

This book is published in the IGI Global book series Advances in Web Technologies and Engineering (AWTE) (ISSN: 2328-2762; eISSN: 2328-2754)

British Cataloguing in Publication Data
A Cataloguing in Publication record for this book is available from the British Library.

For electronic access to this publication, please contact: eresources@igi-global.com.

Advances in Web Technologies and Engineering (AWTE) Book Series

ISSN:2328-2762
EISSN:2328-2754

Editor-in-Chief: Ghazi I. Alkhatib, The Hashemite University, Jordan & David C. Rine, George Mason University, USA

MISSION

The **Advances in Web Technologies and Engineering (AWTE) Book Series** aims to provide a platform for research in the area of Information Technology (IT) concepts, tools, methodologies, and ethnography, in the contexts of global communication systems and Web engineered applications. Organizations are continuously overwhelmed by a variety of new information technologies, many are Web based. These new technologies are capitalizing on the widespread use of network and communication technologies for seamless integration of various issues in information and knowledge sharing within and among organizations. This emphasis on integrated approaches is unique to this book series and dictates cross platform and multidisciplinary strategy to research and practice.

The **Advances in Web Technologies and Engineering (AWTE) Book Series** seeks to create a stage where comprehensive publications are distributed for the objective of bettering and expanding the field of web systems, knowledge capture, and communication technologies. The series will provide researchers and practitioners with solutions for improving how technology is utilized for the purpose of a growing awareness of the importance of web applications and engineering.

COVERAGE

- Strategies for linking business needs and IT
- Integrated user profile, provisioning, and context-based processing
- Web Systems Architectures, Including Distributed, Grid Computer, and Communication Systems Processing
- Human factors and cultural impact of IT-based systems
- Mobile, location-aware, and ubiquitous computing
- Data and knowledge capture and quality issues
- Software agent-based applications
- Security, integrity, privacy, and policy issues
- Virtual teams and virtual enterprises: communication, policies, operation, creativity, and innovation
- Radio Frequency Identification (RFID) research and applications in web engineered systems

IGI Global is currently accepting manuscripts for publication within this series. To submit a proposal for a volume in this series, please contact our Acquisition Editors at Acquisitions@igi-global.com or visit: http://www.igi-global.com/publish/.

Titles in this Series

For a list of additional titles in this series, please visit:
https://www.igi-global.com/book-series/advances-web-technologies-engineering/37158

Dynamic Knowledge Representation in ScientificDomains
Cyril Pshenichny (ITMO University, Russia) Paolo Diviacco (Istituto Nazionale di Oceanografia e di Geofisica Sperimentale, Italy) and Dmitry Mouromtsev (ITMO University, Russia)
Engineering Science Reference • ©2018 • 397pp • H/C (ISBN: 9781522552611) • US $205.00

Innovations, Developments, and Applications of Semantic Web and Information Systems
Miltiadis D. Lytras (American College of Greece, Greece) Naif Aljohani (King Abdulaziz University, Saudi Arabia) Ernesto Damiani (University of Milan, Italy) and Kwok Tai Chui (City University of Hong Kong, Hon Kong)
Engineering Science Reference • ©2018 • 473pp • H/C (ISBN: 9781522550426) • US $245.00

Handbook of Research on Biomimicry in Information Retrieval and Knowledge...
Reda Mohamed Hamou (Dr. Tahar Moulay University of Saida, Algeria)
Engineering Science Reference • ©2018 • 429pp • H/C (ISBN: 9781522530046) • US $325.00

Global Perspectives on Frameworks for Integrated Reporting Emerging Research and...
Ioana Dragu (Babes-Bolyai University, Romania) Adriana Tiron-Tudor (Babes-Bolyai University, Romania) and Szilveszter Fekete Pali-Pista (Babes-Bolyai University, Romania)
Business Science Reference • ©2018 • 160pp • H/C (ISBN: 9781522527534) • US $135.00

Novel Design and the Applications of Smart-M3 Platform in the Internet of Things...
Dmitry Korzun (Petrozavodsk State University (PetrSU), Russia) Alexey Kashevnik (St. Petersburg Institute for Informatics and Automation of the Russian Academy of Sciences (SPIIRAS), Russia & ITMO University, Russia) and Sergey Balandin (FRUCT Oy, Finland & St. Petersburg State University of Aerospace Instrumentation (SUAI), Russia)
Information Science Reference • ©2018 • 150pp • H/C (ISBN: 9781522526537) • US $145.00

For an entire list of titles in this series, please visit:
https://www.igi-global.com/book-series/advances-web-technologies-engineering/37158

701 East Chocolate Avenue, Hershey, PA 17033, USA
Tel: 717-533-8845 x100 • Fax: 717-533-8661
E-Mail: cust@igi-global.com • www.igi-global.com

Table of Contents

Section 1
Introducing IoT Resources Into IoT Services

Chapter 1
IoT Resources and IoT Services

Chapter 2
IoT Resource Access and Management

Section 2
An Integrating and Streamlining Platform for IoT Services

Chapter 3
A Publish/Subscribe-Based Service Bus for Integrating and Streamlining
Event-Driven IoT Services

Chapter 4
Streamlining Service Platform for Integrating IoT Services

Section 3
Flexibly Creating Streamlining IoT Services

Chapter 5
Coordinating Stateful IoT Resources as Event-Driven Distributed IoT
Services

Section 4
Security and Reliability of IoT Services

Section 5
Summary and Example

Preface

BACKGROUND

The Internet of Things (IoT) is a concept in which the virtual world of information technology integrates seamlessly with the real world (Uckelmann et al., 2011). With the development of IoT, large-scale of resources (sensors, actuators, RFID, etc.) and applications on top of them emerge. The reasonable application pattern of IoT is inner-domain high-degree autonomy and inter-domain dynamic coordination. Most of the existing applications, however, are vertical "silos" solutions (Zorzi et al., 2011) because of the characteristics of IoT environment, such as heterogeneity and constrained-resources. This closely-coupled application pattern lacks of effective mechanisms to support applications to share and reuse resources, and interact with each other. In vertical "silos" solutions, the application developer has to bridge this gap between the upper application and the underlying technical details "manually" and has to be an expert in both worlds (Bimschas et al., 2011). But the upper application developers are primarily interested in real-world entities (things, places, and people) and their high-level states rather than in sensors and technical details (Pfisterer et al., 2011). Meanwhile, a large number of existing legacy sensor resources will become an important part of IoT, but they are typically locked into closed systems. Unlocking valuable sensor data from closed systems has the potential to revolutionize how we live.

When physical sensors and devices are opened from their original closed "silo" systems, new architectures need to be adopted in order to support this openness. Over the last decade, IoT applications have driven business transformation by connecting ubiquitous objects and devices together and to cloud-hosted services. However, the need for real-time control, low-latency application responses and local data aggregation mean that the current obligatory cloud connectivity is undesirable for IoT scenarios. In order to sustain the momentum of IoT, a cloud-to-edge continuum is needed, referred to as 'fog computing' in the literature, in which some aspects of computation and storage are placed at the edges of a network and the data centre coordinates with these network edges to achieve low latency for applications. The question of which architectures are appropriate for a cloud-to-things continuum has not yet been comprehensively explored.

Some recent works had focused on applying Service-Oriented Architecture (SOA) on IoT service applications (Guinard et al., 2010; Motwani et al., 2010;Teixeira et al., 2011;Wu et al., 2012;Priyantha et al., 2008). In SOA, the entire application was often broken down into many independent services, which was used to get the functionality reuse and interoperability. But SOA standards are designed to integrate the heavy-weight enterprise services such that some researchers tried to propose light-weight Web service protocol to run in the resource-constrained devices (Castellani et al., 2011; Guinard et al., 2009; Alshahwan et al., 2011). However, only light SOA is not enough (Guinard et al., 2010).

In our work, event-driven architecture (EDA, 2008) is used to realize loosely-coupled application coordination. Due to the physical entities' heterogeneity and dynamic sharing of sensing information in IoT applications, either SOA or EDA has its own limitations and the application scope. But an event-driven architecture can complement service-oriented architecture because services can be driven by triggers fired on incoming events. The event-driven service-oriented architecture (EDSOA) is then defined in our work to address infrastructure and connectivity challenges in IoT scenarios by emphasizing information processing and intelligence at the center-to-edge continuum. EDSOA represents a shift from traditional silo systems and a reliance on cloud-only focused paradigms, which is also complementary to, and an extension of, traditional cloud computing. In our EDSOA-based solution, events are streamlining in open wide-area IoT components and systems, and IoT services are integrated by decoupling and distributed ways, *i.e., the integrating and streamlining of event-driven IoT services moving computation from the cloud to network edges, and potentially right up to the IoT sensors and actuators.*

This book presents an exploration of systematic theories and methods for the design of IoT services based on the principles of streamlining and integration.

WHAT THIS BOOK IS ABOUT

The focus of this book is first and foremost on the design of IoT services based on the principles of streamlining and integration. There is a constant emphasis on how and where design principles can and should be applied, with the ultimate goal of producing high-quality services. More specifically, this book has the following objectives:

1. To clearly establish criteria for solutions involving the streamlining and integrating of IoT services;
2. To provide a complete overview of the IoT service design paradigm;
3. To document specific design characteristics realising the principles of streamlining and integration;
4. To describe how these design principles should be applied;
5. To establish an IoT service platform to support IoT service designs based on the principles of streamlining and integration.

The physical world generates events that reflect its status of operation, and IoT services react to these events in order to monitor and control the physical world; in this way, many events are streamlined for efficient and orderly processing, and these events may also cut across many domains to combine different applications together. This principle is therefore referred to as the 'event-driven principle', and related design paradigms and methods are called event-driven methodologies.

The event-driven principle and methodologies appeal to researchers and engineers when addressing challenging issues related to the Future Internet, and these methodologies can also be adopted in IoT applications for the design of IoT services. For an IoT service system, connecting things together is the most important issue. Although many IoT service systems have been deployed, these are generally specialised systems without a focus on interconnection with other systems; one challenging task for computer science is to guide the creation of society-wide fully-connected information systems. This book focuses on two key issues related to interconnection: integration and scalability. Several approaches and methods are presented, together with a set of designs, platforms and tools for integrating and streamlining event-driven IoT services. An examination is carried out of the creation of large-scale IoT service systems based on distributed events, and a formal foundation is proposed for the decomposition, refinement and re-composition of complex services based on the decoupling features of individual events, signature interfaces, service behaviour, and service properties.

In this book, IoT resource models are introduced that can represent physical entities in the information world; this changes the IoT resource models into a bridge between the physical world and the information world, and distributed events can be represented as traffic flowing across this bridge. Events connect physical states to the information world, and bring back the actuation instructors into the physical world. IoT resources are standardised in order to achieve information sharing and event processing, through which computers can automatically process events and resources, thus building a knowledge base for IoT services.

Using this type of knowledge, physical devices are automatically monitored by access adapters that carry out communication between sensors/actuators and monitor agents. When metered data are received through industrial buses and interpreted as attribute events, IoT communication infrastructure is needed to send the right data at the right time to the right place and the right people. This book proposes a unified message space (UMS) for achieving this task. Atomic IoT services interact with each other based on UMS, in an event-driven way: a composite IoT service is composed of atomic event-driven IoT services. A discussion is also presented of methods for the flexible design of IoT services based on IoT resources, and ways in which scalability can be incorporated. Where IoT service models and resources are given, the design of IoT service security is also discussed.

In summary, this book tries to answer the following key problems: (i) how to converge and share heterogeneous sensors and their metered data; (ii) how to design real-time society-wide IoT services with flexibility and scalability; and (iii) how to guarantee the security and reliability of open social information infrastructures. The designs and technologies in this book can be used in smart cities, smart grids, and Industry 4.0.

WHO THIS BOOK FOR

As a guide to the design of IoT services, this book will be useful for IoT professionals interested in or involved with technology architecture, systems analysis, and solution designs. Specifically, this book will be helpful to developers, analysts, and architects who:

1. Want to know how to design IoT services so that they fully support the goals and benefits of streamlining and integration;

2. Want to understand the event-driven IoT service design paradigm;
3. Want to learn about how event-driven methodologies relate to the implementation of monitoring and control of the physical world;
4. Want in-depth guidance on designing different types of IoT services;
5. Want deep insight into how service contracts support streamlining and integration;
6. Will be involved with the creation of event-driven IoT application solutions.

In summary, this book will be helpful for students, researchers and engineers who are interested in the IoT service community; it can also be used as a textbook for graduate students majoring in computer science.

ORGANIZATION OF THE BOOK

The organization of content is very straightforward. All subsequent chapters have been grouped into the following primary parts:

Section 1: Introducing IoT Resources Into IoT Services

Although this book focuses more on applying and realising IoT services than on understanding the related concepts and terms, it is necessary to take the time to establish and define key concepts and fundamental terms. These concepts and terms are used throughout this book. In Chapter 1, physical systems and devices are introduced into the informational world as the concept of IoT resources, and Chapter 2 describes how to access IoT resources to realise their introduction into the informational world.

Chapter 1: IoT Resources and IoT Services

We begin Part I by establishing the key concepts of IoT resources and IoT services. This chapter then discusses how to integrate Event-driven Architecture (EDA) and Service-oriented Architecture for IoT services with introducing IoT resources as the basis, where we can use resource information to specify IoT services, use independent and shared events to drive the IoT services, and use event session to coordinate the IoT services. In order to integrate EDA and SOA, the event session concept is defined, which was often neglected in most existing works about EDSOA. Based on the event session concept, a graphical modeling method is proposed to describe IoT business processes. Some applications are given to show the concept proof for such event-driven SOA for IoT services.

Chapter 2: IoT Resource Access and Management

This next chapter zooms in on accessing IoT resources. In this chapter, the resource framework is proposed for IoT resource management and utilization, as well as the bridge between the upper layer application and the underlying sensors (actuators). This chapter firstly discusses how to graphically create IoT resources for improving the production performance during deploying IoT systems. We then discuss how to automatically access IoT resources and adapt the resource accessing utility for varying production environments, where raw data metered by sensors are translated into the observation data sent to the resource management platform. Finally, a resource management platform is proposed, where the mechanisms of resource discovery, resource utility, and distributed resource management are discussed, and semantic annotations are imposed on the observation data for resource sharing. In addition, the utilization of IoT resources is discussed as applications, where resource evolution and reverse evolution is illustrated, the coal mine monitor and control system is given as an example for the resource evolution, and the reverse evolution solution is design for the playback of system history.

Section 2: An Integrating and Streamlining Platform for IoT Services

Creating IoT services is the key issue in this book, and we begin Part II by establishing the streamlining and integration principle for IoT service designs. In Chapter 4, how to streamline events is discussed, and Chapter 5 discusses how to integrate IoT services based on the IoT service platform.

Chapter 3: Publish/Subscribe-Based Service Bus for Integrating and Streamlining Event-Driven IoT Service

This chapter begins to make insights on events produced by IoT resources. In this chapter, we design a service-oriented publish/subscribe middleware over SDN (Software-defined Network) and implement it for streamlining events, where the communication capabilities are exposed as services for upper applications to use, and the service routing is supported as well as service programming. We then try to establish an event-driven service bus based on the publish/subscribe middleware, where the publish/subscribe middleware assumes the interaction and coordination functions which are extracted from the upper applications, IoT service can connect to the service bus for publishing and receiving events, and the decoupling features between communication and computation will satisfy the requirements of IoT applications. The behavior coordination logic of event-driven business processes can be translated into the event matching/routing functions for streamlining in the publish/subscribe middleware. The service authorization control can also be combined with the communication fabric, where authorization policies are converted into the event scope and visibility functions.

Chapter 4: A Streamlining Service Platform for Integrating IoT Services

This next chapter focuses on how to streamline and integrate IoT services. In IoT scenarios, there are smart devices hosting Web services and also very simple devices with external Web services. Without unifying the access to different kinds of devices, the construction of IoT service systems would be cumbersome. In our work, integrating distributed events into SOA is the basic principle. The data accessing capability of physical entities is separated from their actuation capability, which acts as a foundation for ultra-scale and elastic IoT applications. We then establish a distributed event-based IoT service platform to support IoT service creation and allow for the hiding of service access complexity, where the IoT services are event-driven, and impedance matching between service computation and event communication is the design goal. The coordination logic of an IoT service system is extracted as an event composition, which supports the distributed execution of the system, with scalability. We finally implement applications over the platform to show its effectiveness and applicability.

Section 3: Flexibly Creating Streamlining IoT Services

In this part, we discuss how to flexibly create streamlining IoT services based on the platform, which is presented in Chapter 5.

Chapter 5: Coordinating Stateful IoT Resources as Event-Driven Distributed IoT Services

The IoT service platform presented in the previous chapters supports decoupling interactions among different IoT services, but how to orchestrate these independent IoT services is not presented. This chapter firstly makes insights into the characteristics of IoT resources: being stateful, orchestrating IoT services is to coordinate stateful IoT resources. Thus, we try to address the issue of flexibly coordinating stateful IoT resources as IoT services in this chapter. In the flexible service creation scheme, the IoT resources are introduced as the action effects by a decoupling way (i.e., via distributed events and causality links), and IoT services are not only compared through their input, output, preconditions, and effects for linking them together, but also bound to and compared with the stateful situations to link to the IoT resources. For an IoT service system, we partition it for deploying IoT services nearby IoT resources to realize real-time monitoring and controlling them. The glitch problem for distributed reactive IoT services is solved by the event separation and composition way. We finally give an evaluation to concept-prove our work.

Section 4: Security and Reliability of IoT Services

An IoT service system often involves informational infrastructures such that this part begins the consideration of IoT service reliability and security. In Chapter 6, the basic security mechanism for IoT service is discussed, and the reliability assurance way is provided for runtime IoT services in Chapter 7.

Chapter 6: Distributed Access Control for IoT Services Based on Publish/Subscribe Paradigm

With IoT services coming open and wide-area, different IoT applications in different sites collaborate to realize the real-time monitoring and controlling of the physical world. The publish/subscribe paradigm makes IoT application collaborations more real-time and flexible because of the space, time and control decoupling of event producer and consumer, which can be used to establish an appropriate communication infrastructure. Unfortunately, a publish/subscribe-based IoT application does not know who consumes its data events, and consumers do not know who produces the events either. In this environment, the IoT application cannot directly control event access because of anonymous and indirect application interactions. To address the above issues, this chapter at first describes the characteristics of IoT communication foundation for wide-area IoT services, and then defines their security model by the data-centric methodology. Based on such models, underpinning network capabilities can be integrated to help IoT applications control event access. The key point in our access control solution is to preserve the application interaction characteristics of the publish/subscribe-based IoT applications: anonymous and multicast. A policy-attaching approach is adopted to preserve the anonymity and multicast features of collaborating IoT services.

Chapter 7: Runtime Monitoring IoT Services for Keeping Properties

Ensuring a critical information infrastructure in a secure and safe state is a mandatory requirement. When its related IoT (Internet of Things) services are open via the Internet, existing execution monitoring technologies do not work well to protect it, because the "inside" malwares may compromise and subvert the monitoring mechanism itself, and its safety property will be interacted by its security property. In this chapter, we propose an isolation-based solution to enforce property policies for runtime IoT services. We firstly address the issue of isolation-based service trace observation by establishing and modeling a virtual channel. We then address the issue of isolation-based policy enforcement by dealing with the incompleteness and inconsistency of trace knowledge observed in the virtual channel. Finally, physical systems are introduced into our runtime monitors, where the controllability of IoT services is discussed as an example of service property enforcement.

Section 5: Summary and Example

This part provides an example that illustrates how to design and implement an IoT service system based on the principles of streamlining and integration, and this is presented in Chapter 8.

Chapter 8: Summary – IoT Service Provisioning With an Illustrative Example

In previous chapters, the design of IoT services using the principles of streamlining and integration was discussed. In this chapter, their use is discussed in terms of a complete IoT service provisioning, and an example is given. The event streamlining problem is initially addressed from an IoT service provisioning perspective, involving how to efficiently disseminate the sensing events among the event producers and consumers on demand. The service integration problem is then discussed, i.e. how to dynamically coordinate the relevant IoT services based on events occurring in the real world. In this chapter, an EDSOA is abstracted from the perspective of utilising the advantages of EDA and SOA, viewing the streamlining and integration principle from an architectural perspective. A combination of SOA and EDA can easily support the on-demand dissemination of sensing information and event-driven service dynamic coordination. The example given here is a deployed coal mine monitor-control system (CMCS) application.

REFERENCES

Alshahwan, F., Moessner, K., & Carrez, F. (2011). Distributing resource intensive mobile web services. *Proceedings of the Innovations in Information Technology (IIT), IEEE International Conference on.* 10.1109/INNOVATIONS.2011.5893861

Baeten, J. C. M., Basten, T., & Renters, M. A. (2010). *Process Algebra: Equational Theories of Communicating Processes.* Cambridge University Press.

Barret, C., Sebastiani, R., Seshia, S. A., & Tinelli, C. (2009). Satisfiability modulo theories. Handbook of Satisfiability, 825–885.

Bimschas, Hasemann, Hauswirth, Karnstedt, & Truong. (2011). Semantic-Service Provisioning for the Internet of Things. *Electronic Communications of the EASST*, 37.

Bultan, T. (2000). Action Language: A specification language for model checking reactive systems. *Proceedings of the 22nd International Conference on Software Engineering (ICSE 2000)*, 335–344. 10.1145/337180.337219

Castellani, A. P., Gheda, M., & Bui, N. (2011). Web Services for the Internet of Things through CoAP and EXI. *IEEE Proceedings of the Communications Workshops (ICC).*

de Moura, L., & Bjørner, N. (2008). *An efficient theorem prover.* Retrieved from http://research.microsoft.com/en-us/um/redmond/projects/z3/

Drescher, C., & Thielscher, M. (2007). Integrating action calculi and description logics. *Lecture Notes in Computer Science*, *4667*, 68–83. doi:10.1007/978-3-540-74565-5_8

EDA. (2008). *Event-Driven Architecture Overview*. Retrieved from http://www.omg.org/soa/ Uploaded%20Docs/EDA/bda2-2-06cc.pdf

Guinard, D., & Trifa, V. (2009). Towards the web of things: Web mashups for embedded devices. *Proceedings of the Workshop on Mashups, Enterprise Mashups and Lightweight Composition on the Web (MEM 2009)*.

Guinard, D., Trifa, V., Karnouskos, S., Spiess, P., & Savio, D. (2010). Interacting with the soa-based internet of things: Discovery, query, selection, and on-demand provisioning of web services. *Services Computing. IEEE Transactions on*, *3*(3), 223–235.

Kowalski, R. A., & Sergot, M. J. (1986). A logic-based calculus of events. *New Generation Computing*, *4*(1), 67–95. doi:10.1007/BF03037383

Kruglov. (2013). *Superposition modulo theory* (Dissertation). Universität des Saarlandes.

McCarthy, J., & Hayes, P. (1969). Some philosophical problems from the standpoint of artificial intelligence. In B. Meltzer & D. Michie (Eds.), *Machine Intelligence* (Vol. 4, pp. 463–502). Edinburgh, UK: Edinburgh University Press.

Motwani, R., Motwani, M., Harris, F., & Dascualu, S. (2010). Towards a scalable and interoperable global environmental sensor network using Service Oriented Architecture. *Proceedings of the Intelligent Sensors, Sensor Networks and Information Processing (ISSNIP), 2010 Sixth International Conference on*. 10.1109/ISSNIP.2010.5706788

Nelson, G., & Oppen, D. C. (1979). Simplication by cooperating decision procedures. *ACM Transactions on Programming Languages and Systems*, *2*(1), 245–257. doi:10.1145/357073.357079

Pfisterer, D., Romer, K., Bimschas, D., Kleine, O., . . . Richardson, R. (2011). SPITFIRE: toward a semantic web of things. IEEE Communications Magazine, 49(11).

Plaisted. (2003). A hierarchical situation calculus. *Journal of Computing Research Repository*.

Priyantha, N. B., Kansal, A., Goraczko, M., & Zhao, F. (2008). Tiny web services: design and implementation of interoperable and evolvable sensor networks. *Proceedings of the 6th ACM conference on Embedded network sensor systems.* 10.1145/1460412.1460438

Reiter. (2001). *Knowledge in action: logical foundations for specifying and implementing dynamical systems.* The MIT Press.

Shostak, R. E. (1984). Deciding combination of theories. *Journal of the Association for Computing Machinery, 1*(31), 1–12. doi:10.1145/2422.322411

Spass-prover. (2015). Retrieved from http://www.spass-prover.org

Teixeira, T., Hamchem, S., Issarny, V., & Georgantas, N. (2011). *Service oriented middleware for the internet of things: a perspective. In Towards a Service-Based Internet.* Springer.

Thielscher, M. (1999). From situation calculus to fluent calculus: State update axioms as a solution to the inferential frame problem. *Artificial Intelligence, 111*(1-2), 277–299. doi:10.1016/S0004-3702(99)00033-8

Thielscher. (2005). *Reasoning Robots: The Art and Science of Programming Robotic Agents.* Springer.

Uckelmann, D., Harrison, M., & Michahelles, F. (2011). *An architectural approach towards the future internet of things. In Architecting the Internet of Things* (pp. 1–24). Springer. doi:10.1007/978-3-642-19157-2

Wu, Y. X., Fan, C. X., & Zou, J. W. (2012). Service-Oriented Middleware for Heterogeneous Environment in Internet of Things. *China Communications, 9*(9), 41–51.

Zorzi, M., Gluhak, A., Lange, S., & Bassi, A. (2010). From today's intranet of things to a future internet of things: A wireless-and mobility-related view. *Wireless Communications, IEEE, 17*(6), 44–51. doi:10.1109/MWC.2010.5675777

Introduction

PRELIMINARIES

Process Algebra

The theory of Process Algebra defined in Baeten et al., (2010) is used to describe IoT services. A signature $\sum$ is a set of functions, and constants are special functions without arity. Term is defined on the signature $\sum$ and a set V of variables, denoting the term set by $T(\sum, V)$. An equational theory is a tuple $(\sum, E)$, where E is a set of equations with the form $s = t$ (*s,t* are terms in $T(\sum, V)$). Process theories are special equational theories, where processes imply the objects described by a process theory. The main functions in our process theory $PA(ACT, PR)$ are as follows (readers can refer to (Plaisted, 2010) for more details):

- *a - means action prefix, and the process executes action then proceeds as term x ;*
- *+*-means alternative composition or choice, and the process x+ y behaves either as term x or y, but not as both;
- $-|-$ means parallel composition, and the process $x \mid y$ *behaves either as term x or y, or as both with arbitrary order or mergence;*
- $[\varphi]$ *- means guard command, and the process* $[\varphi]x$ *executes the term x if the proposition formula* φ *is evaluated to be true;*

where ACT is a set of actions as a parameter of the process theory PA and $a \in ACT$ *, and PR is a set of propositions as a parameter of PA and* $\varphi \in PR$ *.*

In order to express the IoT services' computation model in the process theory, the action set ACT is also defined by another equational theory $(\sum', E')$, where rewrite rules from equations are used to model computing primitives. In this book, the functions of IoT services form the equational theory (Σ', E'). Σ' includes these function symbols, and equations in E' describe the functions' computation model. The set of propositions PR is parameterized to express the states and properties of IoT resources. The IoT service behavior is able to be described by a process defined in *PA(ACT, PR)*, where the action set *ACT* of *PA(ACT, PR)* may be a signature from other equational theories. When the behavior process of an IoT service is executed, an outside observer observes events from and to the process and the observed sequence of events forms *a frame* corresponding to which the sequence of actions in the process forms a trace. In this paper, only IoT services' functions and their equations will be explicitly expressed during discussing the computation model with the equational theory of *PA(ACT, PR)* being implicit.

Satisfiability Modulo Theories

First-order logic is built on a term set $T(\Sigma, V)$, a predicate set *Pre*, and some logical symbols $\neg, \wedge, \vee, \rightarrow, \exists, \forall$, brackets and other punctuation, where the term signature and symbols in *Pre* form an *FOL* signature Σ'. An atom set includes logical constants *False* and *True,* predicates with the terms as input, and equations between terms. A literal is an atom or its negation. A formula consists of a set of literals and logical symbols connecting the literals. Then, a Σ' sentence is a formula with no free variables. A Σ' interpretation over the variable set with a domain is a map, where each variable and constant is respectively mapped into an element in the domain, and functions and predicates are mapped into the domain's functions. A formula is satisfiable if it is *true* under the Σ' interpretation; otherwise, it is unsatisfiable. A theory is a set of sentences over the *FOL* signature Σ'. Determining whether a formula is satisfiable over some theories is a problem of satisfiability modulo theories (SMT) (Kruglov, 2013), (Barret et al., 2009), (Moura et al., 2008).

In first-order logic, the logical symbols include:

1. *Logical constants* false, true *;*
2. *Predicate variables* $x, y, z, \cdots$ *;*
3. *The equality symbol* = *;*
4. *The propositional connectives* $\neg, \wedge, \vee, \rightarrow$ *;*
5. *The quantifiers* $\exists, \forall$ *;*
6. *The punctuation symbols* "(", ")", "," *;*

The signature in first-order logic is defined in Definition 1.

- *Definition 1: Signature*

A domain signature is a set of functions and predictions as follows:

$$\Sigma = \Sigma^C \cup \Sigma^F \cup \Sigma^P,$$

where Σ^C *is a set of functions with zero arity;* Σ^F *is a set of functions with arity* n *and* $n \geq 1$; Σ^P *is a set of predicates.*

- *Definition 2: Term*

Given a signature Σ, *a term set is defined as follows:*

1. *every variable is a term;*
2. *every constant in* Σ^C *is a term;*
3. *an* $n - ary$ *function in* Σ^F *with* n *terms as input is a term.*

$Terms(\Sigma, V)$ *denotes the set of terms built over a variable set* V *and a signature* Σ.

- *Definition 3: Atom*

Given a signature Σ, *the set of atoms is defined as:false, true are atoms;* $P(t_1, t_2, \cdots, t_n)$ *is an atom if* P *is a predicate in* Σ^P *and* $t_1, t_2, \cdots, t_n$ *are terms;* $s = t$ *is a tom if* s, t *are terms.*

- *Definition 4: Formula*

Given a signature Σ, *the set of formulas is defined as:every atom is a formula;* $\neg \omega, \varphi \wedge \omega, \varphi \vee \omega, \varphi \rightarrow \omega, \varphi \leftrightarrow \omega$ *are all formulas if* φ, ω *are formulas;* $(\forall x)\varphi, (\exists x)\varphi$ *are formulas if* φ *is a formula and* x *is a variable.*

- *Definition 5: Literal*

Given a signature Σ, A *and* $\neg A$ *are both literals if* A *is an atom over* Σ.

- *Definition 6: Free Occurrences*

Given a formula on Σ, its included variables are called free occurrences if: each variable in an atom is free; the variable x in $\neg\varphi$ is free if x in φ is free; variables in $\neg\omega, \varphi \wedge \omega, \varphi \vee \omega, \varphi \rightarrow \omega, \varphi \leftrightarrow \omega$ are free if the variables in φ, ω are free; a variable x in $(\forall y)\varphi, (\exists y)\varphi$ is free if x in φ is free and x is different from y.

- **Definition 7: Sentence**

Given a signature Σ, a formula is called a sentence if it does not include free variables.

- **Definition 8: Interpretation**

Given a signature Σ and a variable set V, an interpretation I is defined over a domain D, which is a map as follows:

1. x in V is mapped onto an element x^D in D;
2. A constant c in Σ^C is mapped onto an element c^D in D;
3. for a function f, $f^D : D^n \rightarrow D$;
4. for a predicate P, its interpretation is a subset P^D of D^n.

- **Definition 9: Valid and Satisfiable**

Given a signature Σ and a variable set V, a formula φ over Σ and V is:

1. Valid if $I(\varphi) = $ true *for all interpretations I over Σ and V;*
2. Satisfiable if $I(\varphi) = $ true *for some interpretations I over Σ and V;*
3. Unsatisfiable if $I(\varphi) = $ false *for all interpretations I over Σ and V.*

- **Definition 10: Equivalent**

Given two fomulas φ, ω over a signature Σ and a variable set V:

1. Equivalent if $I(\varphi) = I(\omega)$ for all interpretations I over V and Σ;
2. Equisatisfiable if φ is satisfiable when and only when ω is also satisfiable.

- *Definition 11: Theory*

  Given a signature Σ, a set of sentences over Σ forms a theory over Σ.

- *Definition 12: Theory Interpretation*

  Given a signature Σ and a theory T over Σ, a theory interpretation is an interpretation that makes each sentence in the theory be true.

- *Definition 13: Theory Valid and Theory Satisfiable*

  Given a signature Σ and a theory T over Σ, a formula over Σ and a variable set V is:

1. *Theory Valid if all theory interpretation I makes the formula true;*
2. *Theory Satisfiable if some theory interpretation I makes the formula true;*

There are lots of significant developments of SMT in the past decade, which include fast boolean satisfiability solvers (SAT), some efficient decision procedures for many expressive theories, and modular combination theorems (Nelson et al., 1979;Shostak, 1984; Spass-prover, 2015). SMT solvers have become standard tools in industrial applications to complete automated reasoning and verification.

Action Theory and Fluent Calculus

In classical action theories such as event calculus (Kowalski et al., 1986), situation calculus (McCarthy et al., 1969), and action theory (Bultan, 200), how to describe actions to monitor and control the real world was their focus, where they defined the set of effects to describe the changes which these actions led to. But if only the changed effects that an action would operate were specified, then the frame problem would appear, i.e., how to know the effects which were not changed by the action. Enumerating all effects induced by the action, containing changed ones and unchanged ones, may be a possible solution to the frame problem. However, there may be rich constraints in one actual domain such that the intuitive enumerating method may not be convenient or impossible. Many action theory researchers proposed lots of methods to address the issue, as well as inspecting the ramification problem and the qualification problem (Reiter, 2001;Thielscher, 2005). In our work, we adopt a hierarchy approach to model an IoT service, where physical entities will be specified by IoT resource models at stable bottom to describe direct action effects, and actions and their interactions will be described by IoT services at varied application-related top to specify the indirect action effects and qualification. The knowledge about IoT resources is described as the classical action theories, and the knowledge about the IoT service will be obtained from an environment's observation.

The fluent calculus (Thielscher et al., 1999;Drescher et al., 2007) is a kind of action theory, which is used to specify how an artificial system performs actions over the physical world in a dynamic domain. It is fully based on the first-order logic to support reasoning about actions by addressing the frame problem, the ramification problem, and the qualification problem, where the action's effects, *called fluents*, are defined by terms rather than predicates for realizing flexibility, the frame problem means that the non-changed effects of actions should also be specified by fluents besides specifying the changed effects induced by performing actions, the ramification problem means that the indirect action effects should be defined by fluents besides direct action effects, and the qualification problem means that all preconditions of performing an action should be given by fluents.

The fluent calculus is built over many-sorted first-order logic with equality. The standard sorts are OBJET, ACTION, SITUATION, FLUENT, and STATE. A term of sort FLUENT is a fluent. We analogously speak of states, situations, actions, and objects. Objects are basic terms, and others inherit from them. Situations are sequences of actions rooted in an initial situation. A state is defined by some fluents which hold in one situation.

Signature of Fluent Calculus

The signature of Fluent Calculus is as follows:

1. *A countable function symbols*
    funtion : $OBJECT^n \rightarrow FLUENT \, / \, OBJECT$, *and some of them*
    being $OBJECT^n \rightarrow ACTION$.
2. Two special function symbols for situations:
    a. $S_0 : SITUATION$, *the initial situation.*
    b. $DO : SITUATION \times ACTION \rightarrow SITUATION$, *mapping a situation to its successor after executing an action.*

3. Three special function symbols for states:
   a. $\emptyset : STATE$, *the empty state.*
   b. $\circ : STATE \times STATE \rightarrow STATE$, *conjoining fluents into states, or states into a bigger state.*
   c. $State : SITUATION \rightarrow STATE$, *mapping a situation into a state.*
4. *A predicate symbol* $Poss : ACTION \times SITUATION \rightarrow True \ / \ False$, *denoting the action preconditions.*

In the formalism of actions, most properties in the real world hold for a limited period of validity such that a situation argument is often attached to them, and the situation represents all actions history.

Hold Macro

A fluent f *holds in a state* z *if the latter is composed of* f *and some other state* z' *via* $\circ$; *the same is for a situation* s:

1. $Holds(f, z) \overset{def}{=} (\exists z')z = f \circ z'$;

2. $Holds(f, s) \overset{def}{=} Holds(f, State(s))$.

A finite state is a term $f_1 \circ \cdots \circ f_n$ with each f_i $(1 \leq i \leq n)$ being a fluent.

Fluent Addition/Subtraction

The fluent addition/subtraction is as follows:

1. $z_1 + f \overset{def}{=} z_1 \circ f$

2. $z_1 - f \overset{def}{=} z_2 = (z_1 = z_2 \lor z_2 \circ f = z_1) \land \neg Holds(f, z_2)$

For a fluent such as *Young(Alice)*, there is often a negative fluent *Old(Alice)*. Thus, we introduce $-f$ for a fluent f to denote the negative of f. For the fluents f and $-f$, we define $\forall z, \neg Holds(-f \circ f, z)$. This requires that a set of fluents be checked whether they conflict each other or not, where SMT (Satisfiability Modulo Theories) can be used to assume the checking task by some underlying theories in SMT solvers.

The frame problem is solved by the State Update Axiom, where an action is specified by its positive action effects and negative action effects, as well as the preconditions of action executions.

State Update Axiom

A state update axiom is a formula of the form:

$$Poss(A(x), s) \rightarrow$$
$$(\exists y_1)(\Delta_1(s) \wedge State(Do(A(x), s))) = State(s) - \vartheta_1^- + \vartheta_1^+)$$
$$\vee \cdots \vee$$
$$(\exists y_n)(\Delta_n(s) \wedge State(Do(A(x), s))) = State(s) - \vartheta_n^- + \vartheta_n^+)$$

,

The finite states $\vartheta_i^-, \vartheta_i^+$ with free variables in x, y_i are the negative and positive effects under the condition $\Delta_i(s)$. $\Delta_i(s)$ is a situation formula with free variables in x, y_i and s.

The ramification problem is solved by clarifying the dependence relation between two fluents under some conditions, *i.e., a causality predicate being used.*

Casual Relation

A casual relation is represented by a formula, and we introduce a predicate to specify it as follows:

$$Causes(\, z, \mathit{efffects}, z', \mathit{effects}'),$$

which means that, in state z, the occurrence of effects, causes a state transition from z to z' with the occurrence of effects'.

CONCLUSION

Event-driven methodologies have appealed to researchers and engineers dealing with many challenging issues related to the Future Internet and IoT. This book follows this approach, and starts with an introduction to IoT resource models, which link the physical world to the information world in order to build a knowledge base for IoT services. A unified message space is then used to enable the IoT communication fabric to send out data correctly to sensors/actors, monitoring agents, and IoT services. In the next part, the design of flexible IoT services with scalability is discussed, and a formal foundation for the decomposition, refinement and re-composition of complex services is proposed, involving signature interfaces, service behaviours, and service properties. Finally, the security features and design of IoT services are discussed. In summary, this book presents an overview of prior and current attempts to address key issues relating to the design of IoT services, including: (i) how to converge heterogenous sensors and share their data; (ii) how to design real-time large-scale IoT services with flexibility and scalability; (iii) how to support IoT service realisation and provisioning based on an IoT service platform; and (iv) how to guarantee the security and reliability of open IoT services. The research hypothesis and findings relating to the designs and technologies in this book have a wide range of applications in smart cities, smart grids, and Industry 4.0.

REFERENCES

Alshahwan, F., Moessner, K., & Carrez, F. (2011). Distributing resource intensive mobile web services. *Proceedings of the Innovations in Information Technology (IIT), IEEE International Conference on.* 10.1109/INNOVATIONS.2011.5893861

Baeten, J. C. M., Basten, T., & Renters, M. A. (2010). *Process Algebra: Equational Theories of Communicating Processes.* Cambridge University Press.

Barret, C., Sebastiani, R., Seshia, S. A., & Tinelli, C. (2009). Satisfiability modulo theories. Handbook of Satisfiability, 825–885.

Bimschas, Hasemann, Hauswirth, Karnstedt, & Truong. (2011). Semantic-Service Provisioning for the Internet of Things. *Electronic Communications of the EASST, 37.*

Bultan, T. (2000). Action Language: A specification language for model checking reactive systems. *Proceedings of the 22nd International Conference on Software Engineering (ICSE 200w0),* 335–344. 10.1145/337180.337219

Castellani, A. P., Gheda, M., & Bui, N. (2011). Web Services for the Internet of Things through CoAP and EXI. *IEEE Proceedings of the Communications Workshops (ICC), IEEE International Conference on.*

de Moura, L., & Bjørner, N. (2008). *An efficient theorem prover.* Retrieved from http://research.microsoft.com/en-us/um/redmond/projects/z3/

Drescher, C., & Thielscher, M. (2007). Integrating action calculi and description logics. *Lecture Notes in Computer Science, 4667*, 68–83. doi:10.1007/978-3-540-74565-5_8

EDA. (2008). *Event-Driven Architecture Overview.* Retrieved from http://www.omg.org/soa/ Uploaded%20Docs/EDA/bda2-2-06cc.pdf

Guinard, D., & Trifa, V. (2009). Towards the web of things: Web mashups for embedded devices. *Proceedings of the Workshop on Mashups, Enterprise Mashups and Lightweight Composition on the Web (MEM 2009).*

Guinard, D., Trifa, V., Karnouskos, S., Spiess, P., & Savio, D. (2010). Interacting with the soa-based internet of things: Discovery, query, selection, and on-demand provisioning of web services. *Services Computing. IEEE Transactions on, 3*(3), 223–235.

Kowalski, R. A., & Sergot, M. J. (1986). A logic-based calculus of events. *New Generation Computing, 4*(1), 67–95. doi:10.1007/BF03037383

Kruglov. (2013). *Superposition modulo theory* (Dissertation). Universität des Saarlandes.

McCarthy, J., & Hayes, P. (1969). Some philosophical problems from the standpoint of artificial intelligence. In B. Meltzer & D. Michie (Eds.), *Machine Intelligence* (Vol. 4, pp. 463–502). Edinburgh, UK: Edinburgh University Press.

Motwani, R., Motwani, M., Harris, F., & Dascualu, S. (2010). Towards a scalable and interoperable global environmental sensor network using Service Oriented Architecture. *Proceedings of the Intelligent Sensors, Sensor Networks and Information Processing (ISSNIP), 2010 Sixth International Conference on.* 10.1109/ISSNIP.2010.5706788

Nelson, G., & Oppen, D. C. (1979). Simplication by cooperating decision procedures. *ACM Transactions on Programming Languages and Systems, 2*(1), 245–257. doi:10.1145/357073.357079

Pfisterer, D., Romer, K., Bimschas, D., Kleine, O., . . . Richardson, R. (2011). SPITFIRE: toward a semantic web of things. IEEE Communications Magazine, 49(11).

Plaisted. (2003). A hierarchical situation calculus. *Journal of Computing Research Repository*.

Priyantha, N. B., Kansal, A., Goraczko, M., & Zhao, F. (2008). Tiny web services: design and implementation of interoperable and evolvable sensor networks. *Proceedings of the 6th ACM conference on Embedded network sensor systems*. 10.1145/1460412.1460438

Reiter. (2001). *Knowledge in action: logical foundations for specifying and implementing dynamical systems*. The MIT Press.

Shostak, R. E. (1984). Deciding combination of theories. *Journal of the Association for Computing Machinery*, *1*(31), 1–12. doi:10.1145/2422.322411

Spass-prover. (2015). Retrieved from http://www.spass-prover.org

Teixeira, T., Hamchem, S., Issarny, V., & Georgantas, N. (2011). *Service oriented middleware for the internet of things: a perspective. In Towards a Service-Based Internet*. Springer.

Thielscher, M. (1999). From situation calculus to fluent calculus: State update axioms as a solution to the inferential frame problem. *Artificial Intelligence*, *111*(1-2), 277–299. doi:10.1016/S0004-3702(99)00033-8

Thielscher. (2005). *Reasoning Robots: The Art and Science of Programming Robotic Agents*. Springer.

Uckelmann, D., Harrison, M., & Michahelles, F. (2011). *An architectural approach towards the future internet of things. In Architecting the Internet of Things* (pp. 1–24). Springer. doi:10.1007/978-3-642-19157-2

Wu, Y. X., Fan, C. X., & Zou, J. W. (2012). Service-Oriented Middleware for Heterogeneous Environment in Internet of Things. *China Communications*, *9*(9), 41–51.

Zorzi, M., Gluhak, A., Lange, S., & Bassi, A. (2010). From today's intranet of things to a future internet of things: A wireless-and mobility-related view. *Wireless Communications, IEEE*, *17*(6), 44–51. doi:10.1109/MWC.2010.5675777

Section 1
Introducing IoT Resources Into IoT Services

Chapter 1
IoT Resources and IoT Services

ABSTRACT

Although many IoT applications have been developed, a theoretical basis for interconnecting all things is still obscure. In order to establish a solid foundation for IoT applications, this chapter addresses three issues: how to model physical sensors and devices as IoT resources, how to introduce IoT resources into IoT services, and how to use distributed events to connect IoT resources and IoT services together to form an IoT service system. An IoT resource is defined by its static attributes and dynamic lifecycle; both of these are specified using semantic knowledge to enable automatic sharing and understanding. An IoT service is considered as a set of actions imposed on IoT resources to monitor and control the physical world. An example application is given in order to demonstrate a proof of concept for event-driven IoT services over IoT resources (streamlining events) to integrate IoT services.

INTRODUCTION

The primary aim of IoT services is to introduce physical entities in the physical world into the information world. Digital entities corresponding to physical entities are referred to as IoT resources. A resource provides functionalities allowing access to the physical entity's properties and actuation of the physical entity. We treat this resource, also called a bottom-layer service or resource service, as a primary base for sharing, interaction, composition, and so on.

DOI: 10.4018/978-1-5225-7622-8.ch001

A resource is defined by its object model and its lifecycle model; its object model describes its attributes and the relations it has with other resources, while its lifecycle model describes the way in which it runs and its lifetime state transitions. The interface of the resource service allows access to its attributes and the states in its lifecycle. Business services operate on the resources, inducing state transitions or accessing the resource attributes. The operation of the service is carried out based on events, i.e., it uses an event-driven model.

Distributed events play a key role in communication between business services and underlying resources, driving all these system-building components to progress during operation. Upper-layer IoT services, i.e. business services, use events to access the attributes or actuation capabilities of resources. Each IoT service can obtain events locally, react to their occurrence, and publish its output as a distributed event for other IoT services to use locally. Each event is also required to be independent, meaning that each IoT service should be able to consume it without knowing its 'from' or 'to'.

A hierarchical model is presented here to specify IoT services based on distributed events, including basic IoT services reacting to the occurrence of events, and multiple IoT services interacting via the distribution of events. Although events are independent within the service environment, each service has its own behaviour and interacts with other services. The behaviour and interactions of a service control how events are exchanged among service activities and the reactions to the occurrence of events; that is to say, there are dependency relationships between events in the service system. In order to fill this gap and to maintain consistency with an event-driven methodology, an information-centric session mechanism is proposed here to describe service behaviour and interactions based on distributed events, called an event session. An event session involves using the event itself to correlate the different service activities through which the activity relationship in a service behaviour can be defined.

To the best of the authors' knowledge, there are no existing works that fully explore ways in which to use IoT resources as the basis for event-driven IoT services. The contributions made by this chapter are as follows:

1. First, a semantic method is used to specify physical sensors and actuators based on existing standards and specifications. In most existing works, the physical systems monitored by sensors and initiated by actuators are not comprehensively discussed; these physical systems are therefore modelled here, and together with sensor and actuator models become

IoT resource models. These IoT resource models, which involve ways to interpret sensor data, offer low-layer knowledge for higher-level business applications which are interested in interpreted semantic data rather than sensor deployment and operational details. The IoT resource models are then abstracted to the layers at which they interact with IoT services. This involves two layers of IoT resource models: lower-layer object models that reflect the attributes of physical entities, and higher-layer lifecycle models involving interaction with IoT services. In this way, the lifecycle model of an IoT resource is defined from the perspective of the IoT service that is performing actions on it, i.e. by specifying it using action theories, with an object model specified by Web Ontology Language (OWL) (OWL2, 2012).

2. IoT resources are then introduced into IoT services from two different perspectives: as the effects of actions performed by the IoT services, and as information models in event-driven business processes. From the former perspective, the behaviour of an IoT service is rigidly formalised over IoT resources and the service's IOPE (input, output, pre-condition, effect), and the fluent calculus, a type of action theory, is used to link the lifecycle models of IoT resources to IoT service actions. In IoT business processes, the input or output of an action is specified by the attributes of the IoT resources. In addition, the pre-conditions and effects of IoT processes can also be specified by logical predicates for IoT resources.

3. In order to drive all of the components in an IoT service system and to connect them together, distributed events are introduced, which can realise large-scale and highly concurrent IoT service operation based on the time, space, and control decoupling of event-driven methodologies. Furthermore, event sessions are introduced that can streamline events for different service actions and group these actions together to enable service coordination and transactions. Based on a knowledge of IoT resources and IoT services, service properties are computed and checked from an environmental perspective; in this approach, the environment cannot be predicted and controlled, and is therefore modelled based on its inferring capabilities rather than its behaviour.

The remainder of the chapter is structured as follows. Section 2 presents some preliminaries; Section 3 describes how to model IoT resources; Section 4 gives a specification for IoT services; Section 5 discusses the use of event sessions to coordinate IoT services; Section 6 explains how to model composite IoT services using event-driven business processes; Section 7 describes how to compute the properties of an IoT service; Section 8 presents several applications; Section 9 gives an overview of related work; and finally, conclusions are drawn in Section 10.

PRELIMNARIES

The theory of process algebra is used here, as defined in Cuijpers et al., (2005), and Baeten et al., (2010), to describe the behaviour of IoT services. A signature Σ is a set of functions, and constants are special functions without arity. A term is defined over a set of variables and a signature that consists of constants and function symbols. An equational theory is a tuple *Attr*, where *AP* is a signature and E is a set of equations of the form $s = t$ (*name* := *topic_subject(topic_verbing)*)are terms). Process theories are special equational theories, and objects described by a process theory are referred to as processes.

For example, some event-based processes are as follows:

$$e = command(resourceID = id, control = ON),$$

$$P = [0 \leq time \leq n]1 + \overline{command}(e).P,$$

$$P_1 = [resourceID = id; exclusive = yes]P,$$

$$P_2 = [resourceID = id; status = ready;]command(x),$$

$$M = P_1 \parallel P_2,$$

where e is an event with the name *command* and requires a resource with identifier *id* to carry out an actuation command *ON*; P_1 means that, when the resource has an "exclusive" status (inner state) and the resource has the identifier *id*, it will be enabled to publish a control command e through *command*; P_2 means that when the resource has a "ready" status and *resourceID* = *id* is true, it will be enabled to receive a control command x through *command*. In process M, P_1 and P_2 are able to communicate only when they are enabled.

The behaviour of an IoT service is represented as a process P. The interacting messages/events observed in process P are called a *frame* ω with $\{w_1 \rightarrow m_1, ..., w_n \rightarrow m_n\}$, where $\{w_1, ..., w_n\}$ is an enumerated index set, $\{m_1, ..., m_n\}$ is the set of observed messages/events for the environment, created by P, and $w_i \rightarrow m_i$ means that the index w_i refers to the $i - th$ observed message/event, which is an actual term. In nature, the environment indexes the observable events caused by the service to obtain a *frame*. A term r that is known by the environment is called a *fact*. Based on a frame where events are modelled by terms, the environment can use the equation set E to deduce a term from a known *fact*. Facts represent knowledge about the environment.

We adopt first-order predicate logic to represent the inference capabilities of the environment. We use the definition of knowledge used in Ciobaca, (2011). As in Ciobaca, (2011), and Baader and Nipkowm, (1998), the knowledge of an environment is defined as follows:

```
m ::=              //term
x                  variable
c                  constant
f(m_1, ..., m_n)   function,
fa ::=             //fact
K(w,m)             predicate
pr                 proposition,
cla ::= fa_1 ^ ... ^ fa_n → fa              //clause,
```

IOT RESOURCES

Sensors and Entities

IoT resources are informational representations of sensors, actuators, and physical systems; the last of these is modelled as an entity, the first two are modelled as resources, and both of these are referred to IoT resources (if no confusion will arise).

Sensors detect stimuli in the physical world and transform these stimuli into observations, and these observations form the properties/attributes of physical systems. The stimulus-sensor-observation pattern (SSN, 2017) is used here to describe sensors and actuators, as illustrated in Figure 1. A stimulus is a change that has taken place in the physical world. Sensors detect this stimulus, and an observation is then obtained from the sensors. OWL (OWL2, 2012) can be used to describe this knowledge about sensors and actuators,

Figure 1. The stimulus-sensor-observation pattern

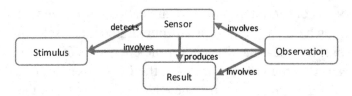

and the ontologies defined by OWL are represented by classes, properties, individuals and data values, which are often exchanged in the form of RDF (RDF, 2001) documents.

In the standard specification of semantic sensor network ontology (SSN, 2017), the classes for sensor and actuators include sosa:Sensor, ssn:Stimulus, sosa:Actuator, sosa:Result, sosa:Observation, sosa:ObservableProperty, sosa:Actuation, sosa:ActuatableProperty, ssn:Property, and so on. The observed object properties (relations) include sosa:madeBySensor (i.e. the relation between an observation and the sensor that made the observation), sosa:madeObservation, sosa:made-Actuation, sosa:madeByActuator, ssn:hasProperty, sosa:hasResult, sosa:actsOnProperty, ssn:detects, and so on. For ssn:Stimulus, the definition (SSN, 2017) is as follows:

IRI: http://www.w3.org/ns/ssn/Stimulus, **an OWL Class**

- **Stimulus**: This is an event in the real world that triggers the **sensor**. The properties associated with this **stimulus** may be different from the eventual **ObservableProperty** recorded. It is an event, rather than an object, that triggers the sensor.
- **Restrictions**: ssn:isProxyFor ONLY sosa:ObservableProperty, inverse Of ssn:wasOriginated- By ONLY sosa:Observation, inverse Of ssn:detects ONLY sosa:Sensor.

```
    For example, a Bosch Sensortec BMP282 sensor instance (SSN,
2017) is created based on the definition of sosa:Sensor, as
follows:
<sensor/35-207306-844818-0/BMP282> rdf:type sosa:Sensor;
    rdfs:label "Bosch Sensortec BMP282"@en ;
sosa:observes <sensor/35-207306-844818-0/BMP282/
atmosphericPressure>.
The observation instance created by the above sensor instance
(SSN, 2017) is as follows:
```

```
<Observation/346344> rdf:type sosa:Observation ;
  sosa:observedProperty <sensor/35-207306-844818-0/BMP282/
atmosphericPressure> ;
  sosa:hasFeatureOfInterest  <earthAtmosphere> ;
  sosa:madeBySensor <sensor/35-207306-844818-0/BMP282> ;
  sosa:hasSimpleResult "1021.45 hPa"^^cdt:ucum ;
  sosa:resultTime "2017-06-06T12:36:12Z"^^xsd:dateTime.
```

The behaviours of sensors and actuators are defined by sosa:Procedure, which is a workflow describing how to perform an observation or impose a change on the state of the world (via an actuator). A *procedure* is designed for re-use, and can be related to many observations, samplings or actuations; it defines the steps required to arrive at reproducible results. For example, the measured wind speed may be different depending on the height of the sensor above the surface, and the corresponding procedures specify an algorithm that defines the use of a standard height for anemometers above ground to obtain the wind speed, typically 10 m for meteorological measures and 2 m in agrometeorology. This algorithm specifying height, sensor placement, and so on can be defined by the procedure.

Sensors detect changes in the physical world, which may be produced by physical systems or objects. These systems and objects are modelled as IoT entities (also called IoT resources) whose attributes/properties are monitored by sensors and are changed by actuators. Although an IoT entity can be represented by the OWL class *sosa:FeatureOfInterest* in the SSN specification (SSN, 2017), the relations between different entities are unspecified, as are certain specific characteristics of entities such as continuous dynamics; that is, IoT entities include not only classes and properties, but also behaviours. The behaviour of an IoT entity involves discrete events and continuous dynamics. The classes and properties of IoT entities can be defined in OWL, and their continuous dynamics can be defined using non-linear, high-order arithmetic functions.

Based on the above discussion, an IoT resource model consists of an object model (i.e. its classes and properties) and a lifecycle model (i.e. its behaviour). An object model represents sensors, actuators, physical entities and their relationships; the sensors are represented by resources which give a definition of the properties of the monitored entities, and physical entities such as those in a smart grid are represented by IoT entities, where their relationship represents the binding between an entity and a resource, i.e. an entity with a specific attribute. The relationships between resources and those among entities are also defined in the object model. In this chapter, IoT resources and entities are both referred to as resources. For example (Zhang et al., 2015), Figure 2a shows a temperature resource model that has different accuracy under different conditions; Figure 2b shows an entity model, which includes the resource and the relationships between entities. In addition, the resource model implies a service interface that allows business services to access the properties in its object model and to operate on its lifecycle states.

A lifecycle model describes the possible ways in which the resource may progress and the transition between two lifetime states. For example, Figure 5 shows a lifecycle model for a boiler (a resource). The boiler has three states: state 1 is represented by the atomic proposition $vmin < v < vmax$, i.e. a normal state with the temperature value in the range $vmin < v < vmax$; state 2 is represented by the atomic proposition $v \geq vmax$, i.e. where the boiler's

Figure 2. Example of a resource

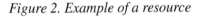
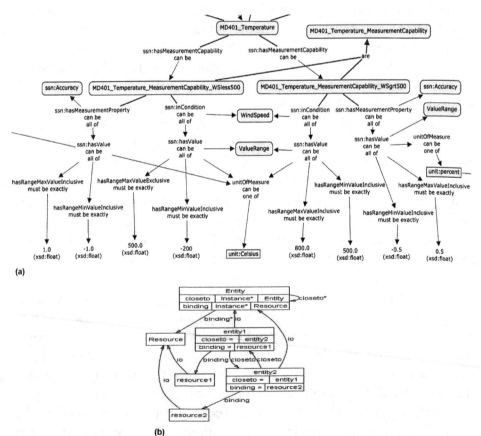

(a)

(b)

temperature exceeds some upper limit; and in state 3, the boiler resource's temperature is below the lower limit, which is represented by the atomic proposition $v \leq v\text{min}$.

Formal Abstraction of IoT Resources

In IoT applications, IoT entities are focal points, and the ways in which stimuli are obtained by sensors and transformed into observations are managed by a low-layer sensor management system, rather than by business services at higher layers. The models of sensors and actuators can therefore be abstracted without requiring information about how stimuli are transformed into observations.

In our work, a resource object model can be represented by a resource description framework (RDF), which is a collection of triples <subject, property, object> (Staab et al., 2009). An RDF graph (Peng et al., 2016) is not only intuitive, but also expressive. The graph partitioning method for a distributed RDF graph presented in Staab et al., (2009), Peng et al., (2016) is used here to circle a resource in the whole knowledge, and to clarify the relationship between two resources represented by crossing edges (see Figure 3). We extend the object model based on the RDF graph by attaching a resource lifecycle model to obtain a complete specification, as given in **Definition 1**.

- **Definition 1: IoT Resource:** *An IoT resource has an RDF graph G and a lifecycle description $T : IoTR ::= (G, T)$.*

- **Definition 2: Object Model:** *An RDF graph G is specified by $(V \cup V^e, E \cup E^c, \Sigma)$ such that*

1. *$V \cup V^e$ is a set of vertices corresponding to subjects and objects in RDF data; $E \cup E^c$ is a multiset of directed edges corresponding to triples in RDF data; $E \subseteq V \times V$; and Σ is a set of edge labels corresponding to properties in RDF data;*

2. *E^c is a set of crossing edges between G and other IoT resources $G_1, \cdots, G_n$, i.e.*

$$E^c = \bigcup_{i=1}^{n} \{\overrightarrow{vv'} \mid v \in V^e \wedge v' \in G_i.V^e \wedge (\overrightarrow{vv'} \in V^e \times G_i.V^e)\};$$

3. *A vertex $v \in V^e$ only when a vertex v' lies in another resource and v is an endpoint of crossing edges, i.e.*

$$V^e = \bigcup_{i=1}^{n} \{v \mid \overrightarrow{vv'} \in E^c \wedge v' \in G_i.V^e\};$$

4. *Vertices in V^e are denoted as external vertices, and all vertices in V are denoted as internal vertices.*

Figure 3 illustrates partial knowledge about the robot and operator resources, where these two resources work on the two common resources of the component and the platform. There are several external edges (e.g. the edge labelled *move*) between the robot and operator resources and the component and platform resources. It is worth pointing out that in resource object models, attributes are defined by predicates, unlike in the fluent calculus, which uses terms to define IoT resource attributes. The mapping method used in Drescher and Thielscher, (2007) can be used to integrate IoT resources into the fluent calculus, and this is straightforward (the mapping is considered to be implicit).

Non-linear constraints are introduced in Definition 2.3 for the continuous variables in the states of IoT resources (Moore et al., 2009; Ninin et al., 2009; Gao et al., 2012); these are suitable for specifying the constraints on complex continuous dynamics in IoT resources, and are not fully supported by RDF (Koubarakis et al., 2010).

- **Definition 3: Non-linear Constraints**: *A non-linear expression $\exp(\vec{x})$ for real numbers R is composed of real constants in R, real variables $\vec{x} = <x_1, \cdots, x_n>$, and real functions (e.g. $+, -, \times, \div$ and the transcendental functions $\sin(x_1), \cos(x_2)$). A non-linear constraint $\exp Con(\vec{x})$ is defined by $\exp(\vec{x}) \Theta c$, $\Theta \in \{=, \neq, >, \geq, <, \leq\}$, $c \in R$, and is called a constraint atom.*

Figure 3. Partial knowledge about robot and human resources

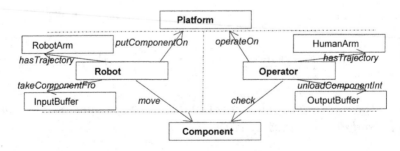

The resource lifecycle model is defined in Definition 2.4, where the causes predicate in the fluent calculus is used to specify that the event labelled in resource transitions is the cause fluent of the resource's transited state.

- **Definition 4: Lifecycle Model:** *The resource lifecycle $T ::= (State, Event, Const, Fun, Mapping, \delta)$ is a graph of states and state transitions, and is defined as follows:*

1. *State is the set of states: $z_0, \cdots, z_m$, where z_0 is the initial state;*
    2. *Event is the set of events $\{e_i\}$ governing state transitions;*
3. *Fun is the set of continuous functions representing complex attributes in resource states $\{attr_i = f_i(x_1, \cdots, x_k)\}$;*
4. *Const is the set of constraints for the resource attributes $\{form_i\}$, and is often represented by a non-linear constraint;*
5. *Mapping defines states as follows: $Mapping : State \rightarrow Const \times Fun$;*
6. *δ represents the state transitions: $Causes(z_j, e(e_i), z'_j, changedEffects'_j)$.*

The lifecycle model for the robot resource in Figure 4, $T ::= (State, Event, Const, Fun, Mapping, \delta)$ is as follows:

- *$State = \{z_0 = empty, z_1 = taking\}$;*
- *$Event = \{take, put\}$;*
- *$Fun = \{\vec{v}_r(t) = \vec{v}_r(0) + \int_0^t \vec{a}_r(\tau)d\tau, \vec{s}_r(t) = \vec{s}_r(0) + \int_0^t \vec{v}_r(\tau)d\tau\}$;*
- *$Const = \{\exp Con_1 ::= (dw_x, udw_y, dw_z) \le \vec{s}_r(t) \le (up_x, up_y, up_z)\}$;*
- *$Mapping : z_1 \rightarrow (\{\exp Con_1\}, \{\vec{v}_r(t), \vec{s}_r(t)\})$;*
- *$Causes(z_0, take, z_1, z_1 = z_0 + taking - empty)$ and $Causes(z_1, put, z_0, z_0 = z_1 - taking + empty)$.*

Figure 4. IoT resources: robot and machine

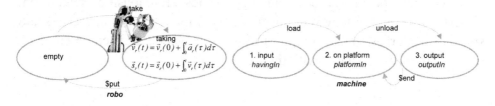

Figure 5. Boiler lifecycle model

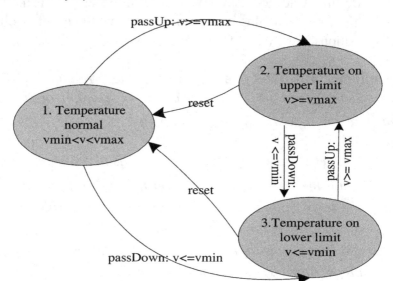

IOT SERVICES

Events, IoT Resources and IoT Services

An example is given here to show the relationships between events, IoT resources and IoT services. Figure 6 illustrates the relationship between a resource and two IoT services. A boiler resource is represented by an object model, i.e. a set of properties such as **SupplyWaterTemperature** and **ReturnWaterTemperature**, and a lifecycle model, as shown in Figure 5, in which the boiler generates heating for residents in winter. The two IoT services are the *Auto temperature control service* and *Energy-saving control service,* both of which read the boiler's attributes/properties and act on the boiler's lifecycle states to induce state transitions. Figure 6 also shows that these IoT services interact with the IoT resource via events, i.e. acting on the boiler's lifecycle states by publishing control events and obtaining the states of the boiler by subscribing to state transition events. These two services may make up a business process and have a causal relationship. In addition, a local resource pool may keep local copies of the attributes/properties and states of resources so that running IoT services can obtain a complete view of all resources associated with their execution.

Figure 6. The relationship between a service and a resource

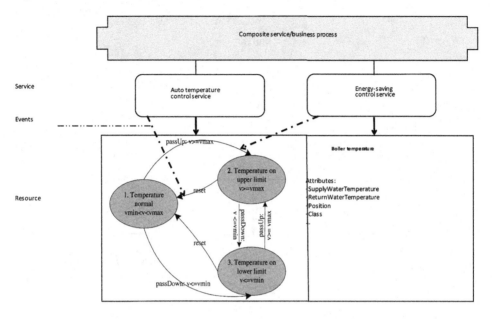

Defining IoT Services

IoT services use events to interact with IoT resources and to coordinate with each other. Events play a primary role in allowing an IoT service to run progressively. In order to enable the sharing of events among different IoT services, these events are named, i.e. a topic name is assigned to each type of event, and the relationship between multiple event names is often represented by a name tree. Figure 7 illustrates an example in which MaDian is a plant running boilers that provide a heating service for residents in winter. There are several types of events, such as analogous, signalling or control events. The analogous event has child topics such as water temperature and water pressure. Using these topic names and consumers' subscriptions, these events can be passed to the consumers. The definition of an event is given in Definition 5 below.

- **Definition 5: Event:** *An event is defined as*

event ::= topic_subject(topic_verbing, content)

Figure 7. A tree of topic names

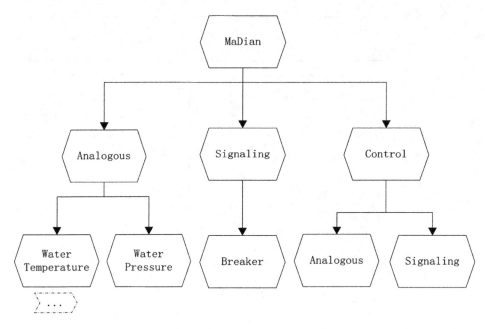

where topic_subject(topic_verbing) forms a topic name representing a type of event, and content represents an event body, which is often defined using an Extensible Markup Language (XML) schema (XML, 2003).

In the above definition, *verbing* may be empty, and Figure 8 illustrates an example of this. Figure 8 presents an XML schema of both an event and its *content*, where the *wsnt:Topic* element denotes a topic name (MaDian/ Analogous/WaterTemperature/AlarmBoiler), and the *wsnt:Message* element denotes the content of an event consisting of a series of name/value pairs such as Level/3 and Value/98.5. When a topic name is given, the elements in its content are defined.

Each IoT service function is reactive; it reacts to the occurrence of events in a similar way to functions in functional programming. In other words, the computational logic of IoT services involving service functions is executed based on events and the properties and states of the IoT resource, and is triggered by the occurrence of these events. The behaviour of an IoT service is described by a process theory *PA(ACT, PR)*; propositions are used as the parameters of *PA* to describe the IoT resource (properties and states) involved in this the behaviour, and service functions as the parameters of *PA* to describe the computation model of the IoT service.

Figure 8. Example of an event

```
<env:Envelope xmlns:env="http://schemas.xmlsoap.org/soap/envelop/"
        xmlns:env="http://www.w3.org/2005/08/addressing/">
  <env:Body>
    <wsnt:Notify xmlns:wsnt="http://docs.oasis-open.org/wsn/b-2/">
      <wsnt:NotificationMessage>
        <wsnt:Topic Dialect=".../wsn/t-1/TopicExpression/Simple">
          MaDian/Analogous/WaterTemperature/Alarm
        </wsnt:Topic>
        <wsnt:Message>
          <TemperatureAlarm>
          <Location>MaDian boiler plant</location>
          <Measure Parameter>Degrees Celsius</Measure Parameter>
          <Information> Upper limit exceeded</Information>
          <Value>98.5</Value>
          <Level>2</Level>
          </TemperatureAlarm>
        </wsnt:Message>
      </wsnt:NotificationMessage>
    </wsnt:Notify>
  </env:Body>
</env:Envelope>
```

- **Definition 6: IoT Service:** *An IoT service $IoTs := (ACT, PR, SUB, PUB, \psi)$ is a 5-tuple, where ACT is a set of actions; PR is a set of propositions composed of three parts, PR_{se}, a session proposition set, PR_{re}, a resource proposition set, and PR_{in}, an inner proposition set; SUB is a set of subscription interfaces represented by $[\phi]n(e,f)$, where $\phi \subseteq PR$, n is a topic name, e is an event with name n, and $f \in ACT$ is a function for reacting to e; PUB is a set of publication interfaces represented by $[\phi]\overline{n}(e,f)$ where $\phi \subseteq PR$, n is a topic name, e is an event with name n, and $f \in ACT$ is a function for producing e; and ψ describes the behaviour of $IoTs$. ψ is defined as follows:*

1. *Obtain a parameterised process theory $PA(PR, ACT)$;*
2. *The service behaviour is represented by a process in $PA(PR, ACT)$, where interfaces such as $[\phi]n(e,f)$ in SUB and PUB are included in the process.*

IoT services are designed based on resources, and are driven by events from these resources. In a service system (business process), however, multiple resources may be involved, and different resource lifecycles should be coordinated as well as different service operations on one resource's lifecycle. For example, a *breaker* resource and a *boiler* resource are illustrated in Figure 9. The breaker should be changed to the *OFF* state in its lifecycle before the boiler is changed into the repair state in its own lifecycle. The *electricity control service* operates on the *breaker's* lifecycle, causing the *breaker* to change from the *ON* state into the *OFF* state. The *boiler repair service* operates on the *breaker's* lifecycle, causing the *breaker* to change from the *normal* state into the *repair* state, indicating that the boiler should repaired by engineers. In order to keep the engineers safe, the *electricity control service* should be invoked before the *boiler repair service* is triggered, i.e. the two services should be coordinated.

Figure 10 gives a detailed specification of the service, corresponding to the components in Figure 9. The *electricity control service*, *RemoteCS*, has two interfaces with parallel behaviour. These two service interfaces include the realisation functions *OffControlSession* and *OnControlSession*, which use events to actuate the physical breaker/switcher using the proposition *switcherId = x*. When these functions are successfully completed, the *SwitcherOff* and *SwitcherOn* events are published. The behaviour of the *electricity control service* forms a process in *PA*. The *boiler repair* service, *RepairS*, is an independent service, and is not coordinated with *RemoteCS*. When we combine *RepairS* and *RemoteCS* into a business process, several event relations are defined between the events for the two services to represent the business requirements, thus defining a causality relation for the existing events. *RepairS* is then revised to get *RepairS'* by specifying an new event

Figure 9. Coordination of lifecycles and services

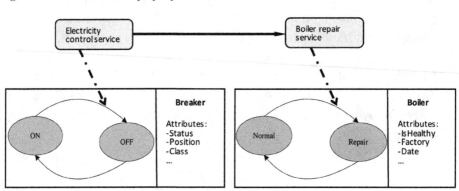

session, where $e(SwitcherOff)$ means the occurrence of event *SwitcherOff* and *switcherId* = x is a proposition about the event *SwitcherOff*, which are used to enable the condition of interface *DeviceAbnormal* in *RepairS'* to execute the function of *BeginRepair*. In other words, the services *RemoteCS* and *RepairS* are coordinated as a composite service based on events, although they are designed independently.

USING AN EVENT SESSION TO COORDINATE IOT SERVICES

In a service system (business process), multiple resources are involved in which a variety of resource lifecycles need to be coordinated, and a variety of service operations also need be coordinated. Although events can be used to drive and coordinate these components, an event-based method of organizing and grouping them is still unavailable. We introduce the concept of an event session as a basis for the coordination task; this retains the decoupling features of events, since the service operations are executed based on events which induce a state transition in the resource lifecycles, and the potential of event-driven methodologies can thus be further exploited. In this way, event sessions are used to ensure event relations (e.g. event causality and event conflict).

In a service environment, events from different services are independent; in a system consisting of these services, each service has its own behaviour, and interactions take place between services that mean that these events are not independent within the system. An event is identified by its topic name, and a single topic name may correspond to multiple events. In order to describe the service behaviour and interactions in a service system, both the event topic and also the content contained within the event are used.

Based on the event content, an event session is defined by a series of name/value pairs in the content (a subset of all the name/value pairs in the content). Two events belong to the same session if they have the same name/value pairs as session identifiers. An action that is constrained by a session proposition in the service behaviour can react to a notified event if the name/value pairs in the event content include those name/value pairs that appear in the session proposition, i.e. if each pair included in the session proposition has the same name and value as the name/value pair in the event content. For example, the action [*Level* = 2;;] *BoilerAlarmTopic*(*content*) can receive the event in shown Figure 8.

Figure 10. Two services and the coordination between them

$RepairS= [;;]DeviceAbnormal(deviceId,BeginRepair(deviceId))[;;]\overline{DeviceNormal(deviceId)}$
$([;;]DeviceNormal(deviceId,NormalAction(deviceId))|[;;]Start(deviceId,NormalAction(deviceId)))$.
$DeviceInspection(deviceId,InspectDevice(deviceId))(\overline{DeviceNormal(deviceId)}+\overline{DeviceAbnormal(deviceId)}$

$RepairS' = [switcherId = x;switcherId.state= OFF, e(SwitcherOff);]DeviceAbnormal(deviceId,BeginRepair(deviceId))$.
$\overline{DeviceNormal(deviceId)}$
$([;switcherId.state= ON;]DeviceNormal(deviceId,NormalAction(deviceId))|$
$[;switcherId.state= ON;]Start(deviceId,NormalAction(deviceId)))$.
$DeviceInspection(deviceId,InspectDevice(deviceId))(\overline{DeviceNormal(deviceId)}+\overline{DeviceAbnormal(deviceId)}$

$RemoteCS=$
$[switcherId = x;state= ON;]On2Off(switcherId,OffControlSession(switcherId))$.
$[switcherId = x;state= OFF;]\overline{SwitcerOff(switcherId)}|$
$[switcherId = x;state= OFF;]Off2On(switcherId,OnControlSession(switcherId))$.
$[switcherId = x;state= ON;]\overline{SwitcerOn(switcherId)}$

While a topic name is used to identify a type of event and can be used as a way of matching events, the session identifier is used to identify a specific event, i.e. different event instances of a given topic name with different values in the name/value pairs. A service uses a topic name to describe the events (changes on the attributes or lifecycle of a resource) that it consumes or produces; it uses a session as a fine-grained mechanism to describe the event instances and content that it consumes or produces. The event causality can be expressed based on the session mechanism; that is, a session proposition for a subscription action describes the event directly causing the action, since the notified event needs to satisfy the session proposition before the action is enabled. Compared with the channel mechanism in a request/reply-based service interaction, the session mechanism for a publish/subscribe- based service interaction is information-centric, and has the following characteristics:

1. The use of a topic name as a subscription is efficient in simply matching the subscription against the events in the service environment. An information-centric network architecture also uses the data name as a basic mechanism for describing a customer's interest and data in the network, which offers efficiency in handling large-scale data.
2. The session mechanism is used to identify the event content and specific instances of the event, to express event causality and conflict, and to create service transactions that cut across multiple services and multiple

interaction rounds. This is in keeping with the event-driven methodology, i.e. reacting to the occurrence of events without being concerned with their 'from' or 'to'.

In the service description (Definition 6) together with event sessions, the action in the publish/subscribe interface is defined by the topic name (event name) and a session proposition, which describes the types of events that are consumed. Session propositions are used to describe the data content and event relations, and $[\phi]a$ is then defined by the event name (topic) and a function condition represented by event sessions (i.e., session propositions), such that the publish/subscribe interface $[\phi]a$ can be viewed as a meaningful independent unit. In other words, if the event name (topic), event content and relation in $[\phi]a$ are satisfied, the functionality represented by $[\phi]a$ is available. Because the publish/subscribe interface $[\phi]a$ is meaningful and independent, event sessions can group multiple such interface units crossing different services and interaction rounds.

An example is given in Figure 11, which illustrates a service behavior crossing multiple services with multiple rounds.

Figure 11 shows a collaboration diagram (Bultan & Fu, 2008) that illustrates the interactions between multiple services in a service system. It is for a remote-controlled service interaction in a typical IoT system, and contains three services: *Prime Dispatcher*, *Slave Dispatcher* and *Actuator*

Figure 11. A remote-control service interaction

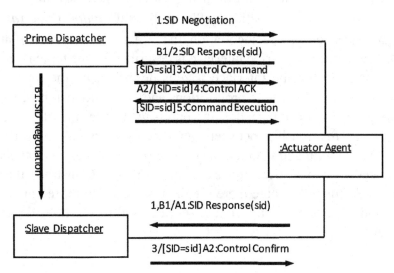

Agent. In this example, the prime dispatcher sends a session negotiation event for remote control. The event is received by the slave dispatcher and the actuator agent. The actuator agent calculates the session identifier, and sends the session response with session identifier *sid* to the prime dispatcher and slave dispatcher. The prime dispatcher then sends a control command event, and the slave dispatcher sends a control confirm event, to confirm the correctness of the control command. This dual dispatcher mechanism is used to assure that critical devices are correctly operated. When the control events from the prime and slave dispatcher are received, the actuator agent prepares the control context, and sends a control ACK event to the prime dispatcher to indicate that preparation is complete. Finally, the prime dispatcher sends the command execution event after receiving the ACK event.

The service behaviour of *Prime Dispatcher* is as follows:

$$\mathrm{Pr}\,imeDispacther = \overline{t}_{1,B1}(random1).\,[random1 = random2;;]$$
$$t_{2,A1}(sid, random2).$$
$$[SID = sid, random1 = random2; ridvalue > limit;]\overline{t}_3(SID, rid, down).$$
$$[SID = sid; ridvalue > \lim it;]t_4(SID, rid').$$
$$[SID = sid, rid = rid'; ridvalue > \lim it;]\overline{t}_5(SID, rid).\,\mathrm{Pr}\,imeDispacther$$

where $t_{1,B_1} = SID\ Negotiation$, $t_{2,A1} = SID\ Response$, $t_3 = Control\ Command$, $t_4 = Control\ ACK$ and $t_5 = Command\ Execution$. $ridvalue > limit$ means that the value of resource with identifier *rid* must be greater than the threshold *limit* in order to enable the action $t_4(SID, rid')$, and *random*1 and *random*2 are initial nonces for session negotiation. In this example, we know that each action in the publish/subscribe interface is described by the topic name, and that the publish/subscribe interface $[\phi]a$ is described by the topic name, session propositions, resource propositions and other propositions.

Although events are independent in a publish/subscribe middleware, there are dependency relationships between events within a service system, because the service behaviour and interactions govern how events are exchanged and how services react to the occurrence of events. Figure 12 illustrates the event causality of Figure 11, where there are three services and three interaction threads, and the events from different services and interactions depend on each other.

Figure 12. An event dependency relation

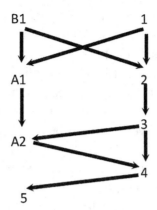

In summary, it is expected that the events in one IoT service system are independent of other service systems at the behaviour layer, although in a specific IoT service system, a dependency relationship often exists among its events where the service behaviour and its structure represented by a process indicates the event relations. For example, a particular service in a system is in charge of actuating a switch, while another service is in charge of dispatching workers to repair certain devices in a power station. Before the *repair event* takes place, an *actuation off event* must have happened. However, in a data storage system, these two events are not required to take place sequentially. We therefore adopt an information-centric principle, giving an event session mechanism where each service operation is a meaningful unit, and multiple publish/subscribe interfaces of different services can be organized and ordered. This gives a basis to realize the behaviour decoupling, meaning that each service system is independent from the others.

GRAPHICAL MODELLING OF BUSINESS PROCESS BASED ON EVENT SESSIONS

In our work, an event has a fine-grained expression. The topic name expresses a type of event that can be used to describe a service interface, and to carry out matching and routing in a service environment, while the event session and the topic name are used to express a specific event instance and identify its content, which is then used to coordinate actions from different services and interaction rounds by placing a number of events into the same group.

For example, in Figure 9, the event *SwitcherOff* contains a session identifier to identify a specific switch being in the off state; this is used to coordinate the *BeginRepair* function of the other service, in order to ensure that work is done under safe conditions. Together with certain session propositions, the event session can be used to describe the causality and conflict relationships between events. In the event-driven process chains (EPC) graphical model (Keller et al., 1992; Scheer, 1998; Aalst, 1999), there is no fine-grained event expression, and subsets of events cannot be grouped together for particular coordination goals. In Mukkamala, (2012), an event-driven method was adopted to graphically model business processes, but this did not address the issues of fine-grained event expression, the grouping of subsets of events for coordination, or the introduction of IoT resources into the model.

Formal Definition of Event Sessions

An event session is defined by a series of name/value pairs in the event content (a subset of all of the name/value pairs in the content).

- **Definition 7: Event Session:** *An event session consists of two parts:*

1. **Session Identifier:** *A session identifier is a set of name/value pairs that is a subset of the name/value pairs in the event content.*
2. **Session Proposition:** *The session proposition of a service function determines whether it belongs to the session. If the session identifier satisfies the proposition, i.e. the values in the identifier mean that the proposition is **True**, the functions governed by the proposition belong to the session identified by the session identifier.*

Two events belong to the same session if they have the same name/value pairs as the session identifier. A service function guarded by a session proposition can react to a notification event if the name/value pairs in the event content include the name/value pairs in the session proposition, i.e. each pair contained in the session proposition has the same name and value as those in the event content. For example, the action [*Level* = 2] *BoilerAlarmTopic*(*content*, *DoAlarm* can react to the event in Figure 8, where {*Level*/2} is a session identifier and [*Level* = 2] is a session proposition which guards the service function *DoAlarm*.

When a session identifier is given, several actions (service functions, their guards and interfaces) from different services can join the session with appropriate guard propositions, and many events from different interaction rounds may be organized into the same session if they include the same name/value pairs as in the identifier.

It should be pointed out that the session mechanism can express a specific event relation. For example, if the session proposition guarding a function is evaluated to be **True** on the basis of an occurring event, this is a causal event for the event produced by the function.

Modelling IoT Business Processes

Multiple IoT services can be combined to form a business process or a composite service. Following the modelling of IoT services, a discussion is needed of how to compose these services to construct an event-driven business process for IoT applications. The event session method can be used for service coordination that cuts across multiple services and multiple rounds of service interactions. However, it is not a complete and graphical business process description, and in this chapter, an EPC graphical modelling method is combined with the event session method to model event-driven business process.

EPC was introduced (Keller et al., 1992; Scheer, 1998) for the graphical description of business logic based on events, and the process is specified as a chain of events and functions, including *Event, Function, Logical Connector, Organization Unit* and *Resource Object*. A function corresponds to a process step (activity, task, a service action, or a service function); logical connectors are used to connect events, representing *AND*, *OR* and *XOR* relationships; the organizational unit determines which structure of an enterprise is in charge of the process step; and resource objects portray entities in the real world. Fine-grained event expression is lacking in EPC. Thus, EPC is adapted here as follows:

1. Each event in EPC is identified by its topic name, i.e. the event icon is filled with the topic name. The topic name can be attached by a session identifier if the corresponding event belongs to the session.
2. Each function in EPC can be attached by a guard, such as resource propositions and session propositions, and the guard is written into the function icon.
3. Two functions are not directly connected, and between these are the events. A directed edge between a function and an event indicates that the function either publishes an event or subscribes to it.

Figure 13 shows a detailed graphical process specification of the example in Figure 9, where an event is denoted by hexagon, a function by a rounded rectangle, and a resource object by a rectangle. The service process is composed of the two services *RemoteCS* and *RepairS* in Figure 9. In the service process, the two services are coordinated using events and one event session. The two events of *On2Off* and *SwitcherOff* have the same session identifier, *switcherId/x*, and belong to the same session. The process activity (service function) *BeginRepair* has the session proposition *switcherId = x*, and belongs to the session identified by the session identifier *switcherId/x*.

IOT SERVICE PROPERTY

In most existing works on the verification of business processes (Aalst, 1999), the checking and asserting of the soundness, liveness, etc. of the processes are considered to be the basic tasks of modelling. IoT services often directly manage and control society-critical physical entities in a physical environment, and the environment needs to be explicitly modelled to ensure high levels of safety, security and so on (Koutsoukos et al., 2002). Furthermore, making each service hold its properties in a composition is a basic criterion for realizing fully behavioural decoupling in the composite system. Three issues can be identified, as follows:

1.   How to model an environment;

Figure 13. A service process for the safe management of devices

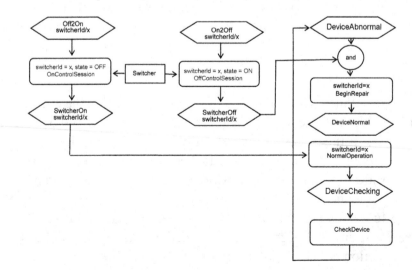

2.   Which properties of an IoT service can be checked and verified;
3.   How to avoid the state explosion problem when verifying a system composed of multiple IoT services.

The environment cannot be controlled or predicted, and it is impossible to completely and accurately define its behaviour; an attempt is therefore made to model it by defining its inferred capabilities. After the environment model has been established, the properties of the IoT service are computed based on the knowledge set for the environment. For example, if we want to know whether an event can eventually take place, a query is formulated as to whether the occurrence of the event is a logical consequence of the knowledge about the environment that can be obtained from the behaviour, computation equations and resource propositions of the service. The authenticity of security checking holds if the causal event can be inferred from the effect event.

For a composite IoT service, the state explosion problem becomes a hindrance to computing its properties meaning that divide-and-conquer methods need to be used. The divide-and-conquer method used here also provides a formal method of computing whether, if the behaviour of a service is decoupled from the service system, its properties are correctly separated; that is, whether the properties of each service can be independently checked without traversing all the states of the whole service system, and whether they hold in the composite system without being impaired by others. This is called fully behavioural decoupling, and can offer a solid basis for the distributed execution of a business process.

Modelling IoT Service Properties From an Environmental Perspective

Given an IoT service specification, including its interfaces, behaviour, computation model and data model, we can compute the properties of the IoT service, such as its safety and security (Aalst, 1999) in a specific environment. In general, the environment can be classified into three types: ideal environments; active environments; and passive environments. In an ideal environment, service events are ideally exchanged, without being discarded, forged or eavesdropped. An active environment may pass any event to the IoT services as input, discard events produced by these services, or forge certain events based on its knowledge. In a passive environment, some service events may be discarded but cannot be forged. In this book, an active environment called a realistic environment is used as an example in our work. An on-demand environment can be defined according to certain specific requirements, i.e. by listing its capabilities.

In a realistic environment, the actions of the service are viewed in terms of traces created by its behaviour process. A frame is an observable trace recorded by the environment, which is translated into facts and clauses in first-order logic, and a deduction based on resolution is carried out to obtain or to forge specific service events (Blanchet et al., 2008; Ciobaca, 2011).

For example, there are two traces in the service *RemoteCS*, as follows (where $\mapsto$ is a sign used to separate two actions):

$$\left[switcherId = x; state = ON; \right] On2Off\left(switcherId, OffControlSession\left(switcherId \right) \right) \mapsto$$
$$\left[switcherId = x; state = OFF; \right] SwitcherOff\left(switcherId \right),$$

$$\left[switcherId = x; state = OFF; \right] Off2On\left(switcherId, OffControlSession\left(switcherId \right) \right) \mapsto$$
$$\left[switcherId = x; state = ON; \right] SwitcherOn\left(switcherId \right),$$

In the first trace, the frame is *{w$_1$ → SwitcherOff(switcherId / x) }*. The environment can observe an event *SwitcherOff(switcherId / x)* produced from the service *RemoteCS*.

The environment observes the running of the behaviour process to obtain its knowledge. In runtime verification, the environment collects the runtime events of the process to make inferences. For verification during the modelling phase, we analyse the behaviour process to obtain knowledge of the environment, traversing each activity in the process to obtain all possible running traces, and using the observable parts of each trace to form a frame, which is translated into facts and clauses. Given an initial knowledge set Λ, a trace *tr* from a service model *P*, a model *P* with equational theory (Σ, E) and a proposition set *PR*, knowledge generation of the environment is carried out as follows:

1. For $\bar{t}(d, f) \in tr$ in *P*, if the frame index for $\bar{t}(d)$ is w_i, then $\Lambda = \Lambda \cup \{\rightarrow K(w_i, t(d)), \rightarrow e(t(d))\}$ when the topic name *t* is public, where $t(d)$ is the output of *f* and $e(t(d))$ is a predicate stating that event $t(d)$ took place;
2. For a public name *n*, $\Lambda = \Lambda \cup \{\rightarrow K(n, n)\}$;

3. For a n-arity function f in Σ, $\Lambda = \Lambda \cup \{K(X_1, x_1), \ldots, K(X_n, x_n) \rightarrow K(f(X_1, \ldots, X_n), f(x_1, \ldots, x_n))\}$ where $X_1, \ldots, X_n$ are distinct names, and $x_1, \ldots, x_n$ are fresh variables;

4. For $[\varphi]\bar{t}(d, f)$ in P corresponding to $\bar{t}(d, f) \in tr$ with index w_i, $\Lambda = \Lambda \cup \{\varphi \rightarrow K(w_1, t(d)), \varphi \rightarrow e(t(d))\}$ where $\varphi \subseteq PR$.

$t(d)$ is not used to generate the knowledge "$\rightarrow K(w_1, t(d))$", because knowledge about d is derived from $\bar{t}(d)$. $\rightarrow K(w_1, t(d))$ means that the environment knows the event $t(d)$ without conditions, and assigns an index w_i to this observed event $t(d)$. Further discussion about the translation between processes and knowledge can be found in Blanchet et al., (2008), and Ciobaca, (2011). For example, the first trace of the service *RemoteCS* is translated as follows:

```
Λ = {  →K(x,x),  →K(ON, ON),
((switcherId of SwitcherOff(switcherId / x) = x), (state = ON))
→ K(w1, OffControlSession(x)),
((switcherId of SwitcherOff(switcherId/x) = x), (state = ON)) →
e(SwitcherOff(switcherId/x)),
K(Y1,y1)  K(OffControSession(Y1), OffControlSession(y1))
}
```

The equation set for the service *RemoteCS* is as follows:

```
{  OffControlSession(y) = SwitcherOff(switcherId / y),
   OnControlSession(y) = SwitcherOn(switcherId/ Y) }.
```

The knowledge about the IoT resource can be viewed as initial knowledge, and is public.

The environment is able to use its knowledge to infer certain results using the resolution method and equation set E in the equational theory (Σ, E). In the resolution method, a unification procedure is repeatedly used (Baader & Snyder, 2001; Baader & Nipkow, 1998). This unification and resolution implies a competition between the environment and the service, since the unification operation means that all possible attacks (giving different inputs to the service) are tried in order to test the response of the service. The equation set E for the existing knowledge set is used to generate more knowledge, and the resolution method is carried out on the enlarged knowledge set (Baader & Snyder, 2001; Baader & Nipkow, 1998; Blanchet et al., 2008; Ciobaca, 2011).

The notation $\sigma| = p$ indicates that the environment's knowledge set $\{\sigma\}$ from trace σ satisfies the property formula p, and the trace-satisfaction is written as follows:

- $\sigma \models \theta_1 \wedge \theta_2$ if $\sigma \models \theta_1$ and $\sigma \models \theta_2$,
- $\sigma \models \theta_1 \vee \theta_2$ if $\sigma \models \theta_1$ or $\sigma \models \theta_2$.

We then define $P \models \theta$, which means that each trace in the IoT service P forms an environmental knowledge set such that the property formula θ holds, where P can be viewed as a trace set.

Composing IoT Service Properties

If two services (or business processes) run concurrently in the same environment, their actions may be coordinated. When the two services are coordinated, the properties of each may be affected by those of the other. We need check the states of the whole composite system in order to verify each original property, and to increase the complexities of the computation. If one service has a property that holds in the composite service, this service is considered to be fully decoupled. The properties of a fully decoupled service are not affected by other services, and can be verified with reference only to the behaviour of the service, without the need to traverse all the states of the composition. A formal criterion is required for the decoupling of a service from others, and a *symmetric circular rule* is therefore proposed to compute the properties of the composite system while avoiding the state explosion problem. This rule is somewhat similar to that used in Namjosh et al., (2010), which did not address the issue of explicitly modelling the environment as an opponent to compute the service properties. In the current work, the environment is able to observe the operation of the service to obtain a *frame,* and to translate this frame into its knowledge set, which also includes service computation knowledge and IoT resource knowledge. The environment can use this knowledge to carry out inferences, and discard or forge events, where the unification procedure (Baader & Snyder, 2001; Baader & Nipkow, 1998) is used for the forging and competing task.

Symmetric Circular Rule

$$P_1 \models (h_2 \rightarrow \phi_1) \wedge h_1$$
$$\frac{P_2 \models (h_1 \rightarrow \phi_2) \wedge h_2}{P_1 \mid P_2 \models \phi_1 \wedge \phi_2}$$

where $P_1 \models (h_2 \rightarrow \phi_1) \wedge h_1$ means that service P_1 in a given environment has the property ϕ_1 if P_2 in the environment assumes h_2; P_1 in the environment assumes another property h_1; $P_2 \models (h_1 \rightarrow \phi_2) \wedge h_2$ means that the service P_2 in the environment has the property ϕ_2 if P_1 in the environment assumes h_1; P_2 in the environment also has another property h_2. The symmetric circular rule says that, if its assumptions hold, then it is guaranteed that $P_1 \mid P_2 \models \phi_1 \wedge \phi_2$, meaning that the parallel composition of P_1 and P_2 has the property $\phi_1 \wedge \phi_2$ in that environment.

APPLICATIONS

An EDSOA-based district heating service system is illustrated in Figure 14, in which heat is generated by a power plant or boiler room and sent to residential homes and commercial buildings in the surrounding district.

In Beijing, China, heating is generally provided by traditional coal-fired and gas-fired boilers. In order to reduce carbon emissions and improve air quality in Beijing, there is a need to establish a new and efficient district heating system, which operates at the highest levels of efficiency. In this new district heating system, there are multiple substation systems in which numerous meters are deployed; these produce real-time metered data collected by a programmable logic controller (PLC), or receive actuation instruction from the PLC through an RS-485 communication interface. The *Monitor Agent Service* communicates with the PLC through the standard Modbus protocol.

The system as a whole consists of three parts: multiple substation service systems, one headquarter service system, and one government heating management system. These are connected with distributed event-based service environments, and there is a local resource pool at each site as well as a local event relation synergising utility. The substation service system is composed of the *Monitor Agent Service*, the *Actuator Agent Service*, and a resource state maintenance service called the *Constructing Resource Service*. The monitor agent service collects sensed raw data at the local site, generates alarm events from these raw data based on the resource model and the resource state in the resource pool, and then publishes the observed data and alarm events to the distributed service environment for other services to consume; the actuator agent service receives actuation events from the distributed service environment and creates a session with an upper remote control service to safely actuate the local devices; and the constructing resource service subscribes the observed data and alarm events to the distributed service environment and maintains the resource states in the resource pool. The resource states in the pool are directly accessed by other services and those considered to be standard services. The headquarters system includes services similar to those in the substation system, together with an *HMI Service*, a *Warning Service*, and other business services. In Figure 14, the DEBS-based service environment utilises a publish/subscribe mechanism to disseminate events, while the event broker acts as a critical component to support the event publication, subscription, notification and routing functions. The headquarters service system uses the distributed events to interact with the government heating management information system, which subscribes emergency events and statistical data. The various substation systems and headquarters system are all connected through event brokers. In general, only one event broker is used by a given substation system to process events among its own different sub-services. At the same time, this broker also delivers events to the headquarters system. Since the different service systems interact with each other in an event-driven pattern, the degree of system coupling is greatly reduced.

Figure 15 shows a typical event flow for the IoT application in Figure 14, in which there are six IoT services: the monitor and control agent (MCA) service, event analysis (EA) service, human machine interface (HMI) service, remote control (RA) service, warning service, and resource model (RM) service. The event flow in Figure 15 is as follows:

1. The sensed data (topic t1) published by MCA (S1) is received by HMI (S3). HMI displays the data to the dispatchers in the form of pictures and tables.
2. The abnormal alarm (topic t2) published by MCA (S1) is received by HMI (S3), the EA (S2), and the warning service (S5). HMI displays the alarm to the dispatchers using pictures and tables. The warning service

Figure 14. An EDSOA-based district heating service system

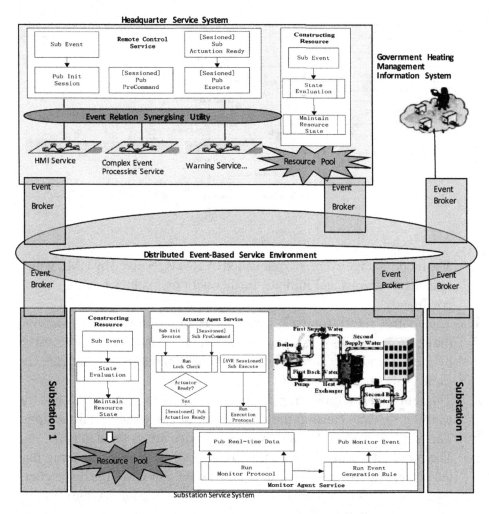

notifies the relevant individuals in various ways, such as via lights, sounds, voice warnings, e-mail, etc. The EA uses the event to evaluate the state of safety of the mine.

3. The control instruction (topic t3) can be sent by HMI or the RA. MCA receives the command. MCA publishes the control result after executing the control according to the command.

4. The control result (topic t4) sent by MCA is received by HMI or the RA if she is the commander, which is handled by the session mechanism. The warning service also receives this.

Figure 15. The event flow

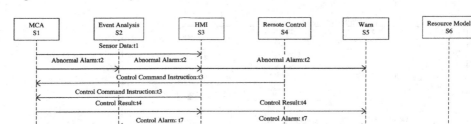

5. The mode change event (t8) published by RM is received by HMI, which updates its graphs and initiates further actions, such as issuing control commands.

6. The control alarm (topic t7) is sent by HMI or the RA after receiving the control result and evaluating the result. The control alarm is received by the EA and the warning service, the responses from which are the same as for step (2).

7. The action alarm (topic t6) published by HMI is received by EA and the warning service, causing the dispatchers to carry out certain actions. The responses of the EA and warning service are as for step (2).

8. The problem alarm (t5) is published by HMI or the EA, meaning that the power system is in a very dangerous state. For HMI, the dispatchers take the decision that there is a serious danger, while for EA, the decision is made by computers.

RELATED WORK

SOA (Erl, 2005) is used to break application silos, and to achieve reuse and interoperability of functionality. In SOA, the complete application is broken down into multiple independent services as described by the standard interface specifications. EDA (2013) is a loosely-coupled application coordination pattern that specifies how to produce, detect, consume and react to events. In EDA, these independent services can be combined together using event flow in a dynamic way. EDA can complement SOA by using events to replace function invocation (Maréchaux, 2006). The work done in Laliwala et al., (2008) explored the integration of SOA with EDA, while the studies in Overbeek et al., (2009), Overbeek et al., (2012), Dasgupta et al., (2009) discussed EDA and SOA for services. Clark and Barn, (2012) proposed a simple extension to UML that supports both SOA and EDA. The study of Zhu et al., (2011) addresses how to use EDSOA in IoT.

EDSOA is information-centric, and an information-centric methodology is often adopted when designing services and business processes such as business artefacts (Cohn & Hull, 2009), (Hull et al., 2011), which are business-relevant objects that are generated, evolved, and stored when they pass through a business. The business artefact is often defined by an information model and a lifecycle model; the information model defines the data used in the lifetime of the business objects, while the lifecycle model defines the possible state transition and timings of business objects, which can be used to describe tasks for these objects. The information model for the business artefacts is not suitable for IoT services, since it includes no concepts of resources or binding between resources and entities. This study also did not discuss how to use events to complete service coordination. The resource service described in the current work can be used in a natural and straightforward way to represent business artefacts.

The authors of Ferrari et al., (2006), Ciancia et al., (2010) addressed the service coordination issue based on distributed events. A formal model of service coordination was proposed in Ciancia et al., (2010), and a middleware based on the former was implemented. This framework allows the design and programming of service coordination policies that rely only on event notifications. The coordination policies were regulated by specifying how services react to events, and the coordination policies are in fact processes in a process calculus. However, in this formal model, receivers must be explicitly specified when an event is published and a point-to-point channel is used; this is not the case in the scenarios in the current work. The work in Ciancia et al., (2010) was an extension of that in Ferrari et al., (2006), which only addressed the service choreography problem. This formal model was tailored to express coordination patterns within the event notification paradigm by combining suitable mechanisms such as event and network hiding, network reconfiguration and multicast communication. The concept of an event session was not introduced.

For collaboration between services, the interaction between multi-participants needs to be managed as a session, which can be explicitly defined and handled, and this is particularly necessary for transactions. The authors

Abreu, (2009), and Guidi and Lucchi, (2008) proposed session handling mechanisms for service-oriented computing. We adopt the method put forward in Guidi and Lucchi, (2008) to handle service sessions, in which a session is defined as a correlation set, that is, a set of name/value (name/name) pairs in processes. If different participants have the same correlation set, i.e. the same process names and same values, they have the same session. These authors did not focus on events.

CONCLUSION

This chapter discusses how to model physical sensors and devices as IoT resources, how to introduce IoT resources into IoT services, and how to use distributed events to connect IoT resources and IoT services together to form an IoT service system. We can use resource information to specify IoT services, use independent and shared events to drive IoT services, and use event sessions to coordinate IoT services. In order to streamline events to integrate IoT services, the concept of an event session is defined, an aspect which has generally been neglected in most existing works on EDSOA. Based on the concept of an event session, a graphical modelling method is proposed to describe IoT business processes and IoT service properties for observed events. Several applications are described as a proof of concept for event-driven IoT services over IoT resources.

REFERENCES

Baader & Snyder. (2001). *Unification Theory*. Academic Press.

Baader, F., & Nipkow, T. (1998). Term rewriting and all that. Cambridge University Press. doi:10.1017/CBO9781139172752

Baeten, J. C. M., Basten, T., & Renters, M. A. (2010). Process algebra: Equational theories of communicating processes. Cambridge University Press.

Blanchet, B., Abadib, M., & Fournet, C. (2008). Automated verification of selected equivalences for security protocols. *Journal of Logic and Algebraic Programming*, 75(1), 3–51. doi:10.1016/j.jlap.2007.06.002

Bultan, T., & Fu, X. (2008). Specification of realizable service conversations using collaboration diagrams. *Service Oriented Computing and Applications, 2*(1), 27–39. doi:10.100711761-008-0022-7

Ciancia, V., Ferrari, G., Guanciale, R., & Strollo, D. (2010). Event based choreography. *Science of Computer Programming, 75*(10), 848–878. doi:10.1016/j.scico.2010.02.009

Ciobaca, S. (2011). *Verification and composition of security protocols with applications to electronic voting.* Dissertation.

Clark, T., & Barn, B. S. (2012). A common basis for modelling service-oriented and event-driven architecture. *Proceedings of the 5th ACM India Software Engineering Conference,* 23-32. 10.1145/2134254.2134258

Cohn, D., & Hull, R. (2009). Business artifacts: A data-centric approach to modeling business operations and processes. *IEEE Data Eng. Bull., 32*(3), 3–9.

Cuijpers, P. J. L., & Reniers, M. A. (2005). Hybrid process algebra. *Journal of Logic and Algebraic Programming, 62*(2), 191–245. doi:10.1016/j.jlap.2004.02.001

Dasgupta, S., Bhat, S., & Lee, Y. (2009). An abstraction framework for service composition in event-driven SOA systems. *Proceedings of IEEE International Conference on Web Services,* 671-678. 10.1109/ICWS.2009.103

de Abreu, J. P. A. (2009). *Modelling business conversations in service component architectures.* Retrieved from http://www.cs.le.ac.uk/~jpad2/publications/thesis_abreu.pdf

Drescher, C., & Thielscher, M. (2007). Integrating action calculi and description logics. *Lecture Notes in Computer Science, 4667,* 68–83. doi:10.1007/978-3-540-74565-5_8

EDA. (2013). *Event-driven architecture overview.* Retrieved from http://www.omg.org/soa/Uploaded%20Docs/EDA/bda2-2-06cc.pdf

Erl, T. (2005). *Service-oriented architecture: Concepts, technology, and design.* Prentice Hall.

Ferrari, G. L., Guanciale, R., & Strollo, D. (2006). Lecture Notes in Computer Science: Vol. 4229. *JSCL: A middleware for service coordination.* Springer.

Gao, S., Avigad, J., & Clarke, E. M. (2012). δ-Complete decision procedures for satisfiability over the reals. *Computer Science, 7364*, 286–300.

Guidi, C., & Lucchi, R. (2008). *Programming service oriented applications. Research technical report of University of Bologna*. Retrieved from ftp://ftp. cs.unibo.it:/pub/TR/UBLCS

Hull, R., Damaggioy, E., De Masellisz, R., & Fourniel, F. (2011). Business artifacts with guard-stage-milestone lifecycles: Managing artifact interactions with conditions and events. *Proceedings of the International Conference on Distributed Event-Based Systems*, 51-62. 10.1145/2002259.2002270

Keller, G., Nuttgens, M., & Scheer, A. W. (1992). *Semantische process modellierungauf der grundlage ereignisgesteuerter processketten (EPK). In Veroffentlichungen des Instituts fur Wirtschaftsinformatik* (Vol. 89). Saarbrucken: University of Saarland. (in German)

Koubarakis, M., & Kyzirakos, K. (2010). Modeling and querying metadata in the Semantic Sensor Web: The model stRDF and the query language stSPARQL. *International Conference on the Semantic Web: Research & Applications, 2*(1), 425-439. 10.1007/978-3-642-13486-9_29

Koutsoukos, X. D., & Antsaklis, P. J. (2002). Design of stabilizing switching control laws for discrete- and continuous-time linear systems using piecewise-linear Lyapunov functions. *International Journal of Control, 75*(12), 932–945. doi:10.1080/00207170210151076

Laliwala, Z., & Chaudhary, S. (2008). Event-driven service-oriented architecture. *Proceedings of IEEE International Conference on Service Systems and Service Management*, 1-6.

Maréchaux, J. L. (2006). *Combining service-oriented architecture and event-driven architecture using an enterprise service bus*. IBM Developer Works.

Moore, R. E., Kearfott, R. B., & Cloud, M. J. (2009). Introduction to interval analysis. Society for Industrial and Applied Mathematics.

Mukkamala, R. R. (2012). *A formal model for declarative workflows: Dynamic condition response graphs* (Dissertation). IT University of Copenhagen.

Namjosh, K. S., & Trefler, R. J. (2010). On the completeness of compositional reasoning methods. *ACM Transactions on Computational Logic, 11*(3), 1–22. doi:10.1145/1740582.1740584

Ninin, Messine, & Hansen. (2009). A reliable affine relaxation method for global optimization. *4OR, 13*(3), 247-277.

Overbeek, S., Janssen, M., & van Bommel, P. (2012). Designing, formalizing, and evaluating a flexible architecture for integrated service delivery: Combining event-driven and service-oriented architectures. *Service Oriented Computing and Applications, 6*(3), 167–188. doi:10.100711761-011-0100-0

Overbeek, S., Klievink, B., & Janssen, M. (2009). A flexible, event-driven, service-oriented architecture for orchestrating service delivery. *IEEE Intelligent Systems, 24*(5), 31–41. doi:10.1109/MIS.2009.90

OWL2. (2012). Retrieved from https://www.w3.org/TR/2012/REC-owl2-overview-20121211/

Peng, P., Zou, L., Özsu, M. T., Chen, L., & Zhao, D. (2016). Processing SPARQL queries over distributed RDF graphs. *The VLDB Journal, 25*(2), 243–268. doi:10.100700778-015-0415-0

RDF. (2001). Retrieved from https://www.w3.org/2001/sw/wiki/RDF

Scheer, A.-W. (1998). *ARIS: Business process modeling* (2nd ed.). Berlin: Springer-Verlag. doi:10.1007/978-3-662-03526-9_24

SSN. (2017). Retrieved from https://www.w3.org/TR/2017/REC-vocab-ssn-20171019/

Staab, S., & Studer, R. (Eds.). (2009). *Handbook on ontologies. International Handbooks on Information Systems* (2nd ed.). Springer.

van der Aalst, W. M. P. (1999). Formalization and verification of event-driven process chains. *Information and Software Technology, 41*(10), 639–650. doi:10.1016/S0950-5849(99)00016-6

XML. (2003). Retrieved from http://www.w3.org/TR/xmlschema-1/

Zhang, Y., & Chen, J. L. (2015). Constructing scalable IoT services based on their event-driven models. *Concurrency and Computation, 27*(17), 4819–4851. doi:10.1002/cpe.3469

Zhu, D., Zhang, Y., Cheng, B., & Chen, J. L. (2011). Towards a flexible event-driven SOA based approach for collaborating interactive business processes. *Proceedings of IEEE International Conference on Services Computing*, 749-750. 10.1109/SCC.2011.62

Chapter 2
IoT Resource Access
and Management

ABSTRACT

In most existing IoT applications, IoT resources are not fully open and shared with "silo" utilization solutions. Although IoT resources are constructed based on semantic models, it is still necessary to establish a resource management platform to support automatic resource access, resource discovery, resource lifecycle management, and resource utilization. This chapter presents an IoT resource management characteristics that can be used to address these issues. Physical systems and devices are connected to the resource accessing utility using a two-layer method, which involves recognizing/installing physical communication drivers and composing communication protocols. A hierarchical mapping method is used to build graphical IoT resource models, helping users to quickly and correctly specify IoT resources and deploy them. A resource platform based on the resource management characteristics is provided to support resource storage, updating, lookup, utilization, and so on.

INTRODUCTION

An IoT application seamlessly integrates the virtual world of information with the real world (Uckelmann et al., 2011). However, most existing applications take the form of vertical "silos" (Zorzi et al., 2010), a closely-coupled application pattern lacking effective mechanisms that can support applications in sharing and reusing resources, and interacting with each other. In a vertical

DOI: 10.4018/978-1-5225-7622-8.ch002

silo solution, IoT engineers must bridge the gap between the higher-level application and the underlying technical details manually, and need to be experts in both domains (Bimschas et al., 2011). This is problematic, since application developers are primarily interested in real-world entities (things, places, and people) and their high-level states, rather than in the details of sensors and actuators (Pfisterer et al., 2011). Meanwhile, a large number of existing legacy sensor resources can offer an important contribution to IoT, but are typically locked into closed systems; unlocking these valuable sensor data from closed systems has the potential to revolutionise how we live. To realise this potential, an infrastructure is needed that can connect sensors to the Internet and publish their output in well-understood, machine-readable formats on the Web, thus making them accessible and usable on a large scale (Pfisterer et al., 2011).

Although the concept of IoT was proposed by the MIT Auto-ID Centre in 1999, the relevant theories and IoT applications still take the form of silos. Huge amounts of resources and information are provided by the IoT, and there is a need to build an IoT resource platform that can open and share IoT resources. Several issues are involved in this:

- **Resource Access:** Dynamic resource access, i.e. realising plug-and-play (PnP) functionality of heterogeneous resources, in which the access system can seamlessly recognise a new resource, and automatically interpret and process the information generated by the resources;
- **Resource Management:** Resource management and maintenance are highly complicated, due to the heterogeneity, instability and evolution of the IoT;
- **Resource Discovery:** A very large number of resources provides more capabilities, but also creates issues in terms of resource discovery. The issue of how to find the most appropriate resource across different domains and networks within an acceptable range of time and space is as yet unsolved;
- **Resource Utilisation:** The real world can be reflected in an increasingly realistic way by the digital world, through an expansion of its range and increased sensing capabilities. Meanwhile, the operations and tasks generated in the digital world are becoming more complicated, and ways in which IoT services can be designed to fully utilise IoT resources should be explored.

Research institutes such as EU FP7, CSIRO have carried out research into resource management architectures for IoT, such as SENSEI, PECES (Villalonga et al., 2010; Haroon et al., 2009), etc. This chapter presents the resource management characteristics involving the access, discovery and management of resources (Haroon et al., 2009; Barnaghi et al., 2011; Han & Crespi, 2017); a resource platform is then implemented based on these resource management characteristics. The resource platform is implemented by the following roadmap:

- It is based on SOA, integrates service component architecture (SCA) and uses the enterprise service bus (ESB). SCA serves as the assembly standard for the service components, while ESB provides protocol translation, message routing, security and management functions for the interactions between components. Hot deployment and cross-platform capabilities are provided by the Open Service Gateway Initiative (OSGi) (OSGI, 2008). These features achieve decoupling between the components and the distributed framework.
- Ontology-based resource models (such as W3C SSN (SSN, 2014) and OWL-S, which are extended to express domain knowledge and business information) act as information bases. The IoT resource platform interprets raw data and automatically promotes observation data to semantic domain information, based on the models.

This chapter first discusses how to build graphical IoT resource models and resource instances; these can help users to quickly and correctly create IoT resources and improve production efficiency during the deployment of developed IoT applications. A discussion is then presented of how to automatically access IoT resources and adapt the resource accessing utility for varying production environments, in which raw data recorded by sensors are translated into observation data and sent to the resource management platform. Finally, a resource management platform is proposed that includes the design of mechanisms for resource discovery, resource utility, and distributed resource management, and in which semantic annotations are imposed on the observation data to enable resource sharing.

The rest of this paper is organised as follows. Section 2 discusses how to build graphical IoT resource models; Section 3 describes resource access in IoT; Section 4 proposes a resource management platform; Section 5 describes applications based on this IoT resource platform; Section 6 discusses related work; and Section 7 draws conclusions.

GRAPHICAL CREATION OF IOT RESOURCE MODELS

When building IoT resource models, several graphical tools are needed in order to help engineers to focus on models, rather than on language formats and details. In addition, these tools should be able to check that the constructed IoT resources are correct and consistent.

A hierarchical mapping method is used here to simplify the creation of IoT resources, as illustrated in Figure 1. In the basic building operations layer, visual tools are provided to define entity templates and their corresponding instances, resource templates and instances, in which some default values are set and the bindings between entities and resources are primary model-building operations. Based on this layer, tools for rapidly building resource models are provided, such as batch operations for resource instances. The built IoT resources are stored as OWL files, and for frequently varying attributes, these are translated into relational data in a real-time database.

Although a resource model is defined by specifying all aspects individually, such as a class and its instance constraints, or a data type and its value constraints, each resource is not often defined from scratch. A new resource is often modelled based on its parent resources, and some attributes do not need to be defined, as they are inherited from the parent. A batch operation is often performed when defining resource instances, since there are often many resource instances corresponding to a single resource template during deployment of an IoT service system, such as numerous switches within a smart grid. The batch operation is often performed as follows:

1. A resource model is selected;
2. A default setting is provided, such as data constraints;
3. Various laws are configured, such as translation of a resource instance into a table record based on some data values;
4. Resource instances are generated based on the default setting, laws that have been established, and instance numbers;
5. Each resource instance may be further modified manually.

In order to be compatible with traditional supervisory control and data acquisition systems (SCADA) and distributed control systems (DCS), the resource models need to be translated into records in the real-time database based on the table structures and definitions in SCADA or DCS. This translation is often as follows:

Figure 1. Method of creation of IoT resource models

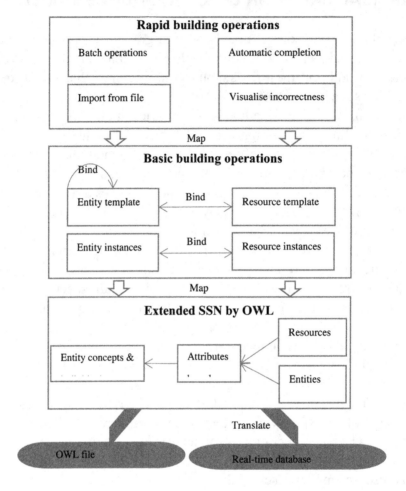

1. Semantic annotations are imposed on the table definitions in SCADA or DCS;
2. Fields in SCADA/DCS tables are linked to the attributes of the resource models;
3. A bidirectional relation between certain resource attributes and table fields is configured;
4. Resource instances are selected for translation;
5. The selected resource instances are translated into records in the SCADA/DCS tables of real-time database, based on the mapping relation.

Figure 2. Graphical resource lifecycle model

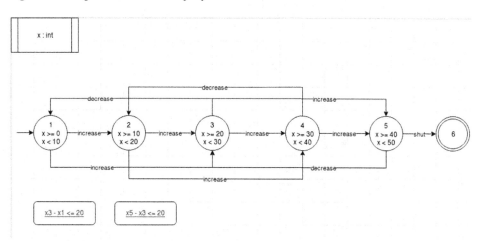

The graphical resource lifecycle model is constructed by visually defining attribute variables and variable-represented states, as illustrated in Figure 2. Visual states and state transitions are specified, and invariants of the resource are also specified, such as $x3 - x1 \leq= 20$ (meaning that the value of the attribute variable x in state 3 should not be more than 20 greater than that in state 1). In a resource state, a complex function may exist, such as a non-linear, high-order differential equation: $\ddot{f}(x) < 10$. Figure 2 is a simple toy example, but it demonstrates that the resource model may be so complex that an error checking tool is needed. In the current work, such tools are designed based on logical reasoning, and a visual tool is designed here to show the incorrectness according to the counter examples from the checking tools.

Human-machine interfaces can be developed for graphical modelling tools using the GUI library in Java. As examples, partial classes for modelling resource instances are illustrated in Figure 3a, and partial classes for specifying resource bindings are illustrated in Figure 3b. An example of real-time table records translated from IoT resource instances is illustrated in Figure 4.

IOT RESOURCE ACCESS

When IoT resources have been modelled, physical systems and devices need to be accessed to obtain fresh monitoring data. Since there are many heterogeneous devices and systems, developing ways in which these can be quickly and easily accessed are important. The resource accessing utility not

Figure 3a. Partial classes for specifying resource instances

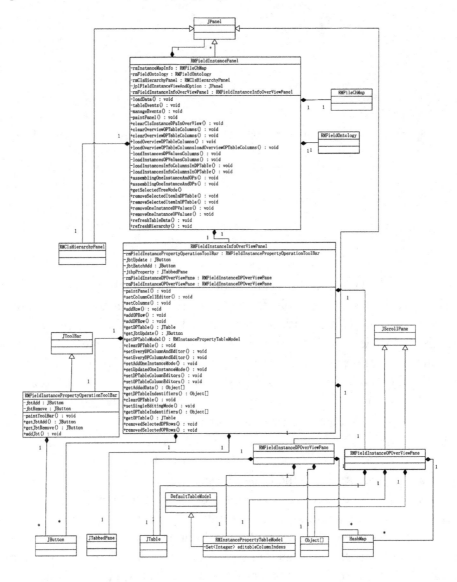

only needs to recognise resources and communicate with them, but also to interpret raw data into observation data. The resource accessing utility used here is illustrated in Figure 5.

Figure 5 shows that the resource accessing utility has two aspects: device insertion and resource adaptation. Observation data are input into the resource platform and are used by applications. In the device insertion layer, physical devices are connected by industrial buses or other communication media, so

Figure 3b. Partial classes for specifying resource binding

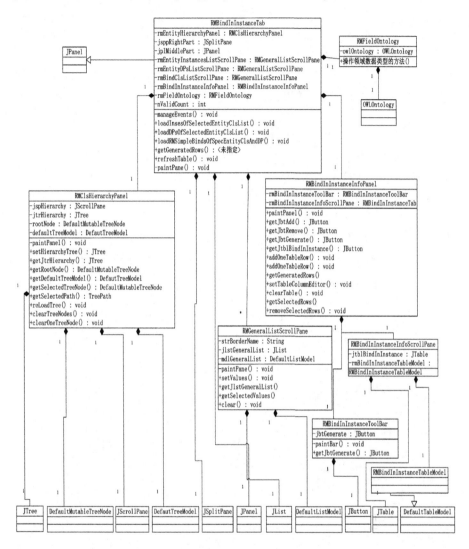

that communication can be configured before the insertion layer is operational. Multiple communication protocols may be combined together to enable communication between the device and the accessing utility. The protocol can be configured or completed using automatic algorithms, known as resource adaptation, and often carries raw data sampled by analogue to digital (AD) converters. The access layer extracts the raw data from the protocol packets, and translates these data into observation data using the real-time database in which calculation parameters are stored. The computation of observation

Figure 4. Real-time table records

DEVICE_ID	SENSOR_ID	PLC_ID	BOILERROOM	BOILER	FIELD	DESCRIPTION	TIMESTAMP	DATE	TIME	MEASURE_TYPE	MEASURE_UNIT	VALUE	FACTOR	OFFSET	STATE	HIGHLIMIT	LOWLIMIT
3	1	1	2	4	RMGL	锅炉房1锅炉1设备1PLC1传感器1	2012-08-13 01:17:25.0	2012-07-27	16:03:58	GSWD	F		25.2705	1.0	0.0	2	30.0	20.0
3	2	1	2	4	RMGL	锅炉房1锅炉1设备1PLC1传感器2	2012-08-13 01:17:25.0	2012-07-27	16:03:59	GSYL	F		29.5607	1.0	0.0	2	30.0	20.0
3	3	1	2	4	RMGL	锅炉房1锅炉1设备1PLC1传感器3	2012-08-13 01:17:25.0	2012-07-27	16:03:59	HSWD	F		28.1708	1.0	0.0	2	30.0	20.0
3	4	1	2	4	RMGL	锅炉房1锅炉1设备1PLC1传感器4	2012-08-13 01:17:25.0	2012-07-27	16:03:59	HSYL	F		24.007	1.0	0.0	2	30.0	20.0
3	5	1	2	4	RMGL	锅炉房1锅炉1设备1PLC1传感器5	2012-08-13 01:17:25.0	2012-07-27	16:03:59	GSLL	F		21.5583	1.0	0.0	2	30.0	20.0
3	6	1	2	4	RMGL	锅炉房1锅炉1设备1PLC1传感器6	2012-08-13 01:17:25.0	2012-07-27	16:03:59	LTWD	F		25.3104	1.0	0.0	2	30.0	20.0
3	7	1	2	4	RMGL	锅炉房1锅炉1设备1PLC1传感器7	2012-08-13 01:17:25.0	2012-07-27	16:03:59	LTFY	F		22.9807	1.0	0.0	2	30.0	20.0
3	8	1	2	4	RMGL	锅炉房1锅炉1设备1PLC1传感器8	2012-08-13 01:17:25.0	2012-07-27	16:03:59	PYWD	F		20.813	1.0	0.0	2	30.0	20.0

Figure 5. Resource accessing utility

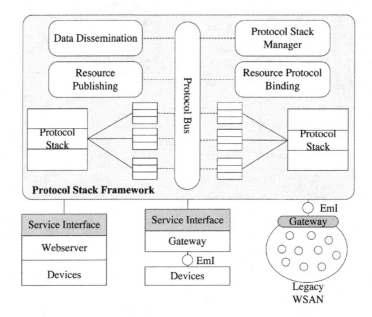

data can be carried out according to parameters such as the base, coefficients and offset.

In an intelligent device or gateway, the semantic procedure interfaces for the translation of observation data are often defined so that the accessing utility can invoke these interfaces to obtain the observation data. In the protocol bus, a protocol repository is used to store different protocols, and a protocol management module is used to manage these protocols, meaning that a protocol can be inserted into or deleted from the protocol bus by the protocol management module.

A package distribution module is used to distribute communication packets to all of the protocol stacks for matching, as illustrated in Figure 6. After these packets are distributed, the resource adaptation layer will analyse them to obtain and interpret the raw data.

As shown in Figure 6, when a new device has been inserted into the system and protocol packets have been sent to the system, the distribution component first distributes these protocol packets to the stack factories, each of which tries to analyse the protocol packets with the existing protocol stacks. If existing protocol stacks can analyse the protocol packets correctly, the devices will then associate with these stacks. When the next protocol packet arrives, the system will distribute this directly to the correct protocol stack. The binding relationship between the protocol stack and the device has a limited period of validity, and the system will try all the protocol stacks again if the binding relationship is out of date.

The protocol stacks are implemented as OSGi bundles (OSGi, 2008), and can be uniquely identified by the protocol type. A new protocol is installed and initiated using OSGi commands, and the OSGi framework will then invoke the 'start' function implemented by users. This function checks the type of the new protocol; if it is in fact a new protocol, it is added to the protocol repository. It is then available and can be used by the other components. Wherever protocol packets of an unknown type arrive, the resource accessing utility will try to use the latest inserted protocol.

Figure 6. Packet distribution module

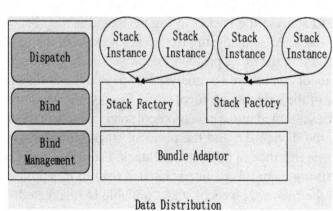

Figure 7. Protocol interface

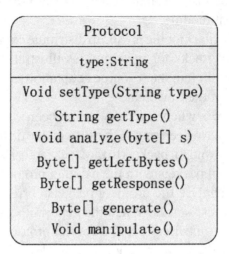

Using OSGi, the resource accessing utility can realize the plug-and-play (PnP) functionality for protocols and dispatching packets from different devices to be analysed. A protocol interface is defined as shown in Figure 7; each protocol has a type that represents the identification of the protocol. Different protocols have different types, and getType and setType functions are used to get and set the type of the protocol. The getLeftBytes function retrieves any remaining packet bytes that were not interpreted in the last round. The getResponse function produces a response message for the received packets, while the generate function forms the packets from the accessing utility to the devices. Using the protocol interface, a protocol can easily be implemented and inserted into the system.

The adaption functionality of the resource accessing utility can be achieved based on the above discussed mechanisms. For example, an H7000 protocol can be used to analyse the packet in Figure 8, and it then becomes part of the protocol stack. After analysing the packet it extracts the payload, which is then published to the other protocols deployed in the protocol stacks. The Modbus protocol can be used to analyse this payload, and thus becomes the highest layer of the example protocol stack. Finally, the Modbus and H7000 protocols are assembled into a new protocol stack, which analyses the packet and extracts the device ID, and the protocol stack manager then binds the device with one instance of this protocol stack. From this point on, this type of packet arriving from this device is handed over to this protocol stack for analysis, i.e. the relevant protocol stacks are able to be created.

Figure 8. Protocol example

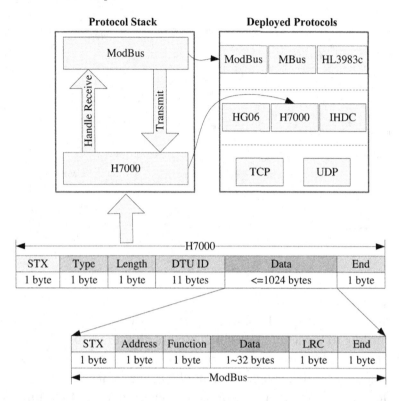

IOT RESOURCE MANAGEMENT PLATFORM

An IoT resource platform is presented in Figure 9. The platform dynamically interprets data, generates semantic information, and publishes events from semantic observations from sensors. Moreover, it can map resource operations to service interfaces and support dynamic resource queries. The resource management platform is established by the characteristics as follows:

1. All resources connect each other, and they can be organized by their inherent relations to form resource directory. In addition, resources can be discovered and selected according to these relations.
2. The ability to access the attributes of IoT resources is separated from the ability to actuate these IoT resources; the former is distributed for concurrent access, while the latter is often deployed at a single site (in an embedded device or on a nearby delegated server) for safe actuation. The reason for this separation lies in the fact that the actuation of physical

Figure 9. Internal function components of a resource management platform

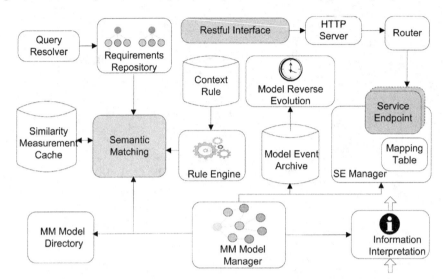

systems is often local, and needs to be strictly checked and executed according to local signals, which are not all known to remote services.

3. Ability to access resource attributes is constructed based on freshly updated sensor data, where each pool management service at each of the different sites builds IoT resource instances in a real-time tuple space, and these are then refreshed by updating events received from multicast notifications.

4. The publish/subscribe paradigm is used to allow multiple pool management/updating services to obtain recent resource attributes at the same time by means of multicast and active notifications.

The key component is MM Model Directory, where all resources are stored and organized for using, and a resource pool supports the concurrent real-time accessing to these stored resources. There are many sensors and actuators in IoT applications, and most of these are simple devices that do not have the ability to provide Web service interfaces. A small number of embedded devices can host low-level and generic services. Distributed resource pools are used as a base to store them and unify interactions between different physical devices.

The distributed resource pool is established over the IoT resource models. Given certain resource models, the resource pool can be designed as illustrated in Figure 10. Tuple space is used to store the resource instances created from their resource models, where only the most recent attributes of the IoT resources are kept, and the distributed independent tuple spaces are connected by a distributed event-based systems (DEBS)-based service environment (Muthusamy & Jacobsen, 2010; Hensa et al., 2004). The pool offers basic resource register interfaces and lookup interfaces. The resource updating service subscribes to data update events in the DEBS-based service environment, and the publish/subscribe service bus pushes these events from sensors to all subscribing services, so that each updating service refreshes the resource instances by using the newly received resource attributes to replace those in the pool. Thus, IoT resource attributes and states can be locally accessed by the other services without being aware of whether they originate from smart devices or from simple devices; in this way, access to the attributes of IoT resources is unified, and is separated from the ability to actuate resources.

This construction of resource pools is sound based on the assumption of weak data consistency, meaning that the attributes of distributed resource instances in different locations are not required to have the same value at every instant, but that these values should stay very close over a given period of time. The soundness of this assumption relies on the fact that the IoT resources' attributes and states are periodically and continuously updated from physical sensors, and partial data loss will not impair the eventual data consistency. We establish distributed resource pools according to this assumption to support access to localised IoT resource instances.

Figure 10. Resource pool

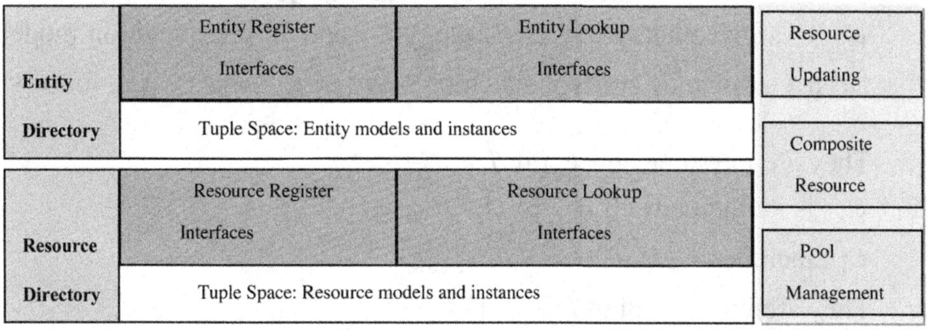

Entity Directory	Entity Register Interfaces	Entity Lookup Interfaces	Resource Updating
	Tuple Space: Entity models and instances		Composite Resource
Resource Directory	Resource Register Interfaces	Resource Lookup Interfaces	
	Tuple Space: Resource models and instances		Pool Management

When services attempt to access remote resources, the pool services look up the resource/entity directory to find the nearest pool with the resource models and their recent instances, and then instantiate the resource models in the local pool and subscribe to the resource updating events according to the models and the topic names.

IoT resource management also assumes the further task of imposing semantic on the observation data, as illustrated in Figure 11. After the resource accessing utility has exported the observation into the resource management, semantic annotations are drawn up according to the IoT resource models, and this is referred to as domain information. The domain information is published by several topic names, and the resource pool will subscribe to them, updating the pool based on the data received.

Selecting IoT Resources

Given a set of resources, we need to select a subset of resources from these according to the users' requirements. The solution used here for resource selection is designed using an intuitive method based on semantic concept matching. In some scenarios such as complex event processing (CEP), physical systems and physical sensors have their own scope of operation, and this forms the basis of resource selection for CEP services. For example, we can select all resources in the Sanjingou Coal Mine for the occurrence of events in this mine system. We then design a resource selection algorithm (the *Selecting IoT Resources* algorithm described below) based on the semantic concept matching method and resource scopes.

- **Definition 1: Semantic Concept Matching:** Given two concepts C_1, C_2, their underlying terminology T, and an interpretation model $\models$ in T, semantic concept matching between C_1 and C_2 is as follows:

1. They are the same concept if $T \models C_1 \equiv C_2$.
2. C_1 is included in C_2 if $T \models C_1 \subseteq C_2$.
3. C_1 includes C_2 if $T \models C_2 \subseteq C_1$
4. They are intersected if $T \not\models C_1 \cap C_2 \subseteq \perp$.
5. They are disjoint if $T \models C_1 \cap C_2 \subseteq \perp$.

Figure 11. Imposing semantics on the observation data

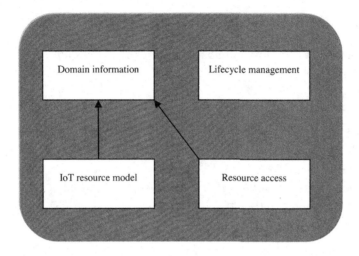

The *Selecting IoT Resources* algorithm is designed to select IoT resources for a resource identifier *resourceIdentifier* to find out resources in a scope of the resource identified by *resourceIdentifier*.

In the scope search algorithm, a resource identifier is a concept, and one resource needs to be identified to have the concept, i.e. using $res_i \in resSet$, which is completed between lines 1 and 3. For each resource, we calculate the intersection of the concepts of operational scope between the resource itself and the resources involved in the identifier, which is completed between lines 4 and 5. If the intersected working scope is not empty and has not been identified, it is a candidate scope. Together, the candidate scopes form a composite concept of resource operational scopes for the event, and this is completed between lines 6 and 10. Based on the concept of a composite scope, all resources within this scope are selected as a resource set, carried out between lines 11 and 13. For example, the operational scope *Sanjingou/ SouthTunnel* of the *Sanjingou* coal mine covers all the operational scopes of the methane gas resources located in the *SouthTunnel* of the *Sanjingou* coal mine.

The rationale for the scope search algorithm is based on the assumption that all physical systems and devices have certain physical boundaries within which they work, and the algorithm is used to determine the least common working scopes for all related resources. For example, *Sanjingou* is the scope for all resources deployed within the *Sanjingou* coal mine, while a resource in

Algorithm 1. Selecting IoT Resources (Scope Search)

Input. *A resource identifier* $resourceIdentifier$ *, a set of resources* $resSet$ *, and a terminology* T *.*
Output. *A set of scoped resource instances* $resScp$ *.*
Data. $Scope \leftarrow 0$ *,* $resScp \leftarrow 0$ *.*
begin
1. for each *resource* $res_i \in resSet$
2.   **if** $T| = resourceIdentifier \equiv res_i.resourceIdentifier$ **then**
3.   break;
4. for each *resource* $res_x \in resSet$
5. $scopeI \equiv res_i.scopeIdentifier \cap res_x.scopeIdentifier$;
6.   **if** $T| \neq scopeI \subseteq \perp$ && $T| \neq res_i.s \cap res_x \subseteq scopeI$ **then**
7. $resScp \leftarrow resScp \cup \{res_x\}$;
8. $Scope \leftarrow Scope \cup \{scopeI\}$;
9. For all *scope identifiers* $scopeI_1, \cdots, scopeI_n \in Scope$
10. $scopeI \equiv scopeI_1 \cap scopeI_2 \cap \cdots \cap scopeI_n$;
11. For each *resource* $res_k \in resScp$
12.   **if** $T| \neq res_k.scopeIdentifier \subseteq scopeI$ **then**
13. $resScp \leftarrow resScp \setminus res_k$, i.e., removing res_k ;
14. return $resScp$ *, golScp*

another mine does not fall within this scope. This algorithm can be used for CEP services to get the set of related resources to derive composite events.

If we replace a given identifier with another requirement of the user, the resource selection algorithm can still be used. User requirements can be represented by RDF queries, and we can achieve this selection using general RDF matching concepts and other criteria (e.g. operational scope).

Using Distributed Memory Databases to Realise Real-Time Tuple Spaces

In order to implement real-time tuple spaces, we utilise memory databases to satisfy soft time constraints, and a distributed management system is imposed on the databases to realise the caching of hot data, metadata and reliability. This is called a distributed real-time data management system.

In our distributed real-time data management system, there are four sub-systems: distributed proxies, a central database, a client database, and dynamic metadata. A distributed proxy for a client can simplify access to data in the entire system if the storage location for the target data is transparent to the client, and the proxy will download these data to cache if they are repeatedly accessed. The central database can store persistent data, and all client databases are initialised by downloading data from this central database. The client database runs in computer memory, and provides soft real-time constraints for local users in terms of access to IoT resources and data. Dynamic metadata is used to manage the mapping information involving the physical locations of storage data, logical access sites, and other meta-information.

In the data centre, a cluster of servers runs the central database, and is partitioned into multiple sets of servers. In each set, there is one master and multiple slave servers, and these servers store the same data, in order to ensure reliability. The central database can replicate its data to other remote central databases to mitigate disasters.

APPLICATIONS

An IoT application often evolves due to the evolution of IoT resources, such as a new tunnel being excavated in a coal mine while the old one is discarded. In this section, the application of IoT resource evolution is discussed, giving an illustration of resource utilisation. In the current work, resource evolution has the following aspects:

- Mobility
- State transition
- New resource appearing/old resource disappearing
- Attribute changes
- Relationship changes

Based on these aspects of evolution, there are three main types of model-event:

- Lifecycle event (changes in resource availability or access, changes to lifecycle state)
- Attribute-changing event (attribute value, state, configuration parameters and performance parameters)

- Relationship-changing event (establish, update, release)

Mobility is one of the most common forms of evolution, and may cause other evolutions. This mainly involves the mobility of resources and entities. Here, the focus is only on the mobility of the resource layer rather than the communication layer. Resource mobility has the following aspects:

- The resource moves but remains connected to the same gateway. The resource access address does not change, although the observation area of the resource may change. The validity of the association between resource and entity should be checked.
- The resource moves and connects to another gateway within the same domain (Payam, 2011). Temporary disconnection may occur as result of the changing radio environment. The communication layer identifiers may change, although the resource layer identifier remains the same. The resource description should be updated based on the resource identifier.
- The resource moves and connects to another gateway in another domain. The communication layer and resource layer identifier may both change, which may affect the availability of the resource.

Entity mobility has the following aspects:

- An entity moves with a resource.
- An entity leaves the observation area of a resource. The association between the resource and this entity becomes invalid and should be removed.
- An entity enters the observation area of a resource. The resource type, observation type and entity attribute should be analysed. Only if the resource capabilities meet the demand of the entity, the association between resource and entity can be established.

Evolution of the IoT resource model may be triggered by manual configuration or certain model-changing events. A resource evolution action often causes other evolution behaviours; for example, release of a resource-entity binding takes place if the resource no longer meets the requirements of the entity. In order to track this evolution, model-changing events are archived and snapshots are periodically taken of the model, allowing the model to be rolled back to a historical state based on a snapshot (closest to that historical moment) and events without interfering with the current model. Thus, the historical model can interpret historical data and events.

Table 1 shows a simplified evolution process. As illustrated in Figure 12, a coal mine CMMCS may evolve based on changes to a resource, as follows:

- **At time** T_0, there are two adjacent entities E_1 and E_2; resource R_1 observes the attribute value of E_1 while resource R_2 observes the attribute value of E_2. In Figure 12, T_0 shows the model view of CMMCS.
- **At time** T_1, the event CH4 (indicating a threshold being exceeded) takes place on E_1 observed by R_1. The T_1 model is shown in Figure 13.
- **At time** T_2, a new resource R_3 creates an access. The context view is shown in Figure 12.

Table 1. Example of resource evolution

Time	Model Event	Model			Snapshot	Data Event
		Entity	Resource	Relationship		
T_0		E_1, E_2	R_1, R_2	$Binding\left(E_1, R_1\right)$ $Binding\left(E_2, R_2\right)$ $Closeto\left(E_1, E_2\right)$		
T_1		E_1, E_2	R_1, R_2	$Binding\left(E_1, R_1\right)$ $Binding\left(E_2, R_2\right)$ $Closeto\left(E_1, E_2\right)$		$Event : E_1$ alarm
T_2	$Event_{1, release}$ $Event_{1, release} < R_3.access$	E_1, E_2	R_1, R_2, R_3	$Binding\left(E_1, R_1\right)$ $Binding\left(E_2, R_2\right)$ $Closeto\left(E_1, E_2\right)$		
T_3	$Event_{1, del} : R_1.delAttribute$ $Event_{1, remove} : R_1.remove$	E_1, E_2	R_2, R_3	$Binding\left(E_2, R_2\right)$ $Closeto\left(E_1, E_2\right)$		
T_4	$Event_2 : Bind(E_1, R_3)$	E_1, E_2	R_2, R_3		$\checkmark$	
T_{Now}	...	...	...	...	...	...

Figure 12. Graphical display of evolution

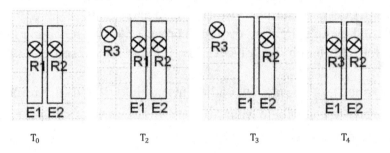

- **At time** T_3, resource R_1 becomes unavailable, and "release relationship", "delete attribute" and "remove resource" events then occur. In order to avoid the problem of relationships and attributes being unable to be restored, all relationships and attributes related to the resource must be released before the resource instance is removed. The view and resource are shown in Figure 12 and Figure 13.
- **At time** T_4, it is assumed that resource R_3 can provide observation service for entity E_1, and a binding between E_1 and R_3 is then established. T_4 is the time of the snapshot, while T_{Now} is the current time.

A comprehensive and thorough analysis of the CH4 threshold-exceeding event cannot be carried out only based only on the current event contents. A reverse evolution mechanism can be applied to restore the model to the historical state.

In a reverse evolution, the system identifies the snapshot that is closest to the historical time desired and then carries out analyzing the actions in the model events which are happened in the time intervals between snapshot time and historical time. In more detail, the system finds the T_4 snapshot that is closest to T_1, and then carried out the replaying actions between T_4 and T_1 in reverse: it releases the relationship between E_1 and R_3; adds resource the instance R_1; restores the attributes of R_1; restores the binding relationship between E_1 and R_1; and removes the resource R_3. In this way, the model can be restored to the state T_1, which expresses the context information at that time. The domain knowledge and the states and relationships of all resources and entities can be used to analyse historical data and events. For example, the cause of the CH4 threshold-exceeding event can be deduced by analysing the historical data and performance of and the threshold configuration of , and by referencing the CH4 attribute value of the neighbouring entity .

In the CMMCS, a resource can be vividly represented by a graphical element relating resource instances to graphic element instances. The resource user can manage and use resources by dragging the graphical element, and this action will be automatically reflected in the model.

Figure 14 shows the process of the dynamic creation of a resource based on domain knowledge. The entity *3302TransportGateRoad* has three attributes: *CH4UpperCorner, CH4ReturnAir* and *CH4Average*. Step 1 of Figure 14 shows that the user defines the domain knowledge so that the attribute *CH4Averagecon* can be calculated from other two attributes. Other, more complicated domain processing, such as the relative abundance of methane, can also be defined. *CH4UpperCorner* and *CH4ReturnAir* are bounded with resources respectively. Based on the conversion relationship of attributes, the system can create the resource *3302TransportCH4Average* dynamically. The observation values of *CH4UpperCorner* and *CH4ReturnAir* form the inputs to the resource *3302TransportCH4Average*. This resource will process these input data according to the domain processing definition, and the result of this processing will be interpreted as the value of the *CH4Average* attribute. Step 2 shows how to configure the sampling description, protocol stack and events related to the resource instance.

Figure 15 shows the process of binding a resource to an entity. Step 1 of Figure 15 shows the binding between sensor resource *CH41-7* and the entity *3302TransportGateRoad*. The binding system will automatically bind the resource to the entity, immediately after the user drags *CH41-7*

Figure 13. Simple example of the evolution and reverse evolution of the ontology

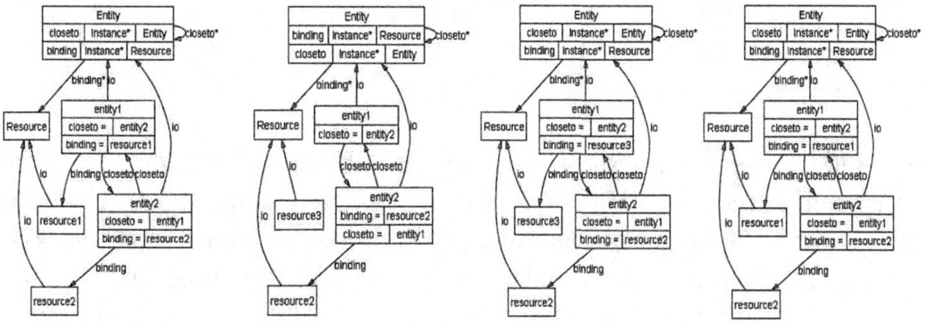

Figure 14. Dynamic creation of a resource

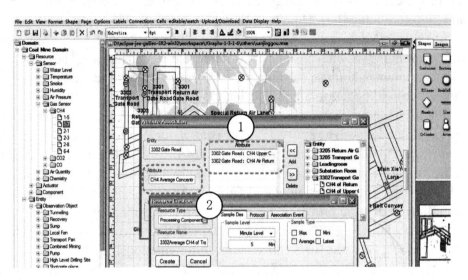

Figure 15. Resource entity binding

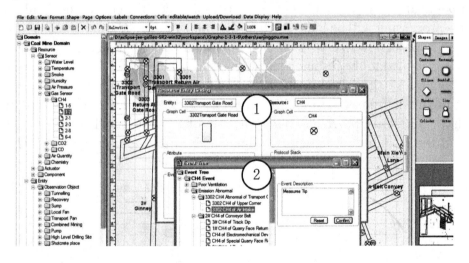

into *3302TransportGateRoad*, and the data observed by *CH41-7* will be interpreted as the value of the *CH4* attribute. Step 2 shows the processes of relating the *CH4* attribute to an event and defining the event conditions. The system will generate an event and trigger an alarm process when the attribute value satisfies certain conditions. Once the binding between the resource and the entity becomes invalid, the system will release it, separate these two graphical elements and generate the corresponding events.

RELATED WORK

In the study in (IEEE1451.2-1997, 1997), smart transducer interfaces for sensors and actuators were standardised. This work did not focus on the semantic interpretation of monitored data. In Botts and Robin, (2007), and SSN, 2014), standard specifications were proposed for the automatic interpretation of raw data from sensors and actuators, and for the linking of this interpretation to real-world systems. Our current work is also based on these semantic specifications for sensors and actuators; however, the position is taken that IoT resources have dynamic running behaviours, and our previous work (Zhang & Chen, 2015) is therefore extended in order to explicitly model their lifecycles. In this study, an IoT resource represents an informational description of one sensor or physical entity in the physical world, and this includes a lifecycle model and an object model.

Linked sensor middleware (LSM) (Le-Phuoc et al., 2011) is used as an IoT resource management platform, allowing some sensor selection and searching functionalities. All searches need to be performed using SPARQL query language. Global Sensor Networks (GSN) (EPFL GSN Project, 2013) is a platform that provides flexible middleware to address the challenges of sensor data integration and distributed query processing. GSN lists all the available sensors in a combo box, from which users are asked to select one. Microsoft has developed SensorMap (Nath et al., 2007), which allows users to select sensors using a location map and based on sensor type and keywords. COSM (Cosm. Platform, 2007) is another platform that connects devices with applications, providing real-time control and data storage. COSM also offers keyword search.

OpenIoT (ICT FP7 OPENIoT Project, 2012) was proposed as an IoT resource management platform for the integration of the physical world with the Web, and has managed millions of resources around the world, enabling people to share, discover, and monitor environmental data from objects connected to the Web.

In the study by Tsiatsis et al., (2010) on resource middleware architecture, the integration of the physical world into the digital world was the primary aim; sensor and actuator networks were used as the means of interaction with the real world, although most of the existing deployments reflected closed, vertically integrated solutions. These authors presented an architecture that enables efficient integration of these heterogeneous and distributed sensor islands into a homogeneous framework for real-world information and interactions, allowing the horizontal reuse of the deployed infrastructure across a variety of application domains. They demonstrated an initial implementation of the architecture, based on the Internet and web technologies.

In the work in Rabah et al., (2016) on a hybrid sensing platform, the dynamic provisioning of hybrid sensing services that integrated both wireless sensor networks and mobile phone sensing was considered, which was a challenging task. The authors proposed a sensing platform that reused the concepts of virtualisation and cloud computing to address these challenges and to overcome the limitations of modern deployment practices. They did not focus on semantic resource models and semantic applications.

In Walewski, (2014), an IoT architecture was presented in which the interoperability of solutions in IoT applications had to be ensured across various platforms. This motivated the creation of a reference model for the IoT domain, in order to promote a common understanding. In addition, businesses wanting to create their own compliant IoT solutions could be supported by a reference architecture that contained essential building blocks and that defined security, privacy, performance, and similar needs. In this work, interfaces were standardised, and best practices in terms of functionality and information usage were provided. This study was similar to the current on in terms of architecture, although these authors did not consider aspects such as the access, discovery, storage and updating of resources.

In the work in Sarkar et al., (2015) on a distributed IoT architecture, the interoperability among various IoT devices and deployments was addressed as one of the major challenges in the realisation of IoT applications. The need for a new architecture that included smart control and actuation had previously been identified by many researchers. In this work, the authors proposed a distributed Internet-like Architecture for Things (DIAT), which tried to overcome most of the obstacles arising from the large-scale expansion of IoT. It specifically addressed the heterogeneity of IoT devices, and enabled the seamless addition of new devices across applications. In addition, they proposed a usage control policy model to support security and privacy in a distributed environment. They described a layered architecture that provided various levels of abstraction to tackle issues such as scalability, heterogeneity, security and interoperability. The proposed architecture was coupled with cognitive capabilities that helped in intelligent decision-making and enabled automated service creation. Our current work is similar to this study, although unique designs and implementations are used.

Other IoT resource platforms have been developed, such as ASPIRE, PECES, and SemsorGrid4Env, which have been evaluated and compared in detail in the literature (Gluhak et al., 2011). Prior work has also been done on building IoT resource models (for example in Neuhaus & Compton, 2009; Goodwin & Russomanno, 2006;Goodwin et al., 2007;Underbrink et al., 2008;Eid et al., 2006;Eid et al., 2007;Compton et al., 2009;Robin & Botts, 2006;Calder et al., 2010;Hu et al., 2007;Stevenson et al., 2009;Madin et al., 2007;Madin et al., 2008;Probst, 2007;Stasch et al., 2009;Barnaghi et al., 2009;Bermudez, 2008;Bermudez, 2008;Werf et al., 2008).

CONCLUSION

How to manage IoT resources is discussed in this chapter, involving supporting automatic resource access, resource discovery, resource lifecycle management, and resource utilisation, and a bridge should be established between the higher-layer application and the underlying sensor (actuator) deployment and running. This chapter first discusses how to create graphical IoT resources to improve production performance when deploying IoT systems. Automatic access to IoT resources is then discussed, alongside ways in which to adapt the resource access utility to varying production environments, where raw data recorded by sensors are translated into observation data and sent to the resource management platform. Finally, a resource management platform is proposed for which the mechanisms of resource discovery, resource utility, and distributed resource management are designed, and semantic annotations are imposed on the observation data to enable resource sharing. In addition, the utilisation of IoT resources is discussed for applications, examples of resource evolution and reverse evolution are given in which the coal mine CMMCS evolves based on resource evolution, and a solution for reverse evolution is designed that enables the restoration of the system's historical states.

REFERENCES

Barnaghi, P., Meissner, S., Presser, M., & Moessner, K. (2009). Sense and sens'ability: Semantic data modelling for sensor networks. *Conference Proceedings of ICT Mobile Summit.*

Bermudez, L. (2008). OGC Ocean science interoperability experiment: Phase 1 report. OGC Engineering Report, 8-124.

Bermudez, L., Delory, E., O'Reilly, T., & del Rio Fernandez, J. (2009). Ocean observing systems demystified. OCEANS 2009, MTS/IEEE Biloxi-Marine Technology for Our Future: Global and Local Challenges, 1-7.

Bimschas, D., Hesmann, H., Hauswirth, M., Karnstedt, M., . . . Truong, C. (2011). Semantic-service provisioning for the Internet of Things. Electronic Communications of the EASST, 37, 1-12.

Botts, M., & Robin, A. (2007). OpenGIS® sensor model language (SensorML) implementation specification (Version 1.0.0). Open Geospatial Consortium Inc.

Calder, M., Morris, R. A., & Peri, F. (2010). Machine reasoning about anomalous sensor data. *Ecological Informatics*, 5(1), 9–18. doi:10.1016/j. ecoinf.2009.08.007

Compton, M., Henson, C. A., Neuhaus, H., Lefort, L., & Sheth, A. P. (2009). *A survey of the semantic specification of sensors*. SSN.

Cosm. (2007). Retrieved from https://cosm.com/

De, S., Barnaghi, P., Bauer, M., & Meissner, S. (2011). Service modeling for the Internet of Things. *Computer Science and Information Systems*, 29(16), 949–955.

Eid, M., Liscano, R., & El Saddik, A. (2006). A novel ontology for sensor networks data. *Computational Intelligence for Measurement Systems and Applications, Proceedings of 2006 IEEE International Conference on*, 75-79. 10.1109/CIMSA.2006.250753

Eid, M., Liscano, R., & El Saddik, A. (2007). A universal ontology for sensor networks data. *Computational Intelligence for Measurement Systems and Applications, IEEE International Conference on (CIMSA 2007)*, 59-62. 10.1109/CIMSA.2007.4362539

EPFL GSN Project. (2013). *Global sensor networks project, 2009*. Retrieved from http://sourceforge.net/apps/trac/gsn/

Esteva, M., Rosell, B., Rodriguez-Aguilar, J. A., & Arcos, J. L. (2004). Ameli. An agent-based middleware for electronic institutions. *Proceedings of the Third International Joint Conference on Autonomous Agents and Multiagent Systems*, 1, 236-243.

Gluhak, A., Hauswirth, M., Krco, S., Stojanovic, N., Bauer, M., Nielsen, R., ... Corcho, O. (2011). *An architectural blueprint for a real-world internet*. The Future Internet. doi:10.1007/978-3-642-20898-0_5

Goodwin, C., & Russomanno, D. J. (2006). An ontology-based sensor network prototype environment. *Proceedings of the Fifth International Conference on Information Processing in Sensor Networks*, 1-2.

Goodwin, J. C., Russomanno, D. J., & Qualls, J. (2007). Survey of semantic extensions to UDDI: Implications for sensor services. *Proceedings of the International Conference on Semantic Web and Web Services*, 16-22.

Han, S. N., & Crespi, N. (2017). Semantic service provisioning for smart objects: Integrating IoT applications into the Web. *Future Generation Computer Systems*, 76, 180–197. doi:10.1016/j.future.2016.12.037

Haroon, M., Handte, M., & Marrón, P. (2009). Generic role assignment: A uniform middleware abstraction for configuration of pervasive systems. Proceedings of Pervasive Computing and Communications 1-6. doi:10.1109/PERCOM.2009.4912852

Hensa, P., Snoecka, M., Poelsb, G., & De Backera, M. (2004). Process fragmentation, distribution and execution using an event-based interaction scheme. *Journal of Systems and Software*, 89, 170–192. doi:10.1016/j.jss.2013.11.1111

Hu, Y., Wu, Z., & Guo, M. (2007). Ontology driven adaptive data processing in wireless sensor networks. *Proceedings of the 2nd International Conference on Scalable Information Systems*, 46. 10.4108/infoscale.2007.897

ICT FP7 OPENIoT Project. (2012). *Open source solution for the internet of things into the cloud*. Retrieved from http://vmusm03.deri.ie/

IEEE1451.2-1997. (1997). *IEEE standard for a smart transducer interface for sensors and actuators—Transducer to microprocessor communication protocols and transducer electronic data sheet (TEDS) formats*. Piscataway, NJ: Institute of Electrical and Electronic Engineers.

Le-Phuoc, D., Quoc, H. N. M., Parreira, J. X., & Hauswirth, M. (2011). The linked sensor middleware—Connecting the real world and the semantic web. In *ISWC 2011 10th International Semantic Web Conference*. Bonn, Germany: IEEE Computer Society.

Li, Muthusamy, & Jacobsen. (2010). A distributed service-oriented architecture for business process execution. *ACM Transactions on the Web*, *4*(1), 2:1-2:33.

Madin, J., Bowers, S., Schildhauer, M., Krivov, S., Pennington, D., & Villa, F. (2007). An ontology for describing and synthesizing ecological observation data. *Ecological Informatics*, *2*(3), 279–296. doi:10.1016/j.ecoinf.2007.05.004

Madin, J. S., Bowers, S., Schildhauer, M. P., & Jones, M. B. (2008). Advancing ecological research with ontologies. *Trends in Ecology & Evolution*, *23*(3), 159–168. doi:10.1016/j.tree.2007.11.007 PMID:18289717

Nath, S., Liu, J., & Zhao, F. (2007). Sensormap for wide-area sensor webs. *Computer*, *40*(7), 90–93. doi:10.1109/MC.2007.250

Neuhaus, H., & Compton, M. (2009). The semantic sensor network ontology. *AGILE Workshop on Challenges in Geospatial Data Harmonisation*, 1-33.

OSGi. (2008). Retrieved from https://www.osgi.org/

Payam. (2011). *D3.6: Final SENSEI Architecture Framework*. Public SENSEI Deliverable. CEA-LETI.

Pfisterer, D., Romer, K., Bimschas, D., Kleine, O., Mietz, R., Truong, C., ... Richardson, R. (2011). SPITFIRE: Toward a semantic web of things. *IEEE Communications Magazine*, *49*(11), 40–48. doi:10.1109/MCOM.2011.6069708

Probst, F. (2007). Semantic reference systems for observations and measurements. University of Münster.

Rabah, S., Belqasmi, F., Mizouni, R., & Dssouli, R. (2016). An elastic hybrid sensing platform: Architecture and research challenges. *Procedia Computer Science*, *94*, 113–120. doi:10.1016/j.procs.2016.08.019

Robin, A., & Botts, M. E. (2006). *Creation of specific SensorML process models*. Earth System Science Center, NSSTC. *University of Alabama in Huntsville*.

Sarkar, C., Akshay Uttama Nambi, S. N., Venkatesha Prasad, R., Rahim, A., Neisse, R., & Baldini, G. (2015). DIAT: A scalable distributed architecture for IoT. *IEEE Internet of Things Journal, 2*(3), 230–239. doi:10.1109/JIOT.2014.2387155

SSN. (2014). Retrieved from http://www.w3.org/2005/Incubator/ssn/XGR-ssn-201 10628/

Stasch, C., Janowicz, K., Bröring, A., Reis, I., & Kuhn, W. (2009). A stimulus-centric algebraic approach to sensors and observations. In *GeoSensor Networks* (pp. 169–179). Springer. doi:10.1007/978-3-642-02903-5_17

Stevenson, G., Knox, S., Dobson, S., & Nixon, P. (2009). Ontonym: A collection of upper ontologies for developing pervasive systems. *Proceedings of the 1st Workshop on Context, Information and Ontologies*, 9. 10.1145/1552262.1552271

Thramboulidis, K., & Foradis, T. (2017). From mechatronic components to industrial automation things: An IoT model for cyber-physical manufacturing systems. *Journal of Software Engineering & Applications, 10*(8), 734–753. doi:10.4236/jsea.2017.108040

Tsiatsis, V., Gluhak, A., Bauge, T., Montagut, F., ... Krco, S. (2010). The SENSEI real world internet architecture. In *Towards the Future Internet* (pp. 247–256). IOS Pr. Inc.

Uckelmann, D., Harrision, M., & Michahelles, F. (2011). *An architectural approach towards the future Internet of Things: Architecting the Internet of Things*. Heidelberg, Germany: Springer. doi:10.1007/978-3-642-19157-2

Underbrink, A., Witt, K., Stanley, J., & Mandl, D. (2008). Autonomous mission operations for sensor webs. *AGU Fall Meeting Abstracts*, 5.

van der Werf, D., Adamescu, M., Ayromlou, M., Bertrand, N., Borovec, J., & Boussard, H. (2008). SERONTO, a socio-ecological research and observation ontology. *Proceedings of TDWG*, 17-25.

Villalonga, C., Bauer, M., López Aguilar, F., Huang, V., & Strohbach, M. (2010). A resource model for the real world Internet. *European Conference on Smart Sensing and Context, EuroSSC 2010*, 163-176. 10.1007/978-3-642-16982-3_13

Walewski, J. W. (2014). *Internet-of-Things Architecture: IoT-A.* Retrieved from http://cocoa.ethz.ch/ downloads/2014/01/1360_D1%202_Initial_ architectural_reference_model_for_IoT.pdf

Zhang, Y., & Chen, J. L. (2015). Constructing scalable IoT services based on their event-driven models. *Concurrency and Computation, 27*(17), 4819–4851. doi:10.1002/cpe.3469

Zorzi, M., Gluhak, A., Lange, S., & Bassi, A. (2010). From today's intranet of things to a future internet of things: A wireless and mobility-related view. *IEEE Wireless Communications, 17*(6), 44–51. doi:10.1109/MWC.2010.5675777

Section 2
An Integrating and Streamlining Platform for IoT Services

Chapter 3

A Publish/Subscribe-Based Service Bus for Integrating and Streamlining Event-Driven IoT Services

ABSTRACT

In IoT scenarios, numerous things and services are connected and coordinated via distributed events. Hence, a service bus needs to be established to streamline these events to enable the efficient and stable coordination of IoT services as an integrated service system. However, without an awareness of the coordination requirements of the application, the publish/subscribe-based service bus will not be optimally utilized to deliver real-time and coherent sensor events, and at the same time, service concurrency and scalability cannot be maximally realized. In this chapter, a service-oriented publish/subscribe middleware is proposed as a base for the construction of a distributed, ultra-scale, and elastic service bus for IoT applications. In order to establish this publish/ subscribe service bus, the service coordination logic is then extracted from an event-driven business process, and the coordination logic is translated into the event matching and routing functions of the publish/subscribe middleware.

INTRODUCTION

In some applications, the communication foundation needs to cooperate with the computation systems. Cloud computing in data centres is based on this idea, enabling elastic and scalable computation with high levels of

DOI: 10.4018/978-1-5225-7622-8.ch003

utility to be realised. Particularly in IoT scenarios, numerous things and real-time services need to connect and coordinate with each other, meaning that cooperation becomes very important in supporting the scalablility and interconnection of IoT services. In the work of Bakken et al. (2011), a special publish/subscribe middleware was proposed for smart grids, involving an adjustment of the communication fabric for higher-layer IoT services. SDNs (O. M. E. Committee, 2012) are similar, and allow an application to control all the operations in the network. These two examples do not involve the redesign of upper applications. In the current work, the communication fabric for IoT services acts as a service bus. In order to enable a service bus and IoT service systems to cooperate, three problems must be addressed:

1. Whether the architecture of the service bus supports the higher-layer applications in utilising its fine-grained functionalities and adjusting it flexibly to adapt to changes.
2. Whether the interaction functionalities can be separated from the upper application and can be assumed by the communication fabric to realise decoupling-based scalability for the application's systems.
3. Whether the higher-layer applications are aware of the underlying communication fabric, enabling adaptation such as adjusting their behaviour and moving.

In the same way as GridStat and SDN enabled a rethinking of the foundations of communication, the work of Li et al. (2010) and Hensa et al. (2014) involved the rethinking of higher-level applications to allow accommodation of the underlying functionality. These authors partitioned a single business process into multiple pieces, which were deployed and executed according to the states of the underlying infrastructure. However, they did not consider two-layer cooperation.

In the current work, the underlying communication fabric which works on the service (SOAP) protocol is designed, followed by the distributed service containers. These two components form the distributed publish/subscribe-based service bus for IoT services, where service routing such as addressing service endpoints and delivering service invocations is supported, and its routing and management capabilities are encapsulated in the form of application interfaces, allowing bus clients to access its functionalities. This bus is called the unified message space (UMS).

The remainder of the paper is structured as follows. Section 2 describes the complete architecture of the service bus. Section 3 describes the service-oriented publish/subscribe middleware over SDN. In Section 4, the service's behaviour coordination functionalities are integrated into the middleware, based on event relations. In Section 5, the authorisation control of the service is combined with the communication fabric, as an example of the integration of service properties. In Section 6, applications and experiments related to this solution are discussed. Section 7 describes related work. Finally, conclusions are drawn in Section 8.

UNIFIED MESSAGE SPACE

A service-oriented publish/subscribe middleware is designed here, and based on this, an event-driven service bus called UMS that can connect together wide-area heterogeneous sensors/actuators and IoT services is presented. The aim of this publish/subscribe middleware design is to converge time-synchronous sensed IoT data and IoT service operations, support interoperation among all IoT participants, and provide a mechanism for coordination between IoT resources and IoT services. Publish/subscribe functionality alone cannot achieve these tasks. Together, the publish/subscribe middleware and the service runtime environment form an event-driven service bus called UMS, in which the names of and relationships between events can be used to describe IoT service interfaces that allow for the convergence of service capabilities and IoT data. Coordination logic can be extracted from the services as an independent modelling unit, and can be integrated into the communication fabric to realise cross-layer coordination in the middleware; collaborating business processes can also be transparently managed without requiring awareness of their deployment sites.

The event-driven service bus, UMS, consists of a service-oriented publish/ subscribe middleware and multiple service containers, as illustrated in Figure 1a and Figure 1b, shows the publish/subscribe middleware. This figure shows IoT scenarios in which the access agent obtains raw data from sensors and uses resource models to translate these data into events. These events enter the UMS, and can be subscribed to by all services. IoT services also use UMS to publish events that can be sent to the sensors in the form of instructions. The coordination interfaces are executed in a distributed service container and use publish/subscribe interfaces as basic activities, which are realised through the WSN local layer.

Figure 1a. Publish/subscribe middleware

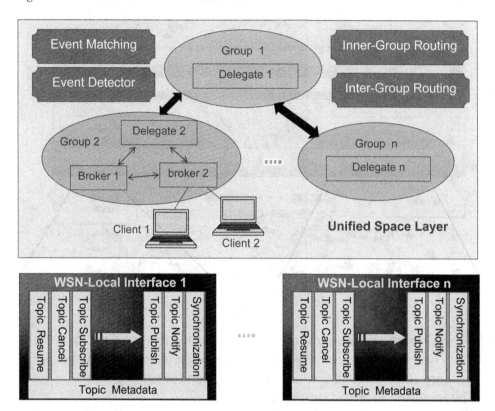

The middleware supports service interaction and routing, and works together with the service container to help provide the service interfaces. The service container creates service instances and manages their concurrency on each network node. The bus is not limited to supporting service interactions, since the interfaces of the service bus itself are also available so that clients can manage the bus.

Within a service environment, service designers can define service interfaces by event topic names, describe service systems/business processes using event relations, and register services to or search within the management centre. The communication fabric includes the event routing layer, an interaction capability exposure layer, and a central management layer. An extension of WSN called web service notification specification (OASIS, 2006), or WSN service, forms the interaction capability exposure layer, in which a set of service interfaces is available to local clients so that they can use the interaction capabilities. The main functionality of the event routing

Figure 1b. The architecture of event-driven service bus

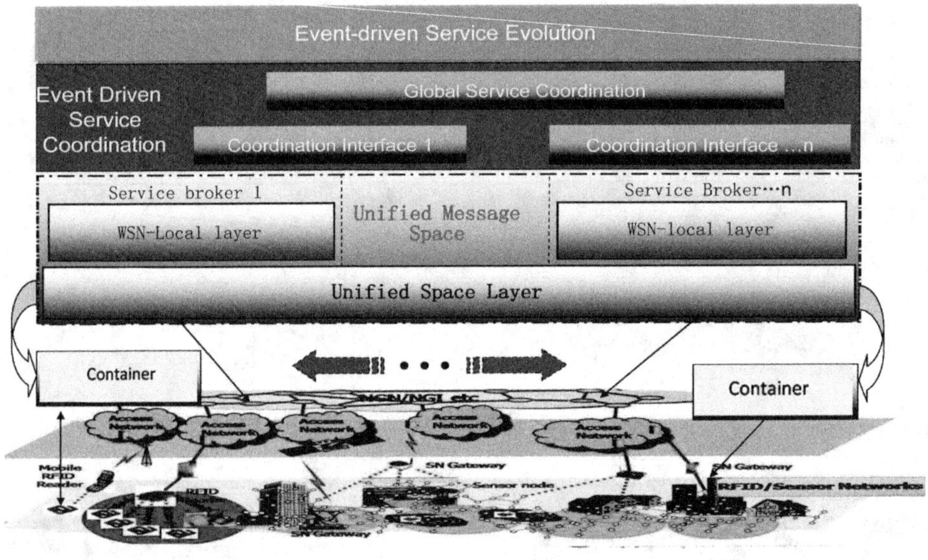

layer is to route events, for example to maintain the topology and update link states. This layer also provides several application interfaces that clients can configure and for which they can adjust the service routing functions, such as by imposing security constraints.

In addition to basic publishing/subscribing operations, the WSN service described here supports service programming. In a programming language, service interfaces are defined by events, and can be invoked without explicitly expressing the publication/subscription details and service locations. For example, a remote service function can be locally invoked by writing *ControlService* ! *Actuation*, i.e. service name + ! + function, where *Actuation* is also an event topic name, and the service is invoked to publish events with a given topic name. The subscribing operation of the WSN service is illustrated in Figure 2, and its notification operation is illustrated in Figure 3. A service placeholder called *MessageReceiver* is introduced to represent the client endpoint, which will be used in the service programming environment to simplify service programming. A *PushPoint* is created in the WSN service to correspond to the *MessageReceiver,* which is used to cache events matched against the subscription, and which actively pushes events to the client's *MessageReceiver.* The service placeholder *MessageReceiver* acts as a bridge connecting the middleware and an event-driven service that can be defined and invoked in the service environment without being aware of the middleware.

Figure 2. Subscribing operation

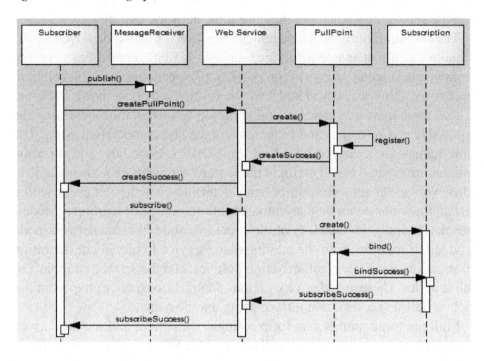

Figure 3. Notification operation

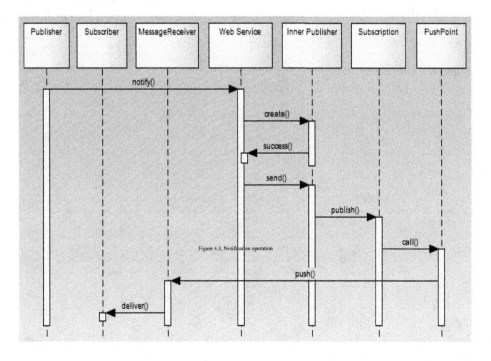

The WSN as a whole acts as a *Web service*, through which clients can find it in the service container and then use it for network operations.

The configuration and management functions are also deployed in the container as a management service, and this is implemented based on the Lightweight Directory Access Protocol (LDAP) specification. In this solution, topic names are hierarchical and have the form of a tree, as shown in Figure 4. Two topic trees may have several common sub-trees, thus increasing the expressiveness of names and reducing storage and computation costs. The topic names are managed based on the LDAP service, and authorisation policies are created based on topic name trees and network node groups. In other words, the authorisation policies determine whether an event with a certain topic name can be disseminated into the scope of a group of nodes, thus determining the visibility of the event to a node. When a network node is added, it registers with the administrator service to obtain configuration information, topic trees, authorisation policies, and the service endpoints of online nodes. These metadata provide data contracts for service programming, such as defining a service interface using a topic name.

Multiple topic names may form a single name tree, and within a given cluster, there are multiple subscribers to different topics in a tree. These subscriptions are aggregated and represented by their common ancestor in the topic tree. Subscriptions from multiple clusters can be aggregated further. Based on these subscriptions and topic name trees, the service bus provides

Figure 4. Topic name tree

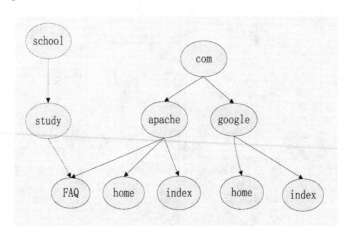

three methods of forwarding events: inner cluster multicasting, non-reliable inter cluster forwarding, and reliable inter cluster forwarding.

QOS-ORIENTED PUBLISH/SUBSCRIBE MIDDLEWARE OVER SDN

The publish/subscribe middleware provides a set of service-oriented interfaces through which clients can express interest in events, publish their own events according to predefined topics and event schema, and adjust event communication functions for special goals. In our event routing scheme, all hosts, routers and clients are organised into clusters, and these clusters and their connections may change over time. Topology maintenance can be achieved by the periodic and event-driven advertising of link states. The routes of subscribers for a given topic name are created in an event-driven way; the link state database, subscriber database, topic name trees and authorisation policies all form the input to the routing algorithm, adapted from the traditional algorithm.

In order to realise real-time event delivery, the publish/subscribe middleware is built over an SDN (Wang et al. 2016). This is illustrated in Figure 5, where the SDN is partitioned into multiple partitions (a partition is also called a

Figure 5. Architecture of publish/subscribe middleware over SDN

77

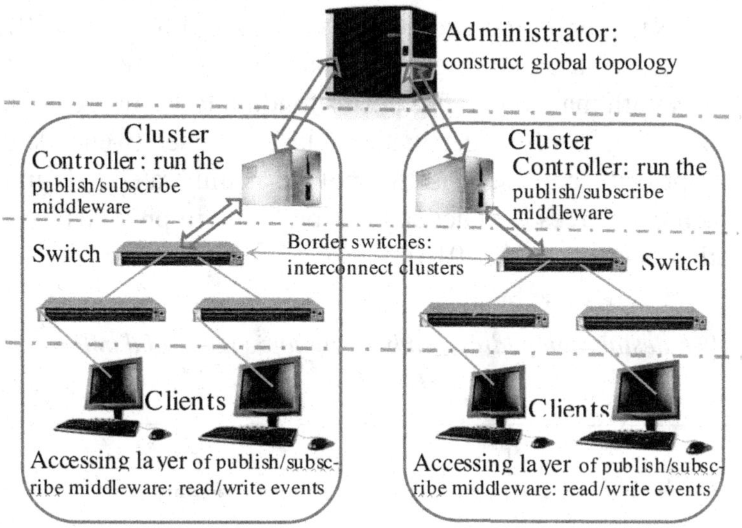

broker, a node or a cluster). Each cluster is managed by a local controller as an interconnected network zone, consisting of a set of SDN-configurable switches and clients, and a pair of border switches connects two neighbouring clusters. A topic-based subscription model is followed here (Chen et al. 2016; Chen et al. 2013), i.e. an event composed of a topic name and a set of attribute-value pairs. Several topics form a topic tree.

Figure 5 shows the middleware, which consists of three layers, as follows:

1. There is a global administrator that manages all the local controllers, forming a three-layer architecture: the *global administrator*, *cluster networking*, and *local access* layers. The global administrator runs on a server, creating and storing event topic trees, event schemes, security policies, and setting configurations and performance strategies. Its key function is to construct a topology for event streams in the middleware.
2. In the cluster networking layer, SDN controllers maintain the clusters, update the link states, advertise subscriptions, compute event routes, and install flow tables on SDN switches. The SDN switches forward event flows using flow tables. The key function of the controllers is to store authorisation credentials and encode authorisation policies into flow entries on SDN switches.
3. The local access layer runs on clients, including publishers and subscribers, and provides these clients with local interfaces to read and write events, i.e. local access to the publish/subscribe middleware.

Each flow can define the content used to match the event header fields, for example VLAN tags or IP addresses (Open Networking Foundation 2013; Open vSwitch 2013). It is assumed here that the publish/subscribe middleware will manage flows with matching fields corresponding to IP multicast addresses (Wang et al., 2016). An IPv6 destination address is used to encode the topic name, event priority, and authorisation policy, as illustrated in Figure 6. The way in which topic trees are encoded can be found in previous work by the current authors (Wang et al., 2016).

Figure 6. IPv6 destination address, embedding topic name and policy

fixed prefix	flag		event type		topic length				
8bits	4bits	4bits	2bits	18bits	7bits	3bits	△		82bits
		scope	policy		priority			topic code	

If the IP destination address of events is not matched against the policy field of the flow entries, the events will be discarded; otherwise, the events are forwarded to the specific ports of the switch to which the subscriber is connected.

In this chapter, it is assumed that the underlying SDN network is only semi-honest; it honestly executes given protocols, but arbitrarily leaks sensitive information in these protocols, and the existence of a special secure SDN is not assumed.

In order to meet end-to-end delay constraints, a subscriber-oriented delay management scheme is designed in which different subscribers have different end-to-end delay constraints for the same event flow. The delay management scheme is implemented using two layers, involving global and local queue management. In the global layer, the multicast tree for a given topic is used to compute the delay constraints on different paths, and allocates delay constraints for each node on each path under the different delay requirements for multiple subscribers. At the local layer, the bandwidth of each port is dynamically allocated to different queues to satisfy the allocated delay constraints on the SDN switch.

The end-to-end event delivery delay includes the propagation, transmission, queue-waiting and processing delays. For a given routing path, the transmission delay and propagation delay are fixed. Here, the queue-waiting and processing delays are of interest, and the queue-waiting delay in particular. Together, the queue-waiting delay and processing delay are referred to here as the processing delay, for convenience and to avoid confusion.

Event Routing

The routing of the publish/subscribe middleware is carried out at two levels: routing between clusters, also known as inter-cluster routing, and routing within a cluster, known as intra-cluster routing. Since it has holistic information about publishing policies, subscriptions, topic trees and a global topology, each controller takes charge of computing the inter-cluster routing.

The topology module running on the controller can sense the topology of the cluster in which it is located. It can also perceive its adjacent clusters based on the link information from the border switches, but needs to adopt a "neighbour-probing" protocol to check the status of its neighbouring controllers. For intra-cluster routing, several IP multicast protocols are used to send a single event to multiple subscribers within a cluster.

When it receives an event, a border switch checks its flow tables; if there is a matched entry, it processes the event according to the matched flow tables. Event routing is accomplished through the flow tables of the switch, which are installed by the controller. The controller first computes a routing table, and then translates items in this routing table into flow table entries in the switch.

By considering each cluster as a node, a cluster-level topology is obtained, and inter-cluster routing is computed over this cluster-level topology. Since each cluster may contain multiple border switches to connect it with adjacent clusters, there are multiple input/output links in a cluster.

When a broker receives an event published by a sensor or other terminal device connected to it, it first identifies the type and the topic (t) of the event, and then searches the topic tree for its binary code. Following this, it multicasts the event using UDP, by encapsulating the type and topic code into the packet header as the IPV6 address. This IP address is the IPV6 multicast address for topic t. The SDN switches route the event at the two levels according to the IPV6 address and its flow tables.

Global Allocation of Delay Constraints From Multiple Subscribers

The global administrator collects the actual event delay in each SDN switch from the controller, and then globally evaluates these congestion states under the constraints of the delay requirements of subscribers, dynamically computing the maximum allowable delay for each SDN switch. At the global layer, longer-term congestion is dealt with by distributing delay constraints on the multicast tree for multiple subscribers, and a simple time ratio is used to link the results of local-layer optimisation to the global optimisation algorithm with conciseness and efficiency.

Given a multicast tree *Nt* for a topic name *tp*, there are processing delay constraints $\{\Lambda_1, \cdots, \Lambda_n\}$ for all paths from a publisher to its subscribers, i.e. there is a delay Λ_i for the $i - th$ path. In fact, this delay Λ_i represents the $i - th$ subscriber's QoS requirement for the end-to-end delay in delivering events with the specific topic *tp*, and the propagation delay and transmission delay are subtracted from this. The subscribers in the multicast tree *Nt* express their different delay requirements for a single event flow, which form the constraint set $\{\Lambda_1, \cdots, \Lambda_n\}$. Then, allowable processing delay constraints

$\{\Delta_{j,i}\}$ allocated for the SDN switches $\{(j, i)|$ *the i – th switch in the j – th path*$\}$ in *Nt* should satisfy the following inequalities:

$$\sum_{i=1}^{m_j} \Delta_{j,i} \leq \Lambda_j, \quad j = 1, \cdots, n \; ;$$

$$\Delta_{j,i} \geq \tau_{j,i}, 1 \leq j \leq n, 1 \leq i \leq m_j$$

where $\Delta_{j,i}$ is the processing delay allowed in the SDN switch *switch*$_{j,i}$ for delay Λ_j in the *j-th* path, and $\tau_{j,i}$ is the requisite floor of the processing delay in switch *switch*$_{j,i}$, i.e. the minimum processing delay which cannot be reduced further.

It is possible that there is no solution for the above inequalities, and thus no $\Delta_{j,i}$ that satisfies the end-to-end delay requirements. In this case, subscribers are notified that their delay requirements cannot be satisfied by the publish/subscribe middleware. After new delay constraints are negotiated, it is assumed that there is at least one solution to the above inequalities, and we obtain an allowable processing delay $\Delta_{j,i}$ allocated for each *switch*$_{j,i}$ at the initial stage.

The most important aspect is the global adjustment of the allowable processing delay during event forwarding. While local queue management is carried out at high frequency on local controllers in order to meet the processing delay constraints in the SDN switches, the global adjustment is periodically carried out on the global administrator with low frequency, or is event-driven for severe traffic congestion.

The global administrator dynamically allocates a processing delay for all SDN switches based on the collected actual event delay in each *switch*$_{j,i}$. The actual delay at each switch varies due to the different congestion states. It is assumed that in the current time period, the delay constraints are $t_{j,i}, 1 \leq j \leq n, 1 \leq i \leq m_j$ times as many as last allowable processing delays for each *switch*$_{j,i}$. $t_{j,i}$ is the ratio of the delay that is actually required to the allowable processing delay computed by the local controllers for the queues (queue scripts are neglected without loss of generality). $t_{j,i}$ may be less than one, meaning that the average processing time of the events in *switch*$_{j,i}$ will be less than the given allowable delay $\Delta_{j,i}$. If $t_{j,i}$ is greater than one, this means that the waiting time for events in $switch_{j,i}$ is long, and the average processing time of these events is greater than the allowable time $\Delta_{j,i}$, i.e. the actually required processing time is $t_{j,i}\Delta_{j,i}$. The global administrator collects $t_{j,i}, 1 \le j \le n, 1 \le i \le m_j$ from the local controllers, and then adjusts the allowable processing delay $\Delta_{j,i}$ for each $switch_{j,i}$, forming the following inequalities:

$$\sum_{i=1}^{m_j} t_{j,i}\Delta_{j,i} \le \Lambda_j, \quad j = 1, \cdots, n \tag{1}$$

$$t_{j,i}\Delta_{j,i} \ge \tau_{j,i}, 1 \le j \le n, 1 \le i \le m_j \tag{2}$$

The new allowable processing delay is computed as follows:

$$\Delta'_{j,i} = t_{j,i}\Lambda_j / \sum_{i=1}^{m_j} t_{j,i}\Delta_{j,i}, \quad 1 \le j \le n, 1 \le i \le m_j \quad .$$

If $\Delta'_{j,i} < \tau_{j,i}$, there are no solutions to the new delay constraints shown in inequalities (a) and (b), and the publishers of events with topic tp will be notified to restrict the publishing speed of their events. Otherwise, a new allowable processing delay $\Delta'_{j,i}, 1 \le j \le n, 1 \le i \le m_j$ as $\Delta_{j,i}$ is sent to local controllers to control each local switch $switch_{j,i}$.

SDN-Based Queue Management Under the Condition of Local Delay Constraints

An ingress event is matched against the flow tables to decide which egress port it should be sent to. In the meantime, the priority of the event is also decided by matching it against the flow tables, and the event is put into a priority queue for the egress port before it is actually forwarded. Three classes of priorities are used here as an example to illustrate this solution. An IPv6 destination address is used to encode the topic name, event priority, and authorisation policy, as illustrated in Figure 6. This IPv6 address not only lies at the header of events, but also fills in the matching field of flow entries in flow tables.

If the destination address of the event is matched against the matching field of the flow entries, the action in the flow entries decides which queue the matched events should enter. An action in the flow entries is a tuple of *<enqueue, port x, queue id>*. Events with the highest priority enter the queue with *queue id* = 1, those with the lowest priority enter the queue with *queue id* = 3, and the remainder enter into the queue with *queue id* = 2. When the event flow is in a congested state, such as for a certain length of queue length, the controller adjusts the bandwidth for each queue.

The local controller adjusts the bandwidth $w_{j,i,q}$ of each priority queue *queue id* = q of one port at the switch *switch$_{j,i}$* in order to reduce the average processing delay of the events in the queue to less than the allowable delay $\Delta_{j,i,q}$, where $w_{j,i,1} + w_{j,i,2} + w_{j,i,3} = w_{j,i}$, i.e. a fixed bandwidth $w_{j,i}$ of the egress port is allocated to the middleware. In this way, the allocation of $w_{j,i}$ for *queue id* = 1, 2, 3 is adjusted to make the average processing delay acceptable, and $w_{j,i,1}$, $w_{j,i,2}$, $w_{j,i,3}$ are then obtained for *queue id* = 1, 2, 3. Before the allocation is adjusted, the average queue length for each priority queue needs to be computed, where the difference between the egress event number $eg_{j,i,q}$ and the ingress event number $ig_{j,i,q}$ is the base, and a weight number $coe_{j,i,q}$ is used to filter temporary congestion. The average queue length $qlen_{j,i,q}$ for each priority queue is as follows:

$$qlen_{j,i,q} = (1 - coe_{j,i,q})qlen_{j,i,q} + coe_{j,i,q}(in_{j,i,q} - eg_{j,i,q}),$$

where $qlen_{j,i,q}$ is iteratively computed, i.e. the last queue length is used as an input to compute the length of this time queue. The monitored queue length is replaced with an average queue length to give resistance against temporary traffic bursts.

After computing the average queue length for each priority queue, the bandwidth allocation needs to satisfy the following constraints:

Goal: *minimize(t$_{j,i,1}$ + t$_{j,i,2}$ + t$_{j,i,3}$)*
Subject to:

$$qlen_{j,i,q} / w_{j,i,q} \leq t_{j,i,q}\Delta_{j,i,q}, \quad q = 1, 2, 3 \tag{3}$$

$$w_{j,i,1} + w_{j,i,2} + w_{j,i,3} = w_{j,i} \tag{4}$$

$$w_{j,i,q} > 0, t_{j,i,q} \geq 0, \quad q = 1, 2, 3 \tag{5}$$

where $t_{j,i,q}, 1 \leq j \leq n, 1 \leq i \leq m_j$ is the ratio of the actually required delay constraint to the allowable processing delay for priority queue q in *switch*$_{j,i}$.

If $t_{j,i,q} >> 1$, (i.e. much greater than one), then the ingress events to the priority queue q are dropped before they actually enter the queue. The local controller sets the corresponding actions of the following entries to drop these events, and all matched events are then directly dropped without being enqueued. In this case, the global controller will also be notified. Otherwise, the controller adjusts the bandwidth for each queue according to the solution of inequalities (3-5).

Theorem 1: The above constraints (3-5) have solutions under conditions of achieving the minimisation goal.

Proof:

According to (3), we have

$$(qlen_{j,i,q} / \Delta_{j,i,q}) / w_{j,i,q} \leq t_{j,i,q}, \quad q = 1, 2, 3 \qquad \Rightarrow$$

$$(qlen_{j,i,1} / \Delta_{j,i,1}) / w_{j,i,1} + (qlen_{j,i,2} / \Delta_{j,i,2}) / w_{j,i,2} + \\ (qlen_{j,i,3} / \Delta_{j,i,3}) / w_{j,i,3} \leq t_{j,i,1} + t_{j,i,2} + t_{j,i,3} \tag{6}$$

Substituting (4) into (6) and adding an arbitrary positive number ε to relax the inequality of (6) gives:

$$(qlen_{j,i,1} / \Delta_{j,i,1}) / w_{j,i,1} + (qlen_{j,i,2} / \Delta_{j,i,2}) / w_{j,i,2} + \\ (qlen_{j,i,3} / \Delta_{j,i,3}) / (w_{j,i} - w_{j,i,1} - w_{j,i,2}) \\ + \varepsilon = t_{j,i,1} + t_{j,i,2} + t_{j,i,3} \tag{7}$$

Let $y = t_{j,i,1} + t_{j,i,2} + t_{j,i,3}$, and take the partial derivative of y with respect to $w_{j,i,1}, w_{j,i,2}, w_{j,i,3}$. Thus

$$dy / dw_{j,i,q} = 0, \quad q = 1, 2 \tag{8}$$

We solve the two equations in (8) to obtain (details are not given):

$$w_{j,i,q} = \frac{w_{j,i}\sqrt{qlen_{j,i,q}/\Delta_{j,i,q}}}{\sqrt{qlen_{j,i,1}/\Delta_{j,i,1}} + \sqrt{qlen_{j,i,2}/\Delta_{j,i,2}} + \sqrt{qlen_{j,i,3}/\Delta_{j,i,3}}},$$
$$q = 1, 2, 3$$

$$t_{j,i,q} = \frac{\sqrt{qlen_{j,i,q}/\Delta_{j,i,q}}\left(\sqrt{qlen_{j,i,1}/\Delta_{j,i,1}} + \sqrt{qlen_{j,i,2}/\Delta_{j,i,2}} + \sqrt{qlen_{j,i,3}/\Delta_{j,i,3}}\right)}{w_{j,i}}$$
$$, \ q = 1, 2, 3.$$

The above method will minimise the average delay of the three queues, with a focus on fairness, when congestion arises. More weight can be given to the queue with highest priority, in order to fully optimise the waiting delay of this queue. $t_{j,i,q}, 1 \leq j \leq n, 1 \leq i \leq m_j$ will be collected from local controllers and passed to the global administrator to represent the required delay allocation, and the global administrator will in turn use these as parameters in the current period to compute the allowable processing delay constraints for the local switches in the multicast tree.

This idea of using time ratios to link together the two-layer optimisation algorithms works well in terms of efficiency and conciseness; the local controllers can always output these time ratios using simple arithmetical calculations, and they are then sent to the administrator without a needing to exchange information about the queue length, event dropping ratio or bandwidth, for example.

QoS Violations

When the QoS goal for end-to-end event delivery delay cannot be realised after trying different allocations of delay constraints, the publish/subscribe middleware will be able to refine subscriptions and split the multicast tree.

In general, all subscriptions in a cluster are merged by the cluster controller, and are represented by their common ancestor in the topic tree *tTree*. The cluster controller then floods the common ancestor as the cluster's subscription, which will be received by all cluster controllers in the middleware. In order to compute the inter-cluster routing paths and install flow tables on border SDN switches, each cluster controller merges all the subscriptions from the clusters, and obtains their common ancestor in *tTree* as the middleware's subscription to *tTree*. Based on this merged subscription and advertisements from the publisher, each cluster controller can compute a multicast tree. Following this, each cluster controller collects all subscriptions from its downstream clusters in the multicast tree, and these collected subscriptions form the sub-topic *stTree* of *tTree*. The cluster controller uses the root topic of *stTree* tree to compute the matching field of the flow entries in the border switches, such that each event will be forwarded if its topic is covered by *stTree*. Thus, the topic of an event is one of the topics in the tree, from the root *tTree* to all leaves of *stTree*.

If the delay QoS is violated, there are two ways to handle this situation. The first is to refine all subscriptions, increasing the accuracy of each cluster's subscription, and then to establish more multicast trees for more subscriptions (forming more independent sub-topic trees). The second is to refine the subscriptions of the downstream clusters in the relevant multicast tree; following this, the cluster controller installs more accurate flow tables on its border switches to bifurcate event flows to more paths, discarding irrelevant events. The core idea used to address this violation involves finding more paths to forward events, and reducing the flow of irrelevant events.

SERVICE COORDINATION BASED ON EVENT RELATIONS

In order to support event-driven, service-oriented service programming, an actor model is introduced here (Agha, 1986; Zhang & Chen, 2005) to represent a service. This listens to one type of messages according to its type string, and reacts to the incoming message by posting its processing result using a name string, as illustrated in Figure 7. There are three types of actors. In the first, each actor is a functionality unit and the chatroom is a service coordination layer, which is used to manage multiple functionality units and to coordinate the service with others to form a composite system. In the second, each actor acts as a service and the chatroom is a composition of multiple services. In the third, a composition of services acts as a service that is assumed by a single actor, and the chatroom is a complex composition of services. Since these services are dynamically created and run, their access interfaces are exposed as endpoints so that other services can interact with them. These endpoints are used by the publish/subscribe middleware to notify these services that events have occurred and to receive their event publications for routing.

Figure 7. Actor-based programming

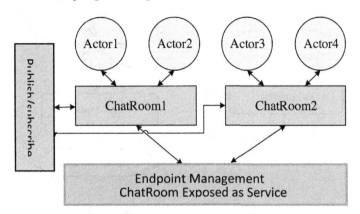

An event-driven business process can be modelled using the EPC graphical language (Scheer 1998; Mendling 2007), which includes objects such as *Function, Event, Logical Connector, Organisation Unit* and *Resource Object*.

Figure 8 shows a simple event-driven business process in which a hexagon denotes an event and a rounded rectangle denotes a function. This business process is composed of two services, *RemoteCS* and *RepairS*, which are coordinated by the event *SwitcherOff*. The two events *DeviceAbnormal* and *SwitcherOff* should both be complete before the activity *BeginRepair* is initiated, in order to protect device maintenance engineers.

Following the work of Mendling (2007), an EPC-based business process is defined as follows.

Definition 1: EPC-Based Business Process (Mendling, 2007): *An EPC-based business process EPC := (E, R, C, F, A) is a 5-tuple, where*

- *E is a set of events;*
- *F is a set of functions;*
- *C is a set of connectors;*
- *R is a set of resources;*
- A is a set of arcs among events, connectors and functions.

For the example shown in Figure 8 above, the event set is

$$E = \{ \ e_1 = On2Off \ , e_2 = SwitcherOff \ ,$$
$$e_3 = DeviceAbnormal, \ e_4 = DeviceNormal \ \}.$$

Figure 8. A simple business process

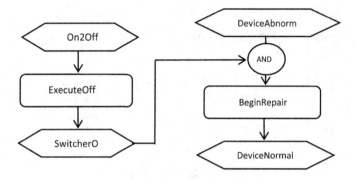

The element in $E \cup C \cup F$ of *EPC* is called a node of *EPC*.

Definition 2: Path, Event Chain, Function Preset and its Incoming Event Relation: *Let epc = (E, R, C, F, A) be an EPC, and let a, b be two nodes in epc. If there is a limited arc sequence $(a, n_1), (n_1, n_2), \cdots, (n_{k-1}, n_k), (n_k, b)$, this sequence is called a path between a and b, and is written as (a, b). If all nodes in the path (a, b) belong to $E \cup C$, the path is called an event chain. The preset of each function f is defined as follows:*

$\bullet f = \{n \mid (n, f)$ *is a path which is aslo an event chain after removing* f *from* $(n, f)\}$

All events in the preset of f are connected by the logical connectors in $\bullet f$, *referred to as the incoming event relation of f and written as* $\bullet_e f$.

In the example shown in Figure 8, the incoming event relation of *BeginRepair* is $\bullet_e f = e_2 \wedge e_3$.

For an EPC-based business process, the extraction of coordination logic involves the extraction of events and their relations. In the current work, this involves computing the incoming event relation for each function; for example, $\bullet_e f = e_2 \wedge e_3$ means that the first service should turn off the switch represented by e_2; the second service can then be coordinated to execute the *BeginRepair* activity if it is also driven by e_3.

From an EPC-based business process, the incoming event relation can be obtained for each function. Only when the event relation is satisfied can the function react, meaning that all events need to be delivered to the service even if the event relation will be unsatisfied or only partly satisfied. The event relation processing function can be placed near the sources to optimise system performance, or at a gateway in the middleware. The position of the function should be consistent with the event routing. Each published event has a routing path, and multiple events may have paths that cross, where the crossing point is in an appropriate position for the location of the event relation processing function for improving cross-layer performance.

For example, consider an incoming event relation $(e_1 \vee e_2) \wedge e_3$ for the function f. The routing paths for events e_1 and e_3 to f have a crossing node that is in an appropriate position to process the event relation $e_1 \wedge e_3$. If there is another position in which the event $e_2 \wedge e_3$ can be processed, the service can receive $(e_1 \wedge e_3)$ or $(e_2 \wedge e_3)$ to obtain $(e_1 \wedge e_3) \vee (e_2 \wedge e_3)$. If the positions of $e_1 \wedge e_3$ and $e_2 \wedge e_3$ are near the sources of the event publication, the transmission cost is reduced, and the composite event of $e_1 \wedge e_3$ and $e_2 \wedge e_3$ appears faster than in the traditional approach.

In a traditional publish/subscribe routing scheme, the relation between events is not used to compute an event's routing path, although the hierarchy of topic names can be used to optimise the event matching/routing procedure. Compared with traditional complex event processing (CEP) systems (Lundberg, 2006; Krumeich et al., 2014), the processing of event relation p has real-time constraints. That is to say, there is no big size window for the event-relation evaluation procedure, and only some recent event instances are stored on the broker node. When another event with the same topic or session identifier arrives, the existing event is replaced. If the event relation is satisfied, a composite event with a composite event name is generated. In this solution, only the event occurrence relations are evaluated, without operations involving the event content.

TRANSLATING AUTHORIZATION POLICY INTO EVENT SCOPE FUNCTIONS

An attribute-based authorization language is used to describe the authorization requirements of event-driven services. The rules for authorization control are based on the structure *<Subject, action, Object>*, meaning that a subject with attributes defined by *Subject* can carry out an action *action* on the event with attributes defined by *Object. action* can also be considered an attribute of *Object*.

For example, in some smart grids, the authorization rule for a remote control service for a control instruction event with topic name *tpc* can be represented as $<(role, =, Control Service)>, <(topic, =, Control Command)>$. This rule means that a service with the attribute $<(role, =, Control Service)>$ can subscribe to and get an event with the topic name *Control Command*.

Given an authorization rule *<Subject, Object>* for an event *e*, this can be translated into a cluster-based authorization rule. When a subscriber *s* subscribes to an event *e*, an evaluation is carried out of whether *s* satisfies the rule *<Subject, Object>*, i.e. whether the attributes of *s* are included in *Subject*. *s* lies within a cluster *clu*, and it can therefore be determined whether *clu* should visit the event *e* according to the evaluation results of the rule. In order to accomplish this cluster-based translation, three assumptions are made:

1. **Localisation:** A group of subscribers in a local cluster may all satisfy the authorisation rule for event *e*, or none of them may satisfy it. For example, finance staff have the right to subscribe to financial events in their department, where their computers, servers and communication networks form a local cluster.
2. **Movability:** Each service running on the service-oriented publish/subscribe middleware is movable. Where a service is established as having the right to read the event, although its cluster does not, it is bound to other border brokers in a cluster that has this privilege, or the service is moved.
3. **Constraint minimisation:** The goal of establishing service-oriented middleware is to share events and deliver them in a timely fashion. The number of unauthorised clusters should be minimised as far as possible.

Given a network topology $G(A, \varepsilon, C)$ and a node set *unN* without privileges to read event *e* represented by a topic name *tName*, the event scope is adjusted as follows:

1. For each node *a* in *unN*, *a* is deleted from $G(A, \varepsilon, C)$. Following this, $G(A, \varepsilon, C)$ becomes $G'(A', \varepsilon', C)$. If G' is connected without isolated nodes, the routing for *tName* is computed on $G'(A', \varepsilon', C)$ in the usual way.

2. $G'(A', \varepsilon', C)$ is not connected and includes several connected sub-graphs, $G_1', G_2', \cdots$. The original neighbour relation is kept intact, and new overlaying neighbour relations are added. That is to say, $G_1', G_2', \cdots$ are treated as new clusters and are connected by a neighbour-establishing algorithm.

3. After the graph $G'(A', \varepsilon', C)$ is connected, the routing for *tName* is computed on $G'(A', \varepsilon', C)$ as usual.

When there are multiple authorisation rules for different events with different topic names, the neighbour-establishing algorithm in Step 2 above should be optimised to reduce the effect on the original topology and the cost of maintaining neighbours. A *label comparing algorithm (LCA)* is designed, which adds the minimal number of edges necessary to connect isolated clusters for different topic names.

An example is given below to illustrate the concept of the *LCA*. A topic name $tName_1$ is attached by an authorisation rule $aRule_1$, and its valid scope graph is $G|_1$, which is split into two connected sub-graphs $G_1|_1$ and $G_2|_1$, as illustrated in Figure 9.

Figure 9. Connected sub-graphs

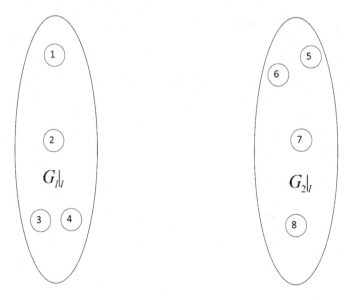

Another topic name $tName_2$ is attached by an authorisation rule $aRule_2$, and its valid scope graph is $G|_2$, which is split into two connected sub-graphs $G_1|_2$ and $G_2|_2$, as illustrated in Figure 10.

When the sub-graphs in $G|_1$ and $G|_2$ are intersected, their intersections are as shown in Figure 11. There are four intersected sub-graphs $< G_1|_1, G_1|_2 >$, $< G_2|_1, G_1|_2 >$, $< G_1|_1, G_2|_2 >$ and $< G_2|_1, G_2|_2 >$. When an edge is added between $< G_1|_1, G_1|_2 >$ and $< G_2|_1, G_2|_2 >$, or between $< G_2|_1, G_1|_2 >$ and $< G_1|_1, G_2|_2 >$, an interconnected graph is added for the two topic names with valid scope and visibility. The aim is to connect sub-graphs with maximal label difference. If $G_1|_1$ and $G_2|_1$ are linked together by adding a neighbour edge between clusters 2 and 7, $G_1|_2$ and $G_2|_2$ are not connected together, since the authorisation rule $aRule_2$ says that events with topic name $tName_2$ cannot be seen by clusters 2 and 7, i.e. these are not within the scope of these two clusters.

The *LCA* is given in Definition 3.

Input: Isolated graphs $G|_1$ with split sub-graphs $G_1|_1, G_2|_1, \cdots, \ldots,$ and $G|_i$ with split sub-graphs $G_1|_i, G_2|_i, \cdots$.

Output: Connected graphs $G|_1, \cdots, G|_i$ with valid scope and visibility.

Figure 10. Connected sub-graphs

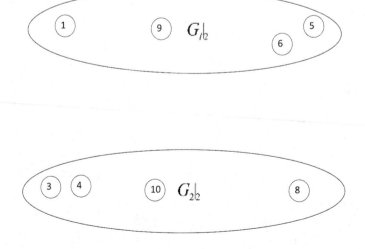

Figure 11. Intersection of scope sub-graphs

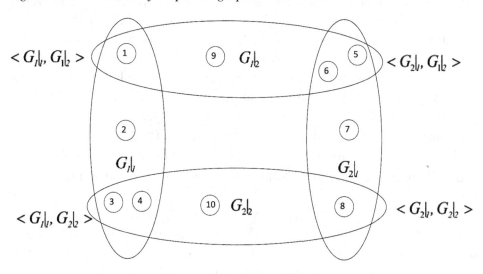

1. The split sub-graphs from different isolated graphs $G\mid_1, \cdots, G\mid_i$ are allowed to intersect. If the intersected set is not empty, the set is labelled with the labels of all the sub-graphs involved in the intersection operation. The divide-and-conquer method can be adopted to improve computation performance.
2. Two intersected sub-graphs are found with the maximal label difference. An edge is added between them, and a label union of the two sub-graphs is obtained.
3. If a split sub-graph has at least one label in the union, its label is replaced with the union label.
4. If all graphs $G\mid_1, \cdots, G\mid_i$ are connected, i.e. all sub-graphs have the same labels, they are output.

APPLICATIONS AND EXPERIMENTS

The proposed service-oriented publish/subscribe middleware and the UMS were deployed in an industrial heating provision environment. The heating provision service system consists mainly of several substation service systems, one headquarters service system, and one governing heating management system. These are connected together through the service-oriented publish/ subscribe middleware to form a distributed IoT service bus. The substation service system obtains sensed raw data at the local site, produces alarm events based on these raw data and the IoT resource model, and then publishes the monitored data and alarm events to the publish/subscribe middleware for other services to consume. The distributed services at different sites coordinate with each other through coordination gateways in the middleware to maintain event relations and drive corresponding service functions. Authorisation policies are created to define the dissemination scope of each event. Figure 12a illustrates a policy application for analogous data update events, in which a cluster G_9 is not allowed to visit an event with topic name GLData/analogData/maDian. Figure 12b illustrates the management of online network nodes.

In this application, the speed of event processing between a client and the WSN services is recorded. Figure 13 shows the average event processing speed of WSN service interfaces, in which the time axis ranges from 5 m 0 s to 5 m 20 s; the average event processing speed is relatively stable at about 422–483 n/s. Based on the application results, it can be seen that this event processing speed satisfies the real-time requirements of the IoT application, for which a specialised SOAP protocol processor is designed and implemented. The service's behavioural decoupling feature based on our method also relaxes the unnecessary limit on the concurrency of event processing units.

Figure 12a. Authorisation policies

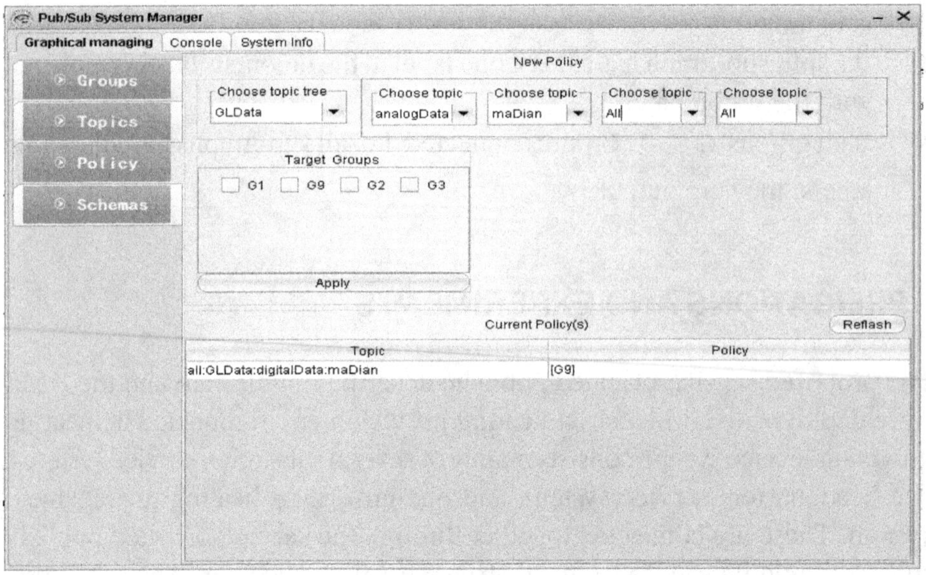

Figure 12b. Network node management

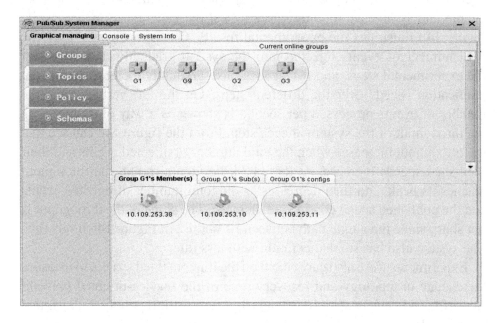

Figure 13. Average event processing speed

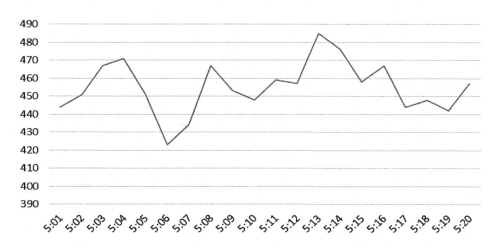

An experiment was also carried out on the implemented system to measure the performance of the service-oriented publish/subscribe middleware in terms of throughput and jitter. There are 10 nodes in the topology, with two senders and four receivers. The experiment was repeated many times, and a different event number was generated by each experiment. Figure 14a illustrates the simple and symmetric topology used to test the basic performance, while Figure 14b illustrates the experimental results. On the horizontal axis, the total number of events injected into the system gradually increases with the experimental steps, and two senders also gradually increase their event publication speeds over the different steps. On the left vertical axis, the number of events processed per second is shown as a way of representing the throughput of the system at each step. From the figure, we can see that the throughput increases when the total number of injected events and their published speeds increase. At the 2400k horizontal point, the throughput reaches its peak, and then decreases as the total number of injected events and the published speed continue to increase. The slope in the throughput is not sharp since the single path between F1 and F2 in Figure 14a limits this. The system also has stable operation with less jitter.

Experiments were also carried out on the implemented system to measure the change in topology and recovery time of the service-oriented publish/subscribe middleware, with 10, 20 and 30 clusters in the topology, as illustrated in Figure 15.

Figure 14a. Topology with 10 nodes

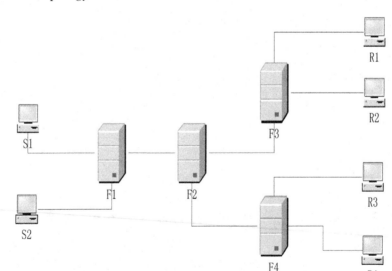

Figure 14b. Throughput and Jitter with 10Node

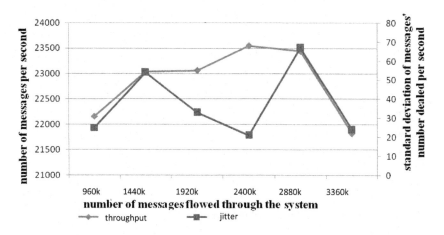

Figure 15a. A 10-cluster topology

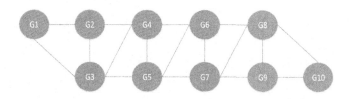

Figure 15b. Route recovery, 10 clusters

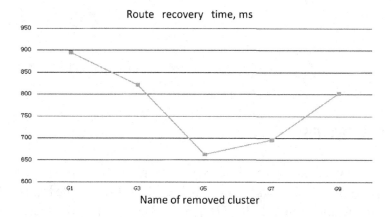

Figure 15c. Route recovery, 20 clusters

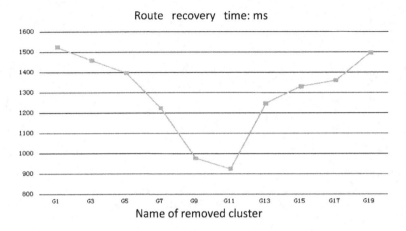

Figure 15d. A 20-cluster topology

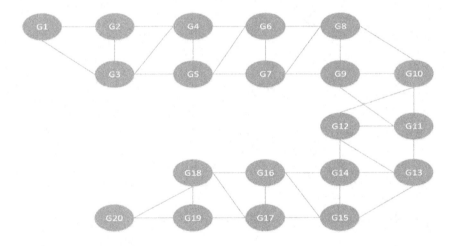

RELATED WORK

There are many existing publish/subscribe systems that aim to provide high levels of performance and scalability, such as SIENA (Scalable Internet Event Notification Architectures, 2008), Gryphon (IBM TJ Watson Research Centre, 2008), JEDI (Cugola, Nitto & Fuggetta, 2001), Rebacca (Mühl 2002), PADRES (Jacobsen, 2010), and SCRIBE (Castro et al., 2002). These schemes do not use a two-layer arrangement for cooperative optimisation. The PLAY project (FP7 PLAY Project, 2012) used an ultra-scale federated service bus based on a dynamic and complex event interaction pattern, which is similar to that used

Figure 15e. A 30-cluster topology

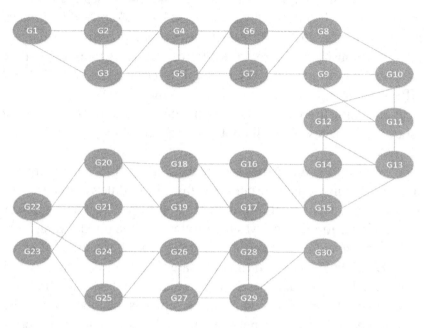

Figure 15f. Route recovery, 30 clusters

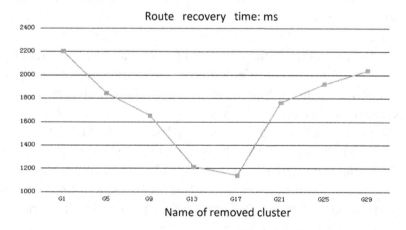

in the current work. Although the goals of the presented work are similar to those of PLAY, the design and implementation are different, for example the distribution of event-relation processing functions at appropriate positions.

There are two types of prior work that are related to the current study: the first is a redesign of the publish/subscribe middleware to accommodate applications, while the other involves redesigning the application to utilise the functionalities of the middleware, in order to achieve scalability and high performance. The GridStat project described by Bakken (2011) proposed a publish/subscribe-based WAMS-DD infrastructure for a smart grid in which different event consumers can express different receiving rates for a particular type of event; for events with strict reliability constraints, the WAMS-DD and IoT services cooperate to meet these, with the WAMS-DD caching event instances and using this caching to respond to requests from the applications for lost event instances. They did not consider adjusting the IoT services to suit the WAMS-DD.

In the work of Li et al. (2010) and Hensa et al. (2014), applications were redesigned to accommodate the publish/subscribe middleware. Both of these studies adopted a decomposition method to partition the upper application such that each partitioned unit was distributed into the middleware, in order to avoid the bottleneck effect arising from the central execution of business processes. Distributed events in the middleware connected distributed units into the logical whole. Unfortunately, these schemes did not consider the issue of the placement of different partitioned units, which is the focus of the current work and requires cooperation between the middleware and upper services.

A non-specialised publish/subscribe middleware designed by Tariq et al. (2014) adopted SDN technologies to improve the middleware's efficiency, and to sustain line-rate performance in dynamic environments. Although it is important to improve the performance of the middleware based on SDN, the concept of the controllable openness of SDN should also be retained. In the current solution, service-oriented principles are adopted to encapsulate network functions at an appropriate level of granularity that is relatively easy for upper applications to invoke and manage .

There are many studies of QoS support for delay in basic SDN networks (Cao et al., 2015; Haiyan et al., 2016; Ishimori et al., 2013; Palma et al., 2014; Ge et al., 2014; Rifai et al., 2015; Jeong et al., 2015). The work in (Haiyan et al., 2016) proposed several queuing estimation methods, and used the results of this estimation to achieve QoS goals in terms of delay by dynamically switching flows to a suitable queue. In the same way as in the current work, the scheme in Cao et al., (2015) proposed a multi-hop scheme for scheduling end-to-end packet routing delay involving the collection and evaluation of both upstream information and downstream resource availability. The work in Jeong et al., (2015) proposed a scheme for cooperative random early detection, which dropped packets early in the edge routers to realise efficiency in core switches if incoming traffic is expected to lead to congestion. These works did not focus on one event flow for multiple subscribers with different end-to-end delay constraints, whereas a two-layer scheme is adopted here to satisfy the delay requirements of multiple subscribers in a given multicast tree.

Some works (Ansell et al., 2016; Mahmood et al., 2015; Hu et al., 2014; Jarschel et al., 2011) adopt queuing theories to optimise the network delay. The work in Ansell et al., (2016) used queuing theory to predict the packet delay in SDN networks, and to optimise the network performance based on the prediction results. The work of Hu et al., (2014) modelled an SDN network by the data plane using a Jackson network and the control plane using M/M/1 queues. Other studies (Bozakov et al., 2013; Azodolmolky et al., 2013) have adopted deterministic network calculus to optimise the network delay. The work in Azodolmolky et al., (2013) adopted a feedback mechanism in the calculus, and then analysed the delay performance of SDN networks. These works provided a good basis to understand the delay optimisation issue in SDN networks, and some of these results were helpful in the present work. However, they did not discuss how to achieve the subscriber-oriented event delivery delay goals in publish/subscribe middleware over SDN networks.

CONCLUSION

This chapter presents a service-oriented publish/subscribe middleware over SDN and describes its implementation. In this middleware, the communication capabilities are exposed as services for upper applications to use, and both service routing and service programming are supported. An event-driven service bus is then designed, based on the publish/subscribe middleware. The middleware carries out assuming the interaction and coordination functions extracted from the upper applications, and this decoupling between communication and computation meets the requirements of IoT applications. The behaviour coordination logic for the event-driven business processes is translated into event matching/routing functions in the publish/subscribe middleware, thus integrating IoT services based on events and the relationships between them. Service authorisation control is also combined with the communication fabric, where authorisation policies are converted into event scope and visibility functions, providing the integration of IoT service properties based on the service bus. Finally, applications and experiments are described that demonstrate the effectiveness and applicability of this solution.

REFERENCES

Agha, G. A. (1986). *ACTORS: A model of concurrent computation in distributed systems. The MIT Press Series in Artificial Intelligence*. Cambridge, MA: MIT Press.

Ansell, J., Seah, W. K., Ng, B., & Marshall, S. (2016). Making queueing theory more palatable to SDN/OpenFlow-based network practitioners. *IEEE/IFIP Network Operations and Management Symposium*, 1119-1124. 10.1109/NOMS.2016.7502973

Azodolmolky, S., Nejabati, R., Pazouki, M., Wieder, P., Yahyapour, R., & Simeonidou, D. (2013). An analytical model for software defined networking: A network calculus-based approach. *Global Communications Conference (GLOBECOM)*, 1397-1402. 10.1109/GLOCOM.2013.6831269

Bakken, D. E., Bose, A., Hauser, C. H., David, E., & Whitehead, G. C. (2011). *Smart generation and transmission with coherent, real-time data*. Retrieved from http://www.gridstat.net/trac/#

Bozakov, Z., & Rizk, A. (2013). Taming SDN controllers in heterogeneous hardware environments. *Software Defined Networks (EWSDN), 2013 Second European Workshop on*, 50-55. 10.1109/EWSDN.2013.15

Cao, X., Dong, Y., & Du, D. H.-C. (2015). Synchronized multi-hop scheduling for real-time traffic on SDNs. *Computer Communication and Networks (ICCCN), 2015 24th International Conference on*, 1-8. 10.1109/ICCCN.2015.7288472

Castro, M., Druschel, P., Kermarrec, A., & Rowstron, A. (2002). Scribe: A large-scale and decentralized application-level multicast infrastructure. *Selected Areas in Communications. IEEE Journal on, 20*(8), 1489–1499.

Chen, A. Y.-R., Radhakrishnan, S., Dhall, S., & Karabuk, S. (2013). On multi-stream multi-source multicast routing. *Computer Networks, 57*(15), 2916–2930. doi:10.1016/j.comnet.2013.05.012

Chen, C., Jacobsen, H.-A., & Vitenberg, R. (2016). Algorithms Based on divide and conquer for topic-based publish/subscribe overlay design. *IEEE/ACM Transactions on Networking, 24*(1), 422–436. doi:10.1109/TNET.2014.2369346

O. M. E. Committee. (2012). *Software-defined networking: The new norm for networks.* Open Networking Foundation.

Cugola, G., Nitto, E. D., & Fuggetta, A. (2001). The JEDI event-based infrastructure and its application to the development of the OPSS WFMS. *IEEE Transactions on Software Engineering, 27*(9), 827–850. doi:10.1109/32.950318

FP7 PLAY Project. (2012). Retrieved from http://cordis.europa.eu/projects/rcn/95864_en.htm

Ge, Z., Gu, R., & Ji, Y. (2014). An active queue management adaptation framework for software defined optical network. *Optical Communications and Networks (ICOCN), 2014 13th International Conference on,* 1-4.

Haiyan, M., Jinyao, Y., Georgopoulos, P., & Plattner, B. (2016). Towards SDN-based queuing delay estimation. *China Communications, 13*(3), 27–36. doi:10.1109/CC.2016.7445500

Hensa, P., Snoecka, M., Poelsb, G., & de Backera, M. (2014). Process fragmentation, distribution and execution using an event-based interaction scheme. *Journal of Systems and Software, 89,* 170–192. doi:10.1016/j.jss.2013.11.1111

Hu, J., Lin, C., Li, X., & Huang, J. (2014). Scalability of control planes for software defined networks: Modeling and evaluation. *Quality of Service (IWQoS), 2014 IEEE 22nd International Symposium on,* 147-152.

IBM TJ Watson Research Center. (2008). *Gryphon: Publish/subscribe over public networks.* Retrieved from http://www.research.ibm.com/distributedmessaging/gryphon.html

Ishimori, A., Farias, F., Cerqueira, E., & Abel'em, A. (2013). Control of multiple packet schedulers for improving QOS on OpenFlow/SDN networking. *Software Defined Networks (EWSDN), 2013 Second European Workshop on. IEEE,* 81-86.

JacobsenH.-A. (2014). *PADRES.* Retrieved from http://msrg.org/project/PADRES

Jarschel, M., Oechsner, S., Schlosser, D., Pries, R., Goll, S., & Tran-Gia, P. (2011). Modeling and performance evaluation of an OpenFlow architecture. *Proceedings of the 23rd International Teletraffic Congress,* 1-7.

Jeong, S., Kim, Y., An, D., & Yeom, I. (2015). Coopred: Cooperative red for software defined networks. *Information Networking (ICOIN), 2015 International Conference on,* 307-308.

Krumeich, J., Weis, B., Werth, D., & Loos, P. (2014). Event-driven business process management: Where are we now? A comprehensive synthesis and analysis of literature. *Business Process Management Journal, 20*(4), 615–633. doi:10.1108/BPMJ-07-2013-0092

Li, G. L., Muthusamy, V., & Jacobsen, H. A. (2010). A distributed service-oriented architecture for business process execution. *ACM Transactions on the Web, 4*(1), 2. doi:10.1145/1658373.1658375

Lundberg, A. (2006). Leverage complex event processing to improve operational performance. *Business Intelligence Journal, 11*(1), 55–65.

Mahmood, K., Chilwan, A., Østerbø, O., & Jarschel, M. (2015). Modelling of OpenFlow-based software-defined networks: The multiple node case. *Networks, IET, 4*(5), 278–284. doi:10.1049/iet-net.2014.0091

Mendling, J. (2007). *Detection and prediction of errors in EPC business process models* (Dissertation). Vienna University of Economics and Business Administration.

Mühl, G. (2002). *Large-scale content-based publish/subscribe systems* (PhD thesis). Darmstadt University of Technology.

OASIS. (2006). *WSN.* Retrieved from http://www.oasis-open.org/committees/wsn/

OASIS. (2007). *Web Services Business Process Execution Language Version 2.0.* Retrieved from http://docs.oasis-open.org/wsbpel/2.0/wsbpel-v2.0.html

Open Networking Foundation. (2013). *OpenFlow management and configuration protocol* (OF-CONFIG v1.1.1). Technical report.

Open vSwitch. (2013). Retrieved from http://openvswitch.org/

Palma, D., Goncalves, J., Sousa, B., Cordeiro, L., Simoes, P., Sharma, S., & Staessens, D. (2014). The queue pusher: Enabling queue management in openflow. *Software Defined Networks (EWSDN), 2014 Third European Workshop on,* 125-126.

Rifai, M., Lopez-Pacheco, D., & Urvoy-Keller, G. (2015). Coarse-grained scheduling with software-defined networking switches. *Proceedings of the 2015 ACM Conference on Special Interest Group on Data Communication*, 95-96. 10.1145/2785956.2790004

Scheer, A.-W. (1998). *ARIS: Business process modeling* (2nd ed.). Berlin: Springer-Verlag. doi:10.1007/978-3-662-03526-9_24

Siena (Scalable Internet Event Notification Architectures). (2008). Retrieved from http://www.inf.usi.ch/carzaniga/siena/index.html

Tariq, Koldehofe, Bhowmik, & Rothermel. (2014). PLEROMA: An SDN-based high performance publish/subscribe middleware. *DEBS 2014*.

Wang, L., Zhang, Y., & Chen, J. L. (2016). Publish/subscribe middleware: A load-balanced topic-based publish/subscribe system in software-defined networking. *Applied Sciences*, *6*(4), 1–21. doi:10.3390/app6040091

Zhang & Chen. (2015). Constructing scalable Internet of Things services based on their event-driven models. *Concurrency and Computation: Practice and Experience*.

Chapter 4

Streamlining Service Platform for Integrating IoT Services

ABSTRACT

IoT scenarios involve both smart devices hosting web services and very simple devices with external web services. Without unified access to these types of devices, the construction of IoT service systems would be cumbersome. The basic principle of this chapter is the integration of distributed events into SOA. The data access capability of physical entities is first separated from their actuation capability, which acts as a foundation for ultra-scale and elastic IoT applications. Then, a distributed event-based IoT service platform is established to support the creation of IoT services and allow the hiding of service access complexity, where the IoT services are event-driven; the design goals are impedance matching between service computation and event communication. The coordination logic of an IoT service system is extracted as an event composition that supports the distributed execution of the system and offers scalability. Finally, an application is implemented on the platform to demonstrate its effectiveness and applicability.

INTRODUCTION

In the study by Guinard et al., (2010), it was advocated that in IoT applications, real-world devices should provide their functionality via SOAP-based Web services or RESTful APIs, thus enabling other components to interact with them dynamically. The functionality provided by these devices was referred

DOI: 10.4018/978-1-5225-7622-8.ch004

to as 'real-world services'. The authors then designed a series of discovery, query, and selection schemes for these services. Unfortunately, many of the sensors and actuators in current use are very simple devices, without the ability to provide Web service interfaces. The use of several different types of physical device is addressed here by integrating distributed events into SOA for service provision, as follows:

1. The data provision functionalities of different types of physical devices are unified in the form of universal IoT services, and their actuation capabilities are separated from these services and often localised. These differences are hidden behind an event-driven service infrastructure for transparent service interactions.
2. IoT applications often have real-time requirements, and the event-based communication fabric should cooperate with IoT service systems in order to satisfy these requirements. A service infrastructure is needed that can be integrated with the cooperation mechanism, the event-based communication fabric, and the service environments.
3. Physical entities often have their own locations, meaning that an IoT service system over these must be a distributed system. An event-based IoT service infrastructure should support a distributed execution with consistency.

In some existing works, a communication foundation has been optimised for IoT applications. For example, in the GridStat project (Bakken et al., 2011), a publish/subscribe-based communication foundation was designed for smart grids, supporting different receiving rates for the same event type, for instance. This work focused on redesigning the underlying communication fabric to support real-time coordination between heterogeneous IoT services, but did not shed light on higher-level applications. It is the belief of the current authors that connecting together all the things in a particular environment requires a reimagining of the communication foundation and higher-level applications simultaneously.

In contrast with GridStat, which focused on the foundation for communication, some works have attempted to redesign higher-level applications to accommodate the underlying structure. In (Li et al., 2010), a business process was decomposed into different types of activities, which were distributed in a DEBS (Distributed Event-based System) system to improve the scalability of the service system. In the study in (Hensa et al., 2014), a business process fragmentation method was proposed based on distributed events, in which each fragment acted as a distributed execution unit connected to several DEBS systems. The partitioning of the business processes was the sole focal point of this work, and the authors did not discuss how to achieve cooperation between the business processes and the DEBS systems.

In our current work, distributed events are integrated into SOA to build an EDSOA infrastructure for distributed IoT services (part of the service platform, as discussed in Chapter 4). Service-oriented principles are used to design the publish/subscribe middleware, and its network operations are based on the service protocol (SOAP) to support service routing, such as addressing service endpoints and delivering service invocations (further details are given in Chapter 4). For higher-level applications, a flexible service process utility and with service run-time environments are built to support the distributed orchestration of IoT services. In this way, distributed resource pools can support the separation of the data access capability from the device actuation capability, and a business process can be partitioned and distributed by enacting its coordination logic as event compositions. Both cross-layer design and the redesign of each layer are carried out.

The rest of this paper is organised as follows. Section 2 presents an EDSOA platform for IoT services; Section 3 describes a DEBS-based service environment; Section 4 proposes a DEBS-based service running environment; Section 5 describes a flexible service process utility; Section 6 discusses how to generate a common operation picture for IoT services as a human-machine interface; Section 7 presents some applications and experiments; Section 8 discusses related work; and Section 9 draws conclusions.

EDSOA PLATFORM FOR IOT SERVICES

A platform is proposed that can support the scalable creation of event-driven IoT services based on IoT resource models. This is called the EDSOA platform, and is illustrated in Figure 1. The EDSOA platform consists of three parts: a distributed resource pool, a DEBS-based service environment, and a flexible service process utility.

There are numerous sensors and actuators in IoT applications, and most of these are simple devices without the ability to provide Web service interfaces; only a proportion of the embedded devices host low-level and generic services.

Figure 1. EDSOA platform for IoT services

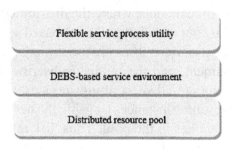

Distributed resource pools are used here as a base to unify interactions with different physical devices, as described below:

1. Physical entities in the physical world are introduced into the information world. The digital entities corresponding to physical entities are modelled as IoT resources managed by IoT services.
2. The capability to access the attributes of IoT resources is separated from the capability to actuate the IoT resources: the former is distributed for concurrent access, and the latter is often deployed on a single site (in an embedded device or on a nearby delegated server) for safe actuation. The rationale for such a separation lies in the fact that the actuation of physical systems is often local, and needs to be strictly checked and executed based on local signals, which are not all known to remote services.
3. The capability to access the resource attributes is constructed based on freshly updated sensor data, whereby each pool management service at each of the different sites builds IoT resource instances in a real-time tuple space. These are then refreshed by updating events received from multicast notifications.
4. The publish/subscribe paradigm allows multiple pool management/ updating services to obtain recent resource attributes at the same time, by means of multicasting and active notifications. Furthermore, the actuation capability is location-transparent, based on the publish/ subscribe paradigm, meaning that remote services can use the local capability of a resource actuation service without searching for its endpoint.

As discussed in Chapter 3, tuple space is used to store the resource instances created from their resource models, where the distributed independent tuple spaces are connected by our distributed DEBS-based service environment.

The resource updating service subscribes to data update events in the DEBS-based service environment, and the publish/subscribe service bus pushes these events from sensors to all subscribing services so that each updating service refreshes the resource instances by using the newly received resource attributes to replace the ones in the pool. Thus, IoT resource attributes and states can be locally accessed by the other services without being aware of whether they originate from smart devices or from simple devices, *that is, unifying the access to the attributes of IoT resources, and separating such access from the capabilities of actuating resources.*

The DEBS-based service environment uses distributed events as the primary mechanism to describe service interfaces, run IoT services, and support the implementation of functional reactive service functions. In this environment, the service-oriented publish/subscribe middleware acts as the distributed service bus core to route services, and works on SOAP messages with WSN (OASIS WSN, 2006) as interfaces. In the original WSN specification (OASIS WSN, 2006), active push primitives were not defined, whereas here the middleware is extended by adding endpoint management and push primitives.

A flexible service process utility is established to support the implementation of service coordination logic in the form of independent event composition blocks, such that the process can be partitioned and each sub-service can be deployed near (or within) the managed physical devices (in order to satisfy some of the real-time requirements encountered). In addition, the partitioned process fragments are flexibly executed under conditions of consistency. The distributed resource pool is established over IoT resource models.

DEBS-BASED SERVICE ENVIRONMENT

A service-oriented publish/subscribe middleware is designed here, based on which an event-driven service bus is established that can connect together wide-area heterogeneous IoT resources and services for transparent interactions, without reference to service locations and online statuses. Service programming is also supported, referred to here as the *service environment*. Its basic functionalities are service programming, service registry, service deployment, service running, and service routing, while the service-oriented publish/subscribe middleware supports cooperation between the underlying event communication fabric and higher-level service systems. The service environment consists of four parts in the service platform: a service-oriented publish/subscribe middleware, multiple service containers, multiple service programming environments, and an administration centre, called *Administrator*. This is illustrated in Figure 2.

The service-oriented publish/subscribe middleware acts as an event-driven service bus core within the UMS. It is combined with service environments, including service containers and programming tools, to build a service bus in which event names can be used to describe IoT service interfaces in order to bridge service capabilities and event communication capabilities. Event schemas are also used to self-describe events in order to realize interoperability. Distributed events are the basic mechanism in this service environment, and these are named so that they can be shared among different IoT services. A topic name is assigned to a particular kind of event, and multiple topic names form a name tree. Based on the topic names and consumers' subscriptions, these events can be pushed to the consumers.

The higher-level applications and the underlying communication fabric are able to cooperate via the UMS. Problems such as the two described below can be solved through this cooperation, as follows:

1.   Even if they subscribe to the same event topic, two different IoT services may have different requirements in terms of event receiving rates. One

Figure 2. The service environment

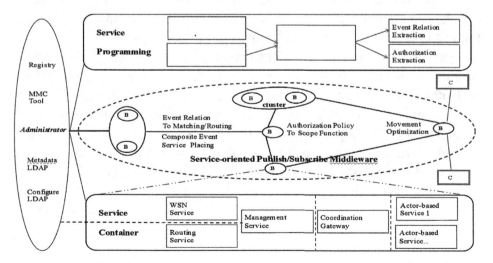

111

service may be able to receive all events over a given period of time, while another may receive only some parts of the event flow. They will adjust their receiving rates to within the allowed range, to avoid congestion in the communication fabric, while the performance of the service environment proposed here can be optimised by appropriately splitting the event flows for the two different subscribers.

2. In the proposed service environment, reliability of event delivery cannot be realised by the re-transmission method, since events are delivered by multicast communication; some cross-layer cooperation is therefore needed. If an IoT service requires events with a particular topic name to be delivered with complete reliability, it actively requests the lost parts. The service environment, having cached multiple event instances, will then directly respond to this request with those in the cache.

From the above discussion, it is clear that compared with existing work (Hensa et al., 2014; Li et al., 2010), the two-layer redesign presented here not only improves the performance of the service environment, but also provides opportunities to overcome several difficulties such as the reliability of event delivery. The main goal is to comprehensively explore the apparent relationships among events, IoT resources, IoT services and the underlying event delivery fabric, in order to realise impedance matching between service computation and event communication. The design principle involves establishing an integrated architecture for a distributed IoT service platform by two-layer redesigns, in which one event name is used to describe a service interface linking to a reactive service function, the same name is also used to represent an event flow for matching and routing in the communication fabric, and the same cross-layer entity can be used to address certain hard issues. For example, in the following sections, a discussion is presented of how IoT services and their interacting events can be protected by integrating access control into event routing. The event-driven IoT services are decoupled from each other and their event access requests are not sent to publishers; thus, the classical request interception mechanism is unavailable for the enforcement of authorisation policy. In addition, the variety and the complexity of the service provision required to access different kinds of physical devices are further hidden by some gluing architectural blocks such as resource pools, which unify resource access.

Service Programming Environment

An actor model (Agha, 1986) is used to abstract event-driven service programming, in which a service listens to incoming messages according to their name strings, and then reacts by posting the processed results using other name strings. There are three types of actors. The first is a functionality unit, which is managed by the second type, called a *chatroom*. A chatroom represents a service consisting of multiple functionality units, and acts as a service coordination layer, coordinating itself to participate in a composite system. The third type of actor is a service composition, and this role can also be assumed by a chatroom. *Scala* software (Schinz & Haller, 2014) is extended to realise actor-based services and maintain service operation, where service interface descriptions, event descriptions, and resource descriptions are created, stored, and referenced.

To enable the rapid development of an IoT service system, it is necessary to establish a service programming environment in which IoT resources are clearly classified and used visually, regardless of their underlying formal specification and storage. Atomic IoT services should have clear and complete descriptions, and certain development tools should be provided.

In Figure 3, atomic IoT services are shown as reactive agents, and are created based on actor models for which development tools are provided to enable the graphical definition of IoT service interfaces (e.g. WSDL). An IoT service system is modelled and created using the graphical language of EPC; IoT resources are introduced into business processes, actual services are bound to EPC functions, and common operation pictures are attached as

Figure 3. Event-driven IoT service programming environment

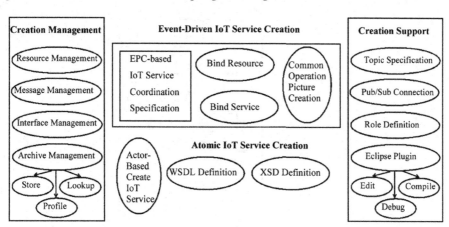

human-machine interfaces for resource-centric IoT applications. Methods for the creation of frequently used operation pictures will be discussed in later sections. The programming of IoT services is contract-oriented, meaning that a service creation management tool is used to manage resource, message and interface contracts. An archive management module is used to store the developed IoT services, organise them based on their profiles, and respond to service discovery and lookup requests. The creation support tool is used to integrate the service creation environment with other tools and middleware, such as Eclipse IDE and publish/subscribe middleware.

An EPC business process produced by the event-driven IoT service environment is exported by EPC makeup language (EPML) format. The structure of EPML documents is illustrated as in Figure 4, where "*epc*" is the root element, and "*event*" and "*func*" are primary elements.

Based on the EPML model, an IoT service system is partitioned for distributed execution, with each atomic IoT service acting as an autonomous agent. A service gate is introduced to mediate between each atomic IoT service and the service system. The service gate subscribes the process-included events that are relevant to the atomic service. When a subscribed event arrives, the service gate dispatches it to the atomic service, and the resource conditions in the process act as conditions on dispatching the event to the atomic service. The class diagram for the service gate is shown in Figure 5.

Figure 4. The structure of EPML documents

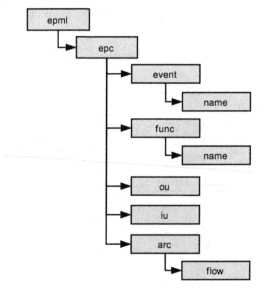

Figure 5. Class diagram for the service gate

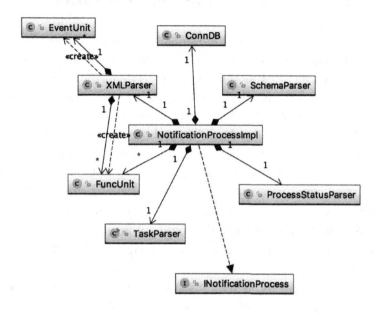

Figure 6. The service-oriented publish/subscribe middleware

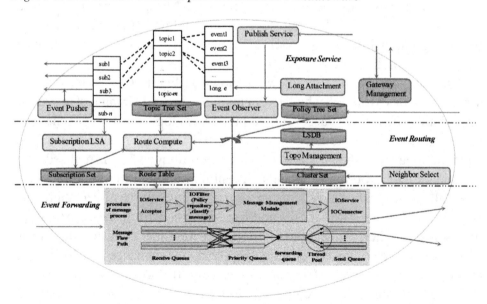

Service-Oriented Publish/Subscribe Middleware

The service-oriented publish/subscribe middleware consists of a communication capability exposure layer, an event routing layer, and a central management layer, as illustrated in Figure 6. The communication capability exposure layer provides local clients with a set of service interfaces that allow communication capabilities to be to used and configured; this is an extension of WSN (OASIS WSN, 2006) and is called the *WSN service*. The event routing layer provides vertical layer application programming interfaces (APIs) to the WSN service; it provides peer-to-peer topology-maintaining, link state update and event forwarding functionality to other routing layers, and called the *routing service*. The central management layer stores configuration information, metadata about topic trees and authorisation policies, and run-time information concerning network nodes. It also provides data access APIs to all network nodes.

All services, including the WSN service and the routing service, are deployed in service containers. The configuration and management functionalities of the middleware are also deployed in the service container as the management service, which is implemented based on a LDAP specification. When a network node is initiated, it registers with the administrator service to get the configuration information, topic trees, authorisation policies, and service endpoints of online nodes.

The publish/subscribe middleware shown in Figure 6 provides a set of service interfaces through which its clients can express their interest in events, publish their own events according to predefined topics and event schemas, and reconfigure the middleware to satisfy their special requirements. The key functionality of the middleware is service routing, which is realised by a combination of a routing layer and an event forwarding layer. In the routing layer, all hosts, routers and clients are organised into clusters by a neighbour selection algorithm. Although the nodes are grouped into clusters, the clusters themselves and their connections often change over time, as clusters disappear and links between clusters change. Topology maintenance is carried out by the periodic and event-triggered advertising of link states. The clients' subscriptions are also disseminated into each cluster, and the topology advertisement and the subscription advertisement are often aggregated to reduce communication costs. In the event forwarding layer, the two prime functionalities are event matching and multiple-priority queue maintenance,

Figure 7. Multicast tree for a single topic

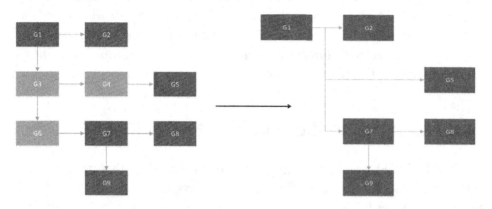

and events are forwarded to neighbouring clusters by looking up routing tables in the routing layer.

Figure 7 illustrates an example of path computation in which the overlay network topology includes clusters G_1, G_2, ?, G_9 in its left column without authorisation constraints: G_1 publishes events with topic t, and G_2, G_5, G_7, G_8,G_9 all subscribe to topic t. The authorisation policy applied in the right-hand column of the figure states that G_3, G_4, G_6 have no rights to visit events with topic name t, and so the multicast tree is changed.

In traditional publish/subscribe systems, brokers evaluate their own authorisation policies against clients' requests for network operations, such as registering topics and reading events, while the requirements in terms of invocation protection for IoT services over these are not considered. Since the proposed event-driven decoupled IoT

services interact indirectly and anonymously, the classical assumption that access to services and their interacting events is controlled by an omniscient monitor performing perfect surveillance on requests becomes impossible. In this work, the cross-layer design is intended to integrate the higher-layer service access control into the lower-layer event routing, which addresses the hard issue of losing omniscient monitors. The basic idea is as follows:

A security policy is efficiently embedded into an event, an independent meaningful entity in the communication fabric, in such a way that the policy can be evaluated independently of its security context. Broker nodes at the edge of the publish/subscribe middleware then make decisions on the delivery of events according to the embedded policies. In addition, the broker network topology of the publish/subscribe middleware can be translated into a graph in which each node is guarded by multiple Boolean values; these are the results of a comparison between the subscribers' attributes and the publishers' policies. Many-to-many multicast trees are then computed over the graph labelled with Boolean values, which does not route an event to unauthorised services or vice versa.

DEBS-BASED SERVICE RUNNING ENVIORNMENT

The DEBS-based service running environment is a utility that manages IoT service interfaces with supporting functional programming, allowing them to create and run IoT service instances and to support service interactions based on events. In the service environment, the event consumers (services) can express their interest to the DEBS-based service environment via subscriptions. The environment delivers a named event to the consumers if these subscriptions match the topic of the event; the topic tree is hierarchical, and each topic is unique, corresponding to a set of events with the same topic. In practice, physical entities, sensors, and IoT applications often have their own geographical boundaries and natural ownership. The DEBS in the service running environment can connect together distributed services and entities from different autonomy domains, since it is a wide-area and Internet-scale service through grouping and isolating on overlay structure. As illustrated in Figure 8, the service running environment provides the DEBS with a service interface layer through which the interfaces and functions of the services can be defined, i.e. by specifying which events are consumed or produced and defining event handling guards. The service running environment also provides a service container in which an IoT service can be deployed, created

Figure 8. Service execution model

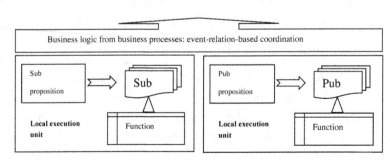

and dispatched, and resource models are mapped in as data contracts to support standardised programming.

The primary task of the publish/subscribe-based service container is to run IoT services with high concurrency. The true dependency of the service functions is determined by removing unnecessary constraints, where event occurrence propositions, event session propositions and resource propositions are used to decompose a service behaviour into multiple independent and concurrent execution units; in other words, coordination logic is explicitly expressed and separated. A sound assumption about event-driven services is taken as a basis for flattening the execution of service functions without depending on the sequential stack structure. This idea is represented by the service execution model in Figure 8, where each service has a business logic layer that is in charge of business process execution, as discussed in the next section, and each publish/subscribe interface has a local execution unit with one guard and one implementation function. Multiple service execution units for the service share the same business logic layer. The focus here is on how to decompose the service behaviour into independent execution units for the execution model.

This decomposition of service behaviour is carried out based on the concept of coordination separation. An IoT service operates on certain IoT resources to produce changes in their attribute or state transition events, and is itself driven by these events. The coordination relation between IoT resources is expressed by the event relation, although the actual operations on these may be completed by different service functions, i.e. by service coordination. In the current work, the coordination of IoT resources is assumed as follows:

1. The publication of an event represents a coordinating action with the event driving service functions or is a result of these.
2. Event relations such as the causality and conflict between events represent the coordination logic. The event session is a fine-grained mechanism for expressing these event relations.
3. Assuring the event relation involves coordinating IoT resources based on the coordination logic.
4. The relation between events can be computed and represented by the event-related propositions in the service formal model.

The separation of coordination logic involves extracting events and their relations from the service, allowing them to act as independent modelling blocks. Following this, the computation logic of the service is executed and its functions run, which often results in changes in several properties and states of resources. If changes take place, the resulting events are published. During decomposition of the service behaviour, therefore, the computation function of the service is represented by its precondition and post-effect. The precondition is defined by its driven events, event propositions and resource propositions (representing resource states), while the post-effect is implicit, and may involve changes in the properties of resources and states or published events. Then, if two actions are sequential, the decomposition is as follows:

1.   The first action is treated as independent.
2.   In order to decompose the second action from the sequence, the first action is represented by an event, i.e. the topic name in its interface together with the topic-related session propositions in its guard.
3.   In the guard for the second action, a proposition is added which states that the representing event occurs. The occurrence of the representing event does not imply that the first action has been executed, but implies that the coordination relation is satisfied. That is to say, there is no concern with the execution of the action. If the result of executing the first action is a prerequisite for executing the second action, an event will be published to implicitly represent the result, and this can also be added into the second action's guard as a proposition.
4.   However, there are other natural choices for modelling the prerequisite for the second action. The IoT resource itself also has the result that resource propositions are used to represent not only the resource properties and states but also certain execution results. When the service is modelled before its execution, its resource guard needs to be defined in these IoT application scenarios. When building the service's execution model from its behaviour model, no additional efforts are required to specify the prerequisite.
5.   When the second action's guard is renewed and coordination relations added, it is valid to treat the second action as an independent one.

When a service action is represented by the representing event, the service behaviour can be decomposed using the principle of coordination separation. In Abrial and Hallerstede (2007), and Klusch et al., (2006), the concepts of precondition and post-effect were also used as modelling blocks to describe services or software systems, which seems to be applicable. However, these works did not consider the issue of coordination separation, and their focus was not on a publish/subscribe paradigm for IoT services. The decomposition procedure is formally described below.

An event e is denoted by $t[session]$, where t is a topic name, and *session* may be a session proposition such as *Level* $= 2$, or may be empty. Event e is identified by its topic name and a specific session identifier, and $t[session]$ is used as an alternative notation; if the content of event e includes a session identifier such as *Level* $/2$, e can be represented by $t[session]$ for the purposes of process analysis. For a service model P_i, each of its publish/subscribe interfaces $[\varphi]a$ can be considered as an execution unit, where φ represents the guard of action a (i.e. $t(e,f)$, $t(e)$ or $\bar{t}(e,f)$, $\bar{t}(e)$) and includes the session proposition set φ_{se}, the resource proposition set φ_{re}, and the inner proposition set φ_{in}. When all propositions in φ are evaluated as *True*, a can be executed, and is therefore referred to as being enabled. During execution, the inner proposition sub-set and resource proposition sub-set in φ are expanded to store the behaviour constraint information for processes. In this way, φ becomes $\bar{\varphi}$; $e(t[session])$ (or $e(t[session])$) means that the event $t[session]$ has taken place; and $e(a[\varphi_{se}])$ is some $e(t[session])$ or $e(t[session])$.

The algorithm used to translate a service model into execution units is as follows:

Algorithm 1. Translation of a service model to execution units
Input: A service model P_i.
Output: Service execution units $P_{E,i}$:

1. For $[\varphi']a'.[\varphi]a$ in P_i, $e(a'[\varphi'_{se}])$ is added into the φ of $[\varphi]a$ as a resource proposition. This gives $[\bar{\varphi}]a$, where φ'_{se} is a collection of session propositions in $[\varphi']a'$, and $e(a'[\varphi'e])$ means that the event $a'[\varphi'_e]$ has occurred. Two execution units, $[\varphi]a'$ and $[\bar{\varphi}]a$, are obtained and inserted into the set $P_{E,i}$.

2. For $[\varphi'_a]a'.[\varphi'_b]b' + [\varphi_a]a.[\varphi_b]b$ in P_i, $\neg e(a'[\varphi'_{se}])$ is added into φ_a and φ_b to get $[\bar{\varphi}_a]a$ and $[\bar{\varphi}_b]b$. $\neg e(a[\varphi_{se}])$ is added into φ'_a and φ'_b to get $[\varphi'_a]a'$ and $[\varphi'_b]b'$. Four execution units, $[\bar{\varphi}_a]a$, $[\bar{\varphi}_b]b$, $[\bar{\varphi}'_a]a'$, $[\bar{\varphi}'_b]b'$ are obtained and inserted into the set $P_{E,i}$.

3. For a recursion sub-process X in P_i, each interface $[\varphi]a$ in X is attached with an unobservable process instance identifier *executionnumber* as $[\varphi]a[execution\ number]$, and the unobservable instance identifier is different for each iteration. The attached X is then translated as in steps 1 and 2.

4.   For two parallel actions in P_i, these are directly inserted into $P_{E,i}$. Other forms of sub-process are neglected and can be handled as in steps 1 and 2. After completing the translation, the algorithm returns.

The parallel composition relation between actions in a service model is not translated, since this is carried out by event-driven communication media such as the service running environment. In Algorithm 1, the sequence relationship $[\varphi']a'.[\varphi]a$ is translated into an event causality $a'[\varphi'_{se}] < a[\varphi'_{se}]$, and $a'[\varphi_{se}] < a[\varphi_{se}]$ is also denoted by $[\varphi']a'.[\varphi]a$ when there is no possibility of confusion. φ'_{se} is the actual session proposition set in φ' of $[\varphi']a'$, but some a'''s name/value pairs related to φ'_{se} are also added as assistant to interpret φ'_{se}. The alternation relationship of process $[\varphi'_a]a'.[\varphi'_b]b' + [\varphi_a]a.[\varphi_b]b$ is translated into an event conflict relationship $a'[\varphi'_{se}] \oplus a[\varphi_{se}]$, and $a'[\varphi'_{se}] \oplus a[\varphi_{se}]$ is also denoted by $[\varphi']a' + [\varphi]a$ when no confusion will arise. The translation of the service RemoteCS is given below; here, an unobservable instance identifier is generated for each action and an inner instance proposition is added to its guard, so that two instances of an action can be correctly matched.

```
RemoteCS =
[switcherId = x; state = ON; instanceId = ins1] On2Off(switcher
Id, OffControlSession (switcherId)) |
[switcherId = x; state = OFF, e(On2Off[switcherId = x]);

instanceId = ins1] SwitcherOff (switcherId) |
[switcherId = x; state = OFF; instanceId = ins2]
Off2On(switcherId, OnControlSession(switcherId)) |
[switcherId = x; state = ON, e(Off2On[switcher Id = x]);

instanceId = ins2] SwitcherOn (switcherId)
```

The translation of a service model can also be expressed using a *PA* process called an *execution process*, in which all execution units are composed in parallel and the set $P_{E,i}$ is viewed as the execution process. As an example, consider two execution units, $[\overline{\varphi}_1]a_1[]$ and $[\overline{\varphi}_2]a_2[]$, whose composition is $[\overline{\varphi}_1]a_1[]\|[\overline{\varphi}_2]a_2[]$. The execution process can be expressed as $P_{E,i} = \prod_j [\overline{\varphi}_j]a_j[\text{execution number}_j]$, where $\prod$ means a parallel composition j (i.e. " | ").

The algorithm is based on the philosophy of EDSOA. This means that a service is constructed based on the event content and IoT resources rather than the event's *from* and *to*, each function is a response to the occurrence of an event, and each event is identified by its name and session. The event naming and session mechanisms act as a cornerstone to express the coordination logic and information flow. When we say that the execution of a service interface $[\varphi]a$ is safe, this means the following:

1. When discussing an event relation, the action a (where a is $t(e,f)$, $t(e)$ or $\bar{t}(e, f)$, $\bar{t}(e)$) is represented by an event, i.e. the topic name t in its interface, together with the session propositions of t in its guard. The causal events of a's representing event are simply called the action (interface) of causal events. It is required that a's causal events have taken place and events conflicting with a have not taken place;
2. The data dependence of $[\varphi]a$'s execution is satisfied by direct access to local resources, the contents of an event that has occurred and service instance information such as the instance identifier.

    Basic Assumption of EDSOA: In EDSOA, each publish/subscribe interface in a service behaviour can be safely executed when its direct causal events have taken place and conflicting events have not taken place; each event is identified by the event naming and session mechanism.

In general, if each event maintains causality with its direct causal event, this does not imply that the event maintains causality with its all causal events; this is because its direct causal event identifier may correspond to a set of detail events, and a different detail event also has different direct causal events. The assumption presented above therefore implies that if each event has a causal relation with its direct causal event, it has causality with all of its causal events. The rationale for this is that developers should design services based on the philosophy of EDSOA, i.e. where each service function is a response to the occurrence of an event. If a series of causal event relationships need to be maintained, the service designer should use the event session mechanism to achieve this goal. The use of a unique session identifier is a general method of maintaining a sequence of event causality. This assumption means that if each event has a causal relation with its direct causal event, the service designer ensures that it maintains causality with its all causal events, or allows for the use of a direct cause-effect relation to replace this event causality, without affecting the business goals. The action can then be successfully executed based on direct access to local resources, the contents of events that have occurred and service instance information. Using this assumption, the behaviour of a service can be decomposed using *Algorithm 1* and each enabled function can be immediately executed when the driven event occurs.

Theorem 1. Given a service model P and its execution model P_E, P_E simulates P, but P cannot simulate P_E.

Proof:

1. P_E simulating P: If P does action $[\varphi]a$, φ is evaluated as True. There is a corresponding execution unit $[\bar{\varphi}]a[number]$, where $\bar{\varphi}$ includes φ and a process structure proposition θ such that $e(a'[\varphi'_{se}])$. φ in $\bar{\varphi}$ is also true. θ is the process structure proposition, as follows:

    a. For $[\varphi']a'.[\varphi]a$, θ is $e(a'[\varphi'_{se}])$. When a occurs, $[\varphi']a'$ must have taken place, and then $e(a'[\varphi'_{se}])$ is true.

    b. For $[\varphi']a' + [\varphi]a$, θ is $\neg e(a'[\varphi'_{se}])$. When a occurs, $[\varphi']a'$ must not have taken place, and then $\neg e(a'[\varphi'_{se}])$ is true.

    c. For the actions in an iterated sub-process, only attachment is attached and the process structure proposition is as above. Process parallel structure information is not included in $\bar{\varphi}$.

2. P simulating P_E: If P_E executes action $[\bar{\varphi}]a[number]$, $\bar{\varphi}$ is evaluated as True. There is a corresponding process action $[\varphi]a$, where $\bar{\varphi}$ includes φ and the process structure proposition θ such that $e(a'[\varphi'_{se}])$. φ in $\bar{\varphi}$ is also true. θ is the process structure proposition, as follows:

    a. For $[\varphi']a'.[\varphi]a$, θ is $e(a'[\varphi'_{se}])$. When θ is True, it does not mean that $[\varphi']a'$ has taken place because the a' in $e(a'[\varphi'_{se}])$ may means a set of events, φ'_{se} may be empty, and other units, sub-process, or processes may send such events. That is to say, $[\varphi]a$ is enabled but $[\varphi']a'$ is not enabled such that P cannot do action a. For example, in $[\varphi_a]a.[\varphi_b]b \mid [\varphi_c]c.[\varphi_a]a.[\varphi_d]d$, $[\varphi_b]b$ cannot take place after the action sequence $c \rightarrow a \rightarrow d$ of the right side occurs. However, in the execution model of $[\varphi_a]a.[\varphi_b]b \mid [\varphi_c]c.[\varphi_a]a.[\varphi_d]d$, $[\varphi_b]b$ may be enabled after the correct action sequence $c \rightarrow a \rightarrow d$ has taken place.

The proof of Theorem 1 also demonstrates the basic assumption of EDSOA from a rigid process view. It is therefore clear that a service's function is decoupled as an independent execution unit, if its behaviour is decomposed using Algorithm 1 and the underlying assumption of EDSOA. The service container maintains the guard of the service in its execution model and triggers the service function when driving events occur. Each service execution unit is independently dispatched by the container, and multiple instances are created and run concurrently when multiple driving events occur. Compared with traditional event-driven computation components, the service function is not only reactive, but is also explicitly coordinated by the business layer. In addition, the event session used here can cut across multiple IoT services to express service transactions with fine-grained event relations, and can be decomposed into guards for different functions without complicating the dispatch by the service container.

FLEXIBLE SERVICE PROPCESS UTILITY

In the *Flexible Service Process Utility,* an IoT business process is partitioned into multiple distributed IoT services and pieces of coordination logic. Each service has a business logic layer that is responsible for distributed coordination, while each publish/subscribe interface in the service is translated into an execution unit running in the service environment. Multiple execution units for the service share the same business logic layer for the business process. Compared with the decomposition of service behaviour, the partition of the business process based on the principle of coordination separation will result in a different problem: that of how to execute distributed fragments of the business process with consistent event relations. This is discussed below.

An IoT business process *Pepc* can be viewed as a composite IoT service, and the translation of activities can be achieved in the same way as for the service model. However, the use of event guards cannot guarantee that the event relations will cut across distributed services during runtime, and an arbitrator is needed in addition to the arbitration algorithm. The translation from *Pepc* to its execution model is carried out as follows:

1. The action $[\varphi]a$ in a service S is integrated into the business process, *Pepc*, and its direct causal event is $a'[\varphi'_{se}]$. $e(a'[\varphi'_{se}])$ is inserted into the proposition guard φ of $[\varphi]a$.
2. The business logic layer of service S listens for event $a'[\varphi'_{se}]$. When $a'[\varphi'_{se}]$ occurs, the business logic layer assigns a value of *True* to $e(a'[\varphi'_{se}])$.
3. For non-deterministic composition in *Pepc*, such as $[\varphi'_a]a'.[\varphi'_b]b' + [\varphi_a]a.[\varphi_b]b$, which happens to belong to the same service S, the business logic layer of S determines which of $\neg e(a'[\varphi'_{se}])$ or $\neg e(a[\varphi_{se}])$ is *True* based on the occurrence of $a'[\varphi'_{se}]$ and $a[\varphi_{se}]$. The business logic layer acts as an arbitrator, with the aim of avoiding inconsistency in the values of $\neg e(a'[\varphi'_{se}])$ and $\neg e(a[\varphi_{se}])$.
4. For a general conflict event relation in *Pepc* such as $[\varphi'_a]a' \oplus [\varphi]a$, the arbitrator can be chosen from the business logic layers of $[\varphi']a'$ or $[\varphi]$

a . This then determines the values of $\neg e(a'[\varphi'_{se}])$ and $\neg e(a[\varphi_{se}])$ during runtime (only one is true at a given time) to avoid inconsistency.

From the above discussion, it can be seen that the business logic layer is required to assume an arbitrator function. However, this intuitive model is not convenient, since complex protocols are required to create consistent consent when a business process is decomposed into multiple distributed IoT services. That is to say, the behaviour decoupling of a business process is different from that of an atomic service, since the distributed execution of different process fragments will result in state inconsistency. The key problem is to obtain consistent event relations for different fragments of the business process. The execution model is therefore revised; the proposition guards for events, such as session propositions and event relation propositions, are not evaluated as propositions, and only the resource proposition guard remains to be checked when events occur. Event-related propositions can be abstracted into a new event name to create a new composite event by aggregating the event composition logic. Different computation logic units in process fragments (the implementing functions of service interfaces) subscribe to and are driven by this composite event with a new name, thus realising consistency of event relations.

In order to enable the use of the event-naming approach to avoid state inconsistency and drive services, a special service is used to create a new event name from event-related propositions. This service handles the propositions and publishes a new event with a new name, representing the result of proposition processing. This result is also an event, and is called a composite event. The service has multiple instances during runtime, and each instance handles one part of the proposition set to avoid the bottleneck effect. The business layer subscribes to the composite event based on its topic name. When the composite event arrives at the business logic layer, the business layer enables the corresponding interfaces.

This service can be carried out by a CEP system such as that in Lundberg, (2006), in which event rules are used to specify how to obtain a composite event from different event sources. The general rules can be expressed as follows (Gao et al., 2014; Qiao et al., 2013):

Rule= (Pattern, Window, RepeatTimes),

where *Pattern* represents the logical relation of several events, and the common relations include *and, or, not, sequence*, etc. *Window* represents the magnitude (size) of the event stream, which often includes a time window (the events in this time interval are computed according to the patterns) and a length window. *RepeatTimes* represents the number of times that a pattern is matched.

Based on the rule expression used in CEP, a session proposition can be expressed using a value comparison of events and logic operators. Event causality can be expressed by the sequence. The event conflict relation between e_1 and e_2 can be expressed by $(\neg e(e_1) \wedge e(e_2)) \vee (e(e_1) \wedge \neg e(e_2))$. The reader is referred to Gao et al., (2014), And Qiao et al., (2013) for more details about this service.

Based on the idea described above, the intuitive execution model is revised as shown in Figure 9, where each publish/subscribe interface is only guarded by inner propositions and resource propositions, and the event related propositions are represented by composite events to which the business logic layer subscribes. Several inner propositions are initialised to *False*. When the composite event arrives at the business logic layer, the business logic layer assigns a value of *True* to the inner propositions of the service's interfaces, which originally have event-related propositions. Multiple CEP service instances can be used to give high levels of concurrency, and each CEP service is in charge of one part of the event relation processing. The main task of the *Flexible Service Process Utility* is then to distribute the event composition rules and enact the rules, meaning that each business process is partitioned into several distributed IoT services and pieces of event composition logic. The service-based approach is then adopted to carry out the distributed execution of the

Figure 9. Revised service execution model

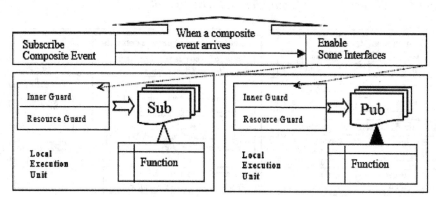

business process, in which IoT services are executed at distributed sites and the separated coordination logic is aggregated into composite events, with one piece of this aggregation being enacted by one instance of the special service, in order to assure the consistency of the event relation for different services. This also provides a direction for the graphical orchestration of or collaboration between services, creating a business process by separately modeling its different parts, and this will be a goal of future work in this area.

COMMON OPERATION PICTURE

For an IoT service system, a well-defined human-machine interface is important, as it allows operators to monitor and control the physical world. Common operation pictures (COP) are used to enable users to operate on these pictures in a visual and conventional way. To help users create COPs, a COP system should first be established. A COP system consists of two parts: a COP creation tool and a COP runtime system.

The COP creation tool is resource-oriented, as illustrated in Figure 10; a set of meta-figures is created for a domain, where each meta-figure corresponds to a single physical entity, and the resource file (including IoT resource models and their instances) forms the basis for creating COPs. Entities and their relations can be extracted from the resource file, and the meta-figures corresponding to particular entities are then identified from the domain meta-figure set. However, meta-figures alone are not sufficient to create a COP. A picture template is used to guide users in laying out meta-figures

Figure 10. IoT resource-oriented picture creation tool

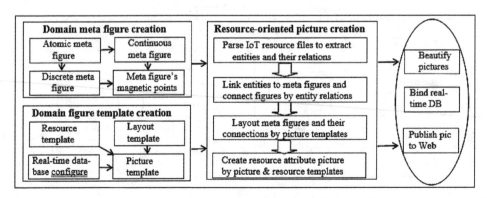

Figure 11. Example of a common operation picture

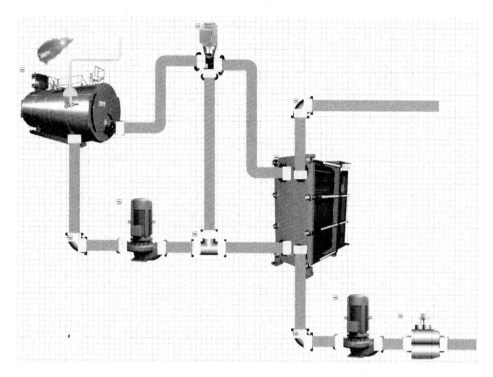

and connecting them together. Figure 11 illustrates an example of a COP in which the boiler graph is a meta-figure corresponding to the physical boiler entity, and is connected to other entities via water pipes.

When a COP has been published to the Web, a user can carry out operations on this in order to monitor and control the physical system and the physical world. These operations include simple actuations, groups of actuations, discrete control, continuous control, configuration of settings and so on. COPs can also be combined to give a single large picture, or merged with other UI components such as tables or reports. COPS can also be published as widgets.

The method of operation of COPS at runtime is illustrated in Figure 12; here, the COPS are wrapped as widgets for display within Web browsers. An operation performed by the user is abstracted as a procedure (denoted as *proc*) and executed on the Web server. For example, one request for a widget is as follows:

```
http://test.bupt.edu.cn/widgets/test5.
```

Figure 12. COP at runtime

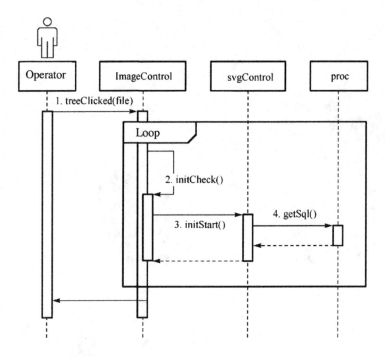

The response to this request is as follows:

```
<widget id="http://test.bupt.edu.cn/widgets/test5" width="500"
height="500" version="0.1">
<name short="">test5</name> <description>test5</description>
<iconsrc="http://localhost:8080/wookie/deploy/test.bupt.edu.cn/
widgets/test5/images/icon.png"/> <author>BUPT</author>
</widget>
```

A request to refresh the resource attributes on the Web is as follows:

```
PREFIXsp:<http://www.test.org/heatExchangeStation/
SenseProperty/> SELECT ?topic
WHERE {?contributor sp:topic ?topic . }
```

APPLICATIONS AND EXPERIMENTS

The EDSOA platform was implemented by deploying it in a CMCS application. The Sanyuan coal company has multiple coal mines in Shanxi province;

each coal mine has a local CMCS, and the CMCSs of all coal mines and the company headquarters collaborate to ensure that coal mining operations are safe and efficient. In each coal mine, there are numerous devices, which generate real-time metered data that is collected by the programmable logic controller (PLC) and/or receive actuation instructions from the PLC.

The applications and experiments of resource pools and unified message space are discussed in previous chapters. This chapter focuses on the service process utility including event compositions and process distribution. CEP is an event processing system that combines events from multiple sources to infer events or patterns that suggest more complicated circumstances. The application architecture of CEP engine is illustrated in Figure 13. To enable the event streaming processing, the CEP engine allows applications to store event queries and run the event through instead of storing the data and running queries against stored data. Input/Output events streaming adapter is in charge of the adaptation of different events representation formats, such as XML or Java Object. In order to support the definition of complex events detection rules, a tailored Event Processing Language (EPL) is used to express rich event conditions, correlation, possibly spanning time windows. EPL is a SQL-like language with SELECT, FROM, WHERE, GROUP BY, HAVING and ORDER BY clauses. The logical operators, such as AND, OR, NOT can be used in event expressions. The temporal sequence of different events can be expressed by "->" operator. For example, A->B represents that event A followed by event B. For the time-related event stream processing, the time-related operators, like timer:interval, timer:at, timer:within, relationship can

Figure 13. CEP service architecture

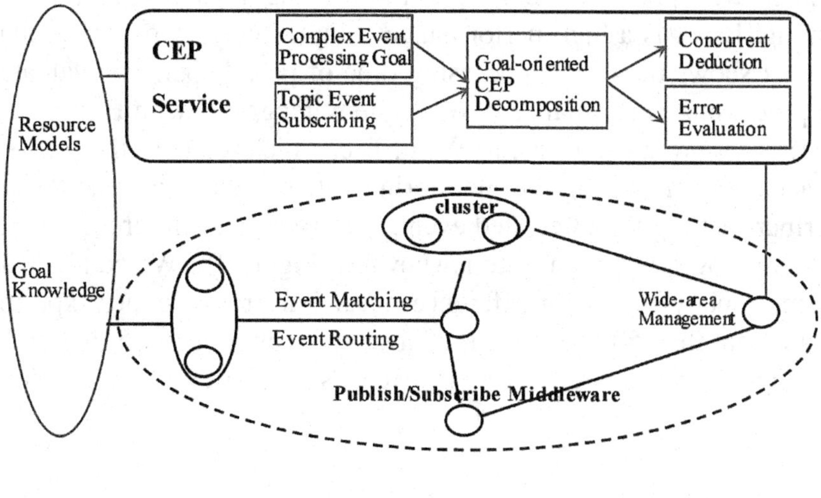

Figure 14. CEP performance for Esper

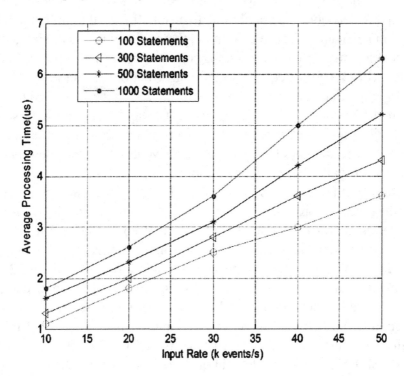

be used in where-conditions to control the lifecycle of sub-expressions. Based on these operators, users can define the interested event detection rules, i.e. statement. Typically, EPL supports pattern matching, joining events on arbitrary criteria and creating time-based windows.

For making experiments, we deployed an open-source CEP system: *Esper*, a complex event processing engine, to filter and aggregate the real-time data streaming. Esper is a high-performance complex event processing engine. Figure 14 shows the event processing time of pure Esper. To evaluate the event processing performance of our system integrated with Esper, we use average event processing time as the metric, which refers to the time spent from access agent getting the monitoring value to the service system (i.e. subscriber) getting the interested event. The average event processing time with increasing input event rate is shown in Figure 15. We conducted the experiment many times with different event arriving rates. In each experiment we send more than 5000 events. It is observed from Figure 15 that with the increasing event input rate from 10 events/s to 100 events/s, the average

Figure 15. CEP performance for service platform

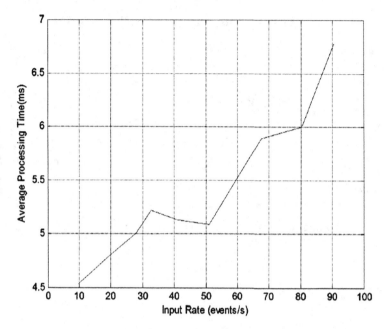

processing time of our whole system remained about 5ms ~ 7ms. Thus, the event processing time can meet the real-time demands for IoT applications.

Process experiments were conducted on the CMCSs to measure the performance of the distributed process execution in terms of throughput and jitter. A simple, symmetric topology was established with 30 broke node in the service platform, and this was used to test the basic performance. On the horizontal axis in Figure 16, the total number of events injected into the system is gradually increased throughout the different experimental steps. On the left-hand vertical axis, the number of events processed per second by the system is given, in order to represent the throughput of the system at each experimental step; the right vertical axis (jitter) means average difference of delivery events per second for services at different sites. From the figure 16, we know that the throughput firstly reached the maximal 24500 events per second and then decreased with the processing pressure increasing; jitter was about 450 events/s~2000 events per second, *i.e., the jitter being about 8%*; and the jitter increased after the system reached its maximal throughput where the system worked very stably and smoothly nearby the maximal throughput to reach the maximal.

Figure 16. Throughput and jitter with 30 nodes

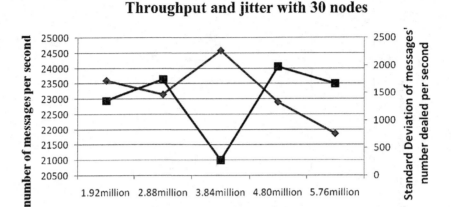

Throughput and jitter with 30 nodes

RELATED WORK

The current authors and their colleagues have previously discussed the use of EDSOA in IoT (Zhang & Chen, 2015;Zhu et al., 2011;Zhao, 2014). The technology surveys (Atzor et al., 2010; Gubbi et al., 2013) also considered the use of an event-driven methodology for IoT applications. However, these papers did not discuss why such an architecture is applicable and how it could be used.

The PLAY project (Stojanovic, 2010) involved the building of an ultra-scale federated service platform based on dynamic and complex event interaction patterns, and this was similar to the work presented here. However, although the two studies share similar goals, the design and implementation are different.

There are two types of prior related work: one involves the redesign of the publish/subscribe middleware to accommodate the applications, while the other involves the redesign of applications to utilise the functionalities of middleware in order to realize scalability and high performance. In Bakken et al., (2011), the GridStat project proposed a publish/subscribe-based WAMS-DD infrastructure for a smart grid in which different event consumers can request different receiving rates for a given type of event. It did not consider adjusting the IoT services to accommodate the WAMS-DD.

In Li et al., (2010) and Hensa, et al., (2014), the redesign of applications to accommodate the publish/subscribe middleware was considered. Both of these studies adopted a decomposition method to partition a higher-level application to avoid the bottleneck effect of the central execution of business processes, but did not consider the consistency issue arising from the running of different partitioned units, which is the focus here, involving the modelling of coordination logic as event compositions.

Matthias Wieland *et al* (2009) proposed a CEP-based method to execute event-driven business processes, where the CEP system produced composite events and sent them to the BPEL engine (OASIS, 2007). In their method, the BPEL was centralized and brought about the bottleneck effect of concurrency. Furthermore, the relation between business computation logic and event composition logic was not clarified. In our works, we establish a service process utility to support appropriately decomposing a business process into distributed business computation logic and event composition logic. The event composition logic is explicitly expressed by the event session and EPC's logical connectors. The distributed execution models of business processes are then derived from our event-driven IoT service models. In the technology survey of event-driven business process management (Krumeich et al., 2014), the authors also emphasized the importance of integrating CEP systems into process engines, but they did not envision how to assume this task.

This method of IoT service creation and support is also suitable for traditional supervisory control and data acquisition (SCADA) systems, which are designed to be close and to consist of one or more remote terminal units (RTU) connected to a variety of sensors and actuators. The works in Chen and Liu, (2002), Qiu et al., (2002), Nithiyanatan and Ramachandran, (2004), Irving et al., (2004), and Santo et al., (2004) discussed Internet-based technologies for improving SCADA systems. The study in Masaud-Wahaishi and Gaouda, (2011) presented an agent-based distribution architecture for power systems that supported ad hoc and automated system configurations, emphasising strategies for achieving, locating and isolating faults without degrading the quality of services. The overall architecture could be viewed as a cooperative, distributed electrical power system compared with traditional monitoring and control technology, which the author found to be highly centralised and not scalable with significant increases in distributed IoT application scenarios.

CONCLUSION

In this chapter, a streamlining service platform is proposed for the integration of IoT services in which a service-oriented publish/subscribe middleware is established to support service interaction and service routing. Its communication capabilities are exposed as services for higher-level applications to use. An event-driven service programming environment and a running environment are then established to converge IoT services and IoT data with scalability; the distributed IoT resource pool supports the separation of the attribute access capabilities and the resource actuation capabilities, and the DEBS-based service environment supports event-based service programming and running. Finally, a service process utility is established which supports the separation of coordination logic from service computation logic for the distributed execution of IoT service processes. Applications and experiments are used to demonstrate the effectiveness and applicability of this solution.

REFERENCES

Abrial, J.-R., & Hallerstede, S. (2007). Refinement, decomposition, and instantiation of discrete models: Application to Event-B. *Fundamenta Informaticae*, 1–28.

Agha, G. A. (1986). *ACTORS: A model of concurrent computation in distributed systems*. Cambridge, MA: MIT Press.

Atzori, L., Iera, A., & Morabito, G. (2010). The Internet of Things: A survey. *Computer Networks*, *54*(15), 2787–2805. doi:10.1016/j.comnet.2010.05.010

Bakken, D. E., Bose, A., Hauser, C. H., Whitehead, D. E., & Zweigle, G. C. (2011). Smart generation and transmission with coherent, real-time data. *Proceedings of the IEEE*, *99*(6), 928–951. doi:10.1109/JPROC.2011.2116110

Chen, S., & Liu, F. Y. (2002). Web based simulations of power systems. *IEEE Trans. on Computer Applications in Power*, *15*(1), 35–40. doi:10.1109/67.976990

Di Santo, M., Ranaldo, N., Villacci, D., & Zimeo, E. (2004). Performing security analysis of large scale power systems with a broker-based computational grid. *IEEE Proceedings of ITCC2004, 2*, 77-82. 10.1109/ITCC.2004.1286593

Gao, F., Curry, E., & Bhiri, S. (2014). *Complex event service provision and composition based on event pattern matchmaking. DEBS'14*. Academic Press.

Gubbi, J., Buyya, R., Marusic, S., & Palaniswami, M. (2013). Internet of Things (IoT): A vision, architectural elements, and future directions. *Future Generation Computer Systems*, *29*(7), 1645–1660. doi:10.1016/j.future.2013.01.010

Guinard, D., Karnouskos, S., Spiess, P., & Savio, D. (2010). Interacting with the SOA-based Internet of Things: Discovery, query, selection, and on-demand provisioning of Web services. *IEEE Transactions on Services Computing, 3*(3), 223–235. doi:10.1109/TSC.2010.3

Hensa, P., Snoecka, M., Poelsb, G., & De Backera, M. (2014). Process fragmentation, distribution and execution using an event-based interaction scheme. *Journal of Systems and Software, 89*, 170–192. doi:10.1016/j. jss.2013.11.1111

Irving, M., Taylor, G., & Hobson, P. (2004). Plug into grid computing. *IEEE Trans. on Power and Energy Magazine, 2*(2), 40–44. doi:10.1109/ MPAE.2004.1269616

Klusch, M., Fries, B., & Sycara, K. (2006). Automated semantic web service discovery with OWLS-MX. *Proceedings of the 5th International Joint Conference on Autonomous Agents and Multiagent Systems*, 915-922. 10.1145/1160633.1160796

Krumeich, J., Weis, B., Werth, D., & Loos, P. (2014). Event-driven business process management: Where are we now? -A comprehensive synthesis and analysis of literature. Business Process Management Journal, 20(4), 615-633.

G. L. Li, V. Muthusamy, H. A. Jacobsen. (2010). A distributed service-oriented architecture for business process execution. *ACM Transactions on the Web, 4*(1), 2:1-2:33.

Lundberg, A. (2006). Leverage complex event processing to improve operational performance. *Business Intelligence Journal, 11*(1), 55–65.

Lundberg, A. (2006). Leverage complex event processing to improve operational performance. *Business Intelligence Journal, 11*(1), 55–65.

Masaud-Wahaishi, A.-M., & Gaouda, A. (2011). Intelligent monitoring and control architecture for future electrical power systems. *2nd International Conference on Ambient Systems, Networks and Technologies*. 10.1016/j. procs.2011.07.101

Mendling, J. (2007). *Detection and prediction of errors in EPC business process models* (Dissertation). Vienna University of Economics and Business Administration.

Nithiyanatan, K., & Ramachandran, V. (2004). RMI based multi-area power system load flow monitoring. *IJECE, 3*(1), 28–30.

OASIS. (2007). *Web Services Business Process Execution Language Version 2.0*. Retrieved from http://docs.oasis-open.org/wsbpel/2.0/wsbpel-v2.0.html, 4 2007.

OASIS WSN. (2006). *OASIS Web Services Notification* (WSN). OASIS Completed Version.

Qiao, X., Liu, Y., Xue, Z., Wu, B., & Chen, J. (2013). Event-driven SOA based district heating service system with complex event processing capability. *International Journal of Web Services Research*, 2013.

Qiu, B., Gooi, H. B., Liu, Y., & Chan, E. K. (2002). Internet based SCADA display system. *IEEE Trans. on Computer Applications in Power*, *15*(1), 14–19. doi:10.1109/67.976986

Schinz & Haller. (2014). *A Scala Tutorial for Java programmers*. Scala Language, Version 1.3.

Stojanovic. (2010). *Pushing dynamic and ubiquitous interaction between services leveraged in the Future Internet by applying complex event processing*. FP7 PLAY Project 258659.

Wieland, Martin, Kopp, & Leymann. (2009). SOEDA: A methodology for specification and implementation of applications on a Service-Oriented Event-Driven Architecture. *Proceedings of the 12th International Conference on Business Information Systems*. 10.1007/978-3-642-01190-0_17

Zhang, Y., & Chen, J. L. (2015). Constructing scalable IoT services based on their event-driven models. *Concurrency and Computation*, *27*(17), 4819–4851. doi:10.1002/cpe.3469

Zhao, S. (2014). *Research on Internet of Things resource management platform and service provision framework* (Dissertation). Beijing University of Posts and Telecommunications.

Zhu, D., Zhang, Y., Cheng, B., & Chen, J. L. (2011). Towards a flexible event-driven SOA-based approach for collaborating interactive business processes. *IEEE International Conference on Services Computing*, 749–750. 10.1109/SCC.2011.62

Section 3
Flexibly Creating Streamlining IoT Services

Chapter 5

Coordinating Stateful IoT Resources as Event-Driven Distributed IoT Services

ABSTRACT

In IoT applications, physical systems have not only discrete behaviors but also continuous dynamics; the corresponding aspects of the information world are called IoT resources. IoT services monitor and control these resources to ensure specific properties such as controllability and stability. An approach is proposed here that links together IoT resources, events, and IoT services based on requirement specifications. IoT resources are explicitly modelled as stateful to express the evolution of their current attributes and states from their previous ones. Multiple actions are modelled by specifying the indirect effects and causalities of their actions, and the interactions between physical processes and information processes are orchestrated as the coordination of the IoT resources (i.e., coordinating stateful IoT resources as IoT services). At runtime, the issue of how to solve the glitch problem is discussed based on an event extraction method. Finally, an evaluation is performed as a proof of concept for this chapter.

DOI: 10.4018/978-1-5225-7622-8.ch005

INTRODUCTION

IoT resources represent physical objects and sensors in ICT systems, and are foundational entities in IoT applications. IoT services are used to manage and coordinate these IoT resources in order to make a physical system work effectively and efficiently, such as robotic assembly lines that machine components.

IoT resources are often specified using specific methods and standards (IEEE1451.2-1997, 1997; SSN, 2014; Botts & Robin, 2007), and are independently deployed at different physical sites. IoT services are often independently developed at different times and places and by different vendors (Erl, 2005). The method of semantic service creation (Hatzi et al., 2012; Stavropoulos et al., 2016) appears to be able to orchestrate these independent IoT services and IoT resources. The fact that IoT resources often have inherent physical processes, including discrete behaviours and continuous dynamics, and their current resource attributes and states are produced only after the previous resource attributes and states (known as a stateful system), means that existing service orchestration methods may not work well.

An IoT service can be considered as a set of actions performed on IoT resources, and appropriate descriptions of these actions are necessary for an artificial system to correctly monitor and control the real world (McCarthy & Hayes, 1969; Kowalski & Sergot, 1986; Gelfond & Lifschitz, 1993; Reiter, 2001). Although existing studies have specified action effects produced by Web services for the definition and composition of semantic services (Hatzi et al., 2012; Stavropoulos et al., 2016), only the dependencies between input and output or between precondition and effect have been explored for the orchestration of services. The way in which the stateful physical process of IoT resources operates and interacts with the information process of IoT services is not fully reflected in the service description of IOPE and classic service orchestration. The orchestration of IoT services needs to be oriented to stateful IoT resources, i.e. allowing the coordination of stateful IoT resources, as follows:

1. The lifecycles of different IoT resources need to be properly matched, since the state of one resource may be a condition on the state transition of another resource. Although a simple matching requirement can be indirectly specified in the service description, complex stateful matching

requirements such as controllability (i.e. distinguishing controllable resource attributes and states from uncontrollable ones, and adjusting them by matching controllable against uncontrollable ones (Zhang & Chen, 2017) are difficult or impossible to define in the service layer.

2. IoT resources have continuous dynamics and discrete behaviours, and their continuous stateful properties such as stability (Smith, 1957; Zhang & Chen, 2015) should also hold; these often do not appear in the IOPE service specification.

3. The attributes of multiple IoT resources may affect each other, and need to be coordinated with each other such that multiple controlling actions over the IoT resources can be performed according to the constraints on resource attributes (e.g. the motion equations of a robot).

For example, robotic resources in a production line should have different motion trajectories without collusion, such as one resource placing components onto a belt and others removing them.

Compared with the coordination of traditional Web services (Tasharofi et al., 2007; Meng & Arbab, 2007; Kokash & Arbab, 2013; Li & Sun, 2015), which focuses on service interactions and constraints on interactions, the coordination of IoT services involves monitoring and controlling IoT resources to make physical systems work well. Cheng et al. (2016) proposed an event-based IoT service coordination method in which event patterns were used to detect events and event-condition-action (ECA) rules were used to coordinate IoT services. Although sensors were introduced in this work, IoT resources were not explicitly and comprehensively modelled, meaning that some properties of IoT resources, such as controllability and continuous dynamics, could not be coordinated. The issue addressed in this chapter is the orchestration of independent IoT services to coordinate stateful IoT resources that need to be integrated into the orchestration as action effects, using a decoupling method. Directly specifying the IoT resources in the IoT services makes it difficult for designers to manage the complexity of orchestrating services. In this chapter, IoT resources are explicitly and independently specified, and the focus is then placed on the interactions between IoT resources and IoT services using an event-driven decoupling method.

In the service orchestration described above, the IoT resources are often distributed at different physical sites, meaning that the IoT services need to be deployed near to the IoT resources for real-time operation (Sill, 2017). Distributed events are used to drive and coordinate these distributed IoT services and resources, including updating events for the attributes of IoT resources, state transition events, actuating events, and so on. Finding a method of solving the glitch problem for the execution of event-driven distributed services (Schuster & Flanagan, 2016), i.e. ensuring consistency of event reactions in distributed environments, is then a challenging task.

IoT resources are often semantically modelled, and semantics-based methods are often used to construct IoT services, such as those in Tzortzis and Spyrou, (2016), Yang et al., (2014). Eshuis et al. (2016) used reusable semantic knowledge to create services in which the semantic description of individual service components acted as the declarative knowledge; the service was then composed to support sequence, choice and parallelism. Data dependency in semantic knowledge was explored as reusable networks for service composition and modification. In our work, IoT service coordination is also based on semantic knowledge with complex action effect descriptions. Hatzi et al. (2012) adopted the Stanford Research Institute planning system (STRIPS) (Fikes & Nilsson, 1971) to model the service orchestration problem over service action effects, and solved this using a planning method. Here, a type of action theory, fluent calculus (Thielscher, 1999; Drescher & Thielscher, 2007; Thielscher, 2005), is used to describe the real-world domain, since it is fully based on first-order logic, and several efficient SMT solvers (Moura & Bjørner, 2008; Gao et al., 2013) can be used to reason about action knowledge. However, the uniqueness assumption for the functions (i.e. different inputs corresponding to different outputs) in fluent calculus is discarded, since an IoT resource may have complex continuous behaviour (different inputs may correspond to the same output), and different names may have compatible meanings, such as allowing for name refinement (e.g. 'bird' is a refinement of 'animal'). The concept of conflict is introduced for fluents (action effects defined in fluent calculus). In other words, different names may have complex relationships such as equivalence, inclusion, parent-child, and conflicts, as discussed in Chapter 1. The fluent relations of causality, conflict, and non-relevance can then be expressed in a distributed concurrent system (Glabbeek & Goltz, 2004). Using these fluent relations, the issue of on-demand orchestration of distributed independent IoT services on stateful IoT resources can be addressed using a decoupling method.

The contributions of this chapter are twofold:

1. A situation-based method is proposed to coordinate stateful IoT resources as distributed IoT services, where the term "situation" represents the stateful features of IoT resources, as discussed in later sections.

a.   An event-based process modelling language called EPC is adapted as a way of graphically expressing the coordination requirements of IoT resources. The requirement specification is an abstract business process that uses only events and event relations to describe service interactions, such as an event involving switches being turned off taking place before an event involving an operator checking electrical devices; this specification focuses on the higher-layer application without diving into the details of the underlying IoT resource specifications. In the requirement specification, function nodes are replaced by action placeholders without binding to actual IoT services, and predicates on IoT resource models are used to express the action effects and preconditions of service actions without binding the actual IoT resources.

b.   In the same way as for the satisfiability reduction method in Berardi et al., (2003), the resource coordination problem is reduced to the SMT (Barret et al., 2009) problem involving a knowledge of IoT service and resource candidates, as represented by the fluent calculus. An exhaustion method is used to search the model of this knowledge, and the model is translated into the required EPC business process, where situations involving historical snapshots of action executions are generated to bind actual IoT services and resources to the EPC business process. The executability of the EPC business process is checked using the satisfiability of action effects in these situations. IoT resource instances are bound to the EPC business process using a decoupling method; that is, events on resource transitions are used to link the resource to the situation-bound service action that produces or receives these events. The concept of resource causality is introduced for changes in IoT resource attributes following events, and this reflects the resource intrinsic running from one state to another state under what conditions. Based on this causality representation, modelled in stateful IoT resources, an event relation indirectly implies coordination between IoT resources.

2. The glitch problem is solved by separating the coordination logic from the service orchestration.

a.   In order to construct a distributed IoT service system, we establish a distributed real-time tuple space to locally store and maintain IoT resource instances. IoT resources are locally instantiated based on their models when IoT services access the attributes of these IoT resources. A special resource maintenance service subscribes to an underlying publish/subscribe middleware to receive the attribute update events published by the services monitoring the sensors and physical systems. IoT services can access local resource pools to read the attributes of resources. The rationale for creating these stateful IoT resources is based on the assumption of eventual consistency of resource attributes.

b. Resource pools provide the basis for the design of a distributed IoT service system that can read the resource states and perform actions on these states in the local resource pool. It is viewed as a stateful service, but does not contain the logic necessary to store resource attributes and states, update them, and maintain their lifecycles. These services can be executed with a high level of concurrency. An actor model (Agha, 1986; SCALA, 2015) is also used to implement an IoT service such that each service action is event-driven, i.e. reacts to the occurrence of events.

c. The event relations are then extracted from the service orchestration in the form of coordination logic. When the coordination logic is separated from the orchestration, all the IoT services become independent and can be distributed. The coordination logic can then be independently enacted as new composite events. Based on the distributed resource pool and separation of coordination logic as composite events, the conditions on solving the glitch problem are described, and the solution is proven.

The remainder of this chapter is structured as follows. Section 2 describes the preliminaries. In Section 3, a discussion of IoT resource properties is given. In Section 4, the specification of the coordination requirements of IoT resources is discussed. Section 5 describes service creation in distributed IoT resources. Section 6 explains how to distribute IoT services with consistency. Experimental results are presented in Section 7. Section 6.8 presents related work. Finally, conclusions are drawn in Section 9.

PRELIMARIES

In previous chapters, an IoT resource was defined as an informational description of a single sensor or physical entity in the physical world, which includes a lifecycle model and an object model. Its object model specifies its

Figure 1. Coordination and services for IoT resources

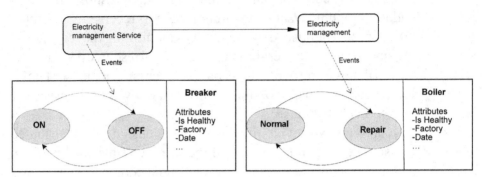

attributes and the relations between them, while its lifecycle model describes the possible ways in which it might progress, and the event-driven transition between two lifetime states.

Multiple IoT resources often affect each other. For example, a *breaker* resource and a *boiler* resource are illustrated in Figure 1; the former is operated by an *electricity management service,* the latter by *a Boiler Maintaining Service*, and the two services are independently developed and operated. The *breaker* resource should be changed to the *OFF* state in its lifecycle before the *boiler* resource is changed to the *repair* state in its lifecycle in order to ensure the safety of the engineers. This means that the two IoT resources need to be coordinated, and this is realised by coordinating the events between the two IoT services.

The fluent calculus is a type of action theory used to specify how an artificial system performs actions over the physical world in a dynamic domain. It is fully based on first-order logic and can support reasoning about actions by addressing the frame problem, the ramification problem, and the qualification problem, where the action effects, called *fluents*, are defined by terms rather than predicates in order to allow flexibility.

SPECIFYING IOT RESOURCE PROPERTIES

Before more technical details are presented, an example is given here to illustrate IoT resources and their properties.

Figure 2 demonstrates two IoT resources. A robot takes a component from its input buffer and puts it on the checking platform; an operator checks the component on the checking platform and unloads the checked component into the output buffer. The *Take* action happens (for convenience, the first

Figure 2. Robot and human resources performing a component check

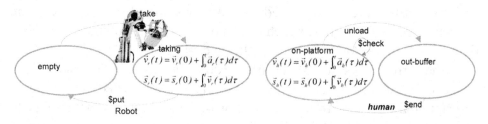

letter of an action name is capitalised, while an event name is written in lower-case letters), i.e. the *take* event occurs, if the robot is in the *empty* state and an IoT service actuates it. The *Put* action will automatically happen, i.e. the *put* event occurs, when the robot is in the *taking* state without an IoT service actuating it. This is called an uncontrollable event, and is denoted by *$put*. The *Check* action is started by a checking operator when the component is placed on the checking platform. A *check* event will be automatically produced during checking, and is denoted as *$check*. The *Unload* action and the *unload* event are controllable. The motion trajectory of the robot moving the component from the input buffer to the platform is simply represented by a velocity vector $\vec{v}_r(t)$ and a position trajectory vector $\vec{s}_r(t)$. The motion trajectory of the operator's arm is simply represented by a velocity vector $\vec{v}_h(t)$ and a position trajectory vector $\vec{s}_h(t)$. Since the *$put* event is uncontrollable, the robot may place two components on the checking platform, which alters the working rhythm. The resource property *safety* appears, as follows:

1.   The uncontrollable event should be indirectly controlled so that only one component is placed on the checking platform.
2.   When the robot places a component and the checking operator begins checking, an injury may occur, i.e. the robot colliding with the operator's hands. The operation zones of the two resources should not intersect.

In the above example, an IoT resource not only interacts with an IoT service, but also has its own running process with specific properties. A resource property defines how a physical entity should work. It can be specified by event relations and nonlinear/linear constraints; the former defines how resource states change, while the latter defines which constraints the resource attributes need to satisfy. The flow event structure (Glabbeek & Goltz, 2004) can be used to define the property relevant to event relations, which is suitable for specifying running systems by event causality and event conflict. Nonlinear or linear constraints can be imposed on continuous variables as a complement to discrete event properties, which can be defined using computer numbers (Ninin et al., 2015; Moore et al., 2009; Gao et al., 2012).

In the current work, an IoT resource is described by an object model and a lifecycle model. A resource object model can be represented by a resource description framework (RDF), a collection of triples in the format <subject, property, object>. An RDF graph (Peng et al., 2016) is not only intuitive, but also expressive. In Peng et al., (2016), the graph partitioning method for a distributed RDF graph is used to circle a resource in the whole knowledge, and clarify the relations between two resources by crossing edges (see Figure 3). We extend the object model based on the RDF graph by attaching a resource lifecycle model to obtain a complete specification, as given in Definitions 1 to 4.

Given a resource model, its properties can be defined as follows.

To protect the operators in Figure 2, the equation set below has no solutions (denoted by $\forall t$, $Eq.1 \models \vec{s}_r(t) \neq \vec{s}_h(t)$):

$$\begin{cases} \vec{s}_r(t) = \vec{s}_r(0) + \int_0^t \vec{v}_r(\tau)d\tau \\ \vec{s}_h(t) = \vec{s}_h(0) + \int_0^t \vec{v}_h(\tau)d\tau \end{cases}. \tag{1}$$

The two resources need to be coordinated with each other in order to maintain safety. The machine platform provides an operating space; the operator's motion trajectory, representing the operating space of the platform, has no positions in common with the robot motion trajectory in order to ensure strict levels of human safety. It is assumed here that two basic IoT services, the *robot management service* and the *human management service,* are used to manage the respective resources.

IOT SERVICES AND CREATION PROBLEM

For an application in one domain, we provide a service architecture in SoaML (SoaML, 2013) to represent its basic structure and functionalities, where the service architecture is a network of participant roles providing and consuming services, and it is a high-level view of how services work. A role defines a basic function or a set of functions. In contrast, a participant specifies the type of a party that fulfills a role in the context of a specific service architecture. A participant may also have its own service architecture.

In this chapter, the service architecture specified by SoaML (SoaML, 2013) is implicit, and the focus is on the behaviour of IoT services. An IoT service is modelled using the EPC language (Karhof et al., 2013; Mendling, 2007; Scheer, 1998), in which an event is represented by a hexagon, a function (also called a service action in a service view of the EPC process) is represented by a rounded rectangle, a logical connector is represented by a circle with *AND, OR,* and *EXCLUSIVE OR,* and a resource is represented by a rectangle.

This event-based process modelling language is adapted here to express the coordination requirements of IoT resources. The specification of requirements is an abstract business process (Berardi et al., 2003) in which function nodes are replaced by action placeholders with filling preconditions and effects, and events and their relations are drawn to represent service interactions. Figure 3 illustrates a specification of the coordination requirements of a component manufacturing/checking process over the IoT resources in Figure 2.

In Figure 4, the *Checking* function, carried out by a checking operator, is triggered by the *$put* event; its precondition is that the operator is authorised. Preconditions are annotated before the semantic placeholder name, and effects are annotated afterwards. The *$put* event from the robot resource is used to coordinate with the operator resource for the *Checking* function.

- **Definition 1: EPC-based IoT Services.** *An EPC-based IoT service specification is a 6-tuple IoTS ::= (E, R, C, F, Ψ, A), where E is a set of events and event session identifiers; R is a set of resource identifiers; C is a set of connectors; F is a set of functions; Ψ is a set of function preconditions pre_F and post-effects eft_F; and A is a set of arcs between events, connectors and functions.*

Figure 3. Specification of requirements for a component manufacturing/checking process

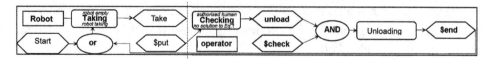

For the example in Figure 4, the specification of requirements (also called IoT service specification) is as follows:

$E = \{start, take, \$put, \$check, unload, \$end\}$;

$R = \{robot, human\}$;

$F = \{a_1 = Taking, a_2 = Checking, \ a_3 = Unloading\}$;

$C = \{c_1 = AND, c_2 = OR\}$;

$$\Psi = \{(a_1, \ pre_{a_1} = \{robot.st = empty\}, \ eft_{a_1} = \{robot.st = taking\}),$$
$$(a_2, \ pre_{a_2} = \{human.right = authorized\}, \ eft_{a_1} = \{\forall t, Eq.1 \models \vec{s}_r(t) \neq \vec{s}_h(t)\}), \ (a_3,,)\} \ ;$$

$$A = \{(start, c_1), \ (end, c_1), \ (c_1, a_1), \ (a_1, take), (\$put, a_2), \ (a_2, unload),$$
$$(unload, c_2), \ (\$check, c_2), \ (c_2, a_3), (a_3, end)\} \qquad .$$

The problem of interest in this chapter is that of how to orchestrate actual IoT services and IoT resource instances based on the specification of requirements. Compared with the classic semantic service orchestration problem, the differences in this orchestration problem for IoT services over IoT resources are as follows:

1. It is insufficient for the effect of one service to match the preconditions of the others. For IoT services, IoT resources are stateful, and should be able to run from an initial state to a final state in the composite action effects induced by a series of service actions, i.e. physical processes that are executable as part of the service orchestration.
2. Although one service does not directly invoke another, causality/conflict relations may still exist between the preconditions and effects of the two services. This not only requires that the service orchestration is executable, but also that atomic services are able to run from an initial event to a final one in the orchestration, and that their implicit fluent relations are checked.

- **Definition 2: The Orchestration Problem for IoT Services over IoT Resources:** *Given an IoT service specification $IoTS_{dest}$, a set of EPC-based IoT services $\{IoTS_i \mid 1 \leq i \leq n\}$, and a set of resources and their instances $\{(IoTR_j, \{IoTR - Ins_{j,k} \mid 1 \leq k \leq m_2\}) \mid 1 \leq j \leq m_1\}$, the orchestration problem for IoT services over IoT resources involves binding some IoT services in $\{IoTS_i \mid 1 \leq i \leq n\}$ to $IoTS_{dest}$ and biIoT resource instances to these services, such that:*

1. *Each function in $IoTS_{dest}$ is bound by one service action in $\{IoTS_i \mid 1 \leq i \leq n\}$, and $IoTS_{dest}$ can run from an initial event to a final one without being blocked by the composite action effects of the bound IoT resources and IoT services of $IoTS_{dest}$.*
2. *If an IoT service $IoTS_i$ is bound to $IoTS_{dest}$, $IoTS_i$ will run from an initial event to a final one without being blocked by the composite action effects in $IoTS_{dest}$.*
3. *If an IoT resource $IoTR_j$ is bound to $IoTS_{dest}$, $IoTR_j$ will run from an initial state to a final state without being blocked by the composite action effects in $IoTS_{dest}$.*

ORCHESTRATING IOT SERVICE FOR IOT RESOURCE COORDINATION

In the fluent calculus, situations are adopted to provide a branching time structure. These situations can be used to represent the stateful relations of IoT resource states and attributes, and to order service actions. However, IoT resources and IoT services are modelled and developed independently, without existing situations to link them together. Solving the service orchestration problem then involves: (i) finding appropriate actual IoT services to bind them to situations; (ii) binding actual IoT resources to the situation-bound IoT services; (iii) correctly ordering service actions and events to satisfy the rules in the service orchestration problem; and (iv) maintaining certain IoT resource properties, such as controllability or safety.

First, situation identifiers are generated for the requirement specifications, and then a linking algorithm is designed to use the situations to link together IoT services to coordinate IoT resources. The solution presented here for orchestrating IoT services is based on an abstract process method that is more practical than automatic semantic service composition methods based on initial states and goals (Stavropoulos et al., 2016). It should be pointed out that in this situation-based approach, an IoT service system can be refined by introducing new actions, i.e. situation identifiers can be refined while keeping the original partial order relation.

- **Definition 3: Situating IoT Services:** *Let* $IoTS ::= (E, R, C, F, \Psi, A)$ *be an EPC-based IoT service specification on which situations are imposed. If there is a limited arc sequence* $(a, n_1), (n_1, n_2), \cdots, (n_{k-1}, n_k), (n_k, b)$, *the sequence is referred to as a path between* a *and* b, *and is denoted by* (a, b). *If* a *is an initial event and* b *is a final event, then all function nodes in the path form a complete trace* $(a_0, a_1, \cdots, a_L)$ *after all non-function nodes are removed from the path. The complete traces form a trace set of* $IoTS$. *For one complete trace* $(a_0, a_1, \cdots, a_L)$ *in the trace set, the situation identifiers on this are produced as follows:*

1. *For* a_0, *a unique number* r_0 *is randomly selected as the identifier of the initial situation, i.e.* $s_0 = < r_0, \cdots >$;

2. *If there exists a situation identifier* $s_i = < r_0, \cdots, r_{i-1}, r_i, \cdots >$ *on* a_i *and a situation identifier* $s_{i-1} = < r_0, \cdots, r'_{i-1}, \cdots >$ *on* a_{i-1} *with* $r_{i-1} = r'_{i-1}$, *then the next action is selected. Otherwise, a unique random number* r_i *is selected to add to* $s_{i-1} = < r_0, \cdots, r'_{i-1}, \cdots >$, *i.e.,* $s_i = < r_0, \cdots, r'_{i-1}, r_i, \cdots >$.

If all nodes in the path (a, b) *belong to* $E \cup C$, *the path is known as an event chain. For each function* a, *its preset is defined as follows:*

$\bullet a = \{n \mid (n, a) \text{ is a path which is aslo an event chain after removing } a \text{ from } (n, a)\}$.

All nodes in the preset of function a *are events and logical connectors; these events are connected by logical connectors that are called the incoming event relations of function* a *and are denoted by* $e \bullet a$. *The output event, preconditions and post-effects of* a *are denoted by* $a \bullet e$, pre_a, *and* eft_a, *respectively.*

Figure 4 illustrates three types of trace: Case *A* shows two concurrent traces; Case B shows multiple traces from the same initial event, without loops; and Case C shows multiple traces from the same initial event, with

Figure 4. Types of trace for an IoT service

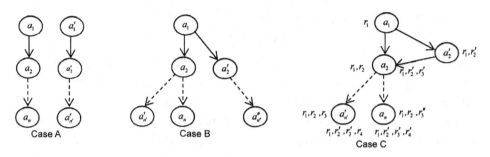

loops. In Case C, there are multiple situation identifiers for the same action, meaning that one IoT service has multiple traces, and some traces may include the same action.

In an IoT service system (e.g. that shown in Figure 3), uncontrollable actions, which are automatically performed by IoT resources such as the *Putting* action in the robot resource, are often left out. In order to impose complete situations on all actions, it is implicitly assumed that uncontrollable actions exist in the current EPC-based service specification.

In the example shown in Figure 4, there is a complete trace, i.e. (*Taking, Putting, Checking, Unloading*); in this case, *Putting* is an uncontrollable action, and the situations on the trace are (<1>, <1, 2>, <1, 2, 3>, <1, 2, 3, 4>). Two actions in an IoT service may or may not take place in a single trace. If two actions such as *Taking, Checking* are in one trace, and one of these actions (e.g. *Taking*) occurs before the other (e.g. *Checking*), this kind of partial order relation is denoted by *Taking* $\prec$ *Checking*. For two situation identifiers in an IoT service, one may or may not be included in the prefix of the other. If two situation identifiers such as <1, 2>, <1, 2, 3, 4> are located in one trace, and one situation identifier (e.g. <1, 2>) is included in the prefix of the other (e.g. <1, 2, 3, 4>), this type of partial order relation is denoted by <1, 2> $\prec$ <1, 2, 3, 4>. For <1, 2>, <1, 2, 3>, this is written as <1, 2> < <1, 2, 3> to denote the inclusion of the immediate prefix. When the partial order relation of the two actions also implies the partial order relation of the situation identifiers, this is denoted by the logical implication, for example *Taking* $\prec$ *Checking* $\rightarrow$ <1, 2> $\prec$ <1, 2, 3, 4>. Resource state transitions may form a partial order relation; this is denoted by $\delta_i \prec \delta_j$, meaning that δ_i occurs before δ_j. A partial order relation in an IoT resource (e.g. $\delta_i \prec \delta_j$) implies the partial order relation of situation identifiers (e.g. $s_i \prec s_j$). This is also written as $\delta_i \prec \delta_j \rightarrow s_i \prec s_j$.

For the *Taking* action shown in Figure 4, $e \bullet Taking ::= start \vee end$, $Taking \bullet e ::= take$, $pre_{Taking} ::= robot.st = empty$, and $eft_{Taking} ::= (robot.st = taking) \wedge (\forall t, Eq.1 \models \vec{s}_r(t) \neq \vec{s}_h(t))$.

$\forall t, Eq.1 \models \vec{s}_r(t) \neq \vec{s}_h(t)$ in eft_{Taking} means that, when the *Taking* action is actuated, the movement of the robot arm should ensure the safety of the human operator, i.e., the checking operator must not be touched.

Two basic procedures are presented here, involving the linking of a resource state to a situation, and the binding of a service action to a placeholder node of the requirement specification's function. Then, a complete solution is given for the IoT service composition problem. In the first procedure, **Link Resource State to Situation**, a situation refers to the point in time at which an action starts or ends. The precondition and effects of the action are used to determine which state of a resource instance is relevant to this action, i.e. the previous state of a resource transition is consistent with the preconditions of the action, and the post state of the resource is consistent with the effects of the action.

In Procedure 1, Line 3 indicates that a state transition labelled by event $a \bullet e$ is selected, and the event comparison is semantically carried out, for example the *Water Temperature Change* event is selected as matching the *Temperature Change* event. Line 4 ensures that the previous state in the resource state transition does not conflict with the preconditions and driving events of the action. Line 5 ensures that the post state of the resource state transition does not conflict with the effect and output events of the action.

In the example shown in Figure 4, the precondition of the *Taking* action conflicts with the *taking* state of the robot resource, *i.e.*

Procedure 1. Link Resource State to Situation St2Sit

```
Input: A state transition δⱼ in an IoT resource instance,
e • a, a • e, preₐ, and eftₐ
Output: A subset of clauses SubS_clause
1. let SubS_clause be empty
2. for δⱼ do
3.     if there is Causes(zⱼ, a • e, z'ⱼ, changedEffects'ⱼ) then
4.         SubS_clause = SubS_clause ∪ {¬Holds(−preₐ, zⱼ), ¬Holds(−e • a, zⱼ)}
5.         SubS_clause = SubS_clause ∪ {¬Holds(−eftₐ, z'ⱼ), Holds(a • e, z'ⱼ)}
6. return SubS_clause
```

$Holds(-(rob.st = empty), taking)$. The precondition of *Taking* is consistent with the *empty* state of the robot resource, *i.e.* $\neg Holds(-(rob.st = empty), empty)$.

In the **Link IoT Service to Requirement Specification** procedure shown below, an IoT service is selected with the same semantic action name as in the requirement specification. A check is then made as to whether the two actions have compatible preconditions and effects. In the same way as the study in Eshuis et al., (2016) compared the service input with output based on ontologies, the comparison of output events is also semantically carried out, and the equality sign is simply used to denote the exact match and parent-child inclusion of two concepts (as shown in Line 2 of Procedure 2).

In the above procedure, Line 2 ensures that the requirement service action has output events that are compatible with the bound IoT service action. Line 4 ensures that the precondition of the function placeholders in the requirement specification does not conflict with the precondition of the bound IoT service action. In Line 5, $Do(a, s)$ means that in situation s, action a is executed and the system transits to the next situation.

For the example shown in Figure 4, the *Taking* node of the manufacturing specification has preconditions and effects that are consistent with those of the *Taking* function of the *robot management service*.

Following these two basic procedures, the exhaustion method is used to design an algorithm for **Linking IoT Services to Coordinate IoT Resources**. Each sub-service with compatible preconditions and effects (Procedure 2) is selected, as is each IoT resource with compatible states (Procedure 1). These choices are combined together in Lines 3-11. A check is then carried out as

Procedure 2. Link IoT Service to Requirement Specification Is2As

Input: An action a in the requirement specification, and a service action a_i
Output: A subset of clauses $SubS_{clause}$
1. **let** $SubS_{clause}$ be empty
2. $SubS_{clause} = \{a \bullet e = a_i \bullet e\}$
3. $SubS_{clause} = SubS_{clause} \cup \{\exists s, \neg Holds(-e \bullet a_i, s) \wedge Holds(e \bullet a, s)\}$
4. $SubS_{clause} = SubS_{clause} \cup \{\exists s, \neg Holds(-pre_{a_i}, s) \wedge Holds(pre_a, s)\}$
5. $SubS_{clause} = $
   $SubS_{clause} \cup \{\exists s, \neg Holds(-eft_{a_i}, Do(a, s)) \wedge Holds(eft_a, Do(a, s))\}$
6. **return** $SubS_{clause}$

to whether or not these choices are desirable; a model of the knowledge of these choices is searched, and the executability of the composed IoT service system is then checked, as follows (Lines 12-19):

1. For a single action, the selected service action needs to be compatible with the EPC specification of its preconditions, effects, input event, and output event. Each action in a complete trace should be bound in the same way as the single action, and any situations between starting and ending events in the trace event are satisfiable, i.e. executable.
2. An IoT service bound to one trace of the composition can also run from an initial event to a final one along the trace, i.e. it is executable.
3. An IoT resource bound to one trace of the composition also can run from an initial state to a final state along the trace, i.e. it is executable and maintains certain properties.

Algorithm 1. Linking IoT Services to Coordinate IoT Resources

Input. An IoT service specification $IoTS_{dest}$, a set of IoT services $Set_s = \{IoTS_i \mid 1 \leq i \leq n\}$, a set of resources and their instances $Set_r = \{(IoTR_j, \{IoTR - Ins_k \mid 1 \leq k \leq m_2\}) \mid 1 \leq j \leq m_1\}$

Output. False or **True**

1. **situating** the IoT service $IoTS_{dest}$ according to Definition 7

2. **let** a clause set Set_{clause} be empty

3. **for** each action a_i in $IoTS_{dest}$ **do**

4.   **find** all actions $Set_{s,a_i} = \{a_{i,j} \mid a_{i,j}.name = a_i.name, 1 \leq j \leq L\}$ in Set_s //get all optional services by semantic name comparison

5.   **find** all transitions $Set_{r,a_i} = \{\delta_{i,j} \mid \delta_{i,j}.e.name = a_i.name, 1 \leq j \leq M\}$ in Set_r //get all optional resources by semantic name comparison

6.   **find** all situation identifiers on it $\{id_{i,j} \mid 1 \leq j \leq N\}$ //get all situation identifiers for an action in the destination specification

7. $Set_{clause} = Set_{clause} \cup \{(x_i.action = a_{i,1}) \vee \cdots \vee (x_i.action = a_{i,L})\}$ //use all optional services to create a formula

continued on following page

Algorithm 1. Continued

8.
$$Set_{clause} = Set_{clause} \cup \{(x_i.transition = \delta_{i,1}) \vee \cdots \vee (x_i.transition = \delta_{i,M})\}$$
`//use all optional resources to create a formula`

9. $\qquad Set_{clause} = Set_{clause} \cup \{(s_i = id_{i,1}) \vee \cdots \vee (s_i = id_{i,N})\}$
`//use all optional situation identifiers to create a formula`

10. $\qquad Set_{clause} = Set_{clause} \cup Is2As(a_i, x_i.action) \qquad$ `//set each`
`optional service comparisons with the destination specification`
`using a formula`

11.
$$Set_{clause} = Set_{clause} \cup St2Sit(x_i.transition, e \bullet x_i.action, a_i \bullet e, pre_{a_i} \circ pre_{x_i.action}, eft_{a_i} \circ eft_{x_i.action})$$
`//set each optional resource comparisons using a formula`

12.`repeat do`

13. $\qquad$ **get** `a model` $Binding$ `of` $Set_{clause} \qquad\qquad$ `//use`
`SMT solvers to find a model for the composition knowledge of`
`IoT services`

14. $\qquad$ **if** $Binding$ `is empty` **then return False**

15. $\qquad$ **if** $x_i.action = a_{i,j}$ `is` **True** `in` $Binding$ `with situation` s_i
then $pre_{a_i} = pre_{a_i} \circ pre_{a_{i,j}}, eft_{a_i} = eft_{a_i} \circ eft_{a_{i,j}}$

$e \bullet a_i = (e \bullet a_i) \circ (e \bullet a_{i,j}) \qquad\qquad$ `//bind a service`

16. $\qquad$ **if** $x_i.transition = \delta_{i,k}$ `is` **True** `in` $Binding$ **then get**
$Causes(z_{i,k}, e(a_i \bullet e), z'_{i,k}, changedEffects'_j)$

$pre_{a_i} = pre_{a_i} \circ z_{i,k}, eft_{a_i} = eft_{a_i} \circ z'_{i,k} \qquad\qquad$ `//bind a resource`

17. $\qquad$ **for** $s_i < s_j$ **do**

18. $\qquad\qquad$ **if** $\neg Holds(eft_{a_i} \circ pre_{a_j}, s_j)$ **then return False**
`//complete traces are executable`

19.`until`
$$Checking(Set_r, Set_s, \{(x_i, s_i, a_{i,j}, \{\delta_{i,k} \mid \delta_{i,k} \in IoTR - Ins_{k'}\}) \mid a_{i,j} \in IoTS_{j'}\})$$
`//sub-services and resources are executable`
20. `return True`

In the above algorithm, Lines 2-3 are carried out semantically based on ontologies, in the same way as in Procedure 2. If the action name of the service is a sub-concept of the action name of the requirement specification, the service can be selected; for example, *run* is a sub-concept of *move*. Lines 7-11 identify all comparisons between possible service candidates and the requirement specifications. The solution is then searched for candidates under these comparison conditions. The model found in this way is checked to ensure an appropriate service orchestration that can effectively coordinate the IoT resources.

The service orchestration for the requirement specification presented in Figure 3 is illustrated in Figure 5. Its controllable actions are bound to respective resource management services, and the preconditions and driving events of the original resource management services have been changed, such

Algorithm 2. Checking

Input. A set of resources and their instances
$Set_r = \{(IoTR_j, \{IoTR - Ins_k \mid 1 \leq k \leq m_2\}) \mid 1 \leq j \leq m_1\}$, a set of IoT services $Set_s = \{IoTS_i \mid 1 \leq i \leq n\}$, a bound relation
$bdR = \{(x_i, s_i, a_{i,j}, \{\delta_{i,k} \mid \delta_{i,k} \in IoTR - Ins_{k'}\}) \mid a_{i,j} \in IoTS_{j'}\}$.
Output. *False* or *True*

1. **for** each bound resource instance $IoTR - Ins$ in Set_r, **do**
// check resources' executability
2.   **if** for one transition δ_j, no $x.transition = \delta_j$ in bdR **then return** *False*
3.   **for** two transitions δ_i, δ_j in $IoTR - Ins$, **do**
4.   **if** no $\delta_i \prec \delta_j \rightarrow s_i \prec s_j$ **then return** *False*
    // complete checking of resources; then check the executability of IoT services
5. **for** $IoTS \in Set_s$, **do**
6.   **if** any action $a_i \in IoTS$, no $x.action = a_i$ in bdR **then continue**
7.   **else** get any complete trace *trace* including a_i in $IoTS$
8.   **if** any action $a'_i \in trace$, no $x.action = a'_i$ in bdR, **then return** *False*
9.   **for** $a_i, a_j \in trace$, **do**
10.   **if** no $a_i \prec a_j \rightarrow s_i \prec s_j$ **then return** *False*
11. **return** *True*

Figure 5. A composite IoT service coordinating robot and human resources

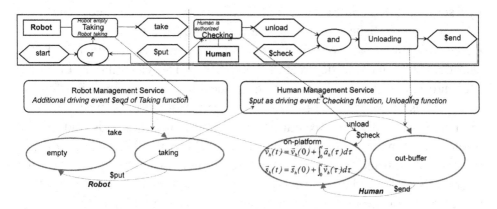

as the *$end* event of the human resource becoming an additional driving event for the *Taking* function of the robot management service. The IoT resources have different types of platforms for the *Robots* and *Machines* that have different motion trajectories, i.e., there are separate operation spaces for robots and humans. From the many possible IoT resource instances, the creation algorithm for IoT services chooses two matched IoT resource instances to bind to one trace, such that the safety condition (no solution to Equation 1) holds. This not only avoids the manual binding of IoT resources, but also provides assistance in deploying these resources.

DISTRIBUTED EXECUTION OF IOT SERVICE

After the actual IoT services are bound, the composed IoT service system is not yet executable even if the bound IoT services are deployed. The event relations between two functions in the service orchestration (also called the EPC business process) should be enacted, i.e. an extracted incoming event relation $e \bullet a$ is enforcing as composite events. An EPC business process is partitioned into multiple distributed IoT services and a set of pieces of coordination logic (extracted event relations), and each service has a business logic layer to carry out distributed coordination. This business logic layer has information about the composite preconditions for the original service and the EPC business process, and it arbitrates on whether or not a function in the service is triggered when the driving event occurs.

The event relations between functions extracted in this way are enacted by a service called complex event processing (CEP), which checks the event relations and publishes composite events with new topic names, i.e. it enacts the coordination logic. When a new composite event arrives at a distributed service, the business logic layer of the distributed service enables the event precondition of the service function. If the service's precondition for IoT resources is also evaluated as *True,* the service function is executed. This kind of distributed service execution is desirable in IoT scenarios, and is often implemented by fog computing (Wen et al., 2017; Sill, 2017), where some of the computation and services are placed at the edges of network for real-time operations, and the data centre collaborates with the edges of the fog, thus achieving low response latency and jitter for IoT applications.

After the EPC business process is decomposed into the bound services and extracted event relations, an executable IoT business process is finally obtained from the requirement specification. When a distributed process is executed, it is also important how to find a method of executing distributed process segments with consistency, *a glitch problem.* The 'glitch problem' is an important issue that arises for event-driven reactive applications (Schuster & Flanagan, 2016). An example illustrating this problem is given below:

$$a_1 : v_1 = 2, \textit{Publish } e_1(v_1);$$

$$a_2 : v_2 = 3 * v_1, \textit{Publish } e_2(v_2);$$

$$a_3 : v_3 = v_1 + v_2, \textit{Publish } e_3(v_3).$$

In the above example, the initial value of v_1 is 1, and v_2 and v_3 have values of 3 and 4 respectively. The glitch problem is a type of update inconsistency, and arises when the sequence process of a_1, a_2 and a_3 is distributed and becomes event-driven. If a_1 is executed and e_1 is published, a_2 and a_3 are driven by event e_1. However, a_3 may not receive event e_1 before e_2, since there is no guarantee of a particular order of events within a network. In this case, the values of v_2 and v_3 change to 6 and 7, respectively, although v_3 is expected to change to 8, as for sequential execution. In the glitch problem, all pre-dependent actions should be executed before a target action is actually executed.

In classical glitch-avoidance methods, the action dependencies are computed to ensure that value updates are consistent (Bainomugisha et al., 2013). In distributed environments, however, these methods do not work well, and state agreement protocols are needed (Salvaneschi et al., 2013). In the current work, the glitch problem is handled in the event-driven process by extracting coordination logic in the form of composite events, where implicit distributed resource pools enable IoT services to locally access most recent local resource attributes and states. Without loss of generality, a simple process of the action sequence can be used as a typical example to explain this method. During service execution, each executed action/function is represented by one event, i.e. an event that has occurred, and this is guarded by the predicates of events and IoT resources. The sequence process in the above example is partitioned, retaining the original causality (giving all pre-dependent actions), as follows:

$$\phi_1 \rightarrow e(e_1), \ (e(e_1) \wedge \phi_2) \rightarrow e(e_2) \ , \ (e(e_2) \wedge e(e_1) \wedge \phi_3) \rightarrow e(e_3),$$

where ϕ_i $(i = 1, 2, 3)$ represents the resource preconditions, and each action is driven by its causal events, for example e_1 drives a_2. For the EPC business process in this work, only the event relation between two functions/actions is extracted, and the above sequence process is partitioned as follows:

$$\phi_1 \rightarrow e(e_1), \ (e(e_1) \wedge \phi_2) \rightarrow e(e_2) \ , \ (e(e_2) \wedge \phi_3) \rightarrow e(e_3),$$

where the execution of a_3 is driven by e_2. The distributed resource pool will record the updated v_1 with e_1 as the resource refreshing event, although e_1 does not drive a_3.

When an event-driven process is partitioned and distributed, the event causality in a sequence process cannot be retained based on the above example. In addition, there are multiple event instances for each specific event name in a runtime service environment. The following assumption and theorem are given for this simple event causality chain.

- **Definition 4: Unique Action Ramification:** *An action that is executed is represented by an occurrence predicate $e(e_i)$ of event e_i, and the causality between the two actions is then represented by the relation between one causal event and one effect event. The causality between* *two actions is called a unique action ramification if the two representation events are both unique and uniquely define the relation.*

Theorem 1. The distribution of event causality chains in a process is correct if all the action ramifications are unique.

Proof. *Given an event causality chain $< e_1, e_2, \cdots, e_n >$ and the corresponding guard predicates $< \phi_1, \phi_2, \cdots, \phi_n >$ (each guard ϕ_i is simply assumed to represent a resource state as an action precondition), the original causality Π for these actions can be represented as follows:*

$$\phi_1 \rightarrow e(e_1),$$

$$(e(e_1) \wedge \phi_2) \rightarrow e(e_2),$$

$$(e(e_1) \wedge e(e_2) \wedge \phi_3) \rightarrow e(e_3),$$

$$\cdots,$$

$$(e(e_1) \wedge e(e_2) \wedge \cdots \wedge e(e_{n-1}) \wedge \phi_n) \rightarrow e(e_n),$$

where each formula (e.g. $(e(e_1) \wedge \phi_2) \rightarrow e(e_2)$) represents the execution of one action (e.g. a_2 / e_2) under its precondition (e.g. $\phi_1 \wedge e(e_1)$), and the underlying resource knowledge implies that if event (e_1) does not happen, the state transition (e.g. from ϕ_1 to ϕ_2: Causes($\phi_1, e_1, \phi_2, \phi_2 - \phi_1$)) does not take place. An action (e_n / a_n) represented by one formula (e.g. $(e(e_1) \wedge e(e_2) \wedge \cdots \wedge e(e_{n-1}) \wedge \phi_n) \rightarrow e(e_n)$) will be executed with holding the corresponding event (e.g. $e(e_n)$) if the formula is True. A single model of Π represents a single service execution instance, and the service cannot be executed if there is no model for Π.

After the business process is flattened and distributed, each action will be executed if its causal event occurs, and the modified causality Π' is represented as follows:

$$\phi_1 \rightarrow e(e_1),$$

$$(e(e_1) \wedge \phi_2) \rightarrow e(e_2),$$

$$(e(e_2) \wedge \phi_3) \rightarrow e(e_3),$$

$$\dots,$$

$$(e(e_{n-1}) \wedge \phi_n) \rightarrow e(e_n),$$

where the business process is partitioned and distributed, and each formula is independently checked at different sites. For each action, a model is found for its independent formula and underlying resource formulas, and the model for each action is found independently.

Assuming that the action e_{n-2} / a_{n-2} is not executed at one site or that e_{n-2} is discarded in the service running environment, a model can still be found for $(e(e_{n-1}) \wedge \phi_n) \rightarrow e(e_n)$ to execute a_n while ensuring $e(e_n)$.

When considering the execution of an action under conditions of unique action ramification, the causality between e_{n-2}, e_{n-1}, e_n is uniquely represented by special event instances, i.e. no causal events occur except the causal action being executed. The model for Π' will be built according to the original causality, and the literal assignments in Π' also satisfy Π by simple induction, and vice versa.

Thus, Π' can represent the action execution in the same way as Π, if all the action ramifications are unique.

If a series of event causality relations that need to be maintained in an IoT service process, fine-grained event instances can be used to achieve this goal. The use of unique event instances is a general way to retain a sequence of event causality. In a hostile environment, certain authentication methods can be used to maintain uniqueness; that is, the distributed resource pool and the event relation extraction approach can be used to solve the glitch problem in a distributed execution of the EPC business process if the assumption of unique action ramification holds. This avoids the use of some state agreement protocols for the coordination of distributed IoT resources.

EVALUATION AND EXPERIMENTS

This section presents a quantitative evaluation of the proposed approach. The purposes of this evaluation are: i) to study the impact of IoT resources on the overall composition performance; ii) to measure the composition performance of the approach over many services; and iii) to measure the performance of the distributed execution of IoT services.

The test sets used to perform experiments were obtained from SemWebCentral OWLS-TC version 4.0 (OWLS, 2018). These included Web services from various domains, such as books, economy, food and travel, and their corresponding ontologies. In the experiments, the entire set of Web services included in specific domains was taken into account, so that the produced domain size was maintained at realistic levels.

In order to evaluate the algorithm over IoT resources, a benchmark of WatDiv (Aluç et al., 2014) was used to generate IoT resources. First, basic RDF data were generated, and then IoT resources were demarcated in the RDF data, with their lifecycle models generated using the attributes in the RDF description. Four data sets were generated with sizes ranging between 100,000 to 1 million triples. Twenty templates were provided by WatDiv (Aluç et al., 2014) including categories such as linear, star, snowflake and 'complex'.

Before the service composition solution was tested, IoT resources were selected from the RDF data set. The performance of IoT resource selection was therefore tested compared with the basic RDF query performance. An additional program for *Apache Jena* (Jena, 2015) was developed to further process the response results of RDF queries, obtaining resources using resource graphs. Experiments were carried out on a personal PC (CPU: Intel i5-3470, 3.20 GHz, 8 GB RAM, 800 GB disk) on the Windows 7 operating system. Figure 6 shows a performance comparison between the RDF query and the resource selection, illustrating that the time spent for resource selection is comparable to that for RDF queries. The selection time is on the order of milliseconds in both cases.

Z3 software (Moura & Bjørner, 2008) was adopted as the underlying SMT solver in this algorithm to test the satisfiability of service composition knowledge. The C++ API of the Z3 SMT solver was used to implement the knowledge of listing candidates for IoT services and resources. Figure 7 illustrates the performance solving the orchestration problem (specially for the controllability problem): the horizontal axis is the round session number

Figure 6. (a) Time for linear-style; (b) time for star-style; (c) time for snowflake-style; (d) time for complex-style

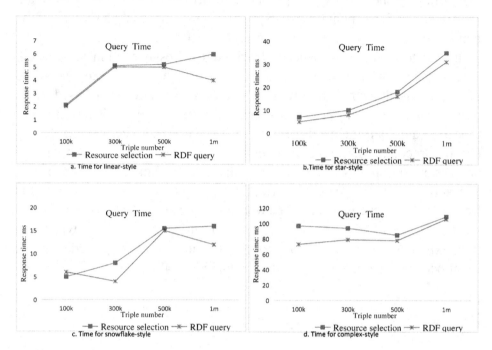

Figure 7. The solving time

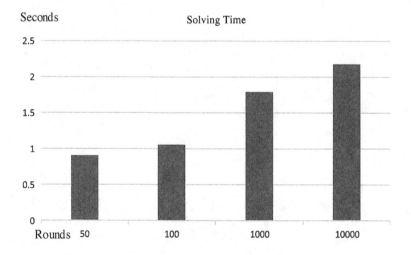

denoting how many times the machine performs machining; and the vertical axis is the time spent solving the problem. From Figure 7, we know the solution is efficient, and the spent time to get a solution is less than 2.5 seconds if the number of event round sessions is fewer than 10000.

In Chapter 4, the performance of distributed process execution is discussed. In this chapter, we focus on the response performance of service reacting to event arrivals rather than the throughput of the whole system, and based on the proposed manufacturing process, experiments were conducted. The businesses processes and their included IoT services were run and scheduled according to their preconditions, running states and post-effects. The performance of process execution was first tested, as illustrated in Figure 7. The incoming and outgoing events per second from the services were recorded, and the frequency of the event occurrences were averaged and used as a performance metric. Figure 7 shows the average event occurrence frequency, where the time axis increases from 5m:00s to 5m:20s, and the average frequency of event occurrence remains between about 435 and 492 n/s.

Figure 8. Average speed of event occurrence

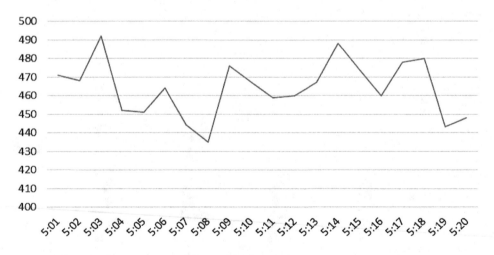

Average speed of event occurrence (number per second)

RELATED WORK

Many works have addressed coordination issues in traditional Web services, such as Tasharofi et al., (2007), Li and Sun, (2015), which proposed a coordination model and language called Reo. Reo uses exogenous connectors to express information flows based on the concept of a point-to-point channel. Each channel imposes its own rules on the information flow at its ends, such as synchronisation or mutual exclusion. Channels can be arranged in a circuit, representing the coordination logic of services. By focusing on service interactions and their constraints, Reo lifts the level of abstraction for the specification of service coordination. These authors did not focus on event-driven methodology and its induced decoupling features. Several other approaches based on coarse events have been proposed for the study of this coordination issue (for example Bellur & Bondre, 2006; Ciancia et al., 2010).

In terms of IoT services, the work in Kaldeli et al., (2013) adopted a service-oriented approach for smart home services to bind physical devices; AI planning technologies were used to dynamically coordinate these services based on contextual information. The work in Mayer et al., (2016) presented a goal-driven service orchestration approach for RESTful IoT services, in which a visual tool was provided that allowed users to configure IoT services and define their goals. The work in Ding et al., (2013) presented a design for a self-organising scheme to compose IoT services for smart devices, where each smart device was considered as an autonomous area, and multiple IoT devices were coordinated based on an information exchange network. The work in Wen et al., (2017) presented a fog-enabled service coordination architecture that linked together fog nodes and IoT services in data centres for real-time operation and system scalability. These authors advocated the distribution of IoT services by coordinating them with the background platform. The study in Cheng et al., (2016) proposed an event-based IoT service coordination method in which event patterns were used to detect events and ECA rules were used to coordinate IoT services. Although physical devices and sensors were introduced in this work, IoT resources were not explicitly and comprehensively modelled, meaning that some properties of IoT resources, such as controllability and continuous dynamics, could not be coordinated. In the current paper, IoT resources are explicitly and formally specified, and the interactions between IoT resources and IoT services are then examined in terms of their rigid and complex coordination.

Many researchers have tried to automatically construct the orchestration of semantic services using semantic reasoning methods. The work in Eshuis et al., (2016) used reusable semantic knowledge to create services; semantics of individual service components were used as the declarative knowledge, and the service was then composed to support sequence, choice and parallelism. Data dependency in semantic knowledge was explored in reusable networks for service composition and modification. The work in Stavropoulos et al., (2016) proposed a lightweight, bottom-up approach framework for orchestrating semantic services. These authors adopted a logic-based strategy and syntactic text-similarity service selection, discovery and matching, and designed a variety of configurable matching algorithms. The study in Mier et al., (2016) carried out a theoretical analysis of service orchestration based on its dependency on service discovery. Based on this analysis, a formal, integrated, graph-based composition framework was proposed, which integrated service discovery with matchmaking. Compared these studies, the current work of creating IoT services is more oriented towards current industrial practices. An IoT service system is developed once, but is often deployed in a range of different environments, meaning that the deployed IoT resource instances and IoT services need to be bound to the IoT service system, and the deployed service system should be verified as being executable and holding the defined properties, i.e. coordinating IoT resources well.

The work in Jergler et al., (2016) adopted the Guard-Stage-Milestone (GSM) meta-model to design a fully-distributed flexible workflow engine. These authors focused on partitioning the GSM model into distributed workflow units for distributed deployment and execution. The work in Hensa et al., (2014) presented a process fragmentation method based on distributed events to realise a distributed process execution; a process model was partitioned into task-level fragments, and each fragment was equipped with starting and ending events, thus becoming a distributed execution unit. The work in Muthusamy and Jacobsen, (2010) presented a distributed business process execution engine, in which a business process was decomposed into different types of activities that were deployed on different publish/subscribe gateways for distributed execution. The service message exchange among these activities was enforced by event matching and event notification mechanisms; however, this work did not consider the glitch problem (Schuster & Flanagan, 2016). In the current work, an event extraction method is proposed in order to distribute the IoT service system for coordinated real-time IoT resources, and the glitch problem in such environments is also discussed.

In classical action theories, such as situation calculus (Reiter, 2001), event calculus (Gelfond & Lifschitz, 1993), and action theory (Bultan, 2000), real-world management is discussed in which actions are listed and the changes due to these actions are described. If only the effects that an action will change are specified, however, then the frame problem arises; that is, the question of how to determine which effects are not changed by the action. Listing all effects induced by an action, including those that are both changed and unchanged, offers a possible solution to the frame problem, although there are many constraints on a real domain such that the intuitive listing method is not available. Numerous researchers have therefore proposed methods of addressing this issue, such as the ramification problem and the qualification problem. In the current work, we adopt a hierarchical approach (Plaisted, 2003) to model an IoT service system in which physical entities are specified by IoT resource models to describe direct action effects. Actions and their interactions are described by IoT services and service processes in various applications, to produce indirect action effects and qualification.

CONCLUSION

In order to address the difficult issue of orchestrating IoT services to coordinate stateful IoT resources, this chapter describes a situation-based service creation scheme in which IoT resources are introduced as the action effects of an event-driven decoupling method (i.e. via distributed events and causality links), and IoT services are not only compared on the basis of their input, output, preconditions, and the effects linking them together, but also are bound to and compared with situations linking IoT resources. A service-oriented coordination requirement of IoT resources is specified using event relations and service properties, while actual services, resources and their executable behaviour are not included. After binding the actual IoT services and IoT resources in the service creation scheme, the proposed service coordination specification is then refined into an executable business process by enacting event relations and composite preconditions in the situations. An IoT service system is partitioned by deploying IoT services near to IoT resources, thus realising the real-time monitoring and controlling of IoT resources. The glitch problem for distributed reactive IoT services is solved through application of the event separation and composition method. Finally, an evaluation is presented as a proof of concept for this work.

REFERENCES

Agha. (1986). *ACTORS: A model of concurrent computation in distributed systems*. MIT Press.

Aluç, G., Hartig, O., Özsu, M. T., & Daudjee, K. (2014). Diversified stress testing of RDF data management systems. *Proc. 13th Int. Semantic Web Conf.*, 197-212.

Bainomugisha, Carreton, van Cutsem, Mostinckx, & de Meuter. (2013). A survey on reactive programming. *Journal ACM Computing Surveys*.

Barret, C., Sebastiani, R., Seshia, S. A., & Tinelli, C. (2009). Satisfiability modulo theories. In Handbook of Satisfiability (pp. 825-885). Academic Press.

Bellur, U., & Bondre, S. (2006). xSpace: a Tuple Space for XML and its application in orchestration of web services. *Proceedings of the 21st ACM Symposium on Applied Computing*, 766-772. 10.1145/1141277.1141453

Berardi, D., Calvanese, D., Giacomo, G. D., Lenzerini, M., & Mecella, M. (2003). Automatic composition of e-services that export their behavior. Lecture Notes in Computer Science, 2910(7), 43-58.

Botts & Robin. (2007). *OpenGIS® Sensor Model Language (SensorML) Implementation Specification (Version 1.0.0)*. Open Geospatial Consortium Inc.

Bultan, T. (2000). Action language: A specification language for model checking reactive systems. *Proceedings of the 22nd International Conference on Software Engineering*, 335–344. 10.1145/337180.337219

Cheng, B., Wang, M., Zhao, S., Zhai, Z. Y., Zhu, D., & Chen, J. L. (2017). Situation-aware dynamic service coordination in an IoT environment. *IEEE/ACM Transactions on Networking*, 25(4), 2082–1095. doi:10.1109/TNET.2017.2705239

Ciancia, V., Ferrari, G., Guanciale, R., & Strollo, D. (2010). Event based choreography. *Science of Computer Programming*, 75(10), 848–878. doi:10.1016/j.scico.2010.02.009

de Moura, L., & Bjørner, N. (2008). *An efficient theorem prover*. Retrieved from http://research.microsoft.com/en-us/um/redmond/ projects/z3/

Ding, Y., Jin, Y., Ren, L., & Hao, K. (2013). An intelligent self-organization scheme for the Internet of Things. *IEEE Computational Intelligence Magazine, 8*(3), 41–53. doi:10.1109/MCI.2013.2264251

Drescher, C., & Thielscher, M. (2007). Integrating action calculi and description logics. *Lecture Notes in Computer Science, 4667*, 68–83. doi:10.1007/978-3-540-74565-5_8

Erl, T. (2005). *Service-oriented architecture: Concepts, technology, and design*. Prentice Hall.

Eshuis, Lecue, & Mehandjiev. (2016). Flexible construction of executable service compositions from reusable semantic knowledge. *ACM Transactions on the Web, 10*(1), 5:1-27.

Fikes, R., & Nilsson, N. J. (1971). STRIPS: A new approach to the application of theorem proving to problem solving. *Artificial Intelligence, 2*(3-4), 189–208. doi:10.1016/0004-3702(71)90010-5

Gao, S., Avigad, J., & Clarke, E. M. (2012). δ-complete decision procedures for satisfiability over the reals. *Computer Science, 7364*, 286–300.

Gao, S., Kong, S., & Clarke, E. M. (2013). dReal: an SMT solver for nonlinear theories over the reals. *International Conference on Automated Deduction, 7898*, 208-214. 10.1007/978-3-642-38574-2_14

Gelfond, M., & Lifschitz, V. (1993). Representing actions in extended logic programming. *Tenth Joint International Conference & Symposium on Logic Programming*, 559-573.

Hatzi, O., Vrakas, D., Nikolaidou, M., Bassiliades, N., Anagnostopoulos, D., & Vlahavas, I. (2012). An integrated approach to automated semantic Web service composition through planning. *IEEE Transactions on Services Computing, 5*(3), 319–332. doi:10.1109/TSC.2011.20

Hensa, P., Snoecka, M., Poelsb, G., & De Backera, M. (2014). Process fragmentation, distribution and execution using an event based interaction scheme. *Journal of Systems and Software, 89*, 170–192. doi:10.1016/j.jss.2013.11.1111

IEEE1451.2-1997. (1997). IEEE Standard for a smart transducer interface for sensors and actuators: Transducer to microprocessor communication protocols and transducer electronic data sheet (TEDS) Formats. Piscataway, NJ: Institute of Electrical and Electronics Engineers, Inc.

Jena. (2015). Retrieved from http://jena.apache.org/

Jergler, M., Sadoghi, M., & Jacobsen, H. A. (2016). Geo-distribution of flexible business processes over publish/subscribe paradigm. *Proceedings of the 17th International Middleware, 15*. 10.1145/2988336.2988351

Kaldeli, E., Warriach, E. U., Lazovik, A., & Aiello, M. (2013). Coordinating the Web of services for a smart home. *ACM Transactions on the Web, 7*(2), 10. doi:10.1145/2460383.2460389

Karhof, J., & Riehle, T., Delfmann, & Becker. (2016). On the de-facto standard of event-driven process chains: Reviewing EPC implementations in process modelling tools. *Proceedings of the Modellierung.*

Kokash, N., & Arbab, F. (2013). Formal design and verification of long-running transactions with extensible coordination tools. *IEEE Transactions on Services Computing, 6*(2), 186–200. doi:10.1109/TSC.2011.46

Koubarakis, M., & Kyzirakos, K. (2010). Modeling and querying metadata in the Semantic Sensor Web: The model stRDF and the query language stSPARQL. *International Conference on the Semantic Web: Research & Applications, 2*(1), 425-439. 10.1007/978-3-642-13486-9_29

Kowalski, R. A., & Sergot, M. J. (1986). A logic-based calculus of events. *New Generation Computing, 4*(1), 67–95. doi:10.1007/BF03037383

Li, G. L., Muthusamy, V., & Jacobsen, H. A. (2010). A distributed service-oriented architecture for business process execution. *ACM Transactions on the Web, 4*(1), 1–33. doi:10.1145/1658373.1658375

Li, Y., & Sun, M. (2015). Modeling and verification of component connectors in Coq. *Science of Computer Programming, 113*, 285–301. doi:10.1016/j.scico.2015.10.016

Mayer, S., Verborgh, R., Kovatsch, M., & Mattern, F. (2016). Smart configuration of smart environments. *IEEE Transactions on Automation Science and Engineering, 13*(3), 1247–1255. doi:10.1109/TASE.2016.2533321

McCarthy & Hayes. (1969). Some philosophical problems from the standpoint of artificial intelligence. *The Mathematical Intelligencer, 4*, 463–502.

Mendling. (2007). *Detection and prediction of errors in EPC business process models* (Dissertation). Vienna University of Economics and Business Administration.

Meng, S., & Arbab, F. (2007). Web services choreography and orchestration in Reo and constraint automata. *Proceedings of 22nd Annual ACM Symposium on Applied Computing*, 346-353. 10.1145/1244002.1244085

Mier, P. R., Pedrinaci, C., Lama, M., & Mucientes, M. (2016). An integrated semantic web service discovery and composition framework. *IEEE Transactions on Services Computing*, 9(4), 537–550. doi:10.1109/TSC.2015.2402679

Moore, Kearfott, & Cloud. (2009). *Introduction to interval analysis*. Society for Industrial and Applied Mathematics.

Ninin, Messine, & Hansen. (2015). A reliable affine relaxation method for global optimization. *4OR*, *13*(3), 247-277.

OWLS. (2018). Retrieved from http://projects.semwebcentral.org/ projects/ owls-tc/

Peng, P., Zou, L., Özsu, M. T., Chen, L., & Zhao, D. (2016). Processing SPARQL queries over distributed RDF graphs. *The VLDB Journal*, *25*(2), 243–268. doi:10.100700778-015-0415-0

Plaisted. (2003). A hierarchical situation calculus. *J. Computing Research Repository*.

Reiter, R. (2001). *Knowledge in action: logical foundations for specifying and implementing dynamical systems*. MIT Press.

Salvaneschi, G., Drechsler, J., & Mezini, M. (2013). Towards distributed reactive programming. *Lecture Notes in Computer Science*, *7890*, 226–235. doi:10.1007/978-3-642-38493-6_16

SCALA. (2015). Retrieved from http://www.scala-lang.org/

Scheer. (1998). *ARIS: Business process modeling* (2nd ed.). Springer-Verlag.

Schuster, C., & Flanagan, C. (2016). Reactive programming with reactive variables. *Proceedings of the 15th International Conference on Modularity*, 29-33.

Sill, A. (2017). Standards at the edge of the cloud. *IEEE Cloud Computing*, *4*(2), 63–67. doi:10.1109/MCC.2017.23

Smith, O. J. M. (1957). Closed control of loops with dead time. *Chemical Engineering Progress*, *53*(5), 217–219.

SoaM. L. (2013). Retrieved from http://www.omg.org/spec/SoaML/

SSN. (2014). Retrieved from http://www.w3.org/2005/Incubator/ssn/XGR-ssn-201 10628/

Staab, S., & Studer, R. (Eds.). (2009). *Handbook on ontologies. International Handbooks on Information Systems* (2nd ed.). Springer.

Stavropoulos, T. G., Andreadis, S., Bassiliades, N., Vrakas, D., & Vlahavas, I. (2016). The Tomaco hybrid matching framework for SAWSDL semantic web services. *IEEE Transactions on Services Computing, 9*(6), 954–967. doi:10.1109/TSC.2015.2430328

Tasharofi, S., Vakilian, M., Ziloochian, R., & Sirjani, M. (2007). Modeling Web services using coordination language Reo. In Lecture Notes in Computer Science: *Vol. 4937. Proceedings of WS-FM07* (pp. 108-123). Springer.

Thielscher. (2005). *Reasoning robots: The art and science of programming robotic agents.* Springer.

Thielscher, M. (1999). From situation calculus to fluent calculus: State update axioms as a solution to the inferential frame problem. *Artificial Intelligence, 111*(1-2), 277–299. doi:10.1016/S0004-3702(99)00033-8

Tzortzis, G., & Spyrou, E. (2016). *A semi-automatic approach for semantic IoT service composition.* Retrieved from https://www.iit.demokritos.gr/sites/default/files/ai_iot_2016_paper_5.pdf

van Glabbeek, R., & Goltz, U. (2004). Well-behaved flow event structures for parallel composition and action refinement. *Theoretical Computer Science, 311*(1-3), 463–478. doi:10.1016/j.tcs.2003.10.031

Wen, Yang, Garraghan, Lin, Xu, & Rovatsos. (2017). Fog orchestration for Internet of Things services. *IEEE Internet Comput., 21*(2), 16-24.

Wen, Z., Yang, R., Garraghan, P., Lin, T., Xu, J., & Rovatsos, M. (2017). Fog orchestration for Internet of Things services. *IEEE Internet Computing, 21*(2), 16–24. doi:10.1109/MIC.2017.36

Yang, R., Li, B., & Cheng, C. (2014). A Petri net-based approach to service composition and monitoring in the IoT. *Asia-Pacific Services Computing Conference.* 10.1109/APSCC.2014.11

Zhang, Y., & Chen, J. L. (2015). Constructing scalable IoT Services based on their event-driven models. *Concurrency and Computation*. doi:10.1002/cpe.3469

Zhang, Y., & Chen, J. L. (2017). Declarative construction of event-driven IoT services based on modular IoT resource models. *IEEE Transactions on Services Computing*.

Section 4
Security and Reliability of IoT Services

Chapter 6
Distributed Access Control for IoT Services Based on a Publish/Subscribe Paradigm

ABSTRACT

With IoT services becoming more open and covering wider areas, different IoT applications at different sites are now collaborating to realize real-time monitoring and controlling of the physical world. The use of a publish/ subscribe paradigm allows IoT applications to collaborate more closely in real time and to be more flexible. This is due to the space, time, and control decoupling of the event producer and consumer, which can be used to establish an appropriate communication infrastructure. Unfortunately, a publish/ subscribe-based IoT application does not know which users are consuming its data events, and consumers do not know where the events originate from. In this environment, the IoT application cannot directly control access, since interactions in the application are anonymous and indirect. To address these issues, this chapter first describes a foundation for communication between wide-area IoT services and then defines a security model supporting a data-centric methodology. Using this model, the underlying network capabilities can be integrated to help IoT applications control event access. The key concept in this access control solution is the preservation of the interaction characteristics of publish/subscribe-based IoT applications, which are both anonymous and multicast. Thus, two specific types of event are used to accomplish requests for and granting of authorization, while remaining consistent with the publish/subscribe paradigm. A policy-attachment method is used to preserve the anonymity and multicast features of the collaborating IoT applications, where policy-matching efficiency, policy privacy, and communication performance are the main points of focus. This access control scheme can also be enhanced with confidentiality.

DOI: 10.4018/978-1-5225-7622-8.ch006

INTRODUCTION

Motivation

Modern wide-area IoT applications can be viewed as an evolutionary system with greater efficiency and openness and use integrated communication technologies and computational intelligence to realise the goal of interconnection. A new communication infrastructure is needed for the delivery of coherent and real-time data in such systems; for example, in a smart grid, a fault in one transmission line can result in a chain reaction and an eventual blackout. This situation requires the visibility of the power system to be improved. If there is no overall picture of the power system and situational awareness is updated only slowly, the significance of the initial event cannot be recognised so that action can be taken to avoid the blackout. In this type of communication infrastructure, informational connections may be made using time-synchronised measurement devices such as a phasor measurement unit (PMU), a phasor data concentrator (PDU) and so on.

Some blackouts take place too quickly to allow operator intervention, and fast control and protection schemes are therefore needed to prevent the power system from reaching instability or collapse. These schemes also depend on coherent, real-time data that are delivered in an appropriate way. Furthermore, the integration of many non-carbon sources of energy, such as wind and solar power, complicates the control procedure, since these behave differently from existing generation sources and are dependent on local weather conditions. To address these issues, a smart grid requires the modernisation not only of the power system but also of its data delivery infrastructure. Time-synchronised measurement technologies should therefore be used, and microsecond-accurate data should be delivered in real time to provide coherent picture of the power system to operators, and to allow closed-loop control and broader protection.

The GridStat (Washington State University) project (Bakken et al. 2011) adopted a publish/subscribe paradigm to build a communication infrastructure in which a data consumer can express interest through a subscription without knowing who produces the data, and the data producer publishes data without knowing who subscribes to these data. This type of communication infrastructure is not aware of where the information is located, but only of which information is needed. A customer can describe her requirements based on the event type, and the infrastructure will deliver data of this type, even if the data producer did not intend to send the data to this customer. Multiple customers are allowed to subscribe to the same type of data, meaning that multicast is an intrinsic method of communication in this infrastructure. This also removes the restrictions on conversation: no source or destination is needed to enable communication, and the event types can be hierarchically structured. In addition, automatic caching is enabled by event type; since each data packet is meaningful, independently of its origin or destination, it can be cached in a real-time database to satisfy future requirements. Although the GridStat project developed a communication architecture for a smart grid, it did not fully address the security issues related to this infrastructure. In addition, this work only described the communication infrastructure itself, and did not discuss its impact on the services (sub-applications) and applications over it.

The caching capacity of a publish/subscribe-based communication infrastructure allows an IoT application to obtain a cached data event without direct access to the producer, even if it did not participate in previous application interactions. The capacity for active subscription allows a IoT service to 'eavesdrop' on the sessions of other IoT applications, and to obtain unexpected data events. The multicast capacity is unlike conventional endpoint-to-endpoint interaction. To some extent, the non-conversational aspect of this system conflicts with the interaction requirement for IoT services, since IoT applications often collaborate to realise a goal involving control and protection. A conversational constraint can be made explicit according to the needs of the designer. The publish/subscribe-based communication infrastructure and data-centric application interaction features require a different security methodology that is data-centric. An example (adapted from (Bakken et al. 2011)) is given below to illustrate the motivation for the current work.

Figure 1. Synchronous distributed control

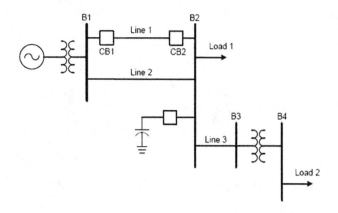

In Figure 1, B1 and B2 are transmission buses in a smart grid, and Lines 1 and 2 are part of the transmission network. B3 and B4 are distribution buses between which there is an on-load tap change transformer. The transmission and distribution networks are connected by Line 3. There is a series of control actions: opening breakers CB1 and CB2 decreases the voltage at B2 due to the increased impedance from the generator to B2; tapping the transformer between B3 and B4 restores the distribution voltage; a parallel capacitor is inserted into the system at B2; and the transformer is tapped back down between B3 and B4. The PDCs at each substation involved execute these sequential operations at exactly the same moment, based on time-synchronised data.

In the above distributed control scheme, six applications/services (sub-applications) are involved: the acquisition and estimation (AE) service, the event analysis (EA) service, the human machine interface (HMI) service, the control agent (CA) service, the warning service, and the resource model (RM) service. AE subscribes to some related time-synchronised measurements and may carry out state estimation. EA also subscribes to some types of data events, carries out event analysis and publishes alarms. HMI subscribes to real-time data events, estimated states and alarms to form an overall picture,

Figure 2. Control-related services

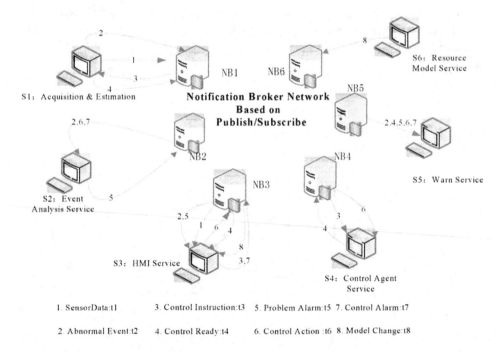

1. SensorData:t1   3. Control Instruction:t3   5. Problem Alarm:t5   7. Control Alarm:t7

2. Abnormal Event:t2   4. Control Ready:t4   6. Control Action :t6   8. Model Change:t8

and an operator uses these for remote control. The warning service uses alarms to warn operators in a timely manner using sounds, lights and so on. RM adapts the display based on the dynamic topology and power resources, as illustrated in Figure 2.

In the example of synchronous distributed control given above, it can be seen that one type of data event can be subscribed to by many services, such as the EA and HMI services, which both subscribe to abnormal events. For control, these data need to be time-synchronised and delivered in real time. Different services have different update requirements for refreshing data; for example, the control application is different from the display services. Data also have varying delivery time constraints, with control data being different from voltage measurements, for example. The WAMS-DD communication infrastructure is based on the publish/subscribe paradigm and provides an appropriate architecture to deliver coherent and real-time data in differentiating QoS. For IoT services and applications, the control procedure in the example actually creates a coordination scheme in which AE provides an accurate state to HMI, EA analyses abnormal online points and gives them to HMI, operators use HMI to make control decisions, multiple control agent services (CAs) collaborate to complete the control task, and all applications collaborate during the control procedure, such that the operators can control each step in the procedure in real time. The acquisition and estimation application interacts with multiple services at the same time, such as the EA, HMI and warning services, although it does not know which abnormal event is used by which application.

In the above example, each data event has its own description, which includes its type, time, location and other semantic metadata, allowing the publish/subscribe network to route and deliver it. Each event is a meaningful entity, independent of its origin and destination, and can be independently cached in real-time databases. For services and applications over this communication paradigm, each data event is also independent of its producer and consumers. In data-centric application interaction environments such as this, the security mechanism should also be data-centric, i.e. self-contained in terms of data, independently of the data producers and consumers. This means that security policies are embedded in the data (referred to as policy attaching) and are independently enforced in order to handle the challenges of identities being anonymous and access being indirect.

Use of an attaching policy alone is not sufficient. For example, consider a remote control service and an actuator agent service in a smart grid, which adjust the voltage of a transmission line. The remote control service publishes a sensitive event to indicate how to adjust the voltage, denoted by *Adjustment Command*, which can be subscribed to by many subscribers. The remote control service will embed an access control policy into the *Adjustment Command* event for protection, which specifies the conditions a customer should meet in order to access the event. The embedded policy thus reflects the requirement of protection for *Adjustment Command*. If the actuator agent service has the capability to match the embedded requirement, it can read the *Adjustment Command* event to execute a command. Unfortunately, this is not adequate for protection. If a malicious publisher publishes a malicious *Adjustment Command* event that embeds the same access control policy as the remote control service, the actuator agent service will damage the smart grid by actuating. It is therefore also necessary to specify the capability of the *Adjustment Command* event. When the actuator agent receives the event and its embedded capability specification, it can check whether the event's capability matches its own requirements, and then decides how to proceed.

From the above example, it can be seen that for IoT applications, events should not only be protected by embedding a requirement specification but should also specify a capability so that bi-direction matching can be carried out. The access control mechanism should include an independent data layer and an application layer. In the independent data layer, event requirements can be represented by embedding an access control policy; the communication infrastructure then decides whether to send the event to a subscriber based on the subscriber's capability. In the application layer, the publisher's event is restricted by its embedded capability, such as its attributes, and this capability is evaluated according to the local policies of the applications. In addition, access control policies and data capabilities are often sensitive, meaning that policy privacy is also required in IoT services. The solution for IoT access control should involve a two-layer framework, policy attaching, policy privacy, and so on. The question of how to satisfy these requirements is as yet unsolved for IoT services.

Most existing approaches to access control for applications are based on the request/reply paradigm. For example, the work in Paci et al. (2011) proposed a conversation-based access control model in which an important requirement for a client is to be able to complete any conversation it engages in with a service. In order to avoid situations in which the client cannot progress with the execution of a conversation because it does not have the proper credentials, an access control model for conversational services is therefore used to initially verify whether a client is able to provide the credentials for authorisation to terminate the conversation. Wang and Li

(2010) proposed a role-and-relation-based access control model (R^{2}BAC) for workflows that may be composed of services, offering another example. For a publish/subscribe-based IoT application, the issue is different, since in this model, consumers do not directly obtain data events from it and cannot be directly rejected from access to its data event. There are three requirements that should be considered in relation to the access control solution for IoT services, as follows:

1. Which access control framework should be adopted in order to realise two-layer protection for IoT applications, policy attaching, policy privacy, and so on. For an event published by a publisher, the IoT communication infrastructure handles the final delivery, and the publisher has no opportunity to directly control the data. It is therefore possible to integrate several network capabilities to help control such data-centric access. In addition, a single data event is subscribed to by many consumers, and these consumers may receive this event from different network nodes. Multiple distributed network nodes are therefore needed to collaborate to allow an application complete access control. The framework combines IoT communication network capabilities and local functionalities of applications for access control, and IoT services should be not aware of the context of applications.

2. When a network node is enforcing policies, direct matching between the clear policies of IoT events and the capabilities of services/applications will result in the disclosure of critical information. For example, a company may not allow people with certain attributes (such as certain positions) to access the data event. Such policies should be kept private. Access control policies should be blinded, and these blinded policies can be efficiently embedded and evaluated.

3. The access control scheme for IoT services should be efficient in terms of its computational and communication costs. There are two methods of realising computational efficiency. One is to design efficient cryptographic algorithms or non-cryptographic schemes, while the other is to utilise all possible cryptographic algorithms by means of synthesis. It is argued here that the latter approach is also available for designing a complete solution. The works in Goyal et al. (2006) and Waters (2011) show that public-key-based cryptographic operations are possible at wire speed in high-speed environments based on particular designs. Methods of reducing communication cost involve compressing or reusing the metadata of access control.

Using the open, multicast and anonymous characteristics of IoT services, an attribute-based access control model is adopted here. Attribute-based policies can be used to represent the protection requirements of IoT events, and attributes can also be used to define the capabilities against which customer requirements can be matched. The access control policies of the IoT events (i.e. protection requirements) and the attributes of IoT events (i.e. capabilities) should both be embedded into the IoT events, so that IoT events can be cached as meaningful independent entities. Attribute-based authorisation policies are then translated into network-integrable policies, enabling integrated network nodes to handle access control for indirect and multicast service interactions. The term "network-integrable" means that delegated policies can be transparently enforced by network nodes without being aware of the policy context or other information.

In the access control framework described here, a new entity is created in terms of network nodes called home brokers, which directly connect to consumers or publishers. The entity stores some metadata for access control and transparent enforcement of policies. The authorisation policies and event attributes are encoded, hiding sensitive information, and the matching between both the requirements of the IoT events and the service capability and between the capability of the event and the service requirements is carried out blindly, without disclosing sensitive information. Two functionalities therefore have to be provided in this framework: one is the embedding of access control policies and attributes into the IoT events, and the other is blind policy matching for control access. The embedding functionality should prevent malicious attackers from attaching access control polices and attributes to IoT events that can be realised by other methods; this is not further discussed in the current paper.

A ciphertext-policy attribute-based encryption (CP-ABE) scheme (Goyal et al., 2006; Waters, 2011) offers a possibility for embedding authorisation policies into ciphertexts. Unfortunately, the traditional CP-ABE model cannot assure flexibility and expressiveness. In the current framework, the policy embedding function needs to be separated from the data encryption function, and the policy embedding function can only be carried out by the event publisher. When encoding policies and attributes, an attempt is made to reduce the volumes of such metadata. In practice, the event names are hierarchical, and take the form of a tree, and a policy may be created for a sub-tree. For efficiency, the encoding procedure is carried out according to the name structure. In order to improve the performance of the access control scheme, the embedding procedure may aggregate attributes and policies according to the attribute relationship and policy relation. This chapter is an extension of work previously reported by the authors (Smart Grid Policy, 2009; Zhang & Chen, 2013).

Related Work

The philosophy of integration requires that the information system used in the wide-area IoT system should be decoupled, composable and open. Traditional SCADA systems for the IoT (Masaud-Wahaishi & Gaouda, 2011), (Smart Grid Policy, 2009) are designed to be closed and to act as the brain of the industrial utility; they consist of one or more remote terminal units (RTUs) connected to a variety of sensors and actuators, and several master stations. When the open wide-area IoT system comes near, new intelligent control and protection systems will also become more open and distributed and can interact with increasing numbers of other services/applications, resulting in heightened security threats to IoT services.

The current authors' previous work in Zhang and Chen (2012) discussed the basic security requirements of a wide-area IoT system and a basic solution to satisfy these requirements. It did not discuss how to address this issue using a two-layer approach or how to embed authorisation policies into events with separation. Policy privacy was also not considered in (Zhang and Chen, 2012), and its main focus was on how to adopt an appropriate encryption scheme to support a distributed security framework. This paper therefore extends this work (Zhang & Chen, 2012), describing a complete security framework, and the issues of policy attaching and policy privacy are fully addressed. The proposed access control framework is also taken from the authors' previous work (Zhang & Chen, 2013), and this paper forms an extension of Zhang and Chen (2013) by adding a description of the embedding and preserving policies.

With respect to access control for Web services, several policy-driven access control models (Anderson, 2007; Wonohoesodo & Tari, 2004; Bhatti et al, 2004; Kagal et al., 2004; Bertino et al., 2006) have been proposed, but none of these have investigated the enforcement of access control for event-driven service collaborations. The industrial effort in this related area is made by OASIS with the WS-XACML profile for Web services (Zhang & Chen, 2012). XACML is a standard specification that consists of an XML-based language for expressing access control policies and a request/

response protocol that specifies how to determine whether a given action is allowed and how to interpret the result. The Web service profile of XACML (WS-XACML) (Anderson, 2007) specifies how to use XACML in a Web services environment. Two new types of policy assertion are introduced in WS-XACML to allow Web service providers and consumers to specify their requirements in terms of authorisation, access control, and privacy, and their capabilities regarding Web service interactions. WS-XACML also proposes an approach to verify whether a client's capabilities and a Web service provider's requirements match and vice versa. The specification focuses on the request/reply interaction paradigm and a one-to-one consumer/service conversation; it does not consider the publish/subscribe interaction paradigm or service collaborations. Wang and Li (2010) proposed an R²BAC model for workflows that could be composed of services. In R²BAC, decentralised authorisation and distributed enforcement are not the main focus.

The policy privacy issue has been discussed in the works of Nishide et al. (2009), Cheung and Newport (2007), and Yu et al. (2008), in which decryptors tried all attribute keys to decrypt ciphertexts, which often limits the efficiency of these schemes. The authors of Li et al. (2012), Doshi and Jinwala (2012), and Muller and Katzenbeisser (2012) also proposed attribute-based encryption schemes based on policy privacy where authorisation policies were hidden in ciphertexts, and where the size of these ciphertexts was reduced. They focused on hiding policies in ciphertexts but did not focus on policy anonymity approaches based on anonymous sets. They also did not focus on the flexible management of policies. In IoT scenarios, authorisation policies for persistent event types could possibly be modified. The updating of authorisation policies is a desirable feature of an access control service. In addition, these schemes did not provide delegation capabilities. The solution proposed here considers that delegation capabilities and flexible authorisation management are both necessary for access control.

Contributions

The contributions of this chapter are as follows:

1. A two-layer framework is developed for access control of IoT services, in which the data layer handles protection of the IoT events and the application layer handles protection of the services/applications. The methodology used for the matching between protection requirements and the entities' capabilities plays a key role in this framework. In order

to establish the data layer, a new network entity is presented to ensure the transparent protection of events with network capabilities that are integrated into the framework.

2. Two building blocks underpin the framework. The first is the policy embedding function in which the policy and attributes can be dynamically generated and embedded. This function is based on the separation between policy embedding and data encryption. The second is the blind encoding function for policies and attributes of IoT events, which realises policy privacy. The encoding procedure is carried out according to the name tree in order to optimise performance. An IoT communication infrastructure is adopted based on the publish/subscribe paradigm.

PRELIMINARIES

A Publish/Subscribe-Based IoT Communication Infrastructure

A publish/subscribe-based IoT communication infrastructure (generally referred to as DEBS) is composed of a set of notification broker (NB) nodes distributed over a network. These NB nodes form an overlay network, which is a logical network built on the physical network. The nodes of the overlay network are brokers and the links are paths in the physical network.

The distributed event-driven IoT service communication infrastructure can be formally represented as a 5-tuple $CF = <B, C, P, S, T>$ where $B = \{NB_1, NB_2, \cdots\}$ is the set of notification broker nodes; $C = \{c_1, c_2, \cdots\}$ is the set of connections between broker nodes; $P = \{p_1, p_2, \cdots\}$ is the set of publishers, which may be IoT services; $S = \{s_1, s_2, \cdots\}$ is the set of subscribers, which may be other IoT services; and $T = \{s_1, s_2, \cdots\}$ is the set of event types.

Each publisher/subscriber is connected to only one of the brokers in Figure 3. The NB that is connected to a subscriber/publisher is called the access broker in the network view and is also referred to as the *home broker* with respect to that subscriber/publisher. The NBs that route events between brokers are called event routers or inter-brokers. Each publisher publishes events to its home broker, and each subscriber receives events from its access broker (home broker). Clients may be publishers and/or subscribers.

Figure 3. SCADA communication infrastructure

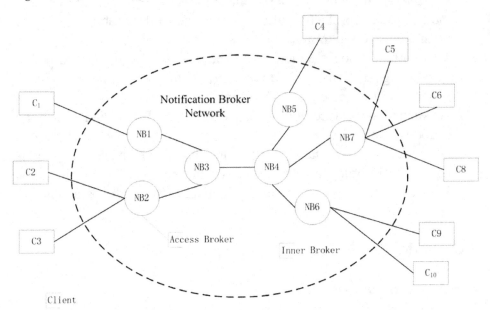

Attribute-Based Authorisation Policy

We adopt the attribute-based access control model in Anderson (2007).

Definition 1: Attribute Tuple: The attribute of a subject S is denoted by $s_k = (s\_attr_k, op_k, value_k)$ and the attribute of an object O as $o_n = (o\_attr_n, op_n, value_n)$, where s_attr and o_attr are attribute names, *value* is the attribute value, and *op* is some attribute operator such as $op \in \{=, <, >, \leq, \geq, in\}$. The action attribute may be one of the object's attributes. The attribute tuple is $< s_1, s_2, \cdots, s_K >$ or $< o_1, o_2, \cdots, o_N >$, where the relationship among the attributes is one of conjunction. S can be represented by the set of attribute tuples $\{< s_1, s_2, \cdots, s_K >\}$, and O by $\{< o_1, o_2, \cdots, o_N >\}$.

In the current work, *op* is simplified as $\{=\}$ by describing digital attributes with careful intervals. Then, S can be written as

$$\left(w_{1,1} \wedge \cdots \wedge w_{1,K_1}\right) \vee \cdots \vee \left(w_{l,1} \wedge \cdots \wedge w_{1,K_l}\right),$$

where

$$w_{i,j} ::= " s\_attr_{i,j} = value_{i,j} ", \ 1 \le i \le l, \ 1 \le j \le K_l.$$

O can be written as

$$\left(w_{1,1} \wedge \cdots \wedge w_{1,N_1} \right) \vee \cdots \vee \left(w_{n,1} \wedge \cdots \wedge w_{n,N_n} \right),$$

where

$$w_{i,j} ::= " o\_attr_{i,j} = value_{i,j} ", \ 1 \le i \le n, \ 1 \le j \le N_n.$$

Definition 2: Authorisation Rule: An attribute-based rule is

$$rule = (< s_1, s_2, \cdots, s_k >, < o_1, o_2, \cdots, o_n >).$$

The $j-th$ subject attribute in *rule* is written as $rule.s_j$. The $j-th$ object attribute in *rule* is written as $rule.o_j$.

An authorisation policy AP_i can be defined as $AP_i = \bigcup\limits_{j=1}^{L} rule_{i,j}$, where $rule_{i,j}$ is the $j-th$ element in the rule set AP_i.

For example, a company called *JingFang* manages the provision of heating for citizens in the winter. Heat consumption data are classified into two classes, *A, B*. The data in class *A* are the detailed records of the heat consumption by each residential home. The data in class *B* are records of statistical information about this heat consumption. *JingFang* publishes these data in the IoT system. Two types of clients access the data, *CL1* and *CL2*. Clients of type *CL1* are individuals who can access their own home consumption data, *A*. One client of type *CL2* is a data mining company serving *JingFang*, which can access the data in class *B*. The attributes of these data and clients are as follows:

A: <(*class*, =, *individual*), (*consumer*, =, *XX*)>, where *XX* is the detail identifier of the consumer who consumes the heat and produces the data. For the data of class *A* from different homes, the identifiers are different.

B: <(*class*, =, *statistics*), (*period*, =, *XX*1)>, which indicates that the data is the list of statistics information for head consumption. That is to say, the data has the following attributes: its class is *statistics*, and the statistics period is *XX*1.

*CL*1: <(*type*, =, *individual*), (*consumer*, =, *YY*)>, where *YY* is a detailed identifier of the consumer. The subject has the following attributes: its class is *individual*, and its consumer identifier is *YY*.

*CL*2: <(*type*, =, *company*), (*service*, =, *dataMining*)>. The subject has the following attributes: its type is *company*, and its service is *dataMining*.

The authorisation policy for data *A* can be represented as $AP_A = \{(<(type, =, individual), (consumer, =, XX)>, <(class, =, individual), (consumer, =, XX)>)\}$. There is one authorisation rule (<(*type*, =, *individual*), (*consumer*, =, *XX*)>, <(*class*, =, *individual*), (*consumer*, =, *XX*)>) in the policy. This means that a client with attribute <(*type*, =, *individual*), (*consumer*, =, *XX*)> can read data with attribute <(*class*, =, *individual*), (*consumer*, =, *XX*)>. The subject attribute tuple is <(*type*, =, *individual*), (*consumer*, =, *XX*)>. The object attribute tuple is <(*class*, =, *individual*), (*consumer*, =, *XX*)>. The subject can be written as "*type = individual*" ∧ "*consumer = XX*". The authorisation policy for data *B* can be represented as $AP_B = \{(<(type, =, company), (service, =, dataMining)>, <(class, =, statistics)>)\}$.

Let Γ be an expression representing the subject attributes of rules in the authorisation policy that are required to access data. This uses logic operators to associate the attributes, which are also referred to as the authorisation policy if no confusion will arise. Based on the authorisation policy *AP*, Γ can be represented as

$$\Gamma = (w_{1,1} \wedge \cdots \wedge w_{1,K_1}) \vee \cdots \vee (w_{l,1} \wedge \cdots \wedge w_{l,K_l}),$$

where

$$w_{i,j} ::= "s\_attr_{i,j} = value_{i,j}", \ 1 \le i \le l, \ 1 \le j \le K_l.$$

For example, according to the authorisation policy for data *B*, i.e. $AP_B = \{(<(type, =, company), (service, =, dataMining)>, <(class, =, statistics)>)\}$, the expression for data *B* is

$$\Gamma_B = " type = company " \wedge " service = dataMining " .$$

If a customer has attributes that match Γ, he/she can access the data. The conjunction of the client's attributes includes the conjunction in Γ of the data. γ often denotes a customer's set of attribute conjunction as the authorisation policy. Another attribute $w'_{i,j}$ is introduced to represent the negative of $w_{i,j}$.

Bloom Filter

A Bloom filter is a simple, space-efficient randomised data structure used to represent a set of strings in a compact way, enabling efficient membership querying (Burton, 1970; Saar et al., 2003; Bonomi et al., 2006).

A Bloom filter representing a set $X = \{x_1, x_2, \cdots, x_n\}$ of n elements is described by an array of m bits, all of which are initially set to 0. A Bloom filter uses k independent hash functions $\{h_1, h_2, \cdots, h_k\}$ with range $\{1, 2, \cdots, m\}$. For each member x belonging to X, the bits $h_i(x)$ are set to one for $1 \leq i \leq k$. The bits can be set to one multiple times, but only the first change has an

Figure 4. The relation between event names and access control policies

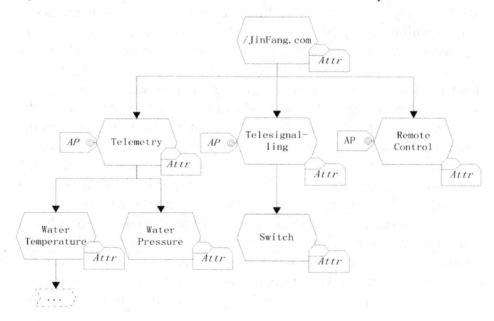

effect. After repeating this procedure for all members of the set, the programming of the filter is complete.

The query process is similar to programming. To determine whether an item y is in X, a check is made as to whether all $h_i(y)$ are set to one.

ACCESS CONTROL FRAMEWORK FOR IOT SERVICES

The access control framework has two layers; the lower layer carries out matching between the protection requirements of the IoT events and the capabilities of the IoT applications, and the upper layer carries out matching between the capabilities of the IoT events and the requirements of the IoT applications. The matching function is carried out based on metadata, such as authorised attributes acting as capabilities and embedded policies acting as requirements. In order to improve the performance of access control schemes, the relation between metadata and event names is defined as shown in Figure 4.

Figure 4 shows JingFang, a company that provides a heating service for residents in winter. The heating system produces and consumes events named *Telemetry, Telesignalling, Remote Control*, and so on. *Telemetry* has some child names, such as *Water Temperature, Water Pressure*, and so on. Each name in the name tree in Figure 1 has its own attributes *Attr*, but an access control policy *AP* is created for the *Telemetry* sub-tree. It should be pointed out that a single event name has many name instances, which appears to conflict with the assumptions made in the publish/subscribe paradigm. In the proposed IoT system, however, if a particular name has its child names with attributes and authorisation policies that do not contain differences, these child names will only be used to tag different data packets and can be regarded as instances. This method will naturally reduce the size of the name tree. For example, consider a sensor that continuously measures the temperature of water and publishes a temperature data event every second, as shown in Figure 4. These temperature data differ only in terms of the timestamp. Temperature data with different timestamps can therefore be regarded as different name instances of the same name: *Water Temperature*. This does not conflict with the assumption of IoT services (in which each data packet has a unique name) since data can be differentiated by the timestamp. An instance identifier can be used to further name a data packet, even if the parent name is common. The concept of *type* is therefore introduced to handle this scenario, meaning that different data packets of the same type may have a common parent name with the same attributes. Multiple types may have a common access control policy. The relation between event names and access control policies is as follows:

1. A event name may have many instances with the same attributes, and thus the same type. A type is defined by attributes, i.e., a subject attribute expression. Two event names may have the same type, although in practice, a type is often unique.
2. Access control policies are often created for sub-trees, and multiple types may have the same access control policy.

The two-layer framework for access control of IoT services is illustrated in Figure 5, which shows an access control engine, and a new network entity (home brokers), shown in the middle column. The engine stores the policies and types of both names and services. When an event arrives at the home broker, the engine identifies the access control policy and type by event name. It then matches the name type and policy, and the application type and policy, if the applications subscribe to events with the name of the received event. If the result of matching is not empty, the engine will enforce policies in the data layer for valid consumers, where the policy of the event is embedded in the access control policy. The embedded policy not only binds the access control policy and type to the event, but also provides an indicator to show that only the event publisher can embed the value, for example using a signature. Access control in the application layer may be carried out by the service itself. The application can also delegate some of the responsibilities for access control in the application layer to the engine in IoT services.

Figure 5 shows that the engine has three functions: finding a name type and policy based on the event name; matching requirements and capabilities; and enforcing policies. In order to realise these functions, two building blocks must be provided. The first involves embedding authorisation policies and types into events; the embedding scheme should provide authentication support, since the bi-directional matching needs to be verified as having been carried out based on actual attributes. For performance optimisation, it is desirable that the scheme itself carries out this authentication task. The second function involves encoding attributes and policies to enable rapid matching and maintenance of privacy.

Figure 6 illustrates an authorisation procedure using two special event names, which is carried out before the publisher publishes events (or service messages) in IoT services. In Step 1, the publisher attaches the name type

Figure 5. Two-layer framework for access control

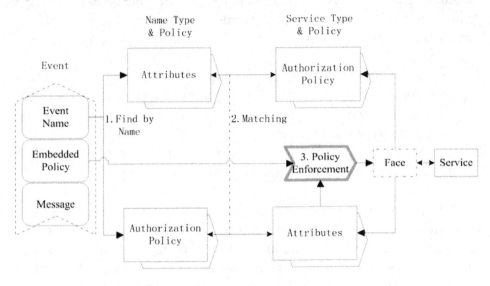

Figure 6. Authorization before dissemination of data

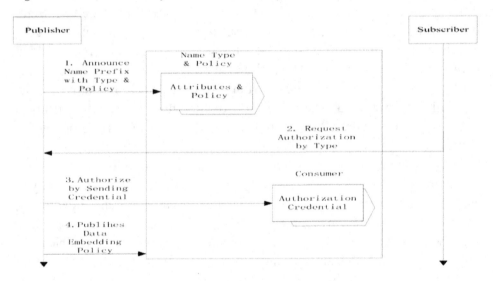

and access control policy to the event prefix announcement. The access control engine stores the received name type and access control policies in a storage database called *Name Type & Policy*. In Step 2, a subscriber publishes an authorisation request for this name based on its type. In Step 3, after receiving the authorisation request, the publisher translates the name policy into a network policy, referred to as its authorisation credentials. The publisher publishes the network policy to the access control engine, which means that home brokers cannot disclose certain sensitive information even if authorisation credentials are stored in the engine. Some parts of the policy are embedded into events in Step 4, thus binding the type and policy to the published events. This authorisation procedure is not the focus of this paper, and readers can refer to Zhang and Chen (2013) for more details.

The event consumers trust their home brokers, and assume that these home brokers are honest, while event producers assume that home brokers are honest but curious, meaning that home brokers will follow predefined protocols but will try to find out as much secret information as possible. It is assumed that home brokers may collude with malicious users and that adversaries control all communication channels, and can eavesdrop, forge, delay and discard messages, and dynamically corrupt any participants in the system.

EMBEDDING SCHEME

In the embedding scheme, each access control policy is expressed by an access expression " , such as:

$$\Gamma = \left(w_{1,1} \wedge \cdots \wedge w_{1,n_1} \right) \vee \cdots \vee \left(w_{l,1} \wedge \cdots \wedge w_{1,n_l} \right),$$

where " is a propositional formula, i.e., a disjunctive normal form; $\left(w_{1,1} \wedge \cdots \wedge w_{1,n_1} \right)$ is a conjunctive clause; and $w_{i,j}$ is a basic proposition such as $attr_{i,j} = value_{i,j}$, i.e. an atomic formula. A type is expressed by a subject attribute expression γ, such as:

$$\left(w_{1,1} \wedge \cdots \wedge w_{1,n_1'} \right) \vee \cdots \vee \left(w_{l',1} \wedge \cdots \wedge w_{1,n_{l'}'} \right),$$

where the subject attributes and object attributes are both represented by type, i.e. the subject and object are relative.

The goal of embedding the type and policy is to compress the variable lengths of the attribute name and value, to enable performance optimisation for matching, communication and storage. Privacy may also be considered in the embedding process. The core idea is to adopt a one-way set hash method to encode the attributes in a conjunctive clause (i.e. a set of attributes) of a disjunctive normal form into a hash value. When evaluating a customer's subscription to some sensitive event data, direct matching of the customer's clear attributes against authorisation policies will result in the disclosure of some critical information about the customer or the publisher. A policy anonymity approach is adopted here; each customer has her/his own attributes, which are a disjunctive normal form of attribute conjunctions, for example:

$$(w_{1,1} \wedge \cdots \wedge w_{1,K_1}) \vee \cdots \vee (w_{l,1} \wedge \cdots \wedge w_{l,K_l}).$$

Each data event also has its attributes as the customer, but attention is paid here to the subject attributes in the authorisation policy for the data event identified by the data attributes, and the same approach is used for the data event. The authorisation policies created by the publisher determine which attributes a customer needs to have in order to access the data event. The home broker makes a decision about the customer's subscription by matching the customer's attributes against the data authorisation policy; that is, it checks whether the customer has an attribute conjunction that includes an attribute conjunction of the authorisation policy.

In order to clarify the idea of policy anonymity, an abstract is given below of an anonymous set based on these requirements. This is then used as a clear and formal basis for designing the policy-attaching and policy-privacy scheme. In the anonymous set, one-way random and compression functionalities, known as a set hash, play a key role in encoding the attributes in a conjunctive clause (i.e. a set of attributes) of disjunctive normal form into a hash value. These are defined as follows:

Definition 3: Random Oracle O_{set} **for Set:** Given a set of string elements, a random bit string called the *Random Oracle for Set* is obtained if the conditions below are satisfied.

1. *For two different sets, the random bit strings output by the oracle* O_{set} *are different;*
2. *The membership of a given element in the set can be checked by the membership checking oracle* $O_{\in}$*;*
3. *The inclusion relation of a subset of the set can be checked by the set inclusion oracle* $O_{\subseteq}$*;*
4. *The union of two sets can be computed by the set union oracle* $O_{\cup}$*;*

5.   The intersection of two sets cannot be computed if no inclusion relation exists;

6.   No elements can be computed from the set hash value (the random bit string) if the set is not publicly known.

Based on the above definition, a set of sensitive attributes can be encoded into a one-way string code in such a way that member elements cannot be directly recovered from the code. A Bloom filter can be used to realise such oracle O_{set}, although this has the following privacy disadvantages:

1.   When encoding a clear authorisation policy into a Bloom filter, some sensitive information can be guessed during the evaluation of customers' requests by testing the membership of clear subject attributes. An attribute-blinding method should be adopted to address this issue.

2.   When attributes are blinded, a membership-checking function is used in many scenarios, and this is carried out on an explicitly specified blinded attribute. When the blinded attribute is explicitly given during this membership checking, it is also a clue to link different Bloom filters for different attribute sets, to link authorisation transactions, and to guess the corresponding clear attributes, since the membership-checking result indicates whether two attribute sets include the same attribute. Hence, the blinded attribute should be hidden from adversaries.

3.   The membership checking function is also a basic function of a set. An alternative method is proposed here in which an anonymous set-inclusion-checking function is used to answer the membership query instead of the member checking function; that is, two Bloom filters are used to complete anonymous membership queries. To the best of the authors' knowledge, there are no existing algorithms that use a set-inclusion-checking function to carry out the anonymous checking function of a set member.

The policy embedding scheme should therefore be designed based on the use of a Bloom filter, with the member-checking function as a key part of the scheme. Use of a set-inclusion function to carry out the member checking function means that for a particular customer's attribute conjunction, the set of attributes of the conjunction that are included in a given authorisation conjunction can be queried using inclusion queries without explicit knowledge of these attributes. Each attribute in the conjunction is ordered using an index, and a method is required that can obtain those indices for which the corresponding attributes satisfy the authorisation conjunction. The same index value in different authorisation conjunctions may correspond to different attributes. When searching for these indices, customer attributes and attributes in the policy are not known or disclosed. These indices are often passed to other functions or used as an indicator to determine whether they are matched; re-encryption keys are also chosen based on these, and the re-encryption operation is carried out using these keys (Goyal et al., 2006; Waters, 2011).

The key idea underlying this alternative method for the member checking function is to sort each attribute conjunction, predefine a series of auxiliary sets for each attribute conjunction of the customer, and then to judge which auxiliary sets include one of the attribute conjunctions in the authorisation policy. When these auxiliary sets are identified, attributes indices are computed according to the indices of these auxiliary sets. This process can be described as follows.

Assume the number of attribute conjunctions for a customer's is x, the number of attributes in a conjunction is y, and the size of the Bloom filter is m. A series of auxiliary sets can be defined for the attributes $w_1, w_2, \cdots, w_y$ in a conjunction

$$CWset_1 = \{w_1, \cdots, w_{y-1}\},$$

$$CWset_2 = \{w_1, \cdots, w_{y-2}, w_y\},$$

$$\cdots, CWset_y = \{w_2, \cdots, w_y\},$$

$$CWset_{y+1} = \{w_1, \cdots, w_{y-1}, w_y\}.$$

If there is a set $AWset$ that is only included in one $CWset_i$ ($1 \leq i \leq y$) and not included in the other sets ($1, \cdots, y$), then $AWset$ includes the attributes in $CWset_i$ and these included attribute indices are $1, \cdots, y - i, y - i + 2, \cdots, y$. If the set $AWset$ is only included in two sets, $CWset_i$ ($1 \leq i \leq y$) and $CWset_j$ ($1 \leq j \leq y$), and not included in other sets ($1, \ldots, y$), then $AWset$ includes the attributes in $CWset_i \cap CWset_j$ and the attribute indices (assume $j > i$) are

$$1, \cdots, y - j, y - j + 2, \cdots, y - i, y - i + 2, \cdots, y \, (j > i + 1)$$

or

$$1, \cdots, y - j, y - i + 2, \cdots, y \ (j = i + 1).$$

The remainder can be treated in the same manner. If the set *AWset* is only included in the set $CWset_{y+1}$, and is not included in other sets $(1, \ldots, y)$, then *AWset* includes all the attributes in $CWset_{y+1}$, and the attribute indices are 1, ..., y.

POLICY ENCODING AND MATCHING

In the proposed solution, three steps are taken to realise policy privacy in the access control service: blinding attributes, encoding blinded attributes into an anonymous set, and carrying out matching between the customer's anonymous attribute set and the anonymous authorisation policy set. The first step is to blind the event attributes, the customer attributes, and authorisation policies, which is described after the encoding procedure and matching procedure. When these attributes and policies have been blinded, the second step is to encode the blinded attribute conjunctions from the authorisation policies and the customer into anonymous sets, which will be stored and embedded. The final step is to compute the set membership, the set inclusion and intersection of two anonymous sets of the data and customer. A Bloom filter is used to encode these blinded attributes. An alternative scheme is designed here that uses a set-inclusion-checking function to complete the membership query, based on two anonymous sets. This scheme, based on the use of anonymous sets, can be used to realise policy privacy.

The encoding procedure describes how to obtain predefined auxiliary sets without disclosing clear attributes. A matching procedure is defined and describes how to identify these auxiliary sets, including the authorisation conjunction, and how to compute attribute indices without disclosing clear attributes.

Definition 4: Encoding Procedure: The encoding procedure has two parts: encoding of the attribute conjunctions of the customers and encoding of the attribute conjunctions of the authorisation policies.

1. Encoding of customers' attributes

Each attribute conjunction is expanded, with the number of attributes in the conjunction set to n, and with random attributes inserted into the conjunction to hide the conjunction length (the attributes and attribute conjunctions are also blinded by the algorithms in Figures 2 and 3, which are discussed in the next section). Table 1 shows the Bloom filters, where Bloom filter BF_t represents the attribute conjunction, BF_1 represents the first auxiliary attribute set, BF_2 represents the second auxiliary attribute set, and so on.

The attributes in the conjunction are distributed across the Bloom filters, as shown in Table 2. The rows of the table represent the Bloom filters, and the columns represent attributes. For example, the $i-th$ row represents BF_i, and the $j-th$ column represents w_j. If BF_i $(1 \leq i \leq n)$ has a value of one in the $j-th$ column, then w_j $(1 \leq j \leq n)$ is encoded into BF_i, i.e. w_j belongs to the $i-th$ auxiliary attribute set. If element (i, j) in the table has a value of one, then w_j $(1 \leq j \leq n)$ is encoded into BF_i. The bottom row, i.e. the $(n + 1)-th$ row, represents BF_t, where all attributes in the conjunction are encoded into BF_t. The right-hand column surrounded by dashed line shows that each row is itself a bit string and is denoted by $b_i (1 \leq i \leq n)$. For example,

$$b_1 = \overbrace{11\cdots10}^{n}, \ b_i = \overbrace{11\cdots1_{n-i}0_{n-i+1}1_{n-i+2}\cdots11}^{n} \ \text{and} \ b = \overbrace{11\cdots11}^{n}.$$

The Bloom filter BF_i $(1 \leq i \leq n)$ is computed as follows:

a. BF_i is initialized to zero;
b. In the $i-th$ row of Table 2, all attributes with a value of one in their position form a set Set_i;
c. A random string is chosen to insert into Set_i;
d. Set_i is encoded into a Bloom filter, which is assigned to BF_i.

The Bloom filter BF_t is computed as follows:

a. BF_t is initialised to zero;

Table 1. Bloom filters in a single attribute conjunction

$BF_t, BF_1, BF_2, ..., BF_n$	w_1	w_2	...	w_n

Table 2. Distribution of attributes among Bloom filters

	w_1	w_2	...	w_{n-1}	w_n	bit strings
BF_1	1	1	...	1	0	b_1
BF_2	1	1	...	0	1	b_2
...			...			...
BF_{n-1}	1	0	...	1	1	b_{n-1}
BF_n	0	1	...	1	1	b_n
BF_t	1	1		1	1	b

    b.   All attributes in the conjunction form a set Set_t;

    c.   A random string is chosen to insert into Set_t if no random string is inserted into the conjunction during expansion;

    d. Set_t is encoded into a Bloom filter which is assigned to BF_t.

2.   Encoding of the attribute conjunction in authorisation policies

The Bloom filter BF_a for the attribute conjunction in an access expression and the mask Bloom filter BF_{a-m} are computed as follows:

    a. BF_a and BF_{a-m} are initialised to zero;

    b.   All attributes in the conjunction form a set Set_a;

    c.   Several random strings are chosen to be inserted into Set_a, and also form a mask set Set_{a-m};

    d. Set_a is encoded into a Bloom filter which is assigned to BF_a;

    e. Set_{a-m} is encoded into a Bloom filter which is assigned to BF_{a-m}.

From the definition of the encoding procedure, we know that each BF_i is encoded from $Set_i = \{w_1, \cdots, w_{n-i}, w_{n-i+2}, \cdots, w_n\}$ and a random string. The random string is a blinded mask for BF_i, and does not affect the process of checking whether an attribute is a member of Set_i and whether an attribute set is included in Set_i.

It is impossible to check whether attribute set Set_a of the access conjunction is included in the attribute set Set_t of the subject conjunction when its Bloom filter BF_a is blinded. To address this issue, the random strings used in the blinding mask are encoded into an independent Bloom filter BF_{a-m}. Since the Bloom filter is a one-way process, it is impossible to remove the blinding mask strings from BF_a, even if BF_a and BF_{a-m} are given. Using a bitwise OR operation, $BF_{a\text{-}m}$ can be added into BF_i, i.e. the blinding mask strings are encoded into BF_i. Then, the inclusion relationship is checked using the equation $BF_a \wedge (BF_{a\text{-}m} \vee BF_i) = BF_a$, thus indicating whether the attribute set Set_a for authorisation conjunction is included in the attribute set Set_t for the customers' attribute conjunction.

Definition 5: Matching Procedure: Given the Bloom filter for the authorisation policies $(BF_a, BF_{a\text{-}m})$, the matching scheme is as follows, where each "0,1" bit string of rows in Table 2 is represented by b_i $(1 \le i \le n)$, $\wedge$ is a bitwise AND operation, and $\vee$ is a bitwise OR operation.

1. A "1" bit string of size n is chosen as b.
2. If $BF_a \wedge (BF_{a\text{-}m} \vee BF_t) \ne BF_a$, the Bloom filter for the authorisation and customer attributes does not match, and the computation is terminated; otherwise, continue to the next step.
3. for $i = 1$ to n
4. If $BF_a \wedge (BF_{a\text{-}m} \vee BF_i) = BF_a$, then $b = b \wedge b_i$.
5. If none of $BF_a \wedge (BF_{a\text{-}m} \vee BF_i) = BF_a$ happens in Steps 3 and 2, the computation is terminated; otherwise,
6. The indices of the matched attributes are the corresponding positions with '1' in b. Those '1' positions are actual column indices in Table 2.

The correctness of the matching procedure is verified since:

1. When $BF_a \wedge (BF_{a\text{-}m} \vee BF_i) = BF_a$, this implies that the attribute set denoted by the $i-th$ row of Table 2 includes the attribute set of the authorisation conjunction denoted by BF_a. The attribute set denoted by the $i-th$ row of Table 2 is written as b_i.
2. When $BF_a \wedge (BF_{a\text{-}m} \vee BF_j) = BF_a$, this implies that the attribute set denoted by the $j-th$ row of Table 2 includes the attribute set of the authorisation conjunction denoted by BF_a. The attribute set denoted by the $j-th$ row of Table 2 is written as b_j.
3. From points 1 and 2, it can be seen that the attribute set of the authorisation conjunction denoted by BF_a is included not only in b_i but also in b_j. Thus, the set is included in the intersection of b_i and b_j. Computing $b_j \wedge b_j$

therefore gives the subset, including the attribute set of the authorisation conjunction.

4. The rows of Table 2 can be used to compute all subsets of attributes in the customers' attribute conjunction. When BF_a matches more $BF_x s$, the set denoted by BF_a includes fewer attribute elements.

An example is given below to illustrate the correctness of the matching scheme. For $Set_a = \{w_1, rw_1, rw_2\}$ and $Set_{a-m} = \{rw_1, rw_2\}$, $BF_1, BF_2, \cdots, BF_{n-1}$ satisfy w $BF_a \wedge (BF_{a-m} \vee BF_i) = BF_a$ $(1 \le i < n)$, and b is computed as follows:

$$b = b \wedge b_1 \wedge b_2 \wedge \cdots \wedge b_{n-1}$$

$$= \overbrace{11\cdots11}^{n} \wedge \overbrace{11\cdots10}^{n} \wedge \overbrace{11\cdots01}^{n} \wedge \cdots \wedge \overbrace{10\cdots11}^{n}$$

$$= \overbrace{10\cdots00}^{n}$$

From $b = \overbrace{10\cdots00}^{n}$, it can be deduced that only the position of w_1 contains a value of one. It is therefore concluded that the attribute with an index of one (although w_1 itself is unknown) is the member of Set_a. For $Set_a = \{w_1, w_2, rw_1, rw_2\}$ and $Set_{a-m} = \{rw_1, rw_2\}$, $BF_1, BF_2, \cdots, BF_{n-2}$ satisfy $BF_a \wedge (BF_{a-m} \vee BF_i) = BF_a$ $(1 \le i < n - 1)$, and b is computed as follows:

$$b = b \wedge b_1 \wedge b_2 \wedge b_3 \wedge \cdots \wedge b_{n-2}$$

$$= \overbrace{111\cdots111}^{n} \wedge \overbrace{111\cdots110}^{n} \wedge \overbrace{111\cdots101}^{n} \wedge \overbrace{111\cdots011}^{n} \wedge \cdots \wedge \overbrace{110\cdots111}^{n}$$

$$= \overbrace{110\cdots000}^{n}$$

Figure 7. Attribute-binding algorithm

Algorithm: Blinding Attributes

Input: A set of attributes $W = \{w_i\}$, with average length of subject attribute expression $length_{sae}$ and anonymity length $length_a$.

Output: A blinded attribute set $\{(w_i, \overline{w}_i, x_i)\}$ where x_i may be empty.

1. Compute a probability $p = (length_a - length_{sae})/ length_a$. If $p < 0$, terminate.

2. For each $w_i \in W$, replace w_i with (w_i, x_i) in W where x_i is chosen with probability p as a random string, and chosen with probability $1 - p$ as an empty string.

3. For each $(w_i, x_i) \in W$, randomly choose a string $\overline{w}_i$ as an alias of w_i, and replace (w_i, x_i) with $(w_i, \overline{w}_i, x_i)$ in W. Output the modified W.

Figure 8. Policy-binding algorithm

Algorithm: Blinding Policies

Input: A set of blinded attributes W, and an authorisation policy $\Gamma = (w_{1,1} \wedge \cdots \wedge w_{1,n_1}) \vee \cdots \vee (w_{l,1} \wedge \cdots \wedge w_{l,n_l})$.

Output: A blinded authorisation policy Γ'.

1. For each conjunction $con_i = (w_{i,1} \wedge \cdots \wedge w_{1,n_i})$ in Γ, compute its blinded counterpart con_i'. con_i' is initialised as empty.

2. For each $w_{i,j}$ in con_i, find $(w_{i,j}, \overline{w}_{i,j}, x_{i,j})$ in W.

3. If $x_{i,j}$ is empty, let $con_i' = con_i' \wedge \overline{w}_{i,j}$. Otherwise, let $con_i' = con_i' \wedge \overline{w}_{i,j} \wedge x_{i,j}$.

4. Let $\Gamma' = con_1' \vee \cdots con_l'$ and output Γ'.

From $\overbrace{110 \cdots 000}^{n}$, we know that only the positions of w_1 and w_2 (w_1 and w_1 themselves are not exposed) contain values of one, and it is therefore concluded that w_1 and w_2 are members of Set_a.

The matching function is efficient, since only a simple bit operation is involved. If the matching function returns *False*, the customer's subscription is rejected; if it returns *True*, the re-encryption component may be invoked, with the matched results from the matching function as an input, to indicate which re-encryption keys should be used by the indices.

The proposed policy embedding scheme, based on a policy anonymity approach, has three parts: the blinding of attributes; the encoding of attribute conjunctions with a mask; and anonymous matching between two anonymous sets. The blinding of attributes is carried out as follows:

1. Given a set of attributes $W = \{w_i\}$ from all attribute conjunctions of all customers, a data owner creates authorisation policies based on this. The elements of W are subject attributes. The data attributes can be discussed as the subject attributes and are not discussed further in this paper.
2. For each $w_i \in W$, a string $\bar{w}_i$ is randomly chosen as an alias of w_i, and w_i is replaced with $\bar{w}_i$. $\bar{w}_i$ is kept secret, so that all elements in W are unknown to home brokers, clients and adversaries.
3. For each $\bar{w}_i \in W$, $\bar{w}_i$ is replaced with $(\bar{w}_i, x_i)$ in W, where x_i is chosen with probability p as a random string, and with probability 1-p as an empty string. Thus, given an attribute conjunction with *length* as input, the length of the output conjunction varies; the attribute w_i in the attribute conjunction is replaced with $\bar{w}_i \wedge x_i$ if x_i is not empty, or with $\bar{w}_i$ if x_i is empty.

After the above steps have been carried out, W becomes $\bar{W}$.

It is assumed here that the average number of attributes in the attribute conjunctions is $length_{sae}$, which is extended to the anonymity length $length_a$ to give each attribute conjunction an anonymity space $length_a$-$length_{sae}$. Attributes are blinded using the attribute-blinding algorithm shown in in Figure 7. From Figure 7, it can be seen that the set of attributes used in the access control service is extended to $((length_a\text{-}length_{sae}) / length_a + 1)$ times the original length by appending the non-empty attributes x_i ($i = 1, 2, \cdots$) to W. For each attribute w_i in the attribute set W, its alias is defined as $\bar{w}_i$, a random string.

Figure 8 shows the algorithm for blinding the authorisation policy. If an element w_i of the authorisation policy has $(w_i, \bar{w}_i, x_i)$ in the blinded attribute set $\bar{W}$ and x_i is not empty, x_i is inserted into the authorisation policy. The element w_i is replaced with its alias $\bar{w}_i$ in the expression. The alias and added x_i are not published, and are known only by the data owner.

AUTHORISATION MANAGEMENT

Using the policy embedding scheme Π_{PE}, authorisation management becomes efficient and simple. The policy privacy authorisation management includes the functions *Customer Subscription Authorisation, New Event Authorisation, Authorisation Update,* and *Customer Revocation.*

Customer Subscription Authorisation

When a new customer B subscribes to the IoT system A, the system uses a traditional authorisation administration tool to decide whether permission is granted. If B is granted permission, A carries out the following computation:

It converts B's subject attribute expression γ into a blinded expression γ' based on Π_{PE}.

It encodes γ' using the encoding procedure in Definition 4 ($\{(BF_t, BF_1, BF_2, \cdots, BF_n)\}$).

It sends the corresponding attribute Bloom filters $\{(BF_t, BF_1, BF_2, \cdots, BF_n)\}$ to B's home brokers.

New Event Authorisation

When a new type of event is published in the IoT system, the management system extracts the authorisation expression Γ from the authorisation policies. It then carries out the following computation:

It converts the authorisation expression Γ into a blinded expression Γ' based on Π_{PE}.

Each conjunction coin' in Γ' is encoded into the Bloom filters BF_a and $BF_{a\text{-}m}$.

It sends the corresponding Bloom filters $\{(BF_a, BF_{a\text{-}m})\}$ to the home brokers.

Only a hash indicator is attached to the published event. If encoding policies have been sent for this event type, policy conversion and transmission are not carried out.

Authorisation Update

When an IoT application modifies the authorisation policy for the type of event it publishes, the access control system computes new Bloom filters $\{(BF'_a, BF'_{a-m})\}$ based on the new authorisation policy. It then sends $\{(BF'_a, BF'_{a-m})\}$ to the home brokers to replace $\{(BF_a, BF_{a-m})\}$.

Customer Revocation

When the access control system revokes a certain privilege for customer B, it computes new Bloom filters $\{(BF'_t, BF'_1, BF'_2, \cdots, BF'_n)\}$, and sends $\{(BF'_t, BF'_1, BF'_2, \cdots, BF'_n)\}$ to the home brokers to replace $\{(BF_t, BF_1, BF_2, \cdots, BF_n)\}$.

POLICY PRIVACY

Since the correctness of this access control solution is obvious, this section clarifies under which attacks from adversaries this scheme can ensure privacy. This is done by defining the concepts of policy privacy and privacy proof. Home brokers are assumed to be semi-honest, meaning that they follow predefined protocols while trying to discover as much secret information as possible. Home brokers may not collude with malicious users but may arbitrarily send any information to users. Given these privacy assumptions, a definition of the policy evaluation scheme Π_{PE} is first given, and the policy privacy model for Π_{PE} is then defined.

Definition 6: Policy Embedding Scheme Π_{PE} **(PES):** Π_{PE} consists of four algorithms, as follows:

1. *Init* : This algorithm generates the attribute set W and $\bar{\text{W}}$.
2. Encode*For*Policy$(\Gamma_i[y])$: On inputting the $y - th$ attribute conjunction of an authorisation policy Γ_i of a data owner i, this outputs some randomised code $BF_i[y]$ by invoking the *encoding procedure*.
3. Encode*ForAttributes*$(\gamma_j[x])$: On inputting the $x - th$ attribute conjunction of an attribute expression γ_j of a customer j, this outputs some randomised code $BF_j[x]$ by invoking the *encoding procedure*.

4. Matching*inPEP(BF$_j$[x], BF$_i$[y])*: On inputting the attribute codes $BF_j[x]$, $BF_i[y]$, this output whether two codes are matched, by invoking the *matching procedure*. If the algorithm outputs a negative result, the access request of the customer is rejected.

A policy embedding scheme Π_{PE} in the access control system has policy privacy if adversaries cannot win (with a non-negligible advantage) the game defined below:

Definition 7: Non-Intersection CPA (Chosen Plaintext Attack) Policy Privacy for Π_{PE}. For a policy evaluation scheme Π_{PE} and a probabilistic polynomial time adversary *Adv* running in two phases, policy privacy holds if *Adv*'s advantage is negligible in the following game:

Setup: The challenger invokes the *Init* algorithm of Π_{PE}.
Phase 1: The adversary is allowed to issue queries for the following oracles:

* O_{Encode} oracle for Encode*ForAttributes* and Encode*For*Policy of Π_{PE}.
* $O_{Match}(BF_1, BF_2)$ oracle for Matching*inPEP* of Π_{PE}.

Challenge: The adversary *Adv* submits two attribute conjunctions with equal length, m_0 and m_1. The challenge flips a random coin $\delta \in \{0,1\}$, and outputs a randomised code BF_δ to the adversary. It is assumed that no attribute of m_0, m_1 has appeared in previous queries.
Phase 2: Phase 1 is repeated, except that the adversary may not query Matching*inPEP* for BF_δ, and may not query oracles with any element in m_0, m_1
Guess: Finally, the adversary outputs its guess $\delta' \in \{0,1\}$, and wins the game if $\delta' = \delta$.

The probability is over the random bits used by the challenger and adversary, and *Adv* makes at most polynomial queries to the oracles.
The above definition implies the following:

1.   For two attribute conjunctions, the adversary cannot distinguish their encoding, i.e. is unable to link a Bloom filter to a specific attribute conjunction.

2.   *Non-intersection* requires that any element in the challenge sets m_0 and m_1 should not have appeared in previous queries, and will not appear in future queries. This indicates that the scheme Π_{PE} has weaker security than that under CPA.

3.   In this definition, the length of the challenged attribute conjunctions is required to be equal. Thus, in this scheme, although some methods are adopted to resist against length attacks, it cannot be shown that Π_{PE} is secure under a length attack.

PRF CPA Assumption: Given a pseudo-random function *PRF(seed, key, input)* in which *seed, key* are secretly set, and two messages, *PRF(seed, key, input)* chooses one message and returns one random number. It is then hard to determine which message is chosen based on the returned random number, without knowing *seed, key*.

PRF_BF Scheme: A Bloom filter *BF* is initialized to zero, and a key and n seeds are secretly generated. Given an element set *eSet*, *PRF(seed, key, input)* is invoked for each element $e \in eSet$ as input with n different seeds, giving n random numbers which are in $(0, m]$, (i.e. greater than zero and less than $m + 1$). The position in *BF* is set to one if any value of n random numbers points to this. When all elements in *eSet* have been iterated, *BF* is output.

Lemma: The PRF_BF scheme is CPA-secure if each element in the challenge set is not queried.

This conclusion is straightforward. In the security proof, multiple random numbers for each element of the challenge set can be seen as multiple oracle queries for the element during a CPA security game, in which the oracle answers each query by attaching different, fixed numbers to the queried element as different inputs. The random numbers for the multiple elements in the challenge set can be seen as multiple oracle queries for different elements. The premise that each element in the challenge set is not queried indicates that, during the *PRF_BF* challenge, no queried elements are challenged. It is natural to require that any element in the challenged set will not be queried afterwards.

Theorem 1. PES Π_{PE} has non-intersectional CPA policy privacy.

Proof. Suppose algorithm B is given a private key. It also generates a series of seeds for random generation. B initializes PRF_BF scheme with the key and seeds.

Init: Given a set W of attributes, B generates a random string $\bar{w}_i$ for each element w_i, and randomly generates $\bar{w}_i'$ based on the probability p. Replacing w_i with $(w_i, \bar{w}_i, \bar{w}_i')$ gives a new set $\bar{W}$ of attributes.

Setup: B maintains a set hash list H^{list}, which is initially empty, and responds to random oracle queries for Adv as described below.

- **Random oracle for set** $H(w_1,, \cdots w_n)$**:** If this query already appears on the H^{list}, then the predefined value is returned; otherwise, the PRF_BF scheme is invoked with the set of $\{w_1,, \cdots w_n\}$ to get a Bloom filter bf. $H(w_1,, \cdots w_n) = bf$ is defined. Finally, the tuple $(\{w_1,, \cdots w_n\}, bf)$ is added to the list H^{list} and $H(w_1,, \cdots w_n)$ is given as a response.

- $O_{\in}(BF, w)$**:** If BF can be found in H^{list} with $BF = bf$ in $(\{w_1,, \cdots w_n\}, bf)$ and $w \in \{w_1,, \cdots w_n\}$, then this returns *True*; otherwise, it returns *False*.

- $O_{\subseteq}(BF_1, BF_2)$**:** If BF_1 and BF_2 cannot be found in H^{list} with $BF_1 = bf_1$ in $(\{w_1^1,, \cdots w_n^1\}, bf_1)$ and $BF_2 = bf_2$ in $(\{w_1^2,, \cdots w_n^2\}, bf_2)$, then this returns *False*; otherwise, if $\{w_1^1,, \cdots w_n^1\} \subseteq \{w_1^2,, \cdots w_n^2\}$, then it returns *True*; otherwise it returns *False*.

Phase 1: In this stage, the adversary Adv issues a series of queries subject to the restrictions of the non-intersectional CPA game. B maintains a list K^{list}, which is initially empty.

1. **Encoding query** $O_{Encode}(w_1, \cdots, w_l)$ $(l \le n)$**:** Algorithm B finds the corresponding $\bar{w}_i, \bar{w}_i'$ for each $w_i \in \{w_1, \cdots, w_l\}$ in $\bar{W}$, and obtains a new set $sT = \{\bar{w}_i, \bar{w}_i', \cdots\}$. If the cardinality of the set sT is less than the parameter k, several random bit strings are generated and are added into sT such that the cardinality of sT is equal to k. Finally, the tuple $(\{w_1,, \cdots w_n\}, sT, H(sT))$ is added to the list K^{list} and it responds with $H(sT)$.

2. **Matching query** $O_{Match}(BF_1, BF_2)$**:** If BF_1 and BF_2 cannot be found in K^{list} with $BF_1 = H(sT_1)$ in $(\{w_1^1,, \cdots w_{l1}^1\}, sT_1, H(sT_1))$ and $BF_2 = H(sT_2)$ in $\{(w_1^1,, \cdots w_{l2}^1\}, sT_2, H(sT_2))$, then it returns *False*. Otherwise, if $\{w_1^1,, \cdots w_{l1}^1\} \subseteq \{w_1^2,, \cdots w_{l2}^2\}$, then it returns *True*; otherwise it returns *False*.

Challenge: When *Adv* decides that Phase 1 is over, it outputs two attribute conjunctions of equal length, m_0, m_1. *B* responds as follows:

1. It finds the corresponding $\bar{w}_i, \bar{w}_i'$ for each w_i of m_0 and m_1 in $\bar{W}$, and keeps w_i unchanged if there are no $\bar{w}_i, \bar{w}_i'$ in $\bar{W}$. It then obtains two new sets $sT_0 = \{\bar{w}_i, \bar{w}_i', \cdots\}$ and $sT_1 = \{\bar{w}_i, \bar{w}_i', \cdots\}$. It is simply assumed here that sT_0 and sT_1 have the same cardinality (otherwise, they are padded with random strings).
2. It submits sT_0 and sT_1 as a challenge to *PRF_BF*.

If *PRF_BF* returns BF_δ, *B* sends it to *Adv*.

Phase 2: Phase 1 is repeated, except that the adversary may not query oracles with any element in m_0, m_1, and Matching*inPEP* for BF_δ.

Guess: Eventually, the adversary *Adv* returns a guess $\delta' \in \{0,1\}$ to *B*. *B* also outputs δ' as the guess for δ for the *PRF_BF* game.

Obviously, if *Adv* has a non-negligible probability of guessing $\delta' = \delta$, *B* then has a non-negligible probability of breaking the CPA security of the *PRF_BF* scheme.

After proving the privacy of Π_{PE}, the false positive probability of the Bloom filter and the cost of Π_{PE} are analysed, since the probability of a false positive is neglected in the proof. Let the length size of a Bloom filter BF be m, the cardinality of the element set n, and the number of hash functions k. Then, the probability p of a random bit being one in BF is $p = (1 - 1/m)^{n \times k} \approx e^{-nk/m}$. The false positive probability p_f of BF is $p_f = (1 - p)^k \approx (1 - e^{-nk/m})^k$.

Let the number of attributes in a conjunction of authorisation policy be x. Then, the false positive probability of x attributes in BF_t and BF_a is

$$p_{BF} = p_f^x + p_f^{x-1}(1 - p_f) + \cdots + p_f^1(1 - p_f)^{x-1}.$$

For $BF_1, \cdots, BF_n$, the probability of false positive in checking whether BF_a is included is

$$p_{vector} = p_{BF}^y + p_{BF}^{y-1}(1 - p_{BF}) + \cdots + p_{BF}^1(1 - p_{BF})^{y-1},$$

where if $x >= n$, then $y = 1$, and otherwise $y = n + 1$.

Assuming that the average number of attributes in a single conjunction is 30, the average number of conjunctions for a customer is 50, and the false positive probability is $< 10^{-10}$ with $(0.6185)^{m/n}$, then the bit size for each conjunction is 1500 with $(0.6185)^{1500/30} = 3.69 \times 10^{-11}$, the byte size for a matrix is 1500/8*32=6000 ≈ 6k, and the byte size for a customer is 50 * 6k = 300k. Thus, a home broker needs to provide 300k of storage for the attribute information of a customer. Calculated in the same way, the storage needed for each rule of a data event is 0.187k=187 bytes, and that for the whole policy for the data event is 9k. If the number of attributes in a conjunction is lower, then the storage cost is greatly reduced. Reusing the stored policies in home brokers can dramatically reduce the communication cost, since event names in IoT are relatively stable, and only certain indicators need to be embedded into a published event.

COMBINING ACCESS CONTROL WITH CONFIDENTIALITY

The publisher may not completely trust the publish/subscribe middleware and the underlying network, and may desire to resist against eavesdropping events. Thus, the access control scheme needs to be improved and end-to-end encryption of events needs to be provided; this improved scheme should work together with a confidentiality mechanism to satisfy all the user's requirements. The access control scheme is improved using SDNs. The policy-matching scheme is the same as in the above discussion, but policy-matching operations are completed by SDN switches, since the flow tables used in these SDN switches are convenient for carrying out the bit-operations of Bloom filters (the bit operations in SDN switches are not discussed here, and the focus is only on key issues). The encryption scheme in this access control solution is separated from the policy-matching scheme, so that a separated confidentiality scheme can flexibly work together with the policy-matching scheme.

Introducing the Encryption Scheme Into the Access Control Solution

The work in Goyal et al. (2006) presented an attribute-based encryption scheme $\Re$ using access trees; however, this cannot be used directly in the current work, since the current scheme has different requirements:

1. It needs to support secret-sharing, which is not considered or supported by $\Re$.
2. When event confidentiality is needed, any encryption schemes should be able to be combined with the policy-matching scheme, and encryption operations should be carried out by clients.

A complete description of the attribute-based encryption representation scheme Π is not given. This is complementary to policy privacy representation, i.e. the latter is a header indicating the operations of the former. For comparison and clarity, the scheme Π is described in Definition 8 below, over parts of the encryption scheme $\Re$ presented in chapter 4 of (Goyal et al., 2006), in which there are four algorithms: *Setup, KeyGeneration, Encryption,* and *Decryption.*

Let G_1, G_2 be two multiplicative cyclic groups with prime order p. Let g be one generator of G_1 and $\dot{e}$ be a bilinear map, $\dot{e}: G_1 \times G_1 \rightarrow G_2$. The Lagrange coefficient $\Delta_{s,S}$ is defined for $s \in Z_p$ and the set S of elements in Z_p (Goyal et al., 2006) as follows: $\Delta_{s,S}(c) = \prod_{t\in S, t\neq s} \dfrac{c-t}{s-t}$.

Definition 8: Attribute-Based Secret Representation Scheme Π for Encryption

1. ***Setup:*** For the universal attributes $\mu = \{1, 2, \cdots, n\}$, the algorithm randomly chooses a number $l_s \in Z_p$ for each $s \in \mu$. The algorithm *Setup* in $\Re$ can be invoked to generate the public parameters *pbPar* $L_1 = g^{l_1}, L_2 = g^{l_2}, \cdots, L_n = g^{l_n}, Y = \dot{e}(g, g)$, with private parameters *pbPar* $l_1, \cdots, l_n$.
2. ***Initialisation:*** For an event topic *tp*, the publisher i creates an access tree $T_{i,tp}$, and prepares a secret random value $\alpha_{i,tp}$ for the root node of

$T_{i,tp}$, i.e. a secret value $\alpha_{i,tp}$ corresponding to $T_{i,tp}$ as the secret base of policy presentation.

3. **KeyGeneration.** Given the attributes γ of a user j, a publisher i will create another access tree $T_{i,tp,j}$ for j (i.e. γ satisfying $T_{i,tp,j}$). It will also generate a secret random value $\beta_{i,tp,j}$ and prepare $\alpha_{i,tp}\beta_{i,tp,j}$ for the root node of $T_{i,tp,j}$.

   a. The publisher i invokes the *KeyGeneration* algorithm in $\Re$ with γ and $T_{i,tp,j}$ as the input, outputting $D'_y = g^{q_y(0)/l_s}$ for each leaf node y in the tree $T_{i,tp,j}$.

   b. The publisher i invokes the *KeyGeneration* algorithm in $\Re$, with γ and $T_{i,tp}$ as the input, outputting $D_x = g^{(q_x(0)-q_x(0)\beta_{i,tp,j})/l_s}$ for the leaf node x of $T_{i,tp}$ with the node attribute in γ.

Then, $creS = \{\{D_x\}, \{D'_y\}\}$.

4. **GeneratingRepresentation**: Given the access tree $T_{i,tp}$ and a certain time period, a publisher i chooses a random number r for this period, and partially invokes the *Encryption* algorithm of $\Re$ to compute $c'_k = (L_k)^r = g^{rl_k}$ for each leaf in $T_{i,tp}$, without encrypting messages.

Publisher i obtains the public parameter set $par = \{c'_k\}$ of the secret policy representation, which is published. The secret policy representation is $dCre = \dot{e}(g,g)^{r\alpha_{i,tp}} = Y^{r\alpha_{i,tp}}$, which is not directly published.

5. **ReconstructingRepresentation**: When the public parameter $pbPar$, representation parameter par, and authorisation credentials $creS = \{\{D_x\}, \{D'_y\}\}$ are given, the secret policy representation can be computed as follows:

   a. When the *DecryptionNode* function in the *Decryption* algorithm of $\Re$ is invoked with $\{D_x\}$, $T_{i,tp}$, and par as input, $RT\_T_{i,tp}(root) = Y^{\alpha_{i,tp}r - \alpha_{i,tp}\beta_{i,tp,j}r}$ is output.

b. When the *DecryptionNode* function in the *Decryption* algorithm of $\Re$ is invoked with $\{D_y'\}$, $T_{i,tp,j}$, and *par* as input, $RT\_T_{i,tp,j}(root) = Y^{\alpha_{i,tp}\beta_{i,tp,j}r}$ is output.

c. The secret policy representation is then computed:

$$RT = RT\_T_{i,tp}(root) \cdot RT\_T_{i,tp,j}(root) = Y^{r\alpha_{i,tp}}.$$

The differences between the current scheme Π and the encryption scheme $\Re$ reported in Goyal et al. (2006) are as follows:

1. **Private keys:** In $\Re$, there is one set of private keys corresponding to the user's attributes, while in Π, there are two sets of private keys, one corresponding to a publisher's topic issued to SDN controllers, and the other corresponding to the subscriber issued to the subscriber itself. This results in secret sharing in Π, i.e. computing the shared secret $Y^{r\alpha_{i,tp}}$.

2. **Ciphertexts:** In Π, *GeneratingRepresentation* and *ReconstructingRepresentation* together output a special ciphetext $c = (\gamma, \{c_i = L_i^r\}_{i\in\gamma}, \dot{Y}^{r-r^2_{tp,j}} \text{ or } \dot{Y}^{r^2_{tp,j}})$, where r is a random number for the current time period; $\{c_i = L_i^r\}$ is computed and published by the publisher (using *GeneratingRepresentation*); the third element in c can be $\dot{Y}^{r-r\beta_{i,tp,j}}$ computed by SDN controllers (using *ReconstructingRepresentation*) or $\dot{Y}^{r\beta_{i,tp,j}}$ computed by the subscriber (using *ReconstructingRepresentation*); and $\dot{Y}^r = Y^{r\alpha_{i,tp}}$ is a shared secret between the controller and subscriber. In $\Re$, the output ciphertext is $c = (\gamma, c' = m\dot{Y}^r, \{c_i = L_i^r\}_{i\in\gamma})$, while in Π no actual message m is encrypted.

Access Control With Encryption

In the current scheme, access control enhanced by confidentiality is constructed over an SDN. During policy matching, the matching between authorisation policies and users' attributes is carried out via matching between the flow entries in SDN switches and event headers, i.e. users' attributes correspond to flow entries in the SDN switches connected to the users (this is based on Bloom filters in the previous sections). Following this, two-party secret sharing is carried out to secretly compute secrets, with the aim of defeating malicious SDN controllers and subscribers. Each subscriber is connected to a local switch and controller, and these are treated as the home broker for the delivery of events, with the local SDN controller regarded as a home controller, and the SDN switch as a home switch.

Credentials are split into two parts, one corresponding to a topic and the other to a subscriber. The former is stored on the home controllers, which can be used to compute one part of the secret. The latter is stored in the accessing layer of the subscriber (i.e. it is transparent to subscribers), and can be used to compute the other part of the secret. The subscriber and its home controller can collaborate to compute the secret without disclosing it.

In order to achieve these objectives, a two-party protocol is used between a subscriber (its access layer for cryptographic operations is transparent to itself) and its home controller, to secretly compute the secret. A homomorphic encryption scheme ise used as the basic confidentiality mechanism (Gentry, 2011; Duan et al., 2016), and a homomorphic hash function (Gazzoni et al., 2006; Krohn et al., 2004) as the two-party computation base. To some extent, a homomorphic deterministic encryption function can be used to realise a homomorphic hash function. The two-party computation protocol Ξ of a secret is illustrated in Figures 9 and 10; this includes a part A, shown in Figure 9, and a part B, shown in Figure 10. The protocol Ξ is formed as follows:

1. The home controller computes its part *dCre.tp* of the secret representation, based on the stored credentials $creS.\{D_x\}$ and the public parameter *par*. *dCre.tp* is then encrypted, *encrypt(dCre.tp)*, under the public key of the publisher, and *encrypt(dCre.tp)* is sent to the subscriber's access layer.
2. The subscriber's access layer computes its part *dCre.subscriber* of the secret policy representation based on the stored authorisation credentials $creS.\{D_y'\}$ and the public parameter *par*. *dCre.subscriber* is encrypted: *encrypt(dCre.subscriber)*. The subscriber's access layer computes the encryption of the secret policy representation *dCre*: *encrypt(dCre)* = *encrypt(dCre.tp)* • *encrypt(dCre.subscriber)* and then stores it.

In the above two-party computation protocol, there is an implicit underlying authentication channel that identifies the controller and the subscriber. When encrypted, the secret is not disclosed to the subscriber's access layer or the home controller.

Figure 9. Part A of protocol Ξ

$\Xi.A:$ **Home controller** Con_j **of** j
1. dCre.tp = Reconstructing Re resentation(creS.{ D_x }, par)
$cipher_{tp} = encrypt(dCre.tp)$
2. $cipher_{tp} \xrightarrow{send} j$

Figure 10. Part B of protocol Ξ

$\Xi.B:$ **Subscriber** j **-** *Access layer*
1. dCre.subscriber =
Reconstruc ting Re resentation(creS.{ D'_y }, par)
$hash_{sub} = Hash(dCre.subscriber)$
2. $hash_{sub} \xrightarrow{send} Con_j$
3. $cipher_{tp} \xleftarrow{receive} Con_j$
4. $encrypt(dCre) = cipher_{tp} \cdot encrypt(dCre.subscriber)$

Given the secret-sharing mechanism of the two-party protocol, the policy matching scheme described in the above sections can be combined with certain homomorphic encryption schemes to resist against collusion and to provide confidentiality. This enhanced policy-matching scheme for the publish/subscribe middleware over SDN has the following characteristics:

1. The home controller of j stores the credentials corresponding to the access tree for event topic tp, i.e. it stores $creS.\{D_x\}$. The access layer of the publish/subscribe middleware deployed on subscriber j (also called the access layer of j) stores the credentials corresponding to the access tree for j, i.e. it stores $creS.\{D'_y\}$.

2. After the publisher publishes the public representation parameter *par* for the current period, the controller and the access layer carry out the two-party computation protocol Ξ, in which the access layer stores the ciphertext of the secret representation.

3. When it publishes an event e, the publisher embeds the secret representation $dCre$ into the event's ciphertext $c = encrypt(e)$ using homomorphic addition, i.e. $c = encrypt(e + dCre)$, where $encrypt()$ is a homomorphic encryption function.

4. Policy matching between the event header and the flow entries is carried out in the same way as described in previous sections.
5. The local access layer of the publish/subscriber middleware carries out the homomorphic operations necessary to remove the embedded secret policy representation by its stored *encrypt(dCre)*. That is to say,

$$c' = c - encrypt(dCre) = encrypt(e + dCre) - encrypt(dCre) = encrypt(e).$$

6. c' is delivered to the subscriber.
7. The subscriber uses its private key to decrypt c' to recover the event e.

In Step 4, the access layer converts a ciphertext under the public key of the publisher into ciphertext under the public key of the subscribers, such that the subscribers only carry out cryptographic operations with respect to their own keys.

This idea is similar to that in Duan et al. (2016), with the following differences:

1. The access tree in the current method provides more expressiveness for authorisation policies and their matching, while the work in Duan et al. (2016) only allows for a linear policy structure, i.e. attribute conjunctions without disjunctions and their mixtures.
2. The access control functions in the current method are separated from the encryption scheme, with the ability to integrate these on demand (e.g. flow-based authorisation enforcement on switches working with independent encryption on clients). This provides flexibility when deploying security mechanisms.
3. Policy matching in the current method is carried out by SDN switches, i.e., matching between flow entries and event headers ensures policy matching.
4. The key difference is that the current solution can resist against collusion between corrupted subscribers and home brokers, i.e. events cannot be sent to uncorrupted subscribers using credentials arising from collusion.

CONCLUSION

In IoT scenarios, named, signed and potentially encrypted content forms a solid foundation for IoT security. The access control mechanism for IoT services should include an independent data layer and an application layer, and these two layers should be both opaque to network entities and suitable for IoT communication features such as event naming, caching, and so on. A two-layer framework for access control for IoT services is therefore proposed. When integrating network capabilities, the data layer ensures protection of the IoT events, and the application layer ensures protection of the services. The principle of anonymous sets is used to design the policy embedding scheme, which is presented as the foundation for an access control service with policy privacy. In this scheme, an alternation method plays a key role; this uses a function that checks for the inclusion of anonymous sets, which assumes the basic function of an anonymous set, i.e. an anonymous set membership-checking function. In the access control system, the IoT application grants flexible authorisation in the same way as traditional access control system; home brokers can securely and efficiently execute the delegated policy enforcing function, in which policies are encoded with a blinded mask and are anonymously matched to realise policy privacy. This access control scheme can be enhanced by confidentiality.

REFERENCES

Anderson, A. (2007). *Web services profile of XACML (WS-XACML), version 1.0*. OASIS standard specification. Retrieved from http://www.oasis-open.org/committees/download.php/24951/xacml-3.0-profile-webservices-spec-v1-wd-10-en.pdf

Bakken, D. E., Bose, A., Hauser, C. H., Whitehead, D. E., & Zweigle, G. C. (2011). *Smart generation and transmission with coherent, real-time data*. Retrieved from http://www.gridstat.net/trac/#

Bertino, E., Squicciarini, A. C., Maritino, L., & Paci, F. (2006). An adaptive access control model for Web services. *International Journal of Web Services Research*, *3*(3), 27–60. doi:10.4018/jwsr.2006070102

Bhatti, R., Bertino, E., & Ghafoor, A. (2004). A trust-based context-aware access control model for Web-services. *Proceedings of the IEEE International Conference on Web Services (ICWS)*. 10.1109/ICWS.2004.1314738

Bonomi, F., Mitzenmacher, M., Panigrah, R., Singh, S., & Varghese, G. (2006). Beyond Bloom filters: From approximate membership checks to approximate state machines. *Computer Communication Review*, *36*(4), 315–326. doi:10.1145/1151659.1159950

Burton, H. B. (1970). Space/time trade-offs in hash coding with allowable errors. *Communications of the ACM*, *13*(7), 422–426. doi:10.1145/362686.362692

Cheung, L., & Newport, C. C. (2007). Provable secure ciphertext policy ABE. *ACM Conference on Computer and Communications Security, CCS 2007*, 456-465.

Doshi, N., & Jinwala, D. (2012). Hidden access structure ciphertext policy attribute based encryption with constant length ciphertext. Advanced Computing. *Network Security*, 515–523.

Duan, L., Liu, D. X., Zhang, Y., Chen, S. P., Liu, R. P., Cheng, B., & Chen, J. L. (2016). Secure data-centric access control for smart grid services based on publish/subscribe systems. ACM Transactions on Internet Technology, 16(4). *Article*, *23*, 1–17.

Gazzoni, Luiz, Filho, & Politécnica. (2006). *Demonstrating data possession and uncheatable data transfer*. IACR Cryptology ePrint Archive.

Gentry, C. (2011). *Fully homomorphic encryption without bootstrapping*. Retrieved from http://eprint.iacr.org

Goyal, V., Pandey, O., Sahai, A., & Waters, B. (2006). Attribute-based encryption for fine-grained access control of encrypted data. *ACM Conference on Computer and Communications Security*, 89-98. 10.1145/1180405.1180418

Goyal, V., Pandey, O., Sahaiz, A., & Waters, B. (2006). Attribute-based encryption for fine-grained access control of encrypted data. *Proceedings of the 13th ACM Conference on Computer & Communications Security*, 89-98. 10.1145/1180405.1180418

Kagal, L., Paolucci, M., Srinivasan, N., Denker, G., Finin, T., & Sycara, K. (2004). Authorization and privacy for semantic Web services. *IEEE Intelligent Systems*, *19*(4), 50–56. doi:10.1109/MIS.2004.23

Kim, Y. S., & Heo, J. (2012). Device authentication protocol for smart grid systems using homomorphic hash. *Journal of Communications and Networks (Seoul)*, *14*(6), 606–613. doi:10.1109/JCN.2012.00026

Krohn, M. N., Freedman, M. J., & Mazieres, D. (2004). On-the-fly verification of rateless erasure codes for efficient content distribution. *IEEE Symposium on Security and Privacy*, 226-240. 10.1109/SECPRI.2004.1301326

Li, X., Gu, D., Ren, Y., Ding, N., & Yuan, K. (2012). *Efficient ciphertext-policy attribute based encryption with hidden policy*. Internet and Distributed Computing Systems. doi:10.1007/978-3-642-34883-9_12

Masaud-Wahaishi, A., & Gaouda, A. (2011). Intelligent monitoring and control architecture for future electrical power systems. *The 2nd International Conference on Ambient Systems, Networks and Technologies*. 10.1016/j.procs.2011.07.101

Muller, S., & Katzenbeisser, S. (2012). *Hiding the policy in cryptographic access control*. Security and Trust Management. doi:10.1007/978-3-642-29963-6_8

Nishide, T., Yoneyama, K., & Ohta, K. (2009). Attribute-based encryption with partially hidden ciphertext policies. *IEICE Transactions*, *92-A*(1), 22–32. doi:10.1587/transfun.E92.A.22

Oggier, F. E., & Datta, A. (2010). Self-repairing homomorphic codes for distributed storage systems. *30th IEEE International Conference on Computer Communications*, 1215-1223.

Paci, F., Mecella, M., Ouzzani, M., & Bertino, E. (2011). ACConv: An access control model for conversational Web services. *ACM Transactions on the Web*, *5*(3), 2011. doi:10.1145/1993053.1993055

Saar, C. (2003). Spectral Bloom filters. In *Proceedings of ACMSIGMOD International Conference on Management of Data*. San Diego, CA: ACM Press.

Smart Grid Policy. (2009). Federal Energy Regulatory Commission. [Docket No. PL09-4-000]

Wang, Q. H., & Li, N. H. (2010). Satisfiability and resiliency in workflow authorization systems. *ACM Transactions on Information and System Security*, *13*(4), 40. doi:10.1145/1880022.1880034

Waters. (2011). Ciphertext-policy attribute-based encryption: An expressive, efficient, and provably secure realization. *Public Key Cryptography*.

Wonohoesodo, R., & Tari, Z. (2004). A role-based access control for Web services. *Proceedings of the IEEE International Conference on Services Computing (SCC)*. 10.1109/SCC.2004.1357989

Yu, S., Ren, K., & Lou, W. (2008). Attribute-based content distribution with hidden policy. *The 4th Workshop on Secure Network Protocols*.

Zhang, Y., & Chen, J. L. (2012). Wide-area IoT system with distributed security framework. *Journal of Communications and Networks (Seoul)*, *14*(6), 597–605. doi:10.1109/JCN.2012.00025

Zhang, Y., & Chen, J. L. (2012). Wide-area SCADA system with distributed security framework. *Journal of Communications and Networks (Seoul)*, *14*(6), 597–605. doi:10.1109/JCN.2012.00025

Zhang & Chen. (2013). Data-centric access control with confidentiality for collaborating smart grid services based on publish subscribe paradigm. *ICDCS-NFSP, 2013*.

Chapter 7

Runtime Monitoring of IoT Services to Guarantee Properties

ABSTRACT

Ensuring that a critical information infrastructure remains in a safe and secure state is a mandatory requirement. When IoT services related to such an infrastructure are open to the internet, existing execution monitoring technologies do not work well to protect it; internal malware may compromise and subvert the monitoring mechanism itself, and the safety properties will interact with its security property. In this chapter, an isolation-based solution is proposed to enforce property policies for runtime IoT services. First, the issue of isolation-based service trace observation is addressed by establishing and modelling a virtual channel. Then, the issue of isolation-based policy enforcement is discussed, and the incompleteness and inconsistency of trace knowledge observed in the virtual channel is addressed. Finally, physical systems are introduced into the proposed runtime monitors, and the controllability of IoT services is discussed as an example of the enforcement of service properties. Several experiments are carried out to demonstrate this solution.

INTRODUCTION

In existing work on execution monitoring technologies, runtime monitors are often embedded into protected systems to check and modify each action using property policies, or to actively build a communication channel between

DOI: 10.4018/978-1-5225-7622-8.ch007

themselves and the targets (unsatisfactory application actions are passed to the monitors for checking/correction). Internal malware may compromise and subvert both these applications and the monitoring mechanism itself, if these are within the same environment. In order to achieve isolation-based protection for IoT services, certain technologies based on virtual machines (VMs) can be utilised, which can place runtime monitors outside of the environment of the protected target with isolation. Although the protected services and the protection monitor are isolated and have no active communication channel, existing VM introspection methods and semantic reconstruction methods (Jiang et al., 2007) can be used to reconstruct the VM memory based on low-level "0/1" snapshots, and to search for execution information about service actions within this reconstructed memory. Event flows on virtual network bridges managed by a virtual machine monitor (VMM) in the physical host are intercepted as a complementary means of VM introspection. Communication packets from VMs on industrial buses can also be intercepted using an isolation method. This type of isolation-based event observation provides a basis for the use of runtime monitors in isolated running environments.

Unfortunately, the semantic reconstruction method is passive (non-intrusive) and inefficient, and cannot conveniently capture all service events (executed service actions). The communication interception method is not trustworthy over virtual network bridges, since adversaries may forge messages/events or interleave these events in realistic interconnecting environments. In other words, the events observed using isolation methods may not have been produced by the protected services; some of these can be trusted as moving from/to the protected target, while others are uncertain. Isolation-based event observation methods can be abstracted in the form of a virtual channel that is controlled by adversaries who can forge events in the channel or discard them. In order to build an isolation-based runtime monitor for the virtual channel, each event is assigned a level of certainty indicating its trustworthiness, and the monitor operates based on the trustworthiness of these events.

In order to enforce property policies for a target system, the work of Basin et al. (2013), Ligatti and Reddy (2010), and Dolzhenko et al. (2015) adopted automata-based runtime monitors to check the system's trace and discarded or edited the actions of the system based on the results of this checking. Although the current work uses the methods and ideas of this study, there are several differences, as follows:

1. **Non-Intrusion:** In existing works, protected systems are recompiled to integrate inline runtime monitors, hooks are placed into the targets, or

communication sinks are embedded to establish active communication channels. These methods are intrusive, i.e. the program code of the protected systems is directly affected or modified. In the current work, the runtime monitor is non-intrusive and transparent, and is based on VM introspection methods. The problem of controlling a non-intrusive action is addressed from two perspectives:

a.   The monitor mediates between a physical system and the IoT services, and checks/enforces each service action from/to the physical system by controlling all physical I/O channels of the VMM host. The primary goal of monitoring is to protect the physical system; each action is checked before it is sent to the physical system through I/O channels. If an action sent to the physical world violates certain properties of the physical targets, it is discarded or edited. A second monitoring goal is to check whether IoT services are in undesirable states and can make the physical system dangerous; these are then regulated based on the results of checking.

b.   In this monitor, besides the editing of actions sent to the physical world, possible runtime enforcement actions for an IoT service include the sending of new events to the target service to adjust its execution, since the service-oriented principle (Erl, 2005) states that the runtime behaviour of a service can be adjusted by invoking its function interfaces and management interfaces, i.e. by publishing events to it. The isolated monitor proposed here can delete, re-install and restore the VMs hosting the services through VM management interfaces provided by VMM.

2.   **Introducing Certainty Into Runtime Monitors:** When the monitor checks the service trace using the property specification, an event with high trustworthiness represents the actual execution of a service action. The certainty of an event is used to reflect the possibility of attacks from adversaries, i.e. attaching a certainty to each observed event can measure its trustworthiness (Dubois et al., 1994; Lang, 2000; Dubois & Prade, 2014).

In classical runtime monitors, a set of events is assumed to be orderly and complete, forming a true trace that reflects an application's actually running states (allowing the application to be corrupted). However, in a virtual channel, adversaries may discard/forge events or interleave them, and a series of observed events ordered temporally may not be a true trace of a given service. The certainty-based reasoning used here handles this incomplete and inconsistent information about the trace, meaning that certainty is introduced into runtime monitors.

3. **Need for Service Models:** The proposed monitor works against security attacks, such as the corruption of a sub-service of an IoT service system; this requires the explicit definition of environments by modelling the virtual channel. These modelling requirements constitute a point of difference for this runtime monitor, since a model of a protected system forms an input for the monitor, alongside property specifications and action traces. It should be assumed that the model is publicly known by adversaries, and that all service properties will be checked over the virtual channel's knowledge. In classical runtime monitors, only the property specifications and action traces are used to generate efficient checking algorithms, and the capabilities of these are limited; for example, they may be unavailable for safety enforcement under certain security attacks. In addition, the certainty of a logical consequence should be greater than the inconsistency level of the observed traces. This requires that service models and definite service running observations are used as a priori knowledge in order to reduce inconsistency. In order to ensure the performance of runtime monitoring, some parts of the model with respect to current system states are instantiated to expand the trace knowledge, and property checking is carried out on the trace.

The proposed monitor works within the mandatory results automata (MRA) framework proposed in (Dolzhenko et al., 2015), in which the monitor provides interfaces for interaction with the protected target system, i.e. for obtaining requests from the target, sending actions to execution environments, and responding to the target with results from the execution system. However, the MRA framework did not explicitly discuss or model the communication channel between the runtime monitor and the applications. In the current work, the communication channel is explicitly modelled, and the outcome of enforcing property policies is a dynamic gaming result between the monitor and the virtual channel.

It is not possible to verify an IoT service's runtime properties based solely on observed events, since the IoT service monitors, controls, and coordinates a physical system, and the nature of this physical system needs to be described. The aim of enforcing IoT service properties is to keep the managed physical system in a desirable state, for example, in a controllable state. IoT resources represent physical entities in the information world and are foundational in IoT applications. An IoT service can be considered as a set of actions performed on IoT resources, and is defined by standard action interfaces, behaviour specifications, and its semantics. Multiple IoT services can interact with each other to act as a composite IoT service. Action theories (McCarthy & Hayes, 1969; Kowalski & Sergot, 1986; Bultan, 2000) are therefore used here to formalise a IoT service for runtime property enforcement. An actual IoT service system is then formally specified using a hierarchical action description method that includes IoT resources and IoT services. In addition, the monitor should also support the checking of continuous dynamics, since this is a common situation for IoT resources.

After descriptions of the hierarchical IoT service and virtual channel model are given, the runtime monitor of IoT services is constructed based on a logical deduction approach using SMT (Barrett et al., 2007), (Sebastiani, 2007), (Kruglov, 2013). The difference between IoT services and general Web services guides the design of this monitor, as shown in Table 1. From Table 1, it can be seen that runtime monitors for IoT services should be physical-system-oriented, reliable, rigidly formalised, actuation-focused, and efficient.

To the best of the authors' knowledge, there are no isolation-based works that construct physical-system-oriented monitors that guard against active attacks from channel-controlling adversaries. The contributions of this chapter are detailed below, and together these support the proposed solution, as illustrated in Figure 1.

1. **The Issue of Isolation-Based Service Trace Observation is Addressed:** A virtual channel is established to observe isolation-based service operation, in which a semantic reconstruction method is used to capture some of the execution traces of service actions in VM memory, and an interception method is used to control all interactions between the

Table 1. Differences between IoT services and Web services

	IoT services	Web services
Scope	Monitor and control physical devices and systems	These are general, and can manage businesses over IoT services
Deployed	Near physical systems for real-time coordination	In data centres
QoS	Reliability, controllability, safety, security; need to be rigid	User experience, service availability; need to be flexible
Interface	Action/behaviour/property interfaces. They are event-driven	Action/behaviour interfaces
Runtime verification	Mandatory. Properties enforced at runtime	Not mandatory

Figure 1. Contributions combine to give a monitoring solution

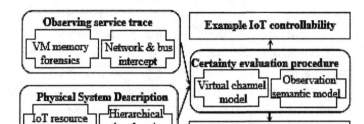

physical world and IoT services. Service events (executed actions) observed in the virtual channel are chaotic without being true service traces. The virtual channel is therefore modelled on an abstraction of the isolation-based runtime environments of monitors for IoT services. A unified monitoring framework is proposed to handle these chaotic events and models.

The most challenging task is to expressively model the virtual channel in such a way that the requirement for the verification of different properties in different environments can be satisfied by enlarging or reducing the knowledge of the virtual channel. For example, in an open and interconnecting environment, the functional safety of IoT services is affected by information security problems or requirements. When a sub-service is corrupted, the knowledge of the virtual channel should be enlarged through knowledge of the inner states and private data of the sub-service, and the safety of the composite service should be checked over this enlarged knowledge and any attacks that can be inferred from this. The expressiveness is achieved from two perspectives, as follows:

a. Service models are as assumed to be public knowledge that is known by adversaries. For online monitoring, runtime service models are used to represent instantiated service models and are then not only used to enlarge trace knowledge but are also integrated into certainty-based logical reasoning.

b. Adversaries are modelled by their inferring capabilities rather than their behaviour, while they cannot be predicted or controlled. Adversaries observe both the events produced by services and publicly known service models to form their knowledge. Based on this knowledge, they can infer and launch attacks. In addition, the trustworthiness of events is introduced to reflect possible attacks from the channel.

2. **The Issue of Isolation-Based Policy Enforcement is Addressed:** An "out-of-the-box" property enforcement solution is proposed for IoT services running in virtual machines, where if the current event cannot satisfy the properties or has low certainty, it is discarded or an alternative action with high certainty is chosen to be sent to the physical system. The handling of the inconsistency and incompleteness of the trace observation depends on certainty-based logical reasoning. A certainty evaluation procedure is designed to act as an underlying decision procedure for SMT solvers (Barrett et al., 2007; Sebastiani, 2007; Kruglov, 2013); this computes a set of alternative actions that can replace a violation action based on a flow event structure (van Glabbeek & Goltz, 2004), i.e. a runtime service model.

    One challenging task is to exhaustively select the possible world with the greatest possible certainty, in order to give a trustworthy verification of an observed trace. Whether or not the certainty evaluation procedure is decidable will be important in improving the performance of exhaustive methods. The construction of the certainty evaluation procedure is presented here, and it is also shown to be decidable. In addition, the high inconsistency of trace knowledge is also handled and reduced in order to ensure that the reasoning is effective, i.e. the certainty of the logical consequence is greater than the level of inconsistency.

3. **The Issue of Introducing Physical Systems Into Runtime Monitors is Addressed:** Physical entities are modelled as IoT resources in the information world, and IoT services are modelled as a set of actions performed on these entities. Using action theories (McCarthy & Hayes, 1969; Kowalski & Sergot, 1986; Bultan, 2000), a hierarchical action description method is proposed that specifies an IoT service system, with IoT resources as action effects and IoT services as a scenario-varying action system with certain preconditions and ramifications. As an example, the enforcement of the controllability of the physical system is discussed, where the controllability problem is defined from a malicious channel viewpoint, and a solution to the problem is sought using a certainty-based prediction method. Unlike the work in (Basin et al., 2013), in which an uncontrollable action means that the action cannot be controlled, in the current work an uncontrollable action cannot be directly controlled but can be indirectly controlled.

Furthermore, unlike the work in Cimatti et al (2013), Gamage et al. (2010), Basin et al. (2013), the proposed monitor can enforce controllability against security attacks such as dynamic corruption of a part of the system. This corruption leads to an expansion of the virtual channel's knowledge. Enforcement of controllability is carried out based on the same knowledge and the attacks that can be inferred from it. In addition, the proposed monitor uses runtime service models and definite observations as a priori knowledge to estimate the certainty of events and to resist attacks from the virtual channel with a high level of trustworthiness. Experiments and evaluations are performed to show that this solution is efficient.

PRELIMARIES

Event Structure

A running service can be represented by a flow event structure. A flow event structure considers a concurrent system as a set of events (van Glabbeek & Goltz, 2004) with "flow", meaning "possible immediate causes".

Definition 1: Flow Event Structure (van Glabbeek & Goltz, 2004): *A flow event structure is represented by a tuple $\Xi = (ES, \prec, \#)$ where:*

$-ES$ *is a set of events;*

$- \prec \subseteq ES \times ES$ *is an irreflexive flow relationship, and $e_1 \prec e_2$ denotes e_1 as the immediate possible cause of e_2;*

$- \# \subseteq ES \times ES$ *is a symmetric conflict relationship, and $e_1 \# e_2$ denotes that e_1 and e_2 do not occur at the same time.*

Given a set of events ES, its causality closures can be computed because the causality relation is transitive, i.e. $e_1 \prec e_2$ and $e_2 \prec e_3$ meaning $e_1 \prec e_3$ to get a closure $\{e_1, e_2, e_3\}$, a subset of ES. For the two conflict relations $e_1 \# e_2$ and $e_2 \# e_3$, there is no $e_1 \# e_3$. The conflict closure $\{e_1, e_2, e_3\}$ of ES means that $e_1 \# e_2$, $e_2 \# e_3$ and $e_1 \# e_3$. If e_1, e_2 have neither causality nor conflict, they are referred to as concurrent, and each can be considered to be a special closure.

Definition 2: Well-Behaved Event Structure. *The flow event structure* $\Xi = (ES, \prec, \#)$ *is called well-behaved if the following conditions hold (the service is also called well-behaved):*

1. *There is no causality cycle in* ES.
2. *For two events in* ES, *causality and conflict relations do not exist at the same time, i.e. no two events have both a causality closure and a conflict closure.*

Assumption 1: Finite Closure Assumption for Service: Given a service, its events form a flow event structure, and the number of event closures included in the flow event structure is a polynomial of the event number in the service if the flow event structure is well-behaved.

Possibilistic Logic

Following the work in Dubois (1994) and Lang, (2000), predicates are also imposed on the behaviour of the protected system to obtain a knowledge set, and the first-order logic (FOL) (Barrett et al., 2007; Sebastiani, 2007; Kruglov, 2013) language is used. An atom set contains the logical constants False (0) and True (1), predicates with terms as input, and certain equations between terms. A literal denotes an atom or its negation. A formula φ is made up of a set of literals and the logical symbols connecting these literals. A sentence is then a formula with no free variables. A formula is called satisfiable if it is True under some interpretation; otherwise, it is unsatisfiable. A theory is described by a set of sentences. The satisfiability of a formula constrained by some theories is called SMT (Barrett et al., 2007; Sebastiani, 2007; Kruglov, 2013). SMT technologies have been extensively studied in recent years, and many efficient SMT solvers have been developed in which desirable decision procedures for background theories have extended SMT into practical industries, such as linear/non-linear arithmetic theory solvers (Basu et al., 2006; Borralleras et al., 2012) and their combinations (Nelson & Oppen, 1979; Shostak, 1984).

When observing the execution of IoT services, the issue of whether an observed event really represents an actual executed service action is uncertain in hostile environments. Inspired by studies of possibilistic logic (Dubois et al., 1994; Lang, 2000; Dubois & Prade, 2014), a level of certainty is attached to literals, thus labelling the trustworthiness of events, and this is called event certainty. Compound certainty is then calculated for formulas.

Possibilistic logic was proposed to enable reasoning under conditions of incomplete and inconsistent knowledge, where the certainty level is expressed by an upper bound and a lower bound, and the latter is called a necessity measure. These two bounds are computed based on possible worlds (i.e. a formula interpretation), and the distribution of possible worlds decides the measures by which the most probable world can be evaluated. Minimisation of the decomposability property of the necessity measures can be used to estimate the most probable world for conjunctions such that the necessity measure is adopted. In addition, Proposition 1 of (Lang, 2000) states that the distribution of possible worlds can be constructed from the certainty attached to literals, and the necessity measure can be computed based on the constructed distribution. Using this method (Lang, 2000; Dubois & Prade, 2014), a definition of necessity measures is given below.

Definition 8: Necessity-Valued Knowledge (Dubois et al., 1994; Lang, 2000): *A necessity-valued knowledge is a finite set with a conjunction relation in the set elements:* $\Lambda = \{(\phi_i, \rho_i) \mid i = 1, \cdots, n\}$, *where:*

1. *A pair* (ϕ_i, ρ_i) *is a necessity-valued formula,* ϕ_i *is a classical first-order closed formula and* ρ_i *is a real number in the range* $[0,1]$;
2. *A necessity measure* N *on a formula is a function from the set of logical formulas to a real number in* $[0,1]$, *and the computation of* N *is as follows:*
   a. $N(True) = 1$;
   b. $N(p \wedge q) = \min(N(p), N(q))$, *and*
   c. $N(p \wedge \neg p) = N(False)$ *is often non-zero;*
   d. $N(p \vee q) \geq \max(N(p), N(q))$;
   e. *if* $p \models q$ *then* $N(p) \geq N(q)$.

Given a necessity-valued set $\Lambda = \{(\phi_i, \rho_i) \mid i = 1, \cdots, n\}$ *and one possible world* ω, *the necessity is computed as follows:*

$$N_\Lambda(\omega) = \begin{cases} 1 & \text{if } \omega \models \phi_1 \wedge \cdots \wedge \phi_n \\ \min\{1 - \rho_i, \mid \omega \models \neg\phi_i, i = 1, \cdots, n\} \end{cases} \qquad (1)$$

The necessity on Λ is then $N(\Lambda) = \max\{N_\Lambda(\omega_j) \mid j = 1, \cdots\}$. In Λ, the necessity of False is then $N(False) = 1 - N(\Lambda)$, representing the inconsistency in Λ. If two sets of formulas are disjunctive, i.e. $\Lambda_1 \vee \Lambda_2$, their necessity under the possible world ω is computed as follows:

$$N_{\Lambda_1 \vee \Lambda_2}(\omega) \geq \max(N_{\Lambda_1}(\omega), N_{\Lambda_2}(\omega)) \tag{2}$$

For example, we have a necessity-valued knowledge set $\{(p \wedge \neg q, 0.3), (q, 0.6)\}$. Its necessity value on different possible worlds is as follows:

$$N_{p \wedge \neg q}(p = 1, q = 1) = \min\{1 - 0.3 \mid p = 1, q = 1 \models \neg(p \wedge \neg q)\} = 0.7,$$

$$N_{p \wedge \neg q}(p = 0, q = 0) = \min\{1 - 0.3 \mid p = 0, q = 0 \models \neg(p \wedge \neg q),$$
$$1 - 0.6 \mid p = 0, q = 0 \models \neg(q)\} = 0.4'$$

$$N_{p \wedge \neg q}(p = 1, q = 0) = \min\{1 - 0.6 \mid p = 1, q = 0 \models \neg(q)\} = 0.4,$$

$$N_{p \wedge \neg q}(p = 0, q = 1) = \min\{1 - 0.3 \mid p = 0, q = 1 \models \neg(p \wedge \neg q)\} = 0.7.$$

The necessity value on the knowledge set is then $N(\{(p \wedge \neg q, 0.3), (q, 0.6)\}) = 0.7$ and the most probable worlds are $(p = 1, q = 1)$ and $(p = 0, q = 1)$. In the current work, we will find out the most possible worlds for evaluating observed service traces.

ISOLATION-BASED OBSERVATION OF SERVICE TRACE

This section presents a non-intrusive runtime protection framework for IoT services and discusses how to model isolation-based service action observations.

Figure 2. Framework for runtime service property enforcement

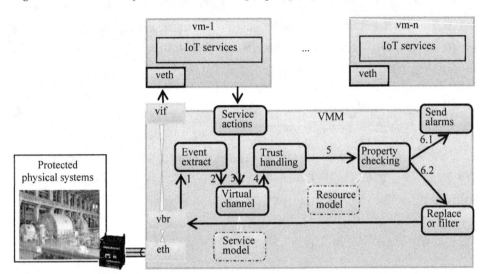

Isolation-Based Protection Framework for Runtime Services

The proposed enforcement framework to guarantee the properties of runtime IoT services in VMs is illustrated in Figure 2. This figure shows multiple IoT services deployed on VMs, and these IoT services collaborate to form a composite service for managing physical systems in which each IoT service on the VMs publishes and subscribes to real-time actuation, alarm and data events based on event names. This framework works in a VMM of the host rather than in VMs, as follows:

1. Establishing a Virtual Channel
   a. The *Event Extract* component in the framework intercepts all communication packets on the virtual network bridge in VMM to filter publish/subscribe events from/to IoT services. Some events may be forged or interleaved by adversaries in a hostile environment, such that the VM memory needs to be reconstructed to determine which service actions are actually executed before the runtime enforcement of property policies is carried out.
   b. When the low-level VM snapshots and states are obtained through external virtual machine management interfaces, semantic reconstruction is used to obtain a high-level view of the VM, for

example process control blocks. The execution states of the IoT services can be further reconstructed from memory kernel structures such as runtime function stacks. These reconstructed service actions can be considered to be actually executed events, and can be used to clean up the intercepted events.

These two isolation-based methods of obtaining service running events are treated as a virtual channel in which an isolated monitor can observe service execution events; some of these are trustworthy, while others are not, and adversaries can control the channel to forge or discard service events.

2. Trust Handling

    a. Each event observed from the virtual channel is assigned a level of certainty that indicates its trustworthiness (e.g. a reconstructed event from a VM memory is a true event with a high level of certainty). The high trustworthiness of an event does not imply the security of executing the service action, and only implies certainty as to whether it was produced by the services in the VMs.

    b. In addition to network interfaces, the *Event Extract* component also controls other I/O ports of computers, such as serial ports. When an event is intercepted in a local communication port, it also has a high level of trustworthiness. The events intercepted in the local industrial bus are cut and interpreted from data packets using IoT resource models that describe physical devices, sensors and the way in which transducers communicate with computers.

3. Property Checking

    a. The runtime monitor operates based on certainty. Unlike classical runtime monitors, this is isolated from the monitored applications, and the transmission of a message from the application to the monitor is modelled as insecure, while other models implicitly assume that the transmission is secure and reliable. Thus, each service event is checked based on its certainty, and a dangerous action is replaced with another that has a high level of trustworthiness.

    b. The runtime monitor is also physical-system-oriented. Models of physical devices clarify the physical action effects performed by service actions, and represent the continuous dynamics. The proposed monitor not only keeps the whole system secure, but also ensures that the IoT service regulates the physical system in a safe state.

From Figure 2, it can be seen that the monitor mediates between IoT services and physical systems, and does not directly control the execution of service actions in VMs (although indirect control of the execution of an action is possible). Each event is checked before it is sent to the physical system; if it violates certain properties of the physical targets, it is discarded or edited. In this isolation-based enforcement framework, a series of observed events may not be a true trace of a service, as described above, and this impedes property checking. Thus, the virtual channel is modelled and certainty introduced into event reasoning in such a way as to handle this incomplete information about the trace knowledge.

Modelling the Virtual Channel

The virtual channel is controlled by adversaries, and only part of the service trace is reliably passed to the runtime monitor. This will be modelled from two perspectives. First, an adversary is modelled based on its inferring capabilities rather than its behaviour; an adversary cannot be predicted or controlled, and it is therefore impossible to accurately describe its behaviour. Certainty is then introduced in order to quantify the trustworthiness of actions/events. This is used to defeat the adversary, and more details are given in later.

An adversary first observes the events from/to IoT services, and then uses these observed events to infer knowledge in order to launch attacks. The adversary is also aware of public knowledge about IoT service models, which include IoT resources representing physical entities and an EPC (Mendling, 2007; Scheer, 1998) representing IoT services in order to monitor and control the IoT resource. Service runtime models correspond to the executed IoT services, and these are represented by flow event structures. Figure 3 presents an example of this.

In Figure 3, a robot that provides a robot management service takes a component part from its input buffer and places this part onto a machine's input buffer. The machine, which provides a machine management service, loads this part into its platform for processing, and then unloads the processed part to its output buffer. The two services form a composite manufacturing service. In the figure, an event is denoted by hexagon, a function (service action) is denoted by rounded rectangle, and event-function chains are created (Mendling, 2007; Scheer, 1998).

The runtime service model is abstracted from its corresponding service model to represent executed service actions (i.e. events that have taken place)

Figure 3. A composite manufacturing service

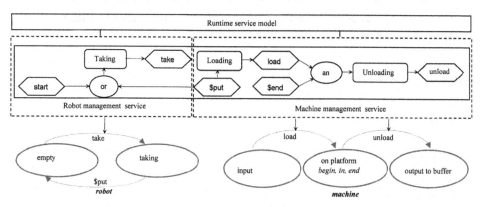

in which event instances are used. The event relations are the focus here, and functions and conditions are removed. An event is defined by a name and an XML schema (a set of name/value pairs). A subset of the XML schema is used to identify event instances at runtime, and this is called an event session identifier (Zhang and Chen, 2015). Thus, an event instance is identified by its name and its session identifier. The relations between event instances are represented by a flow event structure (i.e. runtime service models). For the runtime robot management service, there is a flow event structure Ξ_{robot} for which its event set is $\{start, take[counter \: / \: 0], put[counter \: / \: 0]\}$ where $counter \: / \: 0$ is an event session identifier, its event causality set is $\{start \prec take[counter \: / \: 0], take[counter \: / \: 0] \prec put[counter \: / \: 0]\}$, and its event conflict set is empty.

When an event is observed, the adversary examines the public knowledge to identify the corresponding action effects. Action theories are adopted to construct the knowledge of the virtual channel, where IoT resources represent action effects and IoT services are action agents, monitoring and controlling these IoT resources, i.e. forming an action system. IoT resources offer a stable description of action knowledge, while the IoT services are application-related, reflecting the varying action conditions and action relations. The running of IoT services may be impaired by adversaries, and attention should be paid to the service running in the virtual channel, with IoT resources forming the known basic knowledge.

The running of a service is viewed using traces, where a trace is a sequence of executed service actions. Adversaries cannot observe the execution of the service's inner function or hidden information such as private keys, and can only observe events published by the service. A *frame* is used here to represent observation by adversaries, and this is a sequence of events published by the service. For example, the service

$$volWarn(e_i, fun_i).\overline{control(e_j, fun_j)}$$

has a trace

$$volWarn(e_i, fun_i), \overline{control(e_j, fun_j)}$$

denoted by

$$volWarn(e_i, fun_i) \mapsto \overline{control(e_j, fun_j)}$$

Adversaries observe event e_j to get the frame $\{e_j\}$.

The observed events created by the service are indexed and the *frame* listed as $\{w_1 \to e_1, \ldots, w_n \to e_n\}$ where $\{w_1, \ldots, w_n\}$ is an enumerated index set, $\{e_1, \ldots, e_n\}$ is the observed event set of the adversaries, and $w_i \to e_i$ means that the index w_i refers to the $i - th$ observed event e_i. In order to describe the service trace as knowledge, the predicate $K(w, e)$ is imposed on the frame, meaning that the adversaries know event e with reference to an index w. The predicate $K(w, e)$ is owned by the adversaries. When imposing $K(w, m)$ on frames, service functions and equations are also assumed to be known by the adversaries, thus increase their attacking capabilities (Zhang & Chen, 2015; Ciobaca, 2011). The adversaries thus obtain a knowledge description about a running IoT service from the observed events.

To clarify the above discussion, we give an example involving equations in which there are the functions *encryption* (*publicKey*, *x*) and *decryption* (*privateKey*, *ciphertext*) with the public term *publicKey*, and an equation *decryption*(*privateKey*, *encryption*(*publicKey*, *x*)) = *x*. Then, the knowledge Λ_i is as follows:

1. For the public term *publicKey*,

$$\Lambda_i = \{\to K(publicKey, publicKey)\}.$$

2. For the two functions,

$$\Lambda_i = \Lambda_i \cup \{(K(X_1, x_1), K(X_2, x_2)) \rightarrow K(encryption(X_1, X_2), encryption(x_1, x_2)),$$
$$(K(Y_1, y_1), K(Y_2, y_2))\ K(decryption(Y_1, Y_2), decryption(y_1, y_2))\}.$$

3. For the equation, $\Lambda_i = \Lambda_i \cup \{decryption(privateKey, encryption(publickKey, x)) = x\}$

The above example shows that the adversaries can construct terms based on knowledge of a function, and can use these terms as the input to a service even though they have not been produced by valid participants. When the participant that encrypts messages is corrupted, the adversaries will know the private key and can produce correct ciphertext. Service properties should be checked for knowledge by adversaries, and attacks should be inferred from this knowledge. The proposed monitor can also use this knowledge to defeat the adversaries, thus guaranteeing certain properties, and the certainty of an event certainty is a primary mechanism in this process. Service models are needed not only for adversaries, but also for monitors; the parts of the model which relate to current system states should be instantiated, including the flow event structure and IoT resource instances, and the trace knowledge expanded by this instantiated model knowledge provides a base of operation for runtime monitors.

INTRODUCING CERTAINTY INTO MONITORS

Service actions observed in a virtual channel and represented by events may not arise from actual service executions, i.e. they may be uncertain. In the current approach, an uncertainty number is attached to each observed event. If an event is forensically retrieved from the VM memory, there is a higher level of confidence that the service is executing the action represented by that event, and a high value of certainty $\rho_{confirmed}$ such as 0.9 is attached to it. Certainty is given to literals (e.g., $e(e_i)$ or $K(w_i, e_i)$). If an event is intercepted in virtual network bridges, it is uncertain that the service is executing this action, and a low value of certainty (or variable) such as 0.4 is attached to it. If an event is observed on the industrial bus, a pre-set certainty such as $\rho_{confirmed}$ is attached to it.

Given the certainty of each event, the necessity of a logical consequence needs to be evaluated, and a check should be made as to whether this is greater than a certain threshold indicating that a service property is trustworthy.

When this necessity is low, there is a possibility that some of the events intercepted on the virtual network bridges should not be given a low certainty. However, it is not known whether this event was actually produced by the IoT services. In order to address this issue, a priori knowledge such as runtime service models (e.g. the flow event structure) should be used. The problem of how to efficiently integrate flow event structures into logical reasoning then becomes important.

The flow event structure of a running service describes the allowable possible worlds for certain trace knowledge. Given two events e_1 and e_2, there are four possible worlds: one in which both events occur, i.e. $e(e_1) \wedge e(e_2)$; one where e_1 occurs and e_2 does not, i.e. $e(e_1) \wedge \neg e(e_2)$; one in which e_2 occurs and e_1 does not; and one where neither e_1 or e_2 occur. If e_1 and e_2 conflict within the flow event structure of the service, the first possible world is not allowable, i.e., the distribution of this possible world is zero. Therefore, the flow event structure of this service is combined with possibilistic logic to determine the semantics of certainty-attached formulas for the service trace.

To achieve this combination, the formula is re-evaluated based on the flow event structure of the service. First, a necessity-valued knowledge set (Definition 3) is extended to include disjunctions and assignments to literals. This can still be used to compute the necessity value using Eqs. (1) and (2). The event predicates in the formula are then grouped into multiple subsets corresponding to event relation closures (e.g. event causality closures) in the flow event structure. For example, consider three events e_1, e_2, e_3, and their occurrence predicates $e(e_1), e(e_2), e(e_3)$ that form a formula $(e(e_1) \vee e(e_2)) \wedge e(e_3)$. If the event closures about e_1, e_2, e_3 are $\{e_1, e_2\}, \{e_1, e_3\}, \{e_2, e_3\}$, the formula is grouped into $(e(e_1) \vee e(e_2))_{\#1} \wedge ((e(e_1) \wedge e(e_3))_{\#2} \vee (e(e_2) \wedge e(e_3))_{\#3}$, where each event predicate appears once for each event in a closure, and the extended necessity-valued knowledge set is

$$\{\{(e(e_1), \rho_{e_1}, 0 / 1), (e(e_2), \rho_{e_2}, 0 / 1)\}_\vee, \{(e(e_1), \rho_{e_1}, 0 / 1)_\wedge, (e(e_3), \rho_{e_3}, 0 / 1)\}_\vee,$$
$$\{(e(e_2), \rho_{e_2}, 0 / 1)_\wedge, (e(e_3), \rho_{e_3}, 0 / 1)\}\}$$

where $\rho_{e_1}, \rho_{e_2}, \rho_{e_3}$ are the certainties of the three events, and 0/1 represents the assignments of the three corresponding literals. Since it is straightforward to obtain formula-closure groups such as $\{(e(e_i), \rho_{e_i}, 0 / 1), (e(e_j), \rho_{e_j}, 0 / 1)\}$

from a formula when assignments to these literals, a flow event structure and the certainties of events are known, the transformation procedure is not described here.

Given an extended necessity-valued knowledge set, known as the set of formula-closure groups, two semantic evaluation procedures can be carried out based on the flow event structure of the service, as follows:

1. For a formula-closure group,

$$\{(e(e_i), \rho_{e_i}, \pi_i (= 0 \,/\, 1)), (e(e_j), \rho_{e_j}, \pi_j (= 0 \,/\, 1))\}$$

$$\rho_{e_i} \geq \rho_{e_j} \text{ if } e_i \text{ is the cause event of } e_j. \tag{3}$$

2. For a formula-closure group,

$$\{(e(e_i), \rho_{e_i}, \pi_i (= 0 \,/\, 1)), (e(e_j), \rho_{e_j}, \pi_j (= 0 \,/\, 1))\}$$

$$\pi_i \neq \pi_j \neq 1 \text{ if } e_i \text{ and } e_j \text{ are conflict}. \tag{4}$$

Definition 4: Compatibility Computation: Given a form-closure group CN and its corresponding event closure EC in the flow event structure, the compatibility computation is as follows:

1. If EC is a conflict closure, its corresponding event occurrence atoms in CN are not True at the same time, i.e. Equation (4) is satisfied.
2. If EC is a causality closure, its corresponding event occurrence atoms in CN should have the same assignments, and the certainty of effect event is less than the one of cause event, i.e. Equation (3) is satisfied.

These are said to be compatible if the assignments of CN satisfy Steps 1 and 2 above.

If *Equation* (3) is not satisfied in Definition 4, the certainty of the events can be modified when one of them is confirmed by the service. For example, the certainty of a causal event is replaced with that of an effect event, if the latter is actually produced by the service. For a general predicate that takes multiple events as its input, a variable substitution method is used to compute the certainty. Given the certainties of literals ρ_i and ρ_i', i.e. $(e(e_i), \rho)$ or

$(\neg e(e_i), \rho_i')$, $i = 1, \cdots, n$, the certainty of predicate $pre(e_1, \cdots, e_n)$ is given below (the (#) Rule).

Definition 5: The (#) Rule

1. Variables $x_1, \cdots, x_{i-1}, x_{i+1}, \cdots, x_n$ are introduced to represent the events in $pre(e_1, \cdots, e_n)$, i.e., $x_1 = e_1, \cdots, x_{i-1} = e_{i-1}, x_{i+1} = e_{i+1}, \cdots, x_n = e_n$, and the certainty of $pre(e_1, \cdots, e_n)$ is the necessity on

$$\{pre(x_1, \cdots, x_{i-1}, e_i, x_{i+1}, \cdots, x_n), x_1 = e_1, \cdots, x_{i-1} = e_{i-1},$$
$$x_{i+1} = e_{i+1}, \cdots, x_n = e_n \}$$

where the certainty of $pre(x_1, \cdots, x_{i-1}, e_i, x_{i+1}, \cdots, x_n)$ is ρ_i, the certainty of $x_j = e_j$ is $\acute{A}_j$, $j \neq i, 1 \leq j \leq n$, and each of them is treated as $e(e_x)$.

2. The certainty of $\neg pre(e_1, \cdots, e_n)$ is the necessity of

$$\neg(pre(x_1, \cdots, x_{i-1}, e_i, x_{i+1}, \cdots, x_n) \wedge (x_1 = e_1) \wedge \cdots \wedge (x_{i-1} = e_{i-1}) \wedge$$
$$(x_{i+1} = e_{i+1}) \wedge \cdots \wedge (x_n = e_n)).$$

3. If a function in the predicate takes multiple events as its input, this function is replaced with a variable, and the function itself is then handled as in point 1. It is therefore possible to define the certainty of a predicate that includes nested terms.

ISOLATION-BASED ENFORCEMENT OF PROPERTY POLICIES

This section discusses the construction of a runtime monitor to enforce properties for services, in which the design of the certainty evaluation procedure is a key issue. The isolation-based monitor operates on the *Isolation-based Protection Framework* to complete property checking, in which service properties are verified by resisting against the virtual channel. The certainty algorithms provide a basis for the design of the certainty evaluation procedure.

Runtime Monitor

By embedding the certainty evaluation procedure (described in latter sections) into an SMT solver, a runtime monitor for the virtual channel can be created. First, a step-by-step method for enforcing properties for runtime services is presented.

If an event e_j representing a service action is intercepted on the virtual network bridge without being found in the VM memory, its trustworthiness is uncertain, i.e. it is untrusted. The VM introspection operation is carried out periodically, and a service execution trace may have been missed in the memory. The last service action e_i occurring just before this event is identified, and its possible succeeding actions $e_{j1}, e_{j2}, \cdots$ are listed based on the service model. The next task is to check which of e_j, $e_{j1}, e_{j2}, \cdots$ is the correct event to be sent to actuate the physical system while enforcing the predefined property $goal_{pro}$. Property checking is carried out as follows:

1. e_j, $e_{j1}, e_{j2}, \cdots$ are assigned certainty variables x_j, $x_{j1}, x_{j2}, \cdots$, and prior events have their own assigned certainties. e_j, $e_{j1}, e_{j2}, \cdots$ are modelled as knowledge in the insecure channel view (discussed the above sections), which is added into the existing knowledge set. The proposition about the certainty threshold $\rho_{\lim it}$, the deducted result with its certainty being greater than $\rho_{\lim it}$, is also added into the knowledge set.

2. An action of e_j, $e_{j1}, e_{j2}, \cdots$ that does not violate the property $goal_{pro}$ is then identified. This is achieved by trying these actions together rather than separately. First, $goal_{pro}$ is added into the knowledge set, and then find out its one model. If the most likely model is identified, all of x_j, $x_{j1}, x_{j2}, \cdots$ are assigned a certainty value.

3. It is then shown that the property $goal_{pro}$ is consistent with x_j, $x_{j1}, x_{j2}, \cdots$ being assigned by the certainty value from the found model. Thus, $\neg goal_{pro}$ is added into the knowledge set for the proof.

    a. If no model can be identified from this knowledge set, including $\neg goal_{pro}$, the property $goal_{pro}$ is proved, and the action with the highest certainty value is selected from e_j, $e_{j1}, e_{j2}, \cdots$ as the current executed service action. Its corresponding event is sent to actuate the physical system.

b. If the property $goal_{pro}$ cannot been proved, the assignments for x_j, $x_{j1}, x_{j2}, \cdots$ from the identified model become certainty constraints on x_j, $x_{j1}, x_{j2}, \cdots$, and these are added into the knowledge set. For example, the certainty constraint on x_j is $x_j \neq value_j$ if $x_j = value_j$ is in the identified model. The certainty value of x_j in the model is often an interval $x_j \in [value_{j,low}, value_{j,high}]$, and the certainty constraint is $(0 \leq x_j \leq value_{j,low}) \vee (1 \leq x_j \leq value_{j,high})$. Step 2 is then repeated to find new models.

4. If a model can be found but $goal_{pro}$ cannot be proved, all events with a certainty value greater than $\rho_{\lim it}$ are listed. If e_j appears in this list, the service execution is continued and only a warning is sent. If e_j does not appear in the list, the event with the highest certainty value is selected and used as the current action of the service over IoT resources, and an alarm is sent.

5. If no model can be identified in Step 2, the certainty assigned to the events intercepted on the virtual network bridges is re-estimated based on Eqs. (3) and (4), or is replaced with certainty variables. Step 2 is then repeated. If this attempt also fails, the service execution is suspended and an alarm is sent to administrators.

For example, in Figure 3, a *take* event is intercepted on a virtual network bridge although no *Taking* function can be found in the VM memory. The checking procedure begins by handling this uncertainty problem, where

Figure 4. Runtime monitor

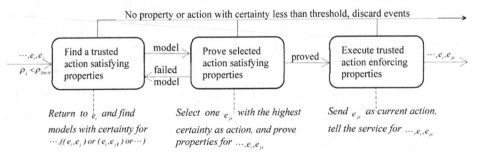

the *Loading* function of the manufacturing service is optional if the *Taking* function is rolled back to the *$put* event (i.e. a one-step prediction is made from the *$put* event). This prediction involves evaluating the certainty variables attached to service events that have not occurred. After checking, the monitor may trigger the *load* event to actuate the machine resource and discard the *take* event over the robot resource, making it possible for the machining line to be resynchronised, in the same way as a beating heart, while enforcing the safety property.

The runtime monitor for services is presented in Figure 4 and includes three function components: searching for events with a high level of certainty, proving service properties, and action enforcement. In the searching component, all optional actions are tried/estimated using SMT solvers in order to predict the action that can enforce properties and which has a certainty that is greater than the threshold. The certainty evaluation procedure underlies this method, and is based on runtime service models. In the proving component, the action with the highest certainty (or the current event if its certainty is greater than the threshold) in the found/predicted model is considered to be a part of the service trace, and the monitor then tries to prove that the service trace satisfies the service property. In the action enforcement component, the monitor discards the current event without carrying out any further actions if it cannot prove the service properties of an alternative action taking the place of the current one. Otherwise, the monitor allows the current event to occur if its certainty is greater than the certainty threshold, or uses the event with the highest certainty replace the current event, telling the service to run this new selected action (invoking the related service interfaces or service management interfaces). In the next two sections, the focus is on the design of the certainty evaluation procedure.

Trace Certainty

After obtaining the service traces, the certainty evaluation procedure is used to check whether a property is consistent with trustworthiness. In this sub-section, a method of computing the necessity of possible worlds prescribed by runtime service models is discussed. In the next sub-section, the evaluation of whether the computed necessity satisfies certain constraints is examined.

When SMT solvers are used to verify service properties, the certainty computation and evaluation will be an underlying procedure, and tentative assignments for formulas can be passed to the procedure by the upper SAT solver. The certainty of the possible world based on these formulas is calculated according to the tentative assignments and the flow event structure of the service. A certainty computation algorithm is presented below.

Algorithm 1: Certainty Computation:

Input: A set of clauses $\{l_{i1} \vee \cdots \vee l_{in_i}\}$ with tentative assignments, where the certainty of the events is unknown x_i or known ρ_j, i.e. $x_1, \cdots, x_m, \rho_{m+1}, \cdots, \rho_K$, certainty threshold $\rho_{\lim it}$, and a service flow event structure IoT.

Output: *Conflict*, or a certainty constraint

1. For each literal l_{ij} in the clause set, the algorithm computes its certainty according to the **(#) Rule**.

2. The algorithm computes event causality closures and conflict closures based on IoT. Then:
    ○   The algorithm groups the clause set $\{l_{i1} \vee \cdots \vee l_{in_i}\}$ into a formula-closure group set $\{CN_i\}$;
    ○   The algorithm carries out the compatibility computation between $\{CN_i\}$ and the event closure sets, i.e. Equation (3) and (4) are executed.

If one CN_i in $\{CN_i\}$ is not compatible with its corresponding event closure, the algorithm returns Conflict.

3. The necessity on the clause set is computed according to Equation (1) and (2).

4. The certainty constraint Π on the clause set is formed as follows:

$$f_{prob}(x_1, \cdots, x_m, \rho_{m+1}, \cdots, \rho_K) \geq \rho_{\lim it},$$

where $f_{prob}(x_1, \cdots, x_m, \rho_{m+1}, \cdots, \rho_K)$ is the necessity value computed in Step 3, including maximal and minimal functions. The certainty constraint Π is returned.

The above necessity is computed for one possible world (constructed using SAT solvers) of the formula. If the computed necessity is greater than a predefined threshold, the possible world from the SAT solvers will be output for the next iteration of processing. Otherwise, the upper SAT solver will construct other new possible worlds for certainty computation. In order to show that this certainty evaluation procedure is decidable, it is first proven that the certainty computation procedure is computable.

Theorem 1: *Certainty computation* is computable for a finite formula if the service model is well-behaved and defined.

Proof: It is proved by induction that Π can be computed. The computation time is a polynomial of the event number, where the checking of one event/logical relation and a real operation (e.g. add) are considered to form a single computational step.

1. Given two events e_1, e_2, the third event e_3 is added.

    1.1 If $e_1 \# e_2$, then

    1.1.1 $e_1 \# e_3$ and $e_2 \# e_3$. These can form a event closure $\{e_1, e_2, e_3\}$ and the necessity on formulas can be computed based on Eqs. 1 and 2 and trial assignments. For example, the conflict closure $\{e_1, e_2, e_3\}$ determines that the evaluation of $e(e_1) \wedge e(e_2) \wedge e(e_3)$ and $(e(e_1) \vee e(e_2)) \wedge e(e_3)$ is False, and the trial assignments for $e(e_1), e(e_2), e(e_3)$ may determine the necessity of $e(e_1) \wedge e(e_2) \wedge e(e_3)$ based on Equation 1 if they are compatible with the conflict closure $\{e_1, e_2, e_3\}$. Thus, $e(e_1) = True(1), e(e_2) = False(0), e(e_3) = False(0)$ determines that the necessity on $e(e_1) \wedge e(e_2) \wedge e(e_3)$ is $\min(1 - \rho_2, 1 - \rho_3)$, where ρ_2, ρ_3 are the certainties attached to the events e_2, e_3 respectively.

    1.1.2 $e_1 \# e_3$ and $e_2 \prec e_3$ or $e_3 \prec e_2$. These form event closures $\{e_1, e_2\}, \{e_1, e_3\}, \{e_2, e_3\}$, and the necessity (or Conflict) of the formulas is computed using the event closures, formula-closure groups, and Equation 1 and 2.

    1.1.3 $e_1 \# e_3$ and e_2, e_3 are concurrent. These form event closures $\{e_1, e_2\}, \{e_1, e_3\}$ and the necessity is computed as above.

    1.1.4 Other cases are similar to the above discussion.

    1.2 If $e_1 \prec e_2$, then

    1.2.1 $e_2 \prec e_3$ or $e_3 \prec e_1$. These form an event closure $\{e_1, e_2, e_3\}$, and the necessity is computed as above.

      1.2.2 $e_1 \prec e_3$ or $e_3 \prec e_2$, . These form two event closures, and the necessity is computed as above.

      1.2.3 Others are similar to 1.1.

    1.3 If e_1, e_2 are concurrent, the discussion is similar to 1.1.

2.   It is assumed that the theorem holds when the number of events considered in the service is $n \geq 2$.

3.   It needs to be shown that the theorem holds when the $n + 1 - th$ event e_{n+1} is added. Regardless of which literals include e_{n+1}, this can be treated as an event occurrence predicate and added according to the (#) Rule.

    3.1 Computing event closures. The event closures in Step 2 and the relations between e_{n+1} and the existing events in Step 2 are used as input to invoke Algorithm 2. The computation time of Algorithm 2 is linearly dependent on the event number and event closure number if the service is defined as well-behaved. Based on Assumption 1 and the incremental computation method of Algorithm 2, the computation time for the event closures adding e_{n+1} is also a polynomial of the event number in the service.

    3.2 Compatibility computation: After computing the event closures, the computation time of compatibility computation is linearly dependent on event closure number and closure size if trial assignments are given for all event occurrence literals. Assumption 1 then also shows that this checking time is a polynomial of the event number.

    3.3 Necessity computation: According to Eqs. 1 and 2, the necessity can be computed, and its computation time is linearly dependent on the formula's literal number, without considering the solution of the maximal/minimal functions. The finite formula means that the literal number of event occurrence is at most a polynomial of the event number. That is, the necessity computation time is a polynomial of the event number.

  This induction therefore shows that the certainty computation time for the finite formula is a polynomial of the event number.

Algorithm 2: Incremental Event Closure Computation:
Input:

1.   The event set $ES = \{e_1, \cdots, e_n\}$ has a conflict closure set $ClC_1, \cdots ClC_x$, a causality closure set $CaC_1, \cdots CaC_y$, and a concurrent event sub-set ES_{conc};

2. The $n+1-th$ event e_{n+1} is added into $ES = \{e_1, \cdots, e_n\}$, where the event relations between e_{n+1} and each event in ES are conflict, causality, or concurrent. The ES events that conflicting with e_{n+1} form a set $ES_{conf \leftrightarrow n+1}$; the ES events that have a causal relation with e_{n+1} form a set $ES_{caus \leftrightarrow n+1}$; and the ES events with a concurrent relation with e_{n+1} form a set $ES_{conc \leftrightarrow n+1}$.

Output: New event closures in $ES \cup \{e_{n+1}\}$.

1. For $ES_{conf \leftrightarrow n+1}$,

   1.1 For each ClC_i, $1 \leq i \leq x$

      1.1.1 If $ClC_i \subseteq ES_{conf \leftrightarrow n+1}$, e_{n+1} is added into ClC_i a new conflict closure is obtained; otherwise, go to 1.1.2;

      1.1.2 If $ClC_i \cap ES_{conf \leftrightarrow n+1} \neq empty$, ClC_i is split into $ClC_i \cap ES_{conf \leftrightarrow n+1}$ and ClC_i-$ClC_i \cap ES_{conf \leftrightarrow n+1}$, and e_{n+1} is added into $ClC_i \cap ES_{conf \leftrightarrow n+1}$ to get two new conflict closures.

   1.2 For $ES_{conf \leftrightarrow n+1}$ events that do not occur in the new conflict closures in 1.1, each of these form a new conflict closure with e_{n+1}.

2. For $ES_{caus \leftrightarrow n+1}$,

   2.1 Each CaC_i, $1 \leq i \leq y$ forms a linear tree from the causal events to the effect events. All CaC_i, $i = 1, \cdots, y$ form a forest that includes multiple linear trees, and e_{n+1} is connected to one linear tree CaC_i, $1 \leq i \leq y$ if $CaC_i \cap ES_{caus \leftrightarrow n+1} \neq empty$. If e_{n+1} is a causal event of e_j in CaC_i, e_{n+1} then becomes a parent node of e_j in the tree CaC_i; otherwise, e_{n+1} becomes a child node of e_j in the tree.

      2.1.1 If two linear trees become a longer linear tree using the above connecting operations, they are merged into a single new causality closure with e_{n+1} being the connector.

      2.1.2 If one original linear tree becomes a normal tree, it is linearised, i.e. each path from the root to one leaf becomes a new linear tree, and the new linearised linear trees become new multiple causality closures.

2.2 For $ES_{caus \leftarrow n+1}$ events that do not occur in the causality closures in 2.1, each of these form a new causality closure with e_{n+1}.

3. The algorithm returns all computed event closures.

Evaluating Certainty Constraints

In Algorithm 1, a certainty constraint is computed for property checking, where the necessity computation in *Equation* (1) and *Equation* (2) introduces the maximal and minimal functions *max, min* into the constraints. However, it is not known whether the constraint is solvable, and this is very important in completing the checking task. An algorithm is given below that evaluates the certainty constraint using existing arithmetic procedures (Borralleras et al., 2006), (Basu et al., 2012); these check whether polynomial equations/inequalities over real numbers are solvable, and the solution is returned.

Algorithm 3: Constraint Evaluation:
Input: A certainty constraint Π including the maximal and minimal functions *max, min* and the variables $x_1, \cdots, x_m$.
Output: *True* (for certainty assignment) or *False*.

1. The algorithm invokes the arithmetic procedure with Π as input;
2. If the arithmetic procedure returns False, the algorithm returns False;
3. If the arithmetic procedure returns True with assignments for $x_1, \cdots, x_m$, the algorithm returns these.

Theorem 2: The *Constraint Evaluation* algorithm is decidable.
Proof:

In the constraint evaluation algorithm, the certainty constraint Π is solved using an arithmetic procedure (Borralleras et al., 2006), (Basu et al, 2012). Following (Borralleras et al., 2006), (Basu et al, 2012), the polynomial constraints over reals can be solved with being decidable. The $\max\{\}$ functions in Π are then translated into polynomial constraints. The translation of $\rho_h = \max\{\rho_1, \rho_2\}$ is $(\rho_h = x) \wedge (((x = \rho_1) \wedge (\rho_1 \geq \rho_2)) \vee ((x = \rho_2) \wedge (\rho_2 \geq \rho_1)))$. That is, for a maximal function $\max\{\rho_1, \rho_2\}$ in the certainty constraint Π, it is replaced with a variable x, and an additional constraint

$((x = \rho_1) \wedge (\rho_1 \geq \rho_2)) \vee ((x = \rho_2) \wedge (\rho_2 \geq \rho_1))$ is added into the certainty constraint Π. The translation for general minimal/maximal functions is also similar to the above. After all maximal/minimal functions are translated, the certainty constraint Π becomes Π'.

Then, Π' has polynomial constraints over reals since the certainty constraint translated from the maximal/minimal functions is linear, and the certainty constraint Π neglecting the maximal/minimal functions is polynomial, according to Algorithm 1. Thus, the theorem holds.

We then design a *certainty evaluation procedure* as a background process for the SMT solvers to handle the trustworthiness of service traces obtained from the virtual channel, i.e. computing certainty on formulas and evaluating certainty constraints.

Definition 8.6: Certainty Evaluation Procedure: The certainty evaluation procedure consists of Algorithm 1 and Algorithm 3, and proceeds as follows:

1. If Algorithm 1 returns Conflict, it returns Conflict;
2. Otherwise, the certainty constraint returned by Algorithm 1 is used as input to invoke Algorithm 3, and it returns the output of Algorithm 3.

Corollary 3. The certainty evaluation procedure is decidable if the service model is defined as well-behaved.

Theorem 1 and Theorem 2 used together shown that Corollary 3 is correct.

The proposed runtime monitor uses SAT solvers to construct possible worlds for service trace formulas, and uses the certainty evaluation procedure to evaluate their certainty. If multiple possible worlds have service properties with a certainty greater than the predefined threshold, the runtime monitor first selects the one with the greatest certainty to prove the properties, or uses it to enforce service actions such as discarding current actuation events. This does not mean that the most probable world is selected from all possible worlds. It is appropriate in practice to find several possible worlds with relatively high certainties for a service trace formula.

It should be pointed out that we should treat with the inconsistency of a service trace formula observed from the virtual channel, when the inconsistency level ($N(False)$ as defined in Definition 3) is high. This means that the certainty attached to the events intercepted in the virtual network bridge is not correct, i.e. the true trustworthiness of these events is different from their predefined assignments. To estimate the true trustworthiness of observed events, runtime service models and definite service running observations (based on *Equation* (3), and (4)) are used as a basis for certainty estimation. This is carried out as follows:

1. The certainty attached to the intercepted events is replaced with certainty variables, $(e(e_1), \rho_1, x_1), \cdots, (e(e_n), \rho_n, x_n)$, where $\rho_1, \cdots, \rho_n$ are the original certainty values, and $x_1, \cdots, x_n$ are unknown variables.

2. Nonlinear programming methods (Bertsekas, 1999) can be used to estimate these unknown variables under the conditions of *Equation* (1) to (4). The nonlinear programming problem here is

    minimize $\sum_{i=1}^{n} | x_i - \rho_i |$

    subject to $N(\mathit{False}) \leq \varepsilon$,

    where $N(\mathit{False})$ is computed as in Definition 3 based on Equation (1) to (4), and ε represents a low value of inconsistency.

Using Definition 8.3, the inconsistency computation iterates over all possible worlds, and this process is inefficient. The process of estimating the true trustworthiness of events can be optimized as follows:

1. The nonlinear programming problem is solved for a possible world, and other possible worlds will be tried if there is no solution for this possible world. At each iteration step, estimation is carried out for one possible world ϖ, and $N(\mathit{False})$ is replaced with $1 - N_\Lambda(\varpi)$. If the estimated certainty for one possible world reduces the inconsistency level to a suitable value, the iteration halts, since the inconsistency of the formula is computed over the maximal certainty of possible worlds.

2. The model-finding algorithm in (Lang, 2000) can be adopted to construct possible worlds for a service trace formula, and inappropriate branches are pruned as soon as possible.

3. It needs to be proved that the predefined service properties are maintained for the estimated certainty of events. Detailed algorithms for this are not given in this book.

MONITORING EXAMPLE FOR A PHYSICAL SYSTEM: CONTROLLABILTY OF IOT SERVICES

The monitoring solution is used as an example of the enforcement of controllability of IoT services. Physical systems are first introduced into the proposed monitor, and the controllability problem is then defined from the perspective of an insecure channel, which is a kind of safety requirement for practical IoT services. Finally, this problem is solved and monitored using a multiple-step prediction.

Description of the Physical System

An IoT service can be considered as a set of actions performed on physical entities. The enforcement of IoT service properties aims to maintain the physical system in a desirable state. Unlike classical runtime monitors, models of both services and physical systems need to be built for IoT scenarios. A physical entity in the physical world is represented by an IoT resource model in the information model, which includes an object model and a lifecycle model. The object model describes the attributes and attribute relations of a resource, while the lifecycle model describes its methods of progressing, state transitions, and continuous resource dynamics.

First-order logic is used to formalise the IoT resources as action effects. The formal specification of an IoT resource involves listing the changed action effects (state transitions following the occurrence of events) induced by the IoT services, and the unchanged action effects (persistence of states when no event occurs). In this chapter, the unchanged action effects are not explicitly discussed, and are used as underlying knowledge. IoT resources involve continuous dynamics such as higher-order differential equations, and these functions are often tested in the background theories of SMT solvers. These are not discussed further here, and it is assumed that SMT solvers can handle several types of continuous variables.

Figure 5 illustrates a robot, which is one type of physical device in the composite manufacturing service illustrated in Figure 3. Two states are possible: state 1 is represented by *rob.st = empty* to indicate that nothing is take, while state 2 is represented by *rob.st = taking* to indicate that it is taking some parts. One state transition from the *empty* state to the *taking* state takes place if the robot is first in the *empty* state and then receives a *take* controlling action/event. A second state transition is possible from the *taking* state to the

Figure 5. A robot resource

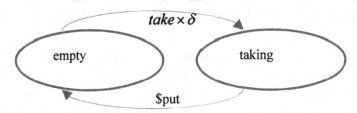

empty state, and this occurs automatically if the robot is in the *taking* state, since a put event is produced that is not controllable. In other words, the *put* event in the *robot* physical device cannot be directly controlled by IoT services; this is referred to as an uncontrollable event and is denoted by *$put* . The knowledge description $\Lambda_{i,rob}$ about the robot resource is as follows:

$$\Lambda_{i,rob} = \{(rob.st = empty) \wedge e(take) \rightarrow (rob.st = taking),$$
$$(rob.st = taking) \rightarrow e(put), e(put) \rightarrow (rob.st = empty)\},$$

where *rob* is a resource identifier; *(rob.st = empty) ∧ e(take) → (rob.st = taking)* means that the robot transits from the *empty* state to the *taking* state if it is first in the empty state and then receives the *take* controllable event (a service action). The changed action effects (the resource state transitions and new resource states) are listed, and the unchanged action effects are implicit.

In order to complete a manufacturing task, the robot resource and machine resource in Figure 3 need to be well coordinated with each other, and uncontrollable events should also be indirectly controlled by adjusting controllable events. The safety of the IoT service is therefore controlled. The safety property is often represented by event relations in the current work using ProVerif (Blanchet, 2015).

For example, Figure 6 illustrates two different cases for the operation of the manufacturing service. Figure 6a represents a safe case, which allows the manufacturing process to continue. However, in Figure 6b, the manufacturing service may produce two *$put* events, which block the manufacturing process. The reason for this is that uncontrollable events exist in the IoT resources, meaning that the use of controllable events is required to adjust uncontrollable events.

A controlling function δ is introduced for each controllable event to try to control these uncontrollable events in an IoT resource model. The controlling

Figure 6. (a) Safe event relation (b) Unsafe event relation

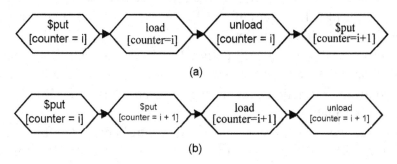

function δ returns *True* if the occurrence of the controllable event enforces the safety property; otherwise, it returns *False,* i.e., the controllable event is disabled. Figure 5 gives an example of this, where the controlling function δ enables the controllable event *take* if δ returns *True*. The controllable event *take* then causes the IoT resource *robot* to enter the *taking* state, which leads to the occurrence of the uncontrollable event *$put* . The robot resource description $\Lambda_{i,rob}$ is then modified as follows:

$$\Lambda_{i,rob} = \{(rob.st = empty) \land e(take) \land \delta \rightarrow (rob.st = taking),$$
$$(rob.st = taking) \rightarrow e(put), e(put) \rightarrow (rob.st = empty)\}.$$

The safety property in Figure 6a is represented as follows:

$$P_{safe} = \{e(put[counter]) \rightarrow e(load[counter + 1]),$$
$$e(load[counter + 1]) \rightarrow e(unload[counter + 1]),$$
$$e(unload[counter + 1]) \rightarrow e(put[counter + 1])\},$$

where *counter* is used to describe the constraints on the entire session of the robot and machine. Formally, the manufacturing service will ensure the property of safety if $sysModel = \; \rangle \cup \neg p_{safe}$ is checked as being unsatisfiable, where Λ includes the observed events $\Lambda_{process}$ and some other models: $\Lambda = \Lambda_{init} \cup \Lambda_{i,function} \cup \Lambda_{i,rob} \cup \Lambda_{i,mac} \cdot \Lambda_{i,rob} \cup \Lambda_{i,mac}$ is the knowledge about the robot and machine resources, and $\Lambda_{init} \cup \Lambda_{i,function}$ is application-related knowledge involving the initial configuration of the IoT service and its functions.

If *sysModel* is unsatisfiable over the modified IoT resource models, then the manufacturing IoT service enforces the safety property. The controllability problem is then defined as follows.

This problem defines how to assign *True/False* to controlling functions to ensure that *sysModel* is unsatisfiable. An assignment scheme is created for the controlling functions, and is used to keep the running IoT service in a state of controllability.

Compared with the classical concept of controllability (Balbiani, 2008), the most important difference in the current work is that the controllability is modelled from the perspective of a virtual channel, and is defined based on the adversary's knowledge rather than the resource description itself. An adversary may carry out attacks based on its knowledge set. The monitor competes with the insecure channel, and outputs an assignment scheme for all controlling functions if it defeats the channel using these assignments.

Enforcing Controllability

The enforcement of controllability aims to solve the controllability problem based on the current states of the running service, and then to enforce the service behaviour based on this solution. Solving the controllability problem involves determining when and where the monitor assigns *True* to controlling functions. In general, the occurrence of any event may offer a good opportunity to enable the controlling functions. In order to filter false chances, the monitor can use an exhaustion-based method to check all of these triggers.

Given the service's future running rounds, the solving algorithms search the assignments for the controlling functions. The monitor then uses the results of this search as knowledge to enforce the controllability as usual. If no solution can be found for the controllability problem, an unsatisfiable core/set (which may include critical actuation events) is sent to administrators, so that a new dispatching scheme can be created to regulate the physical system states in advance. If a solution to the controllability problem can be obtained, the monitor treats the controlling scheme as known knowledge, and then enforces the service execution based on the new knowledge. The service's event flow structure is also dynamically updated according to the assignments of the controlling functions.

The runtime controllability enforcement is illustrated in Figure 7. This scheme tries to determine whether the service operation will satisfy the controllability requirements in several future rounds of operation, and outputs not only *Yes/No* but also an assignment scheme that acts as a solution for the controllability problem. It also carries out complementary actions such as sending alarms, and checks the service is operating as usual by treating the controllability solution as known knowledge. Thus, in the final step of controllability enforcement, the monitor presented in later is used to check an intercepted event with the safety property as its goal.

From the above discussion, it can be seen that the controllability enforcement of IoT services is based on both a service trace and prediction methods. This is different from classical runtime monitors, in which each current service action is detected and corrected. However, for the controllability problem, checking only the current service action may lead to uncontrollable service behaviour; this is because an uncontrollable action can often be indirectly controlled by adjusting multiple controllable actions, and because an adjusted controllable action may occur before the uncontrollable action, with several other actions in between. These controllable actions should be adjusted before the uncontrollable action is actually executed. In order to reduce the computational cost of multiple-step predictions, a prediction based on models can be made independently and in advance, and the predicted results are used as known knowledge during property checking.

PERFORMANCE EVALUATION

The experimental environment is shown in Table 2. The operating systems of the VM and VMM host are both CentOS 6.5. The proposed monitor works in the VMM host to enforce security policies, where it intercepts network packets from/to VMs via a virtual network bridge over VMM by inserting hooks into Netfilter (Netfilter, 2015), and forensically retrieves service traces from VM memory using Volatility (Ligh et al., 2014), a memory forensics tool, and LibVMI (LibVMI, 2014), a VMI library.

Figure 7. Runtime controllability enforcement

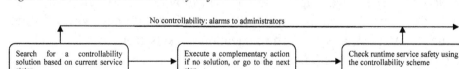

257

Table 2. Experimental environment

Name	The host	The protected VM
OS	CentOS 6.5 with a 64-bit Linux kernel	CentOS 6.5 with a 64-bit Linux kernel
Processor	Intel(R) Core i5 3230M	
RAM	3 GB available	I GB
VMM	KVM with tool qemu-kvm-0.12.1.2	
Related software	*Volatility* 2.4, python 2.7.8, gcc 4.4.7, libVMI 0.10.1	

VM: virtual machine; OS: operating system; VMM: virtual machine monitor.

Volatility and LibVMI are used here as a tool suite for the reconstruction of VM memory. LibVMI provides primitives for accessing the memory of a running VM, while Volatility is a memory analysis tool used to search for digital artefacts in the memory snapshot taken by LibVMI. Using Volatility, the process control block of a process running services can be obtained, and a search for functions (executed service actions) can be carried out in the function stack space based on the kernel memory structure. Although Volatility supports the profiling of functions, the current version is based on the stack pointer register, and obtains execution information for service actions only when the target service is in debugging mode. In order to support dynamically and continuously running services, the existing Volatility is enhanced by iterating the function stack address unity one by one, in order to profile the running service actions.

Figure 8 illustrates the time spent on VM semantic reconstructions. The stack space was analysed using two address intervals: [base, base+0x400] and [base, base+0x800]. The base represents the top of the stack, and the stack size of the latter is larger than that of the former. The experiment was repeated 1000 times, and the time spent on semantic reconstruction for each experiment was recorded. From Figure 8, it can be seen that this reconstruction was effective, and that the stack size affects the semantic reconstruction time. However, there are random peaks in some experiments, which are not related to the stack size. After the service actions are profiled as events, they are assigned a high value of trustworthiness, and are used together with intercepted service events.

Netfilter is a software application provided by the Linux kernel in which hooks can be used to intercept network communications on the virtual bridge of the VMM host, and the communication packets from/to VMs undergo isolation-based filtering. Thus, Netfilter represents a series of hooks inside the Linux kernel, and callback functions can register to the kernel's networking

Figure 8. Time spent on semantic reconstruction

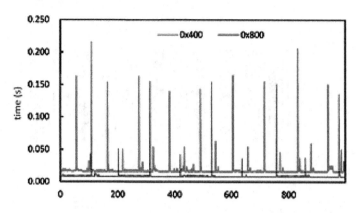

stack for VMM. The extraction of service events in the hooked Netfilter is as follows:

1. When an IP packet is intercepted, the transport protocol type (e.g. TCP or UDP) is analysed according to the IP packet header.
2. Given the transport protocol type, the transport protocol header can also be analysed, and the payload data are cut out.
3. According to the predefined XML schema, service events are extracted from the payload data, and a check is made as to whether the payload data have a valid XML format from/to the target VM services.
4. If these data have a valid format, the extracted service events are sorted and placed into the intercepted event set.

Figure 9 illustrates the performance of this event extraction process, measured using the loss ratio of packets due to the insertion of interception code into communication channels, which may lead to communication congestion, delaying the passing of packets. The intercepting or checking of packets on virtual network bridges will lead to packet loss when the event injection speed becomes high. These interception methods are efficient, with low packet loss ratios.

Figure 10 shows the time for memory retrieval, and the average time for retrieving stack memories less than 3 milliseconds, which is not influenced by the number of service function parameters, the types of service function parameters, the number of service function stack frames, and so on. The time consuming only depends on size of memory retrieved. That is to say, the time

Figure 9. Speed of event extraction

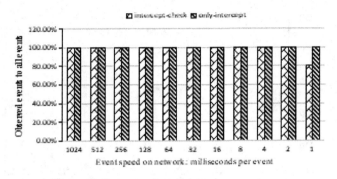

Figure 10. Time for memory retrieval

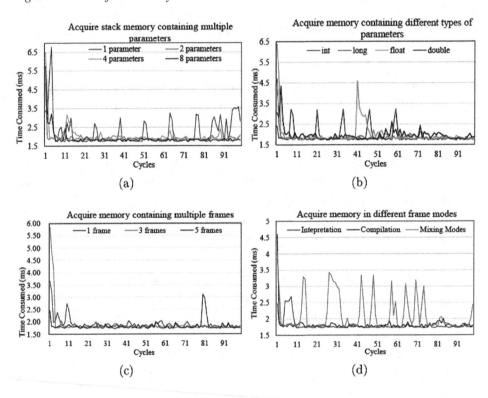

spent on memory acquisition is proportional to the stack size dumped and have nothing to do with the state of each frame of runtime service function stacks.

Figure 11 shows time spent on analyzing JVM stacks in various scenarios. From the figure, we know that the spent time is relevant to contents in each frame and the number of frames analyzed. Obviously, it is proportional to

Figure 11. Time for analyzing function stack memories

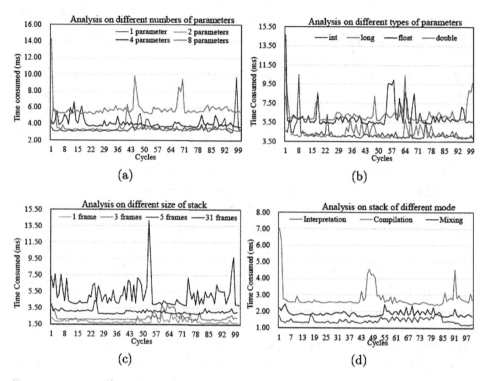

(a) (b) (c) (d)

the number of parameters (Figure 11(a)) and frames (Figure 11(c)) in the retrieved memory. For the given types of parameters, Figure 11(b) shows that the time on analyzing the variable type of *float* and *double* is a little more than that on the type of *int* and *long*. This is because the variables of float and double are also converted from the binary bits and the conversion needs more computation cost.

Figure 11(d) compares the analysis time on frames of different execution mode. It shows that the analysis on interpreted frames consumes the least time, and the analysis on just-in-time compiled frames need the most time. The reason for this is that the stack analysis in our approach is from the bottom to the top of a stack. In this way, when the frame analysis transfers from an interpreted frame to a next compiled frame, the program counter of the compiled frame is unknown. We address the problem by traversing all possible frameSizes to compute it.

So, the analysis on compiled frames consumes more time than on interpreted frames. Based on this, the analysis time spent on mixed frames is in between. From Figure 11 we conclude that the analysis on the JVM stack can be completed at about 7ms averagely. Considering results of memory dump and analysis, time consumed on each reconstruction is maintained mostly within 10ms. For applications with a larger stack size and more frames, the time should be a little more than this.

A point to note here is, the first analysis would spend a relatively considerable amount of time, about 550~580ms in our experiments. This is natural because some initialization on structure of JVM stacks need to be done in the first analysis. And after the initialization is completed, the time consumed will drop down and keep at a few milliseconds.

Z3 software (Moura & Bjørner, 2008) is adopted as the SMT solver for the runtime monitor, and the example shown in Figure 3 is used to evaluate our monitor. The C++ API of the Z3 SMT solver is used to program the knowledge of the manufacturing service: the knowledge set about the *robot resource*, the *machine resource*, the service functions and the observed events is all programmed; event sessions and local timers are expressed using Z3's numerical theories; and the certainty evaluation procedure is embedded as an underlying decidable procedure. The safety property is also programmed using the Z3 C++ API, i.e. the session constraints and logical formulas for the event relations are programmed.

In order to evaluate the proposed solution, five types of experiments are carried out. The first aims to solve the controllability problem based on service models, without any observed service trace that can be monitored. The second involves monitoring a service trace in a secure channel, where events in the trace are not assigned a certainty, in the same way as classical monitors. In the third, the proposed runtime monitor operates in a virtual channel. The fourth compares the proposed monitor with other existing runtime verification methods: no prediction method is used, certainty is assigned without the estimation of unknown certainty variables; and the event processing speed is used as the evaluation metric. The fifth evaluates the performance of the runtime monitor for an IoT service with more states and events than the manufacturing service shown in Figure 3.

For the first three experiments, several different running round thresholds are used as prediction steps when carrying out performance testing. Event session identifiers and local timers represent service running rounds. As an example, part of the knowledge of the machine resource is expressed in Z3 as follows:

s.add(forall(x, cnt, y, ite((x<posCn) && (x >= 0) && (cnt<indCnt) && (cnt >= 0) && (y<indCnt) && (y >= 0), implies(havingIn(cnt, x) && Load(cnt,

x+3) && Sel(iTwo, cnt, y), platformIn(cnt, x)) && implies(platformIn(cnt, x)
&& Unload(cnt, x+5), outputbufferIn(cnt, x)) && implies(platformIn(cnt, x),
End(cnt, x+4)) && implies(outputbufferIn(cnt, x), havingIn(cnt +1, x+5)),
bTrue)), "p4");

where the *load, unload* and *$end* events are expressed by the three functions
Load(cnt, x + 3), Unload(cnt, x+5) and *Unload(cnt, x+5)*, respectively. These
all use the *"cnt"* parameter as the machine's round session identifier and the
"x" parameter as the event order variable (i.e. a local timer). The states are
also expressed by functions such as *platformIn(cnt, x)*.

The monitor's performance in terms of solving the controllability problem,
based only on models and without observing the service traces, is illustrated
in Figure 12, in which the horizontal axis represents the manufacturing
service's running round number; the vertical axis is the time spent on finding
a controllability solution and verifying the manufacturing service's safety
property for each machining round. From Figure 12, it can be seen that this
solution method is also efficient.

In order to test the performance of trace monitoring independently of the
trace length, experiments were carried out multiple times; in each of these, an
executed trace was randomly chosen with a running round number of between
one and ten, and the prediction of controllability was carried out based on this.
Figure 13 illustrates the performance of trace monitoring without assigning
certainty to events, and Figure 14 illustrates the performance including the
assignment of certainty to events using the underlying certainty evaluation
procedure. In these two figures, the time spent on controllability enforcement

Figure 12. Time for the controllability of manufacturing service

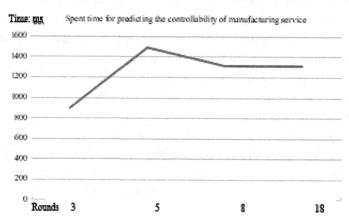

Figure 13. Time spent on monitoring traces without certainty

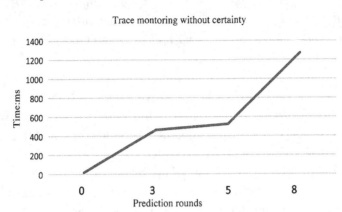

increases when the number of prediction steps increases. The time spent on checking, a current event is less than 20 ms, as shown in Figure 13, and the introduction of certainty processing increases this time (although this is still less than 170 ms), as shown in Figure 14. This is because several unknown certainty variables are estimated in addition to the necessity computation, even though no prediction is required. If the trace length is kept short and no long trace is needed in practice, the time spent on checking current events can be reduced, and this is shown in Figure 15.

In order to compare the proposed monitor with other existing alternatives, the monitor's event processing speed was measured for an observed trace, as used in (Havelund, 2015). In the latter study, the LogScope tool was shown to have an event processing speed of between 0 and 20 events/ms in seven test cases, which was not the fastest and comparable to ours. This demonstrates that the proposed methods is feasible. Figure 15 illustrates the event processing speed of the runtime monitor, where the round number of service operation is gradually increased, incrementally injecting trace events into the monitor. The event processing speed of the runtime monitor increases until the number of injected events reaches 275; this is because there is a fixed computation cost, and the computation capability of our monitor is not fully utilised for lower numbers of events. Above around 22 events/ms, the event processing speed does not increase.

In order to test the runtime monitor on an IoT service with a higher number of states and events, the machine resource in the manufacturing service is enlarged by adding two events and two states; one robot resource serves for two machine resources. The performance of the proposed runtime

Figure 14. Spent time for monitoring traces with certainty

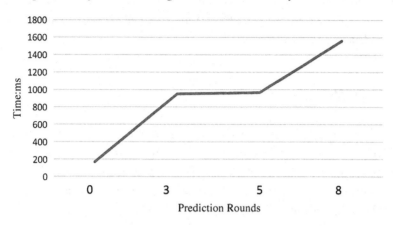

Figure 15. Event processing speed: monitoring traces with certainty

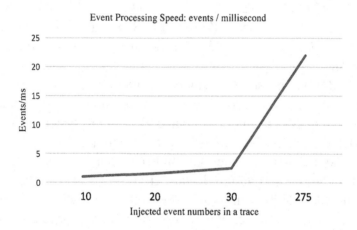

monitor in this case is illustrated in Figure 16, where certainty is assigned to events, and a significant increase can be seen in the time spent. This means that methods need to be found to improve the performance of the proposed monitor in the case where a composite IoT contains many states and events. One possible method is based on the divide-and-conquer principle, and involves independently checking each sub-service at runtime and combining multiple checked results based on assume-and-guarantee rules (Kim et al., 2002). A second method would be the specialised optimisation software Z3 for the checking of runtime IoT services. A third method would be to use dedicated computers with more powerful computation capabilities, and the proposed monitor could be revised to use them. In addition, it should be noted that only events sent to physical systems are fully checked, although all events are intercepted. The development of such optimisation methods will be addressed in future work.

RELATED WORK

Since testing and symbolic verification are not sufficient to protect security-critical IoT services, a method of monitoring a system at runtime is presented here. This monitor observes the system's behaviour and determines whether this is consistent with a certain specification. The monitor is able to provide additional confidence at runtime that the service can enforce certain properties. There are many prior works in this field, such as those in Barringer et al., (2004), Barringer et al., (2005), Kim et al., (1999), Lee et al. (1999), Bhargavan et al., (2002), Kim et al., (2002), Sokolsky et al., (2005), Bhargavan et al., (2001), Bhargavan and Gunter, (2002), and Sen et al. (2004). For example, the Eagle logic (Barringer et al., 2004), and an overview is given in Delgado et al., (2004).

Schneider (2000) investigated which security policies could be enforced by runtime monitors. In this work, an execution monitor observed the execution of the protected system and terminated the target system whenever an action violated a policy. The enforceability of policies also involved raising exceptions, taking corrective actions, and so on, in addition to terminating the execution before a violation. Ligatti et al. (2005), (2009) extended the work of Schneider (2000) by introducing edit automata, which can change the protected system's output actions in order to guarantee security properties. Ligatti and Reddy (2010) further revised the work in (Ligatti et al., 2009) by

Figure 16. Time spent on monitoring traces with multiple rounds

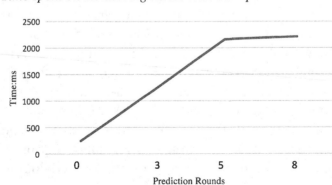

introducing mandatory result automata with powerful expressiveness, which provided interfaces to interact with the target system, for example obtaining requests from the target, sending actions to execution environments, and responding to the target with results from the execution system. Basin et al. (2013) extended Schneider's work on policy enforcement, clarifying the necessary and sufficient conditions for enforcing a security policy; in this work, actions were classified into controllable and uncontrollable types. In the current work, the proposed monitor also obeys the framework of mandatory result automata (Ligatti et al., 2010; Dolzhenk et al., 2015), but operates in isolation, without reliable communication channels between the monitor and the protected target. The virtual channel is modelled by introducing the concept of trustworthiness for each observed event. The editing of actions is based on certainty, and the optional action set is selected based on the possible worlds of running services.

In Lee et al. (1999), the Monitoring and Checking (MaC) toolset was developed as a systematic monitoring-oriented programming framework, targeting soft real-time applications written in Java. The work in (Meredith et al., 2012) surveyed monitoring-oriented programming frameworks and proposed a new framework based on a code design principle and advocating the separation of the core functionality of an application system from the ancillary protection functionality, such as safety and security. This solution organised the program code using a layered onion-style architecture, and a series of tools such as programming editors were provided. The work in (Cassar and Francalanza, 2016) addressed the challenge of implementing a framework of monitoring-oriented programming in the context of software systems in Scala, i.e. based on actor models. In the current work, the VM-based isolation architecture used is also based on the onion style. The focus in this work is on the introduction of certainty into runtime monitors to address the isolation-induced channel insecurity problem, which has not been comprehensively explored in prior work.

There are other works related to this topic, such as (Erlingsson & Schneider, 1999; Falcone et al., 2011; Chabot et al., 2011; Dolzhenko et al., 2015; Havelund, 2014; Garg et al., 2011). An attractive approach involves checking whether a system's behaviour is compliant with regulations and security policies; this is simpler than runtime monitoring to enforce policies, since only policy violations are detected. Runtime monitoring can also be used in compliance checking, for example in the algorithms proposed in Garg et al., (2011), Halle and Villemaire (2012), and Basin et al. (2008). In addition, runtime verification, another technology related to this topic, involves not only execution monitoring but also compliance checking, where violations are detected and reported according to system specifications (Havelund, 2015).

Some researchers have also focused on the verification-based protection of IoT systems. For example, the work in (Gamage et al., 2010) presented a framework to enforce the properties of IoT services; in this case, physical systems formed the focus, and physical properties were the goals of the enforcement. However, these authors did not discuss methods of formally describing general physical resources and correctly describing the relations between IoT service actions and IoT resources. In a similar way to the current work, the authors of (Cimatti et al., 2013) modelled a hybrid system for verification of an IoT system using a first-order logic language and SMT tools. Their work aimed to check whether multiple hybrid automata complied with a desired interaction description, represented by message sequence charts, using bounded model checking and the k-induction method. Their approach was entirely based on the advanced characteristics of modern SMT solvers, such as unsatisfiable core extraction, incrementality and interpolation. Although this approach was similar to that used in the current work, it did not distinguish IoT resources from the system when describing complex actions, and also did not consider the virtual channel model for isolated service running environments or certainty propagation over formulas.

In classical action theories such as event calculus (Kowalski & Sergot, 1986), situation calculus (McCarthy & Hayes, 1969), and action theory (Bultan, 2000), the focus is how to describe actions to monitor and control the real world; the set of effects was defined to describe the changes to which these actions led. However, if only the changed effects resulting from an action are specified, then the frame problem arises, involving how to identify those effects that were not changed by the action. Enumeration of all the effects induced by the action, including both changed and unchanged effects, may be a possible solution to the frame problem, but there may be rich constraints in one domain, meaning that the intuitive enumeration method may not be convenient or possible. Many action theory researchers have proposed methods to address this issue, such as examinations of the ramification and qualification problems. In the current work, a hierarchical approach is used to model an IoT service in which physical entities are specified by IoT resource models at stable bottom to describe direct action effects, and actions and their interactions are described by IoT services at varied application-related top to specify the indirect action effects and qualification. Knowledge about IoT resources is described using the classical action theories, and knowledge about the IoT service is obtained from observation of the environment, i.e. from the perspective of an insecure channel.

The work in Sheeran and Singh (2002) and Shoaei et al. (2014) also utilised a SAT-solver-based method to check the safety property; these authors used induction algorithms and the SAT solver to design a fixed-point solution for invariance checking, and presented preliminary experimental results to verify FPGA cores. In the SAT-solver-based safety checking approaches used by IC3 (Somenzi and Bradley, 2011), the target system was often modelled as a transition system, with propositions representing system states, and an invariant for the system was iteratively solved to show that the safety property could be satisfied. In the scenarios in the current work, the target system is considered to be observed by adversaries, who can record event occurrences to launch attacks through the insecure channel. The safety property of the IoT services, (i.e. controllability), can be realised in a game between the monitor and the insecure channel to resist against these attacks. The above works did not discuss interactions between multiple services, while the proposed virtual-channel-based method can handle this naturally, adding observation objects.

CONCLUSION

A non-intrusive solution is presented here that can guarantee the properties of IoT services at runtime. IoT resource descriptions are used to construct a basis for checking of physical system-oriented properties, and action theories are then adopted to hierarchically formalise those IoT services in terms of the action effects on IoT resources. In this solution, a virtual channel is established to realise isolation-based service observations. In this model, a running service is represented by observed events occurring in the channel, and the concept of the trustworthiness of the occurring events is introduced to reflect possible attacks. A certainty evaluation procedure is presented and embedded into SMT solvers to obtain a unified approach for dealing with uncertainty and rigid logical reasoning, and based on this, the proposed runtime monitor can work in an isolated environment. An example is given to illustrate how to enforce an IoT service's controllability at runtime; the controllability problem is defined from the perspective of a malicious channel, and an exhaustion-based method is adopted to predict the controllability solution as a basis for monitoring. Several experiments demonstrate the efficiency of this non-intrusive runtime monitor.

REFERENCES

Balbiani, P., Cheikh, F., & Feuillade, G. (2008). Composition of interactive Web services based on controller synthesis. 2008 *IEEE International Conference on Services Computing, Web Service Composition and Adaptation Workshop.*

Barrett, C., Sebastiani, R., Seshia, S. A., & Tinelli, C. (2009). Satisfiability modulo theories. Handbook of Satisfiability, 825– 885.

Barringer, H., Goldberg, A., Havelund, K., & Sen, K. (2004). Rule-based runtime verification. In *Verification, Model Checking, and Abstract Interpretation (VMCAI).* Springer-Verlag. doi:10.1007/978-3-540-24622-0_5

Barringer, H., Rydeheard, D., & Havelund, K. (2007). Rule systems for run-time monitoring: From eagle to ruler. In *RV07: Proceedings of Runtime Verification* (pp. 111–125). Springer-Verlag. doi:10.1007/978-3-540-77395-5_10

Basin, D., Juge, V., Klaedtke, F., & Zalinesu, E. (2013). Enforceable Security Policies Revisited. *ACM Transactions on Information and System Security,* *16*(1), A1–A25. doi:10.1145/2487222.2487225

Basin, D., Klaedtke, F., Muller, S., & Pfitzmann, B. (2008). Runtime monitoring of metric first-order temporal properties. In *Proceedings of the 28th Conference on Foundations of Software Technology and Theoretical Computer Science.* Leibniz International Proceedings in Informatics (LIPIcs).

Basu, S., Pollack, R., & Roy, M.-F. (2006). *Algorithms in real algebraic geometry.* Springer.

Bertsekas, D. P. (1999). *Nonlinear Programming* (2nd ed.). Cambridge, MA: Athena Scientific.

Bhargavan, K., Chandra, S., McCann, P., & Gunter, C. A. (2001). What packets may come: Automata for network monitoring. *SIGPLAN Notices,* *35*(3), 209–219.

Bhargavan, K., & Gunter, C. A. (2002). Requirement for a practical network event recognation language. *Electronic Notes in Theoretical Computer Science,* *70*(4), 1–20. doi:10.1016/S1571-0661(04)80574-7

Bhargavan, K., Gunter, C. A., Kim, M., Lee, I., Obradovic, D., Sokolsky, O., & Viswanathan, M. (2002). Verisim: Formal analysis of network simulations. *IEEE Transactions on Software Engineering*, *28*(2), 129–145. doi:10.1109/32.988495

BlanchetB. (2015). Retrieved from http://prosecco.gforge.inria.fr/personal/bblanche/ proverif/

Borralleras, Lucas, & Oliveras, Rodriguez-Carbonell, & Rubio. (2012). SAT modulo linear arithmetic for solving polynomial constraints. *Journal of Automated Reasoning*, *48*(1), 107–131.

Bultan, T. (2000). Action Language: A specification language for model checking reactive systems. *Proceedings of the 22nd International Conference on Software Engineering*, 335–344. 10.1145/337180.337219

Cassar, I., & Francalanza, A. (2016). On implementing a monitor-oriented programming framework for actor systems. *Integrated Formal Methods:* Vol. 9681 of the series. *Lecture Notes in Computer Science*, *9681*, 176–192. doi:10.1007/978-3-319-33693-0_12

Chabot, H., Khoury, R., & Tawbi, N. (2011). Extending the enforcement power of truncation monitors using static analysis. *Computers & Security*, *30*(4), 194–207. doi:10.1016/j.cose.2010.11.004

Cimatti, A., Mover, S., & Tonetta, S. (2013). SMT-based scenario verification for hybrid systems. *Formal Methods in System Design*, *42*(1), 46–66. doi:10.100710703-012-0158-0

Ciobaca, S. (2011). *Verification and composition of security protocols with applications to electronic voting*. Dissertation.

Claessen, K., Een, N., Sheeran, M., Sörensson, N., Voronov, A., & Åkesson, K. (2009, December). SAT-solving in practice, with a tutorial example from supervisory control. *Discrete Event Dynamic Systems*, *19*(4), 495–524. doi:10.100710626-009-0081-8

de Moura, L., & Bjørner, N. (2008). *An efficient theorem prover*. Retrieved from http://research.microsoft.com/en-us/um/redmond/projects/z3/

Delgado, N., Gates, A. Q., & Roach, S. (2004). A taxonomy and catalog of runtime software-fault monitoring tools. *IEEE Transactions on Software Engineering*, *30*(12), 859–872. doi:10.1109/TSE.2004.91

Dolzhenko, E., Ligatti, J., & Reddy, S. (2015). Modeling runtime enforcement with mandatory results automata. *International Journal of Information Security*, *14*(1), 47–60. doi:10.100710207-014-0239-8

Dubois, D., Lang, J., & Prade, H. (1994). Possibilistic logic. (1994). *Fuzzy Sets and Systems*, *144*(1), 439–513.

Dubois, D., & Prade, H. (2014). *Possibilistic logic: An overview. In Handbook of the History of Logic* (pp. 283–342). Elsevier.

Erl, T. (2005). *Service-oriented architecture: concepts, technology, and design*. Prentice Hall.

Erlingsson, U., & Schneider, F. B. (1999). SASI enforcement of security policies: A retrospective. In *Proceedings of the Workshop on New Security Paradigms*. ACM Press. 10.1109/DISCEX.2000.821527

Falcone, Y., Mounier, L., Fernandez, J. C., & Richier, J. L. (2011). Runtime enforcement monitors: Composition, synthesis, and enforcement abilities. *Formal Methods in System Design*, *38*(2), 223–262. doi:10.100710703-011-0114-4

Gamage, T. T., McMillin, B. M., & Roth, T. P. (2010). Enforcing information flow security properties in cyber-physical systems: a generalized framework based on compensation. *Proceedings of the 2010 IEEE 34th Annual Computer Software and Applications Conference Workshops*, 158-163. 10.1109/COMPSACW.2010.36

Garg, D., Jia, L., & Datta, A. (2011). Policy auditing over incomplete logs: Theory, implementation and applications. In *Proceedings of the 18th ACM Conference on Computer and Communications Security*. ACM Press. 10.1145/2046707.2046726

Gelfond, M., & Lifschitz, V. (1993). Representing actions in extended logic programming. *Tenth Joint International Conference & Symposium on Logic Programming*, 559-573.

Halle, S., & Villemaire, R. (2012). Runtime enforcement of web service message contracts with data. *IEEE Transactions on Services Computing*, *5*(2), 192–206. doi:10.1109/TSC.2011.10

Havelund, K. (2014). Rule-based runtime verification revisited. *International Journal of Software Tools for Technology Transfer*, *17*(2), 143–170. doi:10.100710009-014-0309-2

Havelund, K. (2015). Rule-based runtime verification revisited. *International Journal of Software Tools for Technology Transfer, 17*(2), 143–170. doi:10.100710009-014-0309-2

Jiang, X., Wang, X., & Xu, D. (2007). Stealthy malware detection through vmm-based out-of-the-box semantic view reconstruction. *ACM Conference on Computer and Communications Security*, 128-138. 10.1145/1315245.1315262

Kedar, S. N., & Richard, J. T. (2010). On the completeness of compositional reasoning methods. *ACM Transactions on Computational Logic, 11*(3), 1–22. doi:10.1145/1740582.1740584

Kim, M., Lee, I., Sammapun, U., Shin, J., & Sokolsky, O. (2002). Monitoring, checking, and steering of real-time systems. *Proceeding of 2nd International Conference on Runtime Verification.* 10.1016/S1571-0661(04)80579-6

Kim, M., Viswanathan, M., Ben-Abdallah, H., Kannan, S., Lee, I., & Sokolsky, O. (1999). Formally specified monitoring of temporal properties. *11th Euromicro Conference on Real-Time Systems*, 114-122.

Kowalski, R. A., & Sergot, M. J. (1986). A logic-based calculus of events. *New Generation Computing, 4*(1), 67–95. doi:10.1007/BF03037383

Kruglov. (2013). *Superposition modulo theory* (Dissertation). Universität des Saarlandes.

Lang, J. (2000). Possibilistic logic: complexity and algorithms. Handbook of defeasible reasoning & uncertainty management systems.

Lee, I., Kannan, S., Kim, M., Sokolsky, O., & Viswanathan, M. (1999). Runtime assurance based on formal specifications. *International Conference on Parallel and Distributed Processing Techniques and Applications*, 279-287.

LibVMI. (2014). *Simplified virtual machine introspection.* Retrieved from https://github.com/libvmi/libvmi

Ligatti, J., Bauer, L., & Walker, D. (2005). Edit automata: Enforcement mechanisms for run-time security policies. *International Journal of Information Security, 4*(1-2), 2–16. doi:10.100710207-004-0046-8

Ligatti, J., Bauer, L., & Walker, D. (2009). Run-time enforcement of nonsafety policies. *ACM Transactions on Information and System Security, 12*(3), 3. doi:10.1145/1455526.1455532

Ligatti, J., & Reddy, S. (2010). A theory of runtime enforcement, with results. In *Computer Security–ESORICS 2010* (pp. 87–100). Springer. doi:10.1007/978-3-642-15497-3_6

Ligatti, J., & Reddy, S. (2010). A theory of runtime enforcement with results. In *Proceedings of the 15th European Symposium on Research in Computer Security*. Springer. 10.1007/978-3-642-15497-3_6

Ligh, M. H., Case, A., Levy, J., & Walters, A. (2014). *The art of memory forensics*. Indianapolis, IN: John Wiley & Sons, Inc.

Mao, Y. F., Zhang, Y., Hua, Q., & Dai, H. Y. (2015). A non-intrusive solution to guarantee runtime behavior of open SCADA systems. *IEEE International Conference of Web Services*. 10.1109/ICWS.2015.105

McCarthy, J., & Hayes, P. (1969). Some philosophical problems from the standpoint of artificial intelligence. In B. Meltzer & D. Michie (Eds.), *Machine Intelligence* (Vol. 4, pp. 463–502). Edinburgh: Edinburgh University Press.

Mendling. (2007). *Detection and Prediction of Errors in EPC Business Process Models* (Dissertation). Vienna University of Economics and Business Administration.

Nelson, G., & Oppen, D. C. (1979). Simplication by cooperating decision procedures. *ACM Transactions on Programming Languages and Systems*, 2(1), 245–257. doi:10.1145/357073.357079

Netfilter. (2015). *The software of the packet filtering framework inside the Linux 2.4.x*. Retrieved from http://www.nftables.org/

O'Neil Meredith, P., Jin, D., Griffith, D., Chen, F., & Rosu, G. (2012). An overview of the MOP runtime verification framework. *International Journal of Software Tools for Technology Transfer*, 14(3), 249–289. doi:10.100710009-011-0198-6

Plaisted. (2003). A hierarchical situation calculus. *J. Computing Research Repository*.

Reiter, R. (2001). *Knowledge in action: logical foundations for specifying and implementing dynamical systems*. The MIT Press.

Scheer, A. W. (1998). *ARIS: business process modeling* (2nd ed.). Berlin: Springer-Verlag. doi:10.1007/978-3-662-03526-9_24

Schneider, F. B. (2000). Enforceable security policies. *ACM T. Inform. Syst. Se, 3*(1), 30–50. doi:10.1145/353323.353382

Sebastiani. (2007). Lazy satisfiability modulo theories. *Journal on Satisfiability, Boolean Modeling and Computation, 3*(3-4), 141–224.

Sen, K., Vardhan, A., Agha, G., & Rosu, G. (2004). Efficient decentralized monitoring of safety in distributed systems. *ICSE'04: Proceedings of 6th International Conference on Software Engineering*, 418-427. 10.1109/ICSE.2004.1317464

Sheeran, M., & Singh, S. (2002). Checking safety properties using induction and a SAT-solver. FMCAD 2000. *LNCS, 1954*, 127–144.

Shoaei, M. R., Kovács, L., & Lennartson, B. (2014). *Supervisory Control of Discrete-Event Systems via IC3. In Hardware and Software: Verification and Testing* (Vol. 8855, pp. 252–266). Springer.

Shostak, R. E. (1984). Deciding combination of theories. *Journal of the Association for Computing Machinery, 1*(31), 1–12. doi:10.1145/2422.322411

Sokolsky, O., Sammapun, U., Lee, I., & Kim, J. (2005). Run-time checking of dynamic properties. *Proceeding of 5th International Conference on Runtime Verification.*

Somenzi & Bradley. (2011). IC3: Where monolithic and incremental meet. *FMCAD.*

van Glabbeek, R., & Goltz, U. (2004). Well-behaved flow event structures for parallel composition and action refinement. *Theoretical Computer Science, 311*(1-3), 463–478. doi:10.1016/j.tcs.2003.10.031

Zhang, Y., & Chen, J. L. (2015). Constructing scalable IoT services based on their event-driven models. *Concurrency and Computation, 27*(17), 4819–4851. doi:10.1002/cpe.3469

Section 5
Summary and Example

Chapter 8
Summary:
IoT Service Provisioning With an Illustrative Example

ABSTRACT

In previous chapters, the design of IoT services using the streamlining and integration principle was discussed. In this chapter, a summary is given of how to use these principles to achieve IoT service provisioning, and an example is given. The event streamlining problem is first discussed from an IoT service provisioning perspective, involving how to efficiently disseminate the sensing events among event producers and consumers on demand. The service integration problem is then considered, which requires dynamic coordination of the relevant IoT services based on events occurring in the real world. An EDSOA is abstracted from the perspective of utilizing the advantages of EDA and SOA, and the streamlining and integration principle is viewed from an architectural perspective. A combination of SOA and EDA can easily support the on-demand dissemination of sensing information and event-driven service dynamic coordination. The example used here is a deployed CMCS application.

INTRODUCTION

The IoT (ITU Internet Reports, 2005; Ma, 2011; Atzori et al., 2010; Bandyopadhyay et al., 2011) is driving business transformation by connecting ubiquitous objects and devices, both to each other and to cloud-hosted services.

DOI: 10.4018/978-1-5225-7622-8.ch008

Real-time control, low-latency application responses and local data aggregation mean that the current mandatory cloud connectivity is undesirable. To sustain the momentum of the development of IoT, a cloud-to-edge continuum is needed, and this is often referred to as 'fog computing' in the literature. In the current work, an EDSOA is defined to address the challenges related to infrastructure and connectivity in IoT scenarios by emphasising information processing and intelligence at the centre-edge continuum. EDSOA represents a shift away from traditional silo systems and a reliance on cloud-only focused paradigms, and is both complementary to, and an extension of, traditional cloud computing. In the proposed EDSOA service platform, computation can be moved from the cloud to the edges of the network, and potentially right up to the IoT sensors and actuators.

An EDSOA IoT service platform to support various industrial applications is an ideal service provisioning mode. This is described in the previous chapters in this book, and offers several unique advantages over other approaches, for example:

- **Knowledge-Based Intelligence:** The physical world and devices are modelled as knowledge on which applications are established.
- **Low Latency:** Real-time processing and cyber-physical system control are achieved by deploying IoT services near to physical systems and devices.
- **Openness:** Heterogeneous sensors and devices are unified as semantic IoT resources for ubiquitous users, and locations are transparent for IoT services and applications in the proposed UMS (a service-oriented wide-area publish/subscribe system over SDN).
- **Agility:** Rapid service development and affordable scaling are available under a common infrastructure.
- **Overlapping Security:** The safety of physical systems and information security overlaps, and the proposed platform supports physical system-oriented security, thus addressing the problem of their interaction.

From the above discussion, it can be seen that a service provisioning approach based on the EDSOA IoT service platform is crucial for current IoT application systems. The question of how to realise this IoT service provisioning has attracted a great deal of attention. Several works (Fok et al., 2009), (Wang et al., 2008) have explored the integration of real-world and enterprise services using mobile agents and middleware methods, although there is a lack of customised platforms and proprietary technologies of deployed heterogeneous sensor networks or application systems. These authors did not offer uniform interfaces across the system, and this complicated the integration. To ensure interoperability across all systems, several works have adopted SOA for IoT service provisioning (Guinard et al., 2010; Motwani et al., 2010; Teixeira et al., 2011). Since traditional SOA technologies are primarily designed for heavy-weight enterprise services, some researchers have tried to use lightweight services to run on more resource-constrained embedded devices (Priyantha et al., 2008; Castellani et al., 2011).

The above works demonstrate that interoperability and interconnection play a key role in the different entities and enterprise application systems in a dynamic interaction environment. An appropriate architecture is needed that can realise these features; this architecture should be designed to address the event streamlining problem, which involves the question of how to efficiently disseminate sensing events among event producers and consumers on demand, in a loosely coupled, decentralised way; and the IoT service integration problem, which involves dynamic coordination of the relevant enterprise services, based on events occurring in the real world, to meet user requirements. In view of these problems, the new characteristics of IoT services have been analysed in the previous chapters of this book, and the EDSOA-based service provisioning approach, which integrates the advantages of both EDA and SOA, will be discussed in this chapter. Here, the focus is primarily on a provisioning solution by dissemination of on-demand sensing information (event streamlining) and the dynamic coordination of event-driven services (service integration), while other features such as IoT security and intelligence have been discussed in previous chapters. More specifically, this chapter focuses on the following:

- A streamlining IoT service platform to support the efficient dissemination of sensing information among different information providers and consumers, based on a publish/subscribe mechanism, is described from the perspectives of the application and the EDSOA architecture. This can facilitate the asynchronous, on-demand dissemination and sharing of events in a largely distributed, loosely coupled IoT environment.
- An event-driven service dynamic coordination mechanism is presented, based on the IoT service platform, that can rapidly respond to changes in the physical world and in the requirements of the enterprise or individual. This approach minimises both explicit and static service orchestration cost, and uses the streamlined event flow to compose the service logic in a dynamic way. It therefore allows for the rapid

reorganisation of business processes without affecting the existing enterprise application or technical structures.

- Finally, to illustrate the proposed approach, a real CMCS application is described.

The remainder of this article is structured as follows. The chapter shows the new characteristics of the IoT service and the technical challenges involved are described. It also presents an EDSOA-based IoT services provisioning approach, including an architectural framework, key technologies and a service provisioning mechanism. A use case of a deployed CMCS is described. Section 5 presents a discussion, and conclusions are drawn later.

IOT SERVICE CHARACTERISTICS

The Characteristics of IoT Services

In order to integrate physical entities into cyberspace, physical entities become active participants in an information system. IoT services can interact with these "smart objects" over the network, and can query and change their state and any information associated with them. IoT services not only need to interact with the user and information space, but also need to monitor the physical world and to control it with appropriate reactions. An IoT service can make decisions that perform appropriate actions based on the perceived physical situation and the response policy. IoT services are then faced with a 3-tuple problem involving the user, the information and the physical space. Figure 1 illustrates the human/machine/thing interactions involved in IoT services.

Figure 1. System boundary for the IoT service

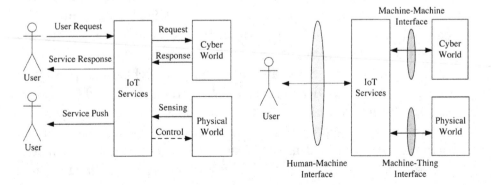

From Figure 1, it can be seen that the IoT service provisioning environment is different from those of Internet and telecommunications services. In IoT scenarios, numerous physical sensors generate vast numbers of events, which need to be shared among different application stakeholders. The IoT service provisioning pattern is shifted to "sensing events → complex event processing → intelligent decision → service coordination". In this chapter, the collection, transmission and fusion of multi-source sensing information in the network is referred to as "cognitive flow". A traditional service delivery mechanism is established based on the bearing flow and control flow, where a bearing flow refers to the range of voice, data and multimedia content that is transported over the network, and a control flow primarily refers to the range of request/response messages, call signalling and management control operations in the network. In this way, the emergence of "cognitive flow" influences the service provisioning mechanism of IoT, as illustrated in Figure 2.

Technical Challenges of IoT Service Provisioning

The integration of the real world with cyberspace has given rise to new challenges for IoT service provisions. The following lists some specific technical challenges.

1. **Event Streamlining Challenge:** Most existing IoT application systems are still based on a silo system, where sensored events are processed in a centralised manner, and the problem of the dissemination and processing of sensing information among different enterprises is not considered, especially in large-scale, distributed computing environments. Event providers and consumers often directly communicate with each other

Figure 2. The concept of cognitive flow

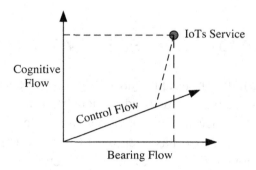

explicitly in a client-server paradigm. In an ideal IoT environment, event providers are often decoupled from event consumers, and need not even be aware of their existence; each can continue to run regardless of the other. Thus, the issue of how to handle numerous events, disseminate them in an orderly way, and establish an event transmission, sharing and integration mechanism for the relevant enterprises and individual users is a key problem in the development of the IoT industry, and this is known as an event streamlining challenge. A wide-area event communication infrastructure and a corresponding decoupling mechanism for the dimensions of space, time, and control therefore need to be explored in order to match the open, collaborative, distributed and dynamic nature of IoT applications.

2. **Event-Driven Service Integration Challenge:** Faced with the 3-tuple problem of "user, information and physical space", IoT service provisioning must address the issues of flexibility and event-reaction. The individual requirements of users are diverse and time-varying, meaning that a business process needs to be flexible, rather than hard coded, and able to react to new, changed requirements. From the perspective of physical space, the decentralised and heterogeneous nature of sensors and entities requires a scalable, open service provisioning mechanism to minimise the coupling degree between the physical space and IoT services, and to respond to changes in the physical world. From an information perspective, IoT services often involve the aggregation of several distributed enterprise application systems that build a larger, composite IoT system. An IoT business process services therefore requires the interaction and collaboration of several decoupled systems in different domains. The development of a new flexible service integration mechanism that can orchestrate distributed and federated applications across enterprises is one of the challenges involved in building IoT applications, and is an event-driven IoT service integration challenge.

EDSOA-BASED IOT SERVICES PROVISION APPROACH

In SOA (Erl, 2005), the entire application is often broken down into many independent services, which are used to achieve functionality reuse and interoperability. EDA (Event-Driven architecture overview, 2008), (Hou et al., 2006; Liu et al., 2010) has been used to realise the coordination of loosely coupled applications. Due to the heterogeneity of physical entities

Figure 3. The event-driven SOA approach

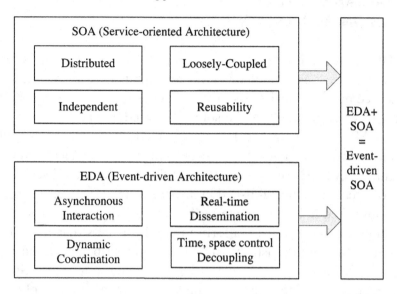

and the dynamic sharing of sensing information in IoT applications, both SOA and EDA have certain limitations on the scope of applications. EDA can complement SOA, since services can be driven by triggers caused by incoming events. Several related works have discussed the integration of SOA with EDA. Overbeek et al. (2009) proposed a flexible, event-driven SOA for orchestrating services in government organisations. Dasgupta et al. (2009) presented a proactive event-driven model in which user activities and services were processed as events to support service composition. However, these works did not resolve the issue of IoT service provisioning by EDSOA. The current authors' research team have presented a preliminary idea related to event-driven SOA for IoT services (Zhu et al., 2011). In the present chapter, a comprehensive EDSOA-based IoT service provisioning approach is presented based on this existing work, as illustrated in Figure 3. In this approach, SOA is used to address the problem of the interoperability and reusability of different heterogeneous services in a distributed, loosely coupled IoT environment. EDA can be used to achieve the on-demand dissemination of sensing events and event-driven service dynamic coordination. This combination of SOA and EDA allows IoT services to react rapidly to real-world changes, and is thus well suited to IoT scenarios.

EDSOA-BASED IOT SERVICES PROVISIONING FRAMEWORK

The EDSOA-based IoT service provisioning framework is illustrated in Figure 4. An access agent collects physical stimuli observed by sensors, and IoT resource models translate the heterogeneous or proprietary information into unified semantic events and resource knowledge. The access agent then uses the UMS in the proposed IoT service platform, invoking the publish/subscribe interface to publish the events to the publish/subscribe-based streamlining UMS, which is responsible for the publication, subscription and routing of events. Events published in the streamlining IoT service platform can be subscribed to by any related IoT services. IoT services can also use the streamlining IoT service platform to publish events that could be sent to the sensors as control instructions. When a subscribed event occurs, the streamlining IoT service platform notifies the related subscribers. Similarly, the IoT application systems can also publish/subscribe high-level business events to realise service coordination among different application systems. For example, when the complex events process service detects an emergency warning event, a notification is sent to the data visualisation portal to show a warning signal; a notification is also sent to the workflow systems to trigger the related business process to deal with this event. Thus, it can be seen that these different systems no longer communicate directly with each other; the streamlining IoT service platform forms a core part of the architecture and further decouples the different IoT application systems. Communication is accomplished through a publish/subscribe mechanism.

UMS: Streamlining IoT Service Platform Based on Publish/Subscribe Paradigms

The streamlining IoT service platform utilises the publish/subscribe mechanism to disseminate the events. A primary component of the streamlining IoT service platform is the event broker, which provides event publication, subscription, notification and routing functions. The event publishers and subscribers use the event broker to communicate with one another, based on a set of subscriptions. Each consumer sends one or more subscription request to the event broker, identifying the types of event that it wants to receive. The event broker in turn delivers events to customers who have subscribed, as these events occur. The broker typically performs a 'store and forward' function

Figure 4. EDSOA-based IoT services provisioning architecture

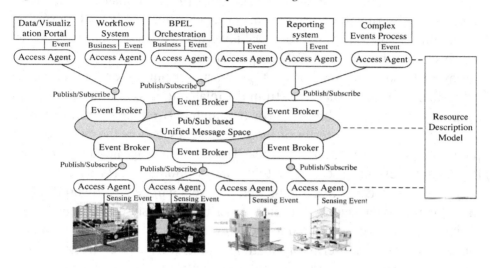

to route messages from publishers to subscribers. As illustrated in Figure 5a, the event broker consists of three parts: a publish/subscribe interface, an event subscription table and the core application functions. The publish/ subscribe interfaces provide services for the publisher and subscriber to use the streamlining IoT service platform. In this approach, a streamlining IoT service platform adopts a topic-based publish/subscribe mechanism. In a topic-based system, events are published to "topics". Subscribers receive all events published to those topics to which they subscribe, and all subscribers to a topic will receive the same events. The subscriber or publisher first

Figure 5a. Framework for the event broker

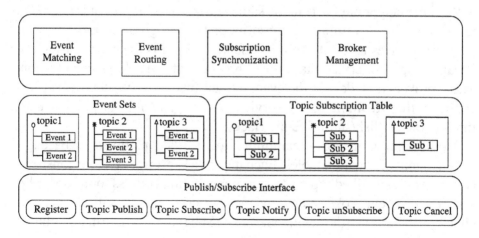

needs to register with the event broker; it can then publish an event as a publisher, subscribe to existing events as a subscriber, or both. In terms of event notification, the event broker achieves the 'event push' function using a web services notification (WSN) specification (WSN, 2005). In addition, the event broker also provides a topic unsubscribing interface, so that a subscriber also can unsubscribe from the related topics. In order to support event routing, the event broker needs to maintain two types of information: event sets and a topic subscription table. The event sets store the most recently published events related to the topics. The event routing module processes the incoming events based on the topic subscription table. If a subscriber is only administrated by this event broker, the event will be directly notified by the topic notify interface. If the subscriber is not registered with this event broker, the event will be routed to the relevant brokers. In order to maintain the consistency of subscription in streamlining IoT service platform, each event broker needs to synchronise the subscriptions.

To support wide-area distributed event dissemination, event brokers can form different groups to provide scalability at the cluster level, and groups of event brokers can then be linked together to allow geographic scaling. The unified space layer is therefore implemented as a distributed overlay network formed by a set of event brokers. In this cluster-based topology, the streamlining IoT service platform needs to support both intra-cluster and inter-cluster routing. Within each cluster, a designated event broker is responsible for inter-cluster routing, and is referred to as a delegate. The concrete topology of streamlining IoT service platform is shown in Figure 5b. Publishers or subscribers connect to one of these brokers, and publish or subscribe through that broker. When a broker receives a subscription from one of its clients, it acts on behalf of the clients and forwards this subscription to the other neighbour hosts in the same cluster; the delegate of this group is responsible for forwarding the subscription to other groups. Similarly, when a broker receives an event from its client, it forwards the event through the streamlining IoT service platform to brokers with matching subscriptions. These brokers then deliver the event to their interested clients. IoT services can view the streamlining IoT service platform as an event pool accessed through the publish/subscribe interfaces.

Event routing in the streamlining IoT service platform is based on subscription information tables. Each item in a subscription table consists of two parts: a subscribed topic and a communication address for a subscriber. The general event broker maintains two subscription tables: the registered_clients_SubTable and the neighbour_hosts_SubTable. The registered_clients_

Figure 5b. Cluster-based streamlining IoT service platform

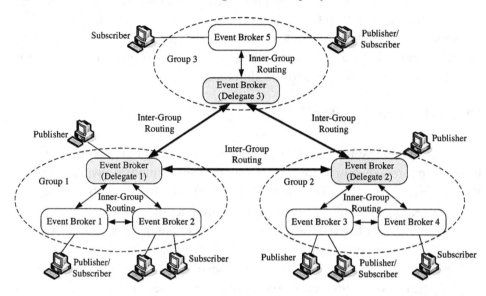

SubTable stores subscription information of clients that directly register with this broker. The neighbour_hosts_SubTable stores subscription information of other event brokers from the same cluster. Since the delegate of each cluster is responsible for inter-cluster routing, with the comparison of general event broker, the delegate also needs to maintain a copy of the clusters_ SubTable in order to store subscription information from other interested clusters. Figure 6 shows the changes in the subscription tables when subscriber 1 of cluster 1 subscribes to topic X and subscriber 2 of cluster 2 subscribes to topic Y.

Figure 6. Topic subscription mechanisms

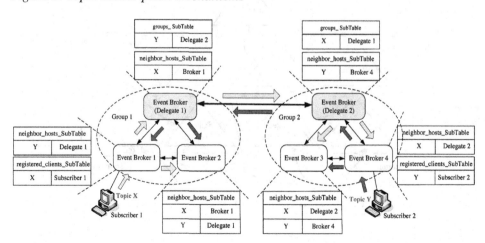

When a broker receives an event published by its own registered client, it looks up the subscription tables and then forwards this event to the relevant subscribers. An event is first routed within a cluster, and is then routed between clusters if other clusters also subscribe to it. Detailed routing algorithms for distributed events can be found in (Shi et al., 2011).

The IoT Resource Model

An extended IoT resource model (for example, linked together based on linked data) can express resource, context information and domain knowledge. Based on this resource model, the proposed access agent can automatically access resources, and generate semantic context information and events.

Figure 7 shows the ontologies used in the semantic model. DOLCE, at the top level, is an ontology used by W3C SSN. The upper layer uses W3C SSN to describe the sensor resources and observation data, although context model and domain knowledge extensions are needed. OWL-Time is used to express time information. SemSOS O&M (Overbeek et al., 2009) and SENSEI O&M are extended, as in the observation data model. Linked data are also used to link the model to ontologies such as FOAF, GeoNames, Linked-GeoData and DBpedia. OWL-S is the upper ontology describing the service. FOAF allows the model to be more generalised, and provides additional information. GeoName and Linked-GeoData are worldwide geographic location ontologies that express the global location of entities

Figure 7. Overview of the ontologies used in the semantic model

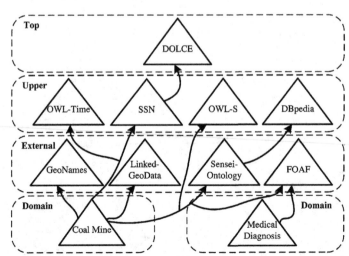

and resources. DBpedia contains structured data extracted from Wikipedia, and provides a relationship between generic concepts. The domain ontologies in the bottom layer extend the ontologies mentioned above, and can express domain knowledge. The proposed resource model contains two parts: a resource description and an entity description. The resource description is used to describe and dynamically maintain sensor/actuator resource information, while the entity description is used to describe the monitored objects and model the context information of business scenarios. In this semantic model, the observation of the resource model is associated with the domain attribute of the entity model. This association is known as resource-entity binding, and is the basis for promoting the observation data to context information. The binding can be static or dynamic, and can be generated automatically or manually. Reasoning and the semantic integration of information such as the resource type, tag, observation type, QoI and cost are needed in order to bind the resource and the entity.

The access agent converts heterogeneous raw sensing information to unified observation information, based on its resource description, and generates observation events. The resource-entity binding relationship can then be used to promote the observation information to context information; context information is related to other existing information to form semantic context information based on domain knowledge. Figure 8 shows a fragment of a simple observation event. The "entity" attribute indicates which entities this event is related to, and the "resource" attribute indicates which resources detect the event. In addition, the event instance contains information such as the alarm level, alarm time, observation value, data unit, threshold value, etc.

Resource Access

After modelling IoT resources, physical systems and devices should be accessed to obtain fresh monitoring data. The resource accessing utility aims not only to recognise resources and communicate with them, but also to interpret raw data into observation data. Resource access points lie between the resource adaptation layer and the information dissemination layer. This utility also generates context information and produces events based on the above resource models. It also maps resource operations to service interfaces.

As shown in Figure 9, a PLC sends a H7000 register packet to the resource platform, in which the resource adaptor selects an appropriate protocol stack to communicate with the PLC, and the access point semantically interprets

Figure 8. Fragment of simple observation event

```
<ClassAssertion>
     <Class IRI="http://www.loa-cnr.it/ontologies/DUL.owl#Event"/>
     <NamedIndividual IRI="#ch4Alarm"/>
</ClassAssertion>
  <ObjectPropertyAssertion>
     <ObjectProperty IRI="#entity"/>
     <NamedIndividual IRI="#ch4Alarm"/>
     <NamedIndividual IRI="#pumping_station_3"/>
  </ObjectPropertyAssertion>
  <ObjectPropertyAssertion>
     <ObjectProperty IRI="#resource"/>
     <NamedIndividual IRI="#ch4Alarm"/>
     <NamedIndividual IRI="#drainage_pumping_station_sensor1"/>
  </ObjectPropertyAssertion>
  <DataPropertyAssertion>
     <DataProperty IRI="#alarm_form"/>
     <NamedIndividual IRI="#ch4Alarm"/>
     <Literal datatypeIRI="&xsd;string">voice</Literal>
  </DataPropertyAssertion>
  <DataPropertyAssertion>
     <DataProperty IRI="#alarm_level"/>
     <NamedIndividual IRI="#ch4Alarm"/>
     <Literal datatypeIRI="&xsd;short">2</Literal>
  </DataPropertyAssertion>
  <DataPropertyAssertion>
     <DataProperty IRI="#alarm_time"/>
     <NamedIndividual IRI="#ch4Alarm"/>
     <Literal datatypeIRI="&xsd;dateTime">2010-10-12T23:05:04</Literal>
  </DataPropertyAssertion>
  <DataPropertyAssertion>
     <DataProperty IRI="#threshold_alarm"/>
     <NamedIndividual IRI="#ch4Alarm"/>
     <Literal datatypeIRI="&xsd;double">0.8</Literal>
  </DataPropertyAssertion>
  <DataPropertyAssertion>
     <DataProperty IRI="#value"/>
     <NamedIndividual IRI="#ch4Alarm"/>
     <Literal datatypeIRI="&xsd;double">1.1</Literal>
  </DataPropertyAssertion>
```

Figure 9. Device access packet

STX	Type	Length	DTU ID	Address	Port	End
		H7000 DTU Register Packet				
0x7B	0x01	0x16	0x16fee0e54f	0x747154	0x5398	0x7B

STX	Type	Length	DTU ID	End
		H7000 DTU Logout Packet		
0x7B	0x02	0x10	0x16fee0e54f	0x7B

the raw data in H7000 DTU. The resource adaptor analyses the H7000 packet and determines whether it is a legal register message. It then extracts the device information from the packet and publishes a device description to the resource platform (see Figure 10a). As Figure 10b shows, the device corresponds to a temperature resource. The quantity type and unit property are linked to the standard physical quantity of QU ontology.

Figure 10a. Device publishing

```
<Device rdf:ID="DTU_98765432143">
  <device_ID rdf:datatype="http://www.w3.org/2001/XMLSchema#string"
  >98765432143</device_ID>
  <port rdf:datatype="http://www.w3.org/2001/XMLSchema#int"
  >21400</port>
  <address rdf:datatype="http://www.w3.org/2001/XMLSchema#string"
  >116.113.84.218</address>
</Device>
```

Figure 10b. Resource description

```
<Resource rdf:about="#98765432143_1_D104">
  <observation_range rdf:datatype="http://www.w3.org/2001/XMLSchema#string"
  >QHBCQ</observation_range>
  <device_ID rdf:datatype="http://www.w3.org/2001/XMLSchema#string"
  >98765432143</device_ID>
  <unit rdf:resource="http://purl.oclc.org/NET/ssnx/qu/unit#degreeCelsius"/>
  <address rdf:datatype="http://www.w3.org/2001/XMLSchema#string"
  >116.113.84.218</address>
  <measure_type rdf:datatype="http://www.w3.org/2001/XMLSchema#string"
  >SWWD</measure_type>
  <description rdf:datatype="http://www.w3.org/2001/XMLSchema#string"
  >2#climate compensator</description>
  <port rdf:datatype="http://www.w3.org/2001/XMLSchema#int"
  >21400</port>
  <PLC rdf:datatype="http://www.w3.org/2001/XMLSchema#string"
  >1</PLC>
  <quantity_type
rdf:resource="http://purl.oclc.org/NET/ssnx/qu/quantity#temperature"/>
  <resource_id rdf:datatype="http://www.w3.org/2001/XMLSchema#string"
  >D104</resource_id>
</Resource>
```

Application developers need only focus on the entities and application logic of application scenarios, without considering the adaptation of, access to or management of resources. They send resource requests to the resource platform, which responds with the appropriate resources. Following this, developers can use the IoT resources, which may belong to different organisations and domains.

Complex Event Processing

From the above descriptions, it can be seen that access agents resolve the information collection and preprocessing problem, and that the streamlining IoT service platform provides a flexible event delivery mechanism between information providers and consumers. The fusion of information also needs to be supported. IoT applications often include a vast amount of sensor information and business events, and the automated analysis of real-time data plays an increasingly important role in IoT applications. IoT applications often need to process streaming event data and to take low-latency, intelligent decisions in response to the changing conditions reflected in these events. The use of real-time or near real-time systems in a variety of IoT application domains demands the ability to extract meaning (e.g. high-level contextual information or potential business opportunities) from potentially disparate events from a variety of sources. The fusion of information or events, also known as complex event processing (CEP), is a crucial technology in smart IoT applications. CEP involves event processing that combines data from multiple sources to infer events or patterns that suggest more complicated circumstances. The goal of CEP is to identify meaningful events and to respond to them as quickly as possible. CEP allows applications to apply real-time intelligence to streaming data by making it easy to identify "complex" sequences of events with temporal constraints.

The functions of classic open-source-Esper CEP are illustrated in Figure 11. To enable streamlining event processing, the CEP engine allows applications to store event queries and to run the data through, rather than storing the data and running queries against stored data. An input/output event flow adapter is responsible for the adaptation of different event representation formats, such as XML or Java Object. In order to support the definition of complex event detection rules, a tailored event processing language (EPL) is used to express rich event conditions and correlations, possibly spanning several time windows. EPL is a SQL-like language with clauses such as SELECT, FROM, WHERE, GROUP BY, HAVING and ORDER BY. The example statement below demonstrates such selections by selecting the locationId, temperature and smoke values of sensors over pairs of events (a TemperatureSensor event followed by a SmokeSensor event for the same location ID, within one minute) occurring in the last two hours, in which the temperature sensor and smoke sensor are all in the "warning" state, and the event query result is grouped by location ID.

To facilitate the definition of event detection patterns, the CEP engine generally provides a visual event pattern editor. Users can define rules and conditions called patterns to filter the events of interest. The generated event detection rules or statements are loaded into the runtime CEP engine. The event pattern detection module then aggregates information from distributed systems in real time, and applies these rules to discern patterns. Upon detection of predefined patterns, alert events are notified to the relevant event listeners. Each event listener can decide on certain actions based on their specific

Box 1.

```
select a.locationId, a.temperature, b.smoke
from pattern [every a=TemperatureSensor ->
    b=SmokeSensor(locationId = a.locationId) where timer:within(1 min)].win:time(2 hour)
where a.Status=' warning' and b.Status=' warning'
group by a.locationId
```

application needs. The derived high-level events can also be republished to the UMS and treated as new events, thus enabling nested patterns. The CEP engine has the ability to process multiple event streams, recognise significant events, and deliver data derived from one or multiple streams when the event is triggered. In addition, in order to facilitate the processing of a customised event type, users can register event types with the CEP engine to simplify the writing of an EPL statement.

Situation-Awareness Service Adaptation Mechanism

Through the perception, on-demand delivery, filtering and aggregation of multi-source sensing information, some high-level events can be derived, such as fire alarms or abnormal movements of goods. Once the events of interest are triggered, the following business actions need to react to the situation. Since a fully automatic service composition is not realistic at present, a flexible, practical service adaptation mechanism is necessary to satisfy the variability

Figure 11. Complex event processing

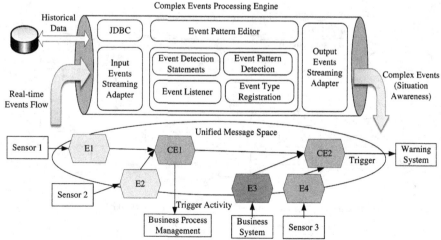

in the application requirements and the dynamic coordination of multiple heterogeneous service systems (see Figure 12). In the current approach, two measures are adopted to enhance the flexible adaptation capability.

- Business systems, whose functions are relatively independent, utilise an event-driven method to collaborate as far as possible. This means that business systems mainly use the event publish/subscribe mechanism to deliver messages. In this method, there are no explicit, centralised service orchestrations to define the order of invocation of web services or other services, and the event flow is used to drive the coordination of different business systems. For example, business system 1 generates and publishes event 1, which is subscribed to by business systems 2 and 5. When business systems 2 and 5 receive event 1, the corresponding business activities are executed. Then, business system 5 generates event 2, which triggers business system 4. In this case, when there are changes in requirements, the user may adjust the event flow to change the business logic, thus changing the publication and subscription of events. For instance, when a new business system 6 is integrated into this system and expresses interest in event 1, it need only subscribe to event 1, without affecting the existing business systems. Event publishers are not aware of the existence of event subscribers. The event-driven service coordination thus enables an asynchronous many-to-many communication approach in which a single specific event can impact many subscribers. This event-driven service coordination

Figure 12. Flexible service adaptation mechanisms

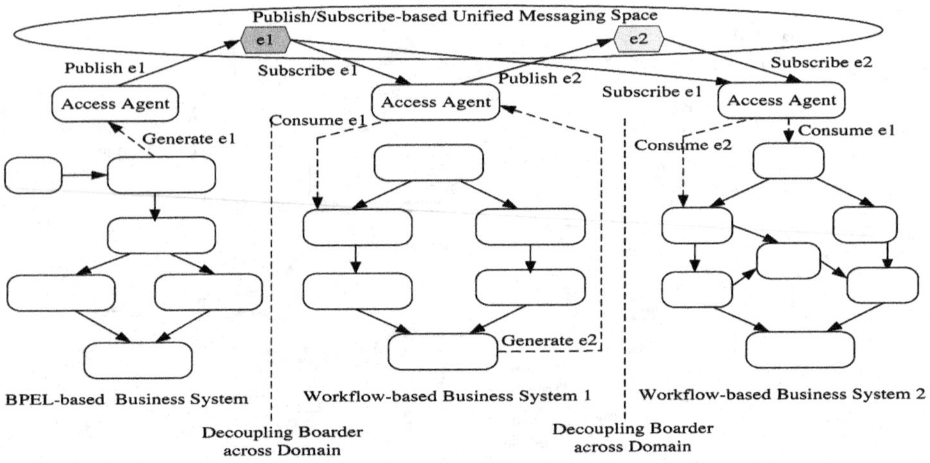

mechanism can therefore help to decouple the different systems and domains, leading to a more flexible and agile architecture.

- However, this does not mean that all request-driven service interactions should be replaced with event-driven ones. For the implementation of a specific business system, traditional request-driven, service-oriented technologies are still encouraged in order to enhance the flexibility of the system. To improve the agility of a business system, several well-defined business functionalities should be built as shared software components (discrete pieces of code and/or data structures) so that they can be reused for different purposes. Services with this characteristic can address novel requirements by recomposing these services in different configurations. When the business requirements undergo changes, users can adjust the business process specified by web services or any other workflow language, to quickly respond to these needs.

PROTOTYPE DEMONSTRATION AND EVALUATION

Prototype Demonstration

In order to verify the proposed EDSOA-based IoT service provisioning mechanism, a CMCS application was developed for this service delivery platform. Figure 13a illustrates the architecture of the event-driven CMCS functions. From this figure, it can be seen that this is a flat structure in which services and components collaborate to achieve the business goal. It provides a set of tools including a UI composition tool, a report generation tool, a warning customisation tool, a CEP definition tool, a resource modelling tool, etc. Using these tools, an engineer can generate specific IoT services with respect to specific requirements such as human-machine interface (HMI) services, report services, warning services, and so on. The application in Figure 14 is constructed using the tools and functions in Figure 13a. In this practical application, the streamlining IoT service platform and the process engine form the service execution environment. The process engine is a set of distributed containers that execute the coordination interfaces. In this real application, a service component architecture (SCA) container is used, and the coordination interfaces are hard-coded in Java and executed in the former. Some snapshots of results from the CMCS application are also illustrated in Figure 13b. More details about the CMCS can be found in (Chen et al., 2011),

Figure 13a. The CMCS function architecture

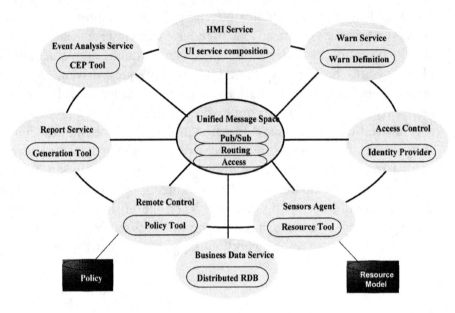

Figure 13b. The CMCS application in a coal mine

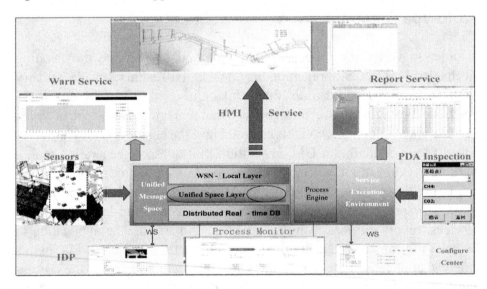

(Huang et al., 2011) including the HMI service, the monitor and control agent (MCA) service, the warning service, and so on.

To demonstrate the work mechanism, a simplified CMCS is shown in Figure 14, where the event flows are illustrated including event publishing

Figure 14. A simplified CMCS

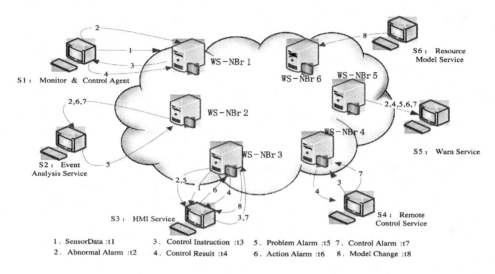

1. SensorData :t1	3. Control Instruction :t3	5. Problem Alarm :t5	7. Control Alarm :t7
2. Abnormal Alarm :t2	4. Control Result :t4	6. Action Alarm :t6	8. Model Change :t8

and event subscribing represented by arrows, and large-scale real-time data are updated every second. In this CMCS, there are six Web services: the MCA service, the EA service, the HMI service, the RA service, the warning service, and the RM Service.

The MCS service collects sensor data, for example on CH4 and CO. The EA service receives data and alarms, and analyses these data to identify system problems. In the HMI service, a coal mine picture is used with an industrial configuration graph showing real-time data and abnormal alarms; safety operators use this to dispatch and control the devices and employees within the mine. Based on the level of abnormal data, the warning service will notify certain responsible individuals in different ways, using lights, sounds, voice recordings, e-mail, SMS, etc. The RA service can control devices in the mine automatically. The RM service is in charge of modifying device and sensor models when tunnels are changed in the mine.

Experimental Evaluation

To evaluate the performance of the proposed approach, a publish/subscribe-based experimental environment for the streamlining IoT service platform was deployed, consisting of nine physical machines and 10 virtual machines. Figure 15 illustrates the receiving rate when there is only one publishing services. When the load exceeds 504 events/s published by one service, some events will be discarded. Figure 16 illustrates the multiple receiving

Figure 15. Receiving rate

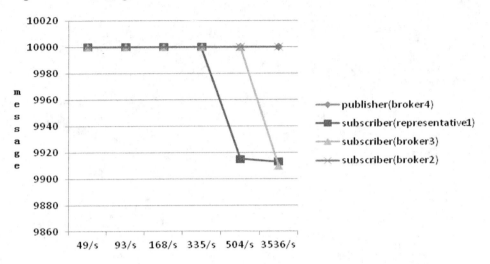

Figure 16. Multiple receiving rates

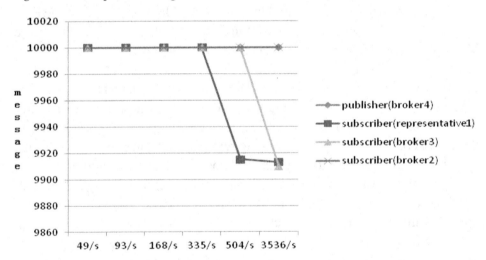

rates when multiple services publish events at rates exceeding 504 events/s. From the figure, it can be seen that the receiving rate decreases when the publishing rate increases.

Figure 17a illustrates the structure of the services when the jitter is measured in multiple clusters. Figure 17b illustrates the jitter in multiple clusters.

In order to compare the event-driven IoT service coordination with the classic service orchestration, several experiments were carried out using the LoadRunner (2008) testing tool. S1 and S2 were chosen as two basic

Figure 17a. Multiple clusters

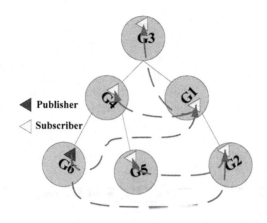

Figure 17b. Jitter in multiple clusters

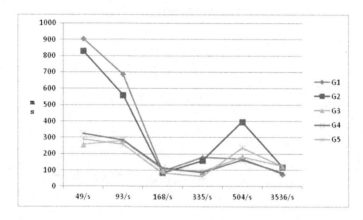

services, Apache ODE (2008) was used as a BPEL orchestrator, in which the processing logic was programmed as a BPEL process, and S1 and S2 provided only plain WSDL interfaces. For event-driven service coordination, the CMCS system was used, and only S1 and S2 were run. The sensors were simulated using LoadRunner scripts. The raw data from the sensors included only CH4 and CO, and the number of randomised data points was 10,000, with CH4 and CO taking 50% each. These were deployed on a PC cluster, and the focus was on the response time and hits per second.

From Figure 18a, it can be seen that the orchestrator needs 3 min and 20 s to complete all processing; the maximum number of hits per s was 69, and the average number of hits per s was 48.309. From Figure 18b, the average response time is 0.136 s.

Figure 18a. Hits/s for orchestrator

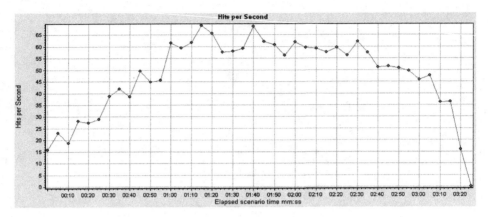

Figure 18b. Response time of orchestrator

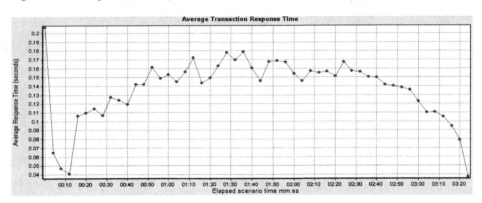

For event-driven IoT service coordination, S1 and S2 are simultaneous, and the longest running time is therefore chosen, i.e. S1. Figure 19a shows that CMCS only needs 1 min 52 s to complete all processing, the maximum number of hits per s is 117.6, and the average number of hits per s is 85.47. From Figure 19b, it can be seen that the average response times are 0.052 and 0.053 s for S1 and S2. It is therefore clear that the processing speed of the orchestrator is lower than for CMCS, and that the event-driven service coordination is more suitable for time-critical applications. The reason for this is that there is a central control point in the BPEL process, such that all messages travel along longer paths and await their turn in the central processing queue.

Figure 19a. Hits per second for CMCS

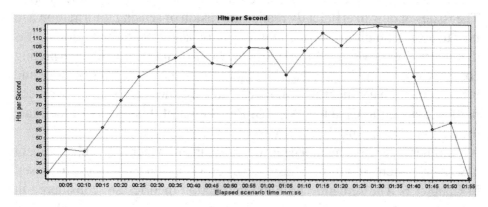

Figure 19b. Response time of CMCS

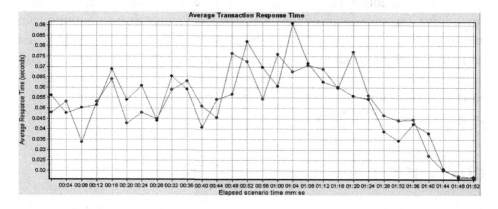

DISCUSSION

It can be seen that the event-driven, service-oriented architecture provides a flexible, loosely coupled service provisioning approach which can satisfy the new service characteristics of IoT. In order to provide smart and autonomous IoT applications, several issues need to be considered that are not discussed in this chapter such as IoT service security, although these have been covered in previous chapters. Since the heterogeneous entities and devices often move and interact dynamically with different application systems, the meanings of events require a consistent semantic understanding by different devices and systems. In addition, in an IoT environment, various entities and devices will (actively or passively) generate massive amounts of sensing information, which has multi-source, dynamic, uncertain and heterogeneous characteristics. The issues of how to efficiently realise the fusion of sensing information and how to abstract high-level context information also need to be explored. It is therefore necessary to further explore methods of automatically interpreting complex events, adding semantic annotation (what will happen next and what precautionary measures should be taken); these questions have been partly discussed in Chapters 2 and 3. Resolution of this issue will facilitate the advent of more intelligent IoT services.

Another aspect that has not been discussed in this paper is the enhancement of semantic interoperability in the service description specifications discussed in Chapter 6. The semantic problem and action theories are considered in the service description. This mode is more suited to service coordination between definite entities, devices and enterprises or organisations application system. In the highly dynamic and ad hoc service interaction mode, it becomes imperative for service providers and service requestors to communicate meaningfully with each other. In order to support seamless machine-to-machine and thing-to-thing semantic interoperation over a network, the devices and application systems must understand the meaning of services. For massive resource-constrained embedded devices, semantics for lightweight service protocols also need to be considered.

CONCLUSION

Over the past decade, the movement of computing, control and data storage into data centres has become an important trend; computing, storage and network service functions are being shifted to centralised clouds, backbone networks and cellular core networks. Today, however, IoT applications need to push cloud computing towards cloud-edge-continuum computing, using the streamlining and integration principle. The construction of IoT services aims to reconcile the physical world with the cyber world, along the cloud-to-thing continuum. However, IoT service provisioning is essentially faced with a 3-tuple challenge of "user requirements, information and physical space". The issues of how to efficiently disseminate the perceived information in an open, distributed computing environment and multiple tuples, (i.e. event streamlining), and then to realise dynamic service coordination among heterogeneous systems or entities (i.e. IoT service integration), are cores in IoT service provisioning.

In this chapter, this book is summarised in terms of the authors' understanding and thinking about the core IoT issues, and in terms of how to use the technologies and methods presented in prior chapters to achieve IoT service provisioning. The concept of "cognitive flow" is introduced into IoT applications, and based on this, a new IoT research idea involving the convergence of "bearing flow, control flow and cognitive flow" is proposed. An EDSOA-based service provisioning approach is then proposed that integrates the advantages of EDA and SOA, where SOA technology is employed to address the interoperability and reusability of different heterogeneous services in the distributed, loosely coupled IoT environment, and EDA is used to implement the on-demand dissemination of sensing information and dynamic coordination of event-driven services. For clarification, a CMCS prototype is demonstrated and experimental results from this prototype are presented.

REFERENCES

Abril, J. P. (2009). *Modelling business conversations in service component architectures.* Retrieved from http://hdl.handle.net/2381/8657

Apache ODE. (2008). Retrieved from http://ode.apache.org/

Atzori, L., Iera, A., & Morabito, G. (2010). The Internet of Things: A survey. *Computer Networks, 54*(15), 2787–2805. doi:10.1016/j.comnet.2010.05.010

Bandyopadhyay, S., Sengupta, M., Maiti, S., & Dutta, S. (2011). A survey of middleware for Internet of Things: Recent trends in wireless and mobile networks. Communications in Computer and Information Science, 162, 288-296.

Bruni, R., Lanese, I., Melgratti, H. C., & Tuosto, E. (2008). *Multiparty sessions in SOC.* Oslo, Norway: Proc. Coordination.

Castellani, A. P., Gheda, M., Bui, N., Rossi, M., & Zorzi, M. (2011). Web services for the Internet of Things through CoAP and EXI. *Proc. IEEE International Conference on Communications Workshops (ICC),* 1-6. 10.1109/iccw.2011.5963563

Chen, Y. Y., Zhang, Y., & Chen, J. L. (2011). A graph configuration method based on UI service composition. *Proc. 7th International Conference on Mobile Ad-hoc and Sensor Networks,* 339-340. 10.1109/MSN.2011.61

Dasgupta, S., Bhat, S., & Lee, Y. (2009). An abstraction framework for service composition in event-driven SOA systems. *Proc. IEEE International Conference on Web Services (ICWS 2009)*, 671-678. 10.1109/ICWS.2009.103

Ene, C., & Muntean, T. (1999). Expressiveness of point-to-point versus broadcast communications. *Fundamentals of Computation Theory*, *1684*, 258–268.

Erl, T. (2005). *Service-oriented architecture: Concepts, technology, and design*. Upper Saddle River, NJ: Prentice Hall PTR.

Event-Driven architecture overview. (2008). Retrieved from http://www.omg.org/soa/Uploaded%20Docs/ EDA/bda2-2-06cc.pdf

Fok, C. L., Roman, G. C., Lu, C., & Agilla, Y. (2009). A mobile agent middleware for self-adaptive wireless sensor networks. *ACM Trans. Auton. Adap.*, *4*, 1–26. doi:10.1145/1552297.1552299

Guidi, C., & Lucchi, R. (2008). *Programming service oriented applications*. Research Technical Report of the University of Bologna. Retrieved from ftp://ftp.cs.unibo.it:/pub/TR/UBLCS

Guidi, C., Lucchi, R., & Mazzara, M. (2007). A formal framework for web services coordination. *Electronic Notes in Theoretical Computer Science*, *180*(2), 55–70. doi:10.1016/j.entcs.2006.10.046

Guinard, D., Trifa, V., Karnouskos, S., Spiess, P., & Savio, D. (2010). Interacting with the SOA-based Internet of Things: Discovery, query, selection, and on-demand provisioning of web services. *IEEE Transactions on Services Computing*, *3*(3), 223–235. doi:10.1109/TSC.2010.3

Hennessy, M., & Rathke, J. (1995). Bisimulations for a calculus of broadcasting systems. *CONCUR '95 Concurrency Theory*, *962*, 486–500.

Hou, L. S., Jin, Z., & Wu, B. D. (2006). Modeling and verifying web services driven by requirements: An ontology based approach. *Science in China*, *49*(6), 792–820.

Huang, L. T., Zhang, Y., & Chen, J. L. (2011). Research and implementation of an ontology-based semantic reporting system. *Proc. 7th International Conference on Mobile Ad-hoc and Sensor Networks*. 337-338.

ITU Internet Reports. (2005). *The Internet of Things*. Retrieved from http://www.itu.int/osg/spu/publications/ internetofthings/ index.html

Liu, X. Z., Huang, G., & Mei, H. (2010). A community-centric approach to automated service composition. *Science in China, 53*(1), 50–63.

LoadRunner. (2008). Retrieved from http://www8.hp.com/us/en/software/software-product.html? compURI=tcm:245-935 779

Ma, H. D. (2011). Internet of things: Objectives and scientific challenges. *J. Comput. Sci. Technol., 26*(6), 919–924. doi:10.100711390-011-1189-5

Milner, R., Parrow, J., & Walker, D. (1992). A calculus for mobile processes. *Journal of Information and Computation, 100*(1), 1–40. doi:10.1016/0890-5401(92)90008-4

Motwani, R., Motwani, M., Harris, F., & Dascalu, S. (2010). Towards a scalable and interoperable global environmental sensor network using service oriented architecture. *Proc. Sixth International Conference on Intelligent Sensors, Sensor Networks and Information Processing (ISSNIP)*, 15-156. 10.1109/ISSNIP.2010.5706788

Overbeek, S., Klievink, B., & Janssen, M. (2009). A flexible, event-driven, service-oriented architecture for orchestrating service delivery. *IEEE Intelligent Systems, 24*(5), 31–41. doi:10.1109/MIS.2009.90

Prasd, K. V. S. (1995). A calculus of broadcasting system. *Science of Computer Programming, 25*(2-3), 285–327. doi:10.1016/0167-6423(95)00017-8

Priyantha, N. B., Kansal, A., Goraczko, M., & Zhao, F. (2008). Tiny web services: Design and implementation of interoperable and evolvable sensor networks. *Proc. Sixth ACM Conf. Embedded Network Sensor Systems*, 253-266. 10.1145/1460412.1460438

Shi, R. S., Liu, F. Q., Zhang, Y., Cheng, B., & Chen, J. L. (2011). MID-based load balancing approach for topic-based pub-sub overlay construction. *Tsinghua Science and Technology, 16*(6), 589–600. doi:10.1016/S1007-0214(11)70079-7

Teixeira, T., Hachem, S., Issarny, V., & Georgantas, N. (2011). *Service oriented middleware for the Internet of Things: A perspective* (pp. 220–229). Poznan, Poland: Proc. ServiceWave.

Wang, M. M., Cao, J. N., Li, J., & Dasi, S. K. (2008). Middleware for wireless sensor networks: A survey. *J. Comput. Sci. Technol., 23*(3), 305–326. doi:10.100711390-008-9135-x

WSN. (2005). Retrieved from http://www.oasis-open.org/committees/wsn/

Zhu, D., Zhang, Y., Cheng, B., & Chen, J. L. (2011). Towards a flexible event-driven SOA based approach for collaborating interactive business processes. *Proc. IEEE International Conference on Services Computing*, 749–750. 10.1109/SCC.2011.62

About the Authors

Yang Zhang has a degree in computer applied technology from the Institute of Software, Chinese Academy of Sciences in 2007. His research interests include service-oriented computing, the Internet of Things, and service security and privacy. He currently works at the State Key Laboratory of Networking and Switching Technology, Beijing University of Posts & Telecommunications (BUPT), China. He leads a team doing scientific research on the theoretic foundation of EDSOA for IoT services.

Yanmeng Guo is an associate professor in Institute of Acoustics, Chinese Academy of Sciences. His research interest is signal processing. His education background includes the Chinese Academy of Sciences Institute of Acoustics (PhD, 2003-2006), the Chinese Academy of Sciences Institute of Acoustics (Master's, 1999-2002), and Southeast University Radio Engineering (Bachelor's, 1995-1999).

Index

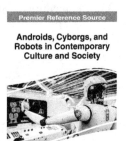

Ensure Quality Research is Introduced to the Academic Community

Become an IGI Global Reviewer for Authored Book Projects

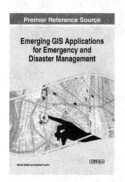

Premier Reference Source

Emerging GIS Applications for Emergency and Disaster Management

Premier Reference Source

Managerial Strategies and Green Solutions for Project Sustainability

Premier Reference Source

Comparative Approaches to Using R and Python for Statistical Data Analysis

Premier Reference Source

Solutions for High-Touch Communications in a High-Tech World

The overall success of an authored book project is dependent on quality and timely reviews.

In this competitive age of scholarly publishing, constructive and timely feedback significantly expedites the turnaround time of manuscripts from submission to acceptance, allowing the publication and discovery of forward-thinking research at a much more expeditious rate. Several IGI Global authored book projects are currently seeking highly qualified experts in the field to fill vacancies on their respective editorial review boards:

Applications may be sent to:
development@igi-global.com

Applicants must have a doctorate (or an equivalent degree) as well as publishing and reviewing experience. Reviewers are asked to write reviews in a timely, collegial, and constructive manner. All reviewers will begin their role on an ad-hoc basis for a period of one year, and upon successful completion of this term can be considered for full editorial review board status, with the potential for a subsequent promotion to Associate Editor.

If you have a colleague that may be interested in this opportunity, we encourage you to share this information with them.

Printed in the United States
By Bookmasters